C# Programming With the Public Beta

Burton Harvey

Simon Robinson

Julian Templeman

Karli Watson

Wrox Press Ltd. ®

C# Programming With the Public Beta

© 2000 Wrox Press

wrox

Published by Wrox Press Ltd,
Arden House, 1102 Warwick Road, Acocks Green,
Birmingham, B27 6BH, UK
Printed in the United States
ISBN 1-861004-87-7

Trademark Acknowledgements

Wrox has endeavored to provide trademark information about all the companies and products mentioned in this book by the appropriate use of capitals. However, Wrox cannot guarantee the accuracy of this information.

Credits

Authors

Burton Harvey

Simon Robinson

Julian Templeman

Karli Watson

Technical Architect

Julian Skinner

Technical Editors

Ben Egan

Gary Evans

Paul Jeffcoat

Gareth Oakley

Adrian Young

Project Administration

Cilmara Lion

Category Manager

Bruce Lawson

Author Agent

Sarah Bowers

Technical Reviewers

Richard Anderson

Steve Danielson

Robin Dewson

Jacob Hammer Pedersen

Hope Hatfield

Robert Howard

Davide Marcato

Shawn Murphy

Jonathan Pinnock

Scott Robertson

John Roth

Chris Sanchez

Radomir Zaric

Production Co-Ordinator

Pip Wonson

Figures

Shabnam Hussain

Cover Design

Shelley Frazier

Index

Martin Brooks

About the Authors

Burton Harvey

Burton Harvey is a software development consultant for Oakwood Systems Group, a Microsoft Partner company specializing in Internet solutions. An MCSD with fifteen years' experience using Microsoft development tools, Burt enjoys teaching others how to program and architecting software that elegantly fulfills clients' needs. In 1998, Burt founded the online journal of scientific research, *Scientia*. His areas of interest include compiler theory, UML, and the object-oriented paradigm. His Master's thesis, "The Outlaw Method for Solving Multimodal Functions with Parallel Genetic Algorithms", was presented at the International Conference on Evolutionary Computation.

Simon Robinson

Simon Robinson lives in Lancaster in the UK, where he shares a house with some students. He first encountered serious programming when he was doing his PhD in physics, modeling all sorts of weird things to do with superconductors and quantum mechanics. The experience of programming was nearly enough to put him off computers for life (though, oddly, he seems to have survived all the quantum mechanics), and he tried for a while being a sports massage therapist instead. But he then realized how much money was in computers compared to sports massage, and rapidly got a job as a C++ programmer/researcher instead. Simon is clearly the charitable, deep, spiritual type, who understands the true meaning of life.

His programming work eventually lead him into writing, and he now makes a living mostly from writing great books for programmers. He is also an honorary research associate at Lancaster University, where he does research in computational fluid dynamics with the environmental science department. You can visit Simon's web site at http://www.SimonRobinson.com.

Julian Templeman

Julian has been a programmer for just over thirty years, and still enjoys it. He started as a real programmer, and so is pleased to see that Fortran may have a place in the .NET world. He spends most of his time running a training and consultancy company in London, mainly on Java, C++, and COM, and writes articles and books on programming topics.

Karli Watson

Karli Watson is an in-house author for Wrox Press with a penchant for multicolored clothing. He started out with the intention of becoming a world famous nanotechnologist, so perhaps one day you might recognize his name as he receives a Nobel Prize. For now, though, Karli's computing interests include all things mobile, and upcoming technologies such as C#. He can often be found preaching about these technologies at conferences, as well as after hours in drinking establishments. Karli is also a snowboarding enthusiast, and wishes he had a cat.

Acknowledgement:

"Thanks go to the Wrox team, both for helping me get into writing, and then dealing with the results when I started. Finally, and most importantly, thanks to my wife Donna for continuing to put up with me."

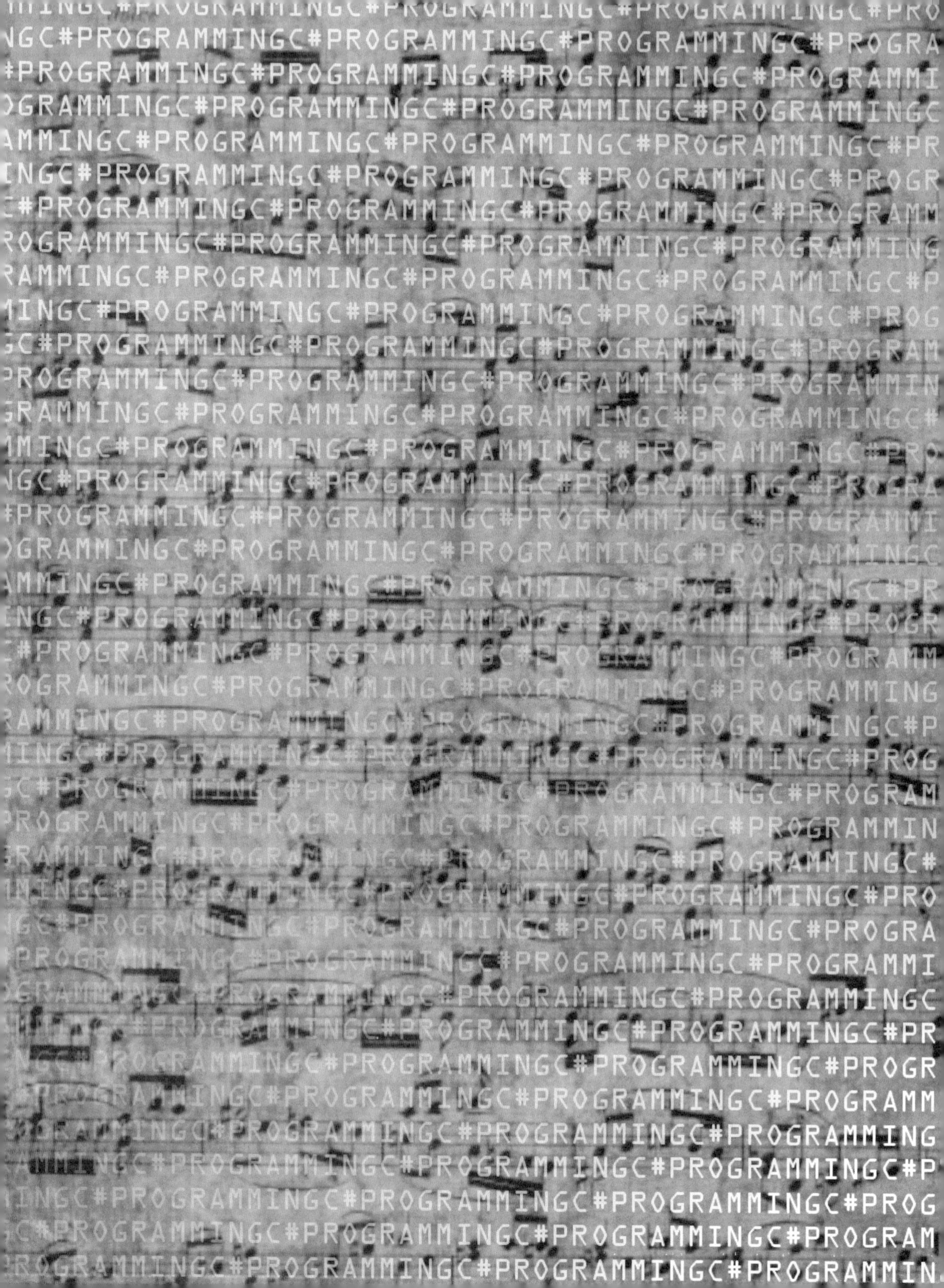
C#PROGRAMMING

Table of Contents

Table of Contents

Table of Contents

Table of Contents

Table of Contents

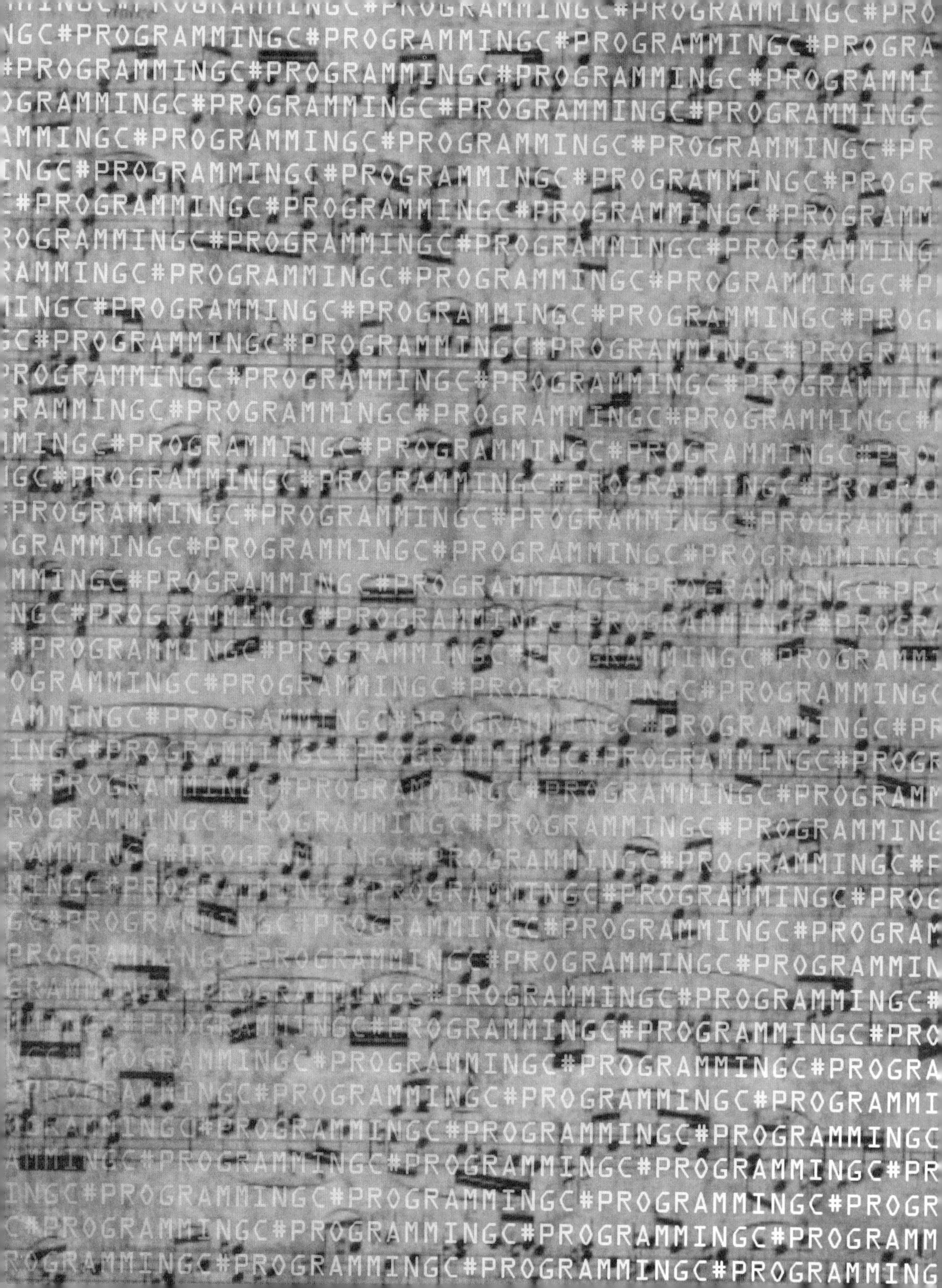
C#PROGRAMMING

Introduction

A New Platform

C# (pronounced 'C Sharp') is Microsoft's new language, designed specifically for their new platform, the .NET Framework. This platform is currently in beta, but is freely available from Microsoft's web site, and a final release is expected some time around the middle 2001.

The .NET framework promises to revolutionize programming on the Windows platform. The basic premise is quite simple: all .NET programs are compiled to an intermediate language (IL, or MSIL) rather than to native code which can be understood by the computer's processor. This IL code is then compiled to native code either when the application is installed, or when the application is run. Code run on the .NET Framework is managed by a runtime environment called the Common Language Runtime (CLR). This runtime provides memory-management features such as automatic garbage collection and type-safety checking, and is similar in some ways to Java's Virtual Machine.

The .NET Framework also provides a large number of base classes, whose functionality is available to all languages which use the CLR, and which allow the developer to achieve many common programming tasks. This provides a high degree of language independence. In the long term (if the .NET Framework is migrated to non-Windows platforms), these classes may provide a degree of platform-independence by avoiding the necessity of calling OS-specific APIs.

A New Language

For the last few years, developers working chiefly on Microsoft platforms have had two principal languages to work with: they could choose the power of Visual C++, or the ease of use of Visual Basic. Although Visual Basic did allow a lot of power to those who were prepared to stretch it to its limits, and Visual C++ had a host of AppWizards designed to simplify life for the C++ developer, as a general rule applications built in Visual C++ took longer to develop, but had much better performance than those developed in Visual Basic.

The release of the .NET Framework changes all that in two ways. Firstly, Visual Basic.NET is much more powerful than its predecessor. All .NET languages compile to Intermediate Language, and can take advantage of the features supplied by the Common Language Runtime. Added to this are a number of more powerful features in Visual Basic.NET, such as true object-oriented features and exception handling with `Try...Catch`. However, probably the more important development is the creation of an entirely new language – C#, the subject of this book.

C# is a new language derived from C++, but designed to support Rapid Application Development (RAD) in a similar way to Visual Basic. Visual C# allows us to design both Windows and web applications quickly and easily using form designers; Visual Studio takes care of much of the code, such as instantiating the controls and writing the definitions for event handlers. This of course comes on top of the features provided by the Common Language Runtime, such as automatic garbage collection. However, C# also gives us most of the power of C++, even allowing the use of direct access to memory addresses through pointers in blocks of "unsafe" code (code which bypasses C#'s type safety features). Add to this the fact that C# is the only language designed from the ground up for the .NET Framework, and it's clear why C# looks set to become the language of choice for .NET programming.

Who Is This Book For?

This book is for anybody who wants to learn about C# and.NET. This book is not a beginner's book – we've assumed that you've got some programming experience, perhaps in Windows programming with Visual Basic or Visual C++. Alternatively, you may be coming from a Java background and want to see what all the fuss is about. Some of the later chapters assume some basic knowledge of Microsoft technologies such as ASP and ADO.

What Does It Cover?

This book is designed to provide an introduction to programming in C# on the .NET platform. As we have already implied, these two topics are closely connected. Because all code written for the .NET Framework will make extensive use of the .NET base classes, for example for input/output, data manipulation and file handling, we cover these extensively, as well as the syntax of the C# language itself.

We start off by taking quick overviews of the .NET Framework, C#, and Visual Studio.NET, before moving on to look at the C# language in detail. Next we cover the basics of .NET programming – namespaces, building Windows applications, data access with ADO.NET, and building components. Finally, we look at a few more advanced topics: integrating C# programs with COM and with Component Services, and building ASP.NET web applications and web services in C#.

Let's take a brief look at what we cover in each of the individual chapters of this book:

Chapter 1: Overview of the .NET Framework

In this chapter we look at the .NET Framework, and at some of the problems that it addresses. The Common Language Runtime (CLR) is discussed, along with Intermediate Language (IL) and interoperability between .NET language components and COM+ components.

Chapter 2: Introduction to C#

This chapter introduces at the C# language – it starts with a very brief history of Windows programming, and discusses why we need another programming language. C# is also compared to other programming languages currently in use. The chapter then looks at the types of application that can be built using C# in the .NET environment. Finally, we look at how to compile and run C# programs.

Chapter 3: A Tour of VS.NET

This chapter looks at the Visual Studio IDE, which is now common to all .NET languages. We look at the different windows which are used in the development of C# projects. Features of the code window, such as code collapsing and Intellisense, are discussed. We look at how code is compiled, and then we look at the available debugging tools.

Chapter 4: C# Syntax

This chapter is the start of the detailed look at C#. Throughout the chapter, any similarities and differences between C# and C++ and Java are noted. We look at the features of a C# program, including the data types, operators, and statements used in the language. Program control and loops are examined, and also the calling of methods and method overloading. Errors and how to handle them are discussed. The chapter ends with an explanation of namespaces.

Chapter 5: Object-Oriented Programming

This chapter looks at the functionality built into C# for working with objects. We begin with a discussion of user-defined data types – structs and enumerations – before going on to look at classes. The members of classes – fields, properties, methods, and events – are all discussed. We also look at OO concepts such as inheritance, and see how they are implemented in C#. Other topics covered include interfaces and abstract classes, boxing, operator overloading, indexers, and delegates.

Chapter 6: Advanced C# Concepts

In this chapter we will examine some advanced techniques involved with working with classes, such as variable argument lists. We then look at implementing collections, and using reflection to find out about the members of classes at runtime. Next we look at C#'s preprocessor directives, which we can use to modify how our code is compiled, using .NET attributes in C#, unsafe code, and XML documentation.

Chapter 7: Namespaces and the Base Classes

This chapter takes a closer look at namespaces and the most commonly used base classes. We see how the WinCV tool allows us to interrogate the classes for their methods. Example programs are written which show the base classes in action, and demonstrate how to perform common programming tasks in C#, such as file handling, working with dates, and accessing the Registry.

Chapter 8: Windows Applications

This chapter uses WinForms to aid Rapid Application Development. After a quick look at creating WinForms applications without Visual Studio, the Visual Studio IDE is used to add controls onto Windows forms. A sample Windows application is used to demonstrate creating menus, handling events, and other aspects of building Windows applications. We then look at how Windows applications are deployed.

Chapter 9: ADO.NET

ADO.NET isthe latest of Microsoft's Data Access technologies. After a quick look at the object model and some of the advantages of ADO.NET, we discuss using the dataset to access and update a database. We also see how to bind a dataset to a datagrid, and examine some of the ADO.NET's functionality for working with XML. Next we look at another way of accessing data with ADO.NET – using the forward-only, read-only data reader. Finally, we introduce some of Visual Studio's built-in features for data access.

Chapter 10: Assemblies and Manifests

In this chapter, we see how to create components in C#, and look at the concepts of assemblies and manifests. Assemblies are .NET components which include both the code itself, and all the metadata needed to describe the component – its manifest. The .NET Framework uses shared names to locate assemblies regardless of their physical location in the file system, so we see how we can create shared names for our assemblies. This allows assemblies to be shared by multiple applications. Finally, we look at some of the cross-language features enabled by the Common Language Runtime.

Chapter 11: COM Interoperability

Next, we come on to look at integrating C# applications and components with existing code. First, we see how to call existing COM components from C# applications, using both early and late binding. Next, we discuss calling C# components as if they were COM components, by creating a wrapper COM object and exporting a type library. Finally, we look at calling unmanaged functions using PInvoke (Platform Invocation Services).

Chapter 12: COM+ Services

After an overview of Component Services and the advantages of hosting components in COM+, we see how to use these features with .NET components. We look at creating transactional components under .NET and registering them with COM+ Services, and we see how to take advantage of some of the other main features of COM+ from our C# component, such as object pooling and auto-completing transactions.

Chapter 13: ASP.NET

In our penultimate chapter, we see how to create web applications using ASP.NET, the latest incarnation of ASP. After an overview of the new features on offer, we show an example of creating a simple ASP.NET web application. We demonstrate the use of server-side controls in maintaining state and in validating user input, and finally we see how ASP.NET allows us to upload files from the client easily, without any additional components.

Chapter 14: Web Services

Finally, we look at another, new kind of web application – the web service. Web services are a way of exposing the application logic on a server over the Internet. This allows the client to use the data on the server, without being tied to particular pre-constructed static or dynamic web pages. After a look at what web services are, and the protocols they use, we demonstrate how to build a web service and a client which will consume this service. Finally, we take a look at the discovery files which are used when checking which web services are available on a server.

What Do You Need To Use This Book?

To run the samples in this book, you'll need the Microsoft .NET SDK. This can be downloaded for free from Microsoft's web site, at `http://msdn.microsoft.com/code/sample.asp?` `url=/msdn-files/027/000/976/msdncompositedoc.xml`. To make full use of the book, you'll also need Visual Studio.NET, which can be downloaded for free by MSDN Universal subscribers, or ordered on CD for a nominal fee by other users, at `http://msdn.microsoft.com/vstudio/nextgen/beta.asp`. All the code samples in this book have been tested on the Beta 1 release of the .NET SDK.

We provide the source code for the samples that you'll see in this book on our web site. You can get the code samples from the Support page of the Wrox Press web site, at `http://www.wrox.com`. This site also contains a range of other resources and reference material, including other books, which you might find useful.

Conventions

We have used a number of different styles of text and layout in the book to help differentiate between the different kinds of information. Here are examples of the styles we use and an explanation of what they mean:

Bullets appear indented, with each new bullet marked as follows:

- ❑ **Important Words** are in a bold type font
- ❑ Words that appear on the screen in menus like the File or Window are in a similar font to the one that you see on screen
- ❑ Keys that you press on the keyboard, like *Ctrl* and *Enter*, are in italics

Code has several fonts. If it's a word that we're talking about in the text, for example, when discussing the `if...else` loop, it's in `this font`. If it's a block of code that you can type in as a program and run, then it's also in a gray box:

```
public static int Main()
{
    AFunc(1,2,"abc");
    return 0;
}
```

Sometimes you'll see code in a mixture of styles, like this:

```
// If we haven't reached the end, return true, otherwise
// set the position to invalid, and return false.
pos++;
if (pos < 4)
    return true;
else {
    pos = -1;
    return false;
}
```

The code with a white background is code we've already looked at and that we don't wish to examine further.

> *Advice, hints, and background information come in an italicized, indented font like this.*

Important pieces of information come in boxes like this.

We demonstrate the syntactical usage of methods, properties (and so on) using the following format:

```
Regsvcs BookDistributor.dll [COM+AppName] [TypeLibrary.tbl]
```

Here, italicized parts indicate object references, variables, or parameter values to be inserted; the square braces indicate optional parameters.

Customer Support

We've tried to make this book as accurate and useful as possible, but what really matters is what the book actually does for you. Please let us know your views, either by returning the reply card at the back of the book, or by writing to us at feedback@wrox.com.

The **source code** for this book is available for download at http://www.wrox.com.

We've made every effort to ensure there are no errors in this book. However, to err is human, and we recognize the need to keep you informed of errors as they're spotted and corrected. **Errata sheets** are available for all our books, at http://www.wrox.com. If you find an error that hasn't already been reported, please let us know.

Our web site acts as a focus for other information and support, including the code from all our books, sample chapters, and previews of forthcoming titles.

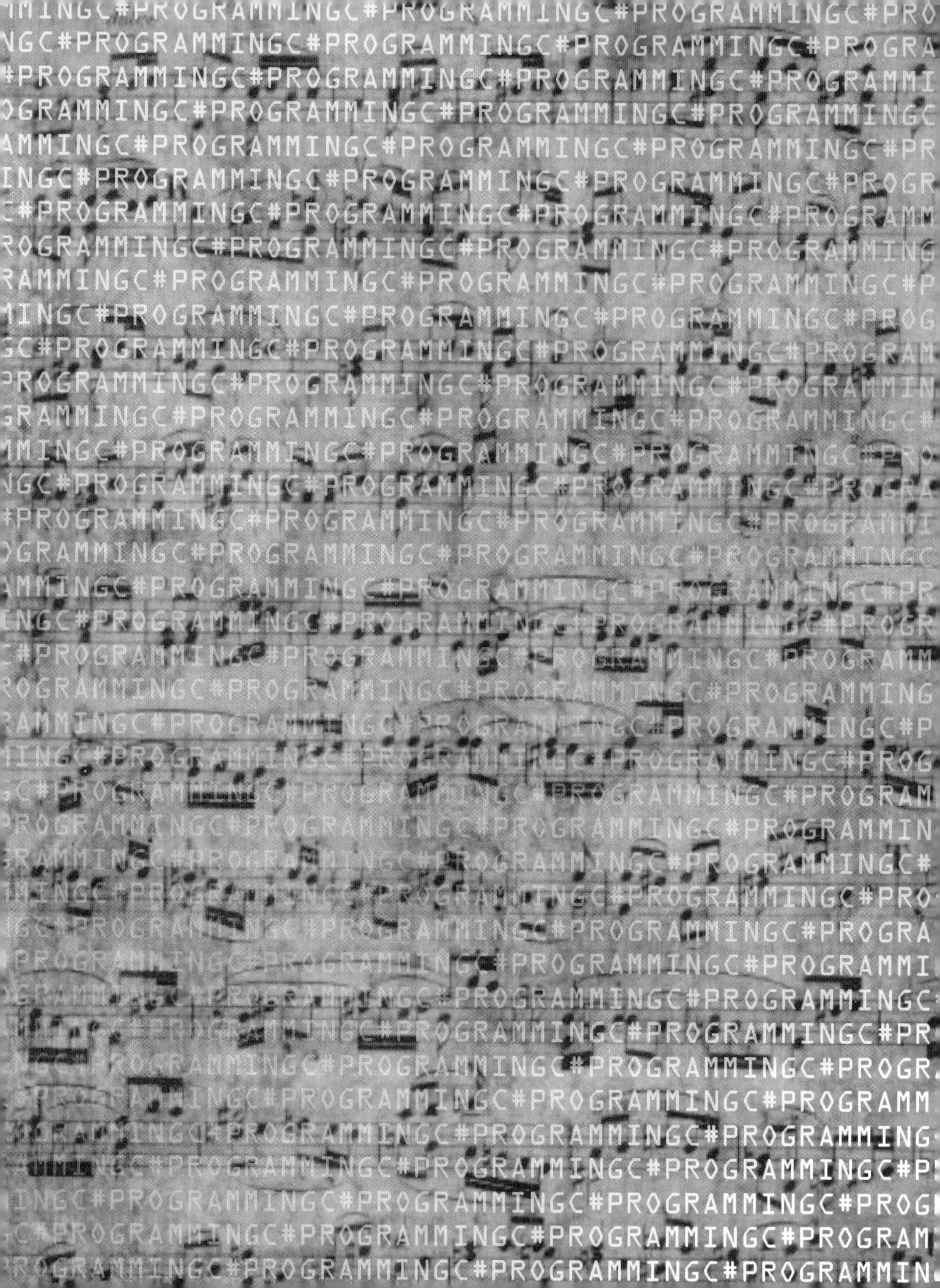
C#PROGRAMMING

1

Overview of the .NET Framework

Introduction

It's taken decades to determine what developers really need from a programming language, what they don't need from one, and what they want to rely on the operating system to do. The product of this accumulated understanding is C#. C# is a concise, clean, and modern language that combines the best features of many commonly used languages: the productivity of VB, the elegance of Java, and the power of C++.

Because it was drawn on a clean slate, C# has a lean and consistent syntax. Another virtue of having been invented recently, is that C# is intrinsically object-oriented and Web-enabled. Because it can rely on housekeeping services provided by intelligent and modern operating systems, C# embodies today's concern for productivity, security, and robustness.

Microsoft has submitted a C# standard for ratification by ECMA (the European Computer Manufacturers' Association). Once this standard is in place, vendors worldwide will be able to use it to develop C# compilers that target their own platforms (in contrast, Java has not been submitted to an independent standards body). Until then, C# will be used in the context of the platform for which it was originally invented – that is .NET.

This chapter will explain the .NET development framework and C#'s place within it.

Microsoft .NET

One amazing aspect of the Microsoft Corporation is its chameleon-like ability to re-invent itself, to morph into a new organization with a new strategy. Today, in response to the popularity of Java and the exponential growth of the Web, and in the face of legal problems, Microsoft has invented itself yet again. Its new identity is **.NET**, a development platform that makes it easier for programmers using different languages to quickly create robust internet applications.

The benefits of internet applications are obvious. Internet applications allow businesses to communicate vital information with each other across existing communication lines and also to market goods to consumers. Unfortunately, internet development has traditionally been a very difficult endeavor. In fact, in order to author an n-tier application using Microsoft tools, a developer might have to use the following set of languages and technologies: SQL, ADO, COM(+), VB, C++, MTS, ASP, VBScript, HTML, DHTML, and JavaScript. Developers possessing sufficient skill in all of these areas are few and costly. Even developers who use these skills to successfully develop Internet applications can spend hours battling component version conflicts (otherwise known as DLL Hell) when the time comes to install their products.

To better understand how .NET makes internet development easier, let's look at how it affects the various entities associated with it.

Microsoft has made the specifications for the .NET development platform freely available to compiler vendors in the form of the **Common Language Specification** (CLS). Vendors can then use this specification to develop compilers that plug into the environment and produce a standardized binary code format. A developer picks the .NET language that he likes most, writes components in it, and shares the compiled binary versions of his components with developers using other .NET languages. When executed, the components use the .NET runtime component for security and memory management. To avoid versioning and registration problems – in that different versions of the same components can run side-by-side on the same machine, requiring only a file copy for deployment – all the version information and other information is included in the metadata that is distributed with the component.

For developers, .NET offers other advantages besides the language interoperability just mentioned. By liberally applying the "drag-and-drop" metaphor, the up-and-coming VS.NET development environment eliminates a lot of hand-coding drudgery. Even better, the .NET base classes, which provide the standard .NET application programming interface (API), provide a rich library of built-in functionality that developers can use to quickly develop powerful subclasses, including forms and controls. Because the same .NET base class library is shared between all programming languages, a developer can take his knowledge of this library with him as he migrates from language to language.

In short, .NET allows internet developers to write less plumbing code and to write applications in the language with which they are most comfortable, and it enables their applications and components to be shared with and used by developers who program in other languages.

Now that we understand *what* .NET does, let's look at *how* it does it.

The Common Language Runtime

Traditionally, a "runtime" was a component that a computer had to have in order to execute programs written in a particular programming language. In order to execute VB6 programs, for instance, a machine had to have the VB runtime (`msvbvm.dll`) installed. VC++ programs and Java programs required unique runtime components too. A language's runtime component implemented core language features needed by programs written in that language. When executed, a program can dynamically link to the runtime component of its source code language to get basic functionality that it needs.

The fact that different languages required different runtimes made life more difficult for developers. VB developers, for example, had to think twice before using VB to develop ActiveX controls for web pages. One reason for this was that in addition to downloading an ActiveX control, a web surfer might also have to download the rather hefty VB runtime that the ActiveX control needs, if the VB runtime happened not to be installed on his machine – he'd have even more problems if Windows wasn't installed either. Add to this the component versioning concerns and you have the formula for a distribution nightmare.

To avoid such dilemmas, .NET introduces a single, **Common Language Runtime** (the CLR) that all .NET languages share. This is a diagram of the CLR and the main activities that go on there.

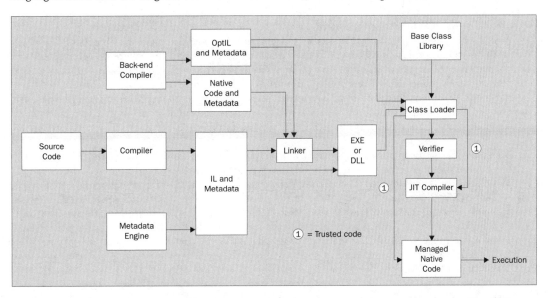

Here is a very quick summary of how the CLR works. A fuller, more technical explanation can be found in the .NET framework SDK documentation. The source code gets compiled to IL and the same time meta data information is created using the meta data engine. These are optionally linked with other code compiled by different compilers and the result is an EXE or DLL containing the IL code, which is saved to disk. The compiler's work is now done. Then on execution, the IL code and any functionality from the .NET base class library is brought together using the class loader, the combined code is optionally tested for type safety using the verifier before the JIT (Just-in-Time) compiler comes into play. The JIT compiler processes the IL creating managed native code which is passed on to the .NET runtime manager.

We'll take a closer look at how a single runtime can serve multiple languages in the section on IL, the Intermediate Language; for now, be satisfied in knowing that .NET languages compile to a common format that the CLR understands. This format is specified in the **Common Language Specification**, or CLS, to which the compiler of a programming language must adhere in order to be considered .NET-compatible.

So that as many different languages as possible can use the CLR, the CLS describes a bare minimum of external requirements, including set of settings for specifying component accessibility and a set of basic data types. Like the COM specification, the CLS specification is an unobtrusive one, allowing languages to implement themselves however they desire, and regulating only the connection mechanism between those languages and the CLR.

Code Management

Unlike previous runtimes, the CLR is not merely a required component providing useful routines to clients, but is an integral part of those clients' lifecycles, managing their compilations, executions, and privileges. The VB and VC++ runtimes provided functions that could be called by compiled VB and VC++ programs. By contrast, .NET programs are stored in a common format that the CLR compiles to machine code on an as-needed basis. Furthermore, as this dynamically generated machine code is executed, the CLR watches to make sure that no unauthorized actions are performed and that no memory leaks develop.

Before .NET, each Windows component was in charge of allocating and de-allocating the memory resources that it needed. If a class inside a component was coded incorrectly, objects of that class might fail to release the memory back to the operating system when they were de-referenced. This loss of system memory is what's known as a **memory leak**. Although it might take weeks or even months, an application using these faulty, memory-leaking components could eventually eat up all available RAM and crash the system, leaving engineers to puzzle over a periodic, mysterious, and hard-to-replicate failure. What's more, unless the system is continually running or regularly reaching its RAM capacity, minor memory leaks may largely go unnoticed.

In .NET, the CLR thwarts memory leaks by managing objects' lifetimes for them. The CLR's **garbage collector** periodically checks the memory heap for unreferenced objects, and frees up the memory used by these objects. The garbage collector uses an algorithm to determine whether objects in memory can be reached by the application. If the object cannot be accessed, it can be considered garbage, and its memory allocation can be released. Client applications written in C# and VB make use of the CLR's garbage collector implicitly. In contrast, .NET code written in managed C++ must explicitly indicate that the garbage collector object is to be used. For C# and VB programmers who want maximum control, the garbage collector object is exposed as a class in the .NET base class library.

> For a detailed description of garbage collection in the CLR, see Jeffrey Richter's two-part article at
> `http://msdn.microsoft.com/msdnmag/issues/1100/`
> `GCI/GCI.asp`.

It is a common mistake to confuse *unsafe* code with code that is *unmanaged* by the .NET runtime. The term **unmanaged** describes native code that does not execute in the context of the runtime, such as code written using VB6 or earlier and C++ without the managed extensions. By contrast, all C# code is managed, though you can specify blocks of C# code as **unsafe**, which means that it sidesteps C#'s type-checking mechanism and enables the programmer to carry out some traditional C/C++ activities such as using pointers to manipulate memory directly (see Chapter 6 for more details). However, it must be stressed that all .NET programs are managed by the CLR, whether or not they have unsafe blocks of code embedded within them.

As you can see, the CLR effectively functions as a middle-layer between .NET programs and the operating system. Like the police, the CLR's professed duty is to protect and serve. Like a Java virtual machine, the CLR creates a virtual "sandbox" in which it is permissible for components to play. If components want to perform a potentially dangerous action – such as write to the file system – they must be granted a trust, an explicit allowance from the system administrator.

IL – Intermediate Language

Compilation is typically taken to mean the transformation of high-level source code (such as VB) into low level machine code (1's and 0's). When linked, the sequences of 1's and 0's in the machine code correspond to instructions recognized by the target machine's microprocessor. Execution of a compiled program involves setting the instruction counter to the first instruction in the machine code and allowing the chain reaction of instruction fetches and instruction performances to proceed. Technically, however, compilation can refer to the transformation from code in one language to code in any other target language – even if code in that target language must be interpreted before it can be executed by a microprocessor. This point is important because .NET programs are effectively compiled *twice*.

The first compilation occurs immediately after a developer finishes coding a .NET component or program. When the developer chooses Build from the Visual Studio IDE, the compiler compiles the C#, VB.NET, or managed C++ code not into machine code, but instead into a language called **IL** (**Intermediate Language**). The IL code is persisted to files on disk. This step is typically the slower one.

The second compilation occurs when these IL files are executed, and the CLR dynamically transforms them to machine code that the system's microprocessor can understand. (We'll talk more about this second compilation in an upcoming section where we discuss the Just in Time compilers (JITters). This step can be fast.

The use of IL has two implications, of which only one has been realized.

The first implication is language interoperability. Because .NET languages compile to a standardized IL, they can be used together to form "software quilts", which are applications stitched together out of components originally created in diverse source code languages. IL is the same no matter whether is was created by a VB compiler, a C# compiler or any other .NET compatible compiler. It is because the .NET base classes are stored as IL, that all the .NET languages can make use of them.

The second implication, which exists today only as a rumor, is platform independence. IL is more abstract than any single microprocessor's machine code instruction set. Theoretically, the same IL file could be executed on any architecture that is equipped with a suitable CLR interpreter and a base class library. Although Microsoft has not even breathed the words "platform independence", it's a logical conclusion, and has been the subject of gossip on the Internet for several months prior to this book's publication. Windows is the only platform for which an IL runtime has been developed, but this situation is expected to change. Even if the Microsoft Corporation doesn't produce the Macintosh, UNIX, and IBM runtimes, someone else probably will in order to enjoy the reduced development costs associated with platform independence.

Visual Studio.NET will host at least four Microsoft languages capable of generating IL: managed Visual C++, VB.NET, C#, and JScript. At the time of writing, other vendors are offering many other IL languages that plug into the Visual Studio IDE:

- ❑ COBOL
- ❑ Eiffel
- ❑ Mercury
- ❑ Perl
- ❑ Python
- ❑ SmallTalk
- ❑ Scheme

Although IL code is not bytecode, its simple binary instructions mirror those in any modern microprocessor's instruction set. There are IL instructions, for instance, for shuttling values between free memory addresses and a virtual stack maintained by the CLR. Because of this close correlation between IL commands their machine code equivalents, the compilation from IL to machine code occurs quickly. In addition to fine-grained commands that are close to the instruction set, IL also possesses higher-level commands for accessing objects and methods, for example, special instructions target virtual method calls. One can rightly think of IL as an assembly language with extra commands for objects. A look at some raw IL can be enlightening. ILDASM.EXE, the IL disassembler provided with the .NET SDK, was used to extract the following snippet of "Hello World" code from an IL component:

```
/ Test::Main : void(class System.String[])                              _ □ ×
.method public hidebysig static void  Main(class System.String[] args) il managed
{
  .entrypoint
  // Code size       11 (0xb)
  .maxstack  8
  IL_0000:  ldstr      "Hello World"
  IL_0005:  call       void [mscorlib]System.Console::WriteLine(class System.String)
  IL_000a:  ret
} // end of method Test::Main
```

What this code shows you is that the string "Hello World" is loaded into memory and written to the console using the `Console.WriteLine()` method from the base classes library (`mscorlib`).

As a .NET application is executed, its IL code is translated into machine code. For efficiency, this compiled code is cached and users can select the caching schemes that best fit their execution environments.

There is a tendency among programmers – particularly among those who started programming with early computers that were much less powerful than today's – to sneer at interpreted languages. While it is true that interpreted programs tend to execute more slowly than their machine code counterparts, today's high speed processors and gargantuan RAM stores blunt the discrepancies, and as processors become even faster, the validity of this criticism will continue to diminish. In most real world situations, code that ships on time with 90% efficiency is preferable to code that ships 6 months late with 100% efficiency.

The Just in Time (JIT) Compilers

In order for a .NET application to run, the IL within it has to be translated into machine code that a computer's microprocessor can understand. In the parlance of .NET, a program capable of performing such translation is a **Just in Time Compiler**, or a **JITter**. .NET will ship with two different JITters. Because each JITter balances compilation speed, code execution speed, and memory usage differently, each is appropriate for a different kind of platform.

Standard JIT

The default JITter, **Standard JIT** or just **JIT**, produces highly optimized machine code as it is needed and retains it in case it is needed again. When an IL function or method is invoked, JIT analyzes, compiles, and caches it with a sophistication that is reminiscent of a full-blown compiler. This sophisticated compilation is relatively slow, but the code that it produces is very, very fast. For this reason, JIT makes sense for platforms with enough RAM to cache the compiled code for re-use. Platforms without enough RAM to cache JIT's compiled code would have to call JIT over and over again, thereby suffering the slow compilation speed that results from its precision. Interestingly, .NET programs using JIT tend to become faster and faster as the various branches of execution within them are converted to pure native code.

EconoJIT

The second JITter, **EconoJIT**, targets small hardware platforms that don't have a lot of RAM. Because code cannot be cached, it must be continually recompiled. So that tolerable execution speeds are achieved, EconoJIT produces machine code that is efficient but not optimal. Because EconoJIT performs fewer optimizations than JIT does, it compiles faster.

PreJIT

PreJIT is not really a JITter in its own right. Rather, it is the invocation of the Standard JIT at the time that an application is installed on a system. With PreJIT, the entire application is completely converted from IL to machine code so that it subsequently executes at optimal speed. Obviously, PreJIT is right for an application that requires consistently high-performance from its very first use.

.NET, COM, and COM+

Code re-use is one of the ideals to which all good developers aspire. It allows you to more quickly produce applications that have greater robustness. With .NET, Microsoft proposes a new approach to code re-use that improves upon methods it has championed in the past.

There are two types of code re-use: **white box** and **black box**. White box code re-use refers to simply pasting together passages of source code and compiling the conglomeration into one monolithic executable. The second and somewhat more sophisticated and useful approach, black box code re-use, involves the linking together of segments of previously compiled machine code. Using black box code re-use to build a software application is a lot like assembling a circuit from stock, prefabricated components such as resistors, capacitors, and diodes. Hence, in Microspeak, a compiled, black box class library from which client applications can create objects is the **component**. .NET provides developers with a new way of building and using components. Because this new approach resembles previous efforts like COM, and because Microsoft has applied terminology inconsistently as .NET was developed, it's easy to confuse .NET componentization with separate, distinct approaches such as COM+. In order to eliminate this confusion, let's take a quick look at the history of Microsoft componentization and how .NET's approach differs from those of its predecessors.

DLLs

Even in the early days of programming, developers maintained archives of object files containing function libraries compiled into machine code. If a developer wanted to use a function library in a program, he compiled the client portion of his program to machine code and then relied on the linker to join this machine code with the library's object file into a single executable. All that was really saved was the time spent compiling the function library. Storage space was wasted because separate executables referencing the same class library would each have separate, unused copies of the class library embedded within them. Maintenance was difficult, too. For example, if a bug was discovered in a function library, executables using the library had to be completely re-compiled and re-distributed.

With .NET, executables reference compiled functions *stored in separate files*. No longer is it necessary to compile client programs and the function libraries as single, gigantic executables. With **dynamic link libraries** (DLLs), a developer could simply place an executable file into the same folder as the library file that it referenced and rely on the operating system to do the linking dynamically at runtime. This space-saving scheme resulted in smaller executables that could share copies of function libraries between them. This approach made maintenance easier too. Developers could upgrade programs by simply replacing old DLL files with new ones without having to re-distribute huge executables. As you'll soon see, components built with .NET are, from the standpoint of installation, a throwback to the early days of DLLs.

15

COM

Despite the benefits that dynamic linking provided, it had one serious limitation: only executables and DLLs written in the same programming language could easily be used together. There was no easy way, for example, for an executable written in QuickBasic to reference a DLL built with C++. This limitation was due to the fact that different programming environments used different naming schemes to reference methods and classes (called DLL symbols), making it difficult to resolve function names as represented in the compiled client code with function names as represented in the compiled server code. To overcome this limitation, Microsoft developed COM (the Component Object Model). Although the COM approach to componentization provides some of the same benefits as the .NET approach, and although the two approaches can be used together, the underlying mechanisms that make them work are completely different.

With COM, an EXE written in Visual Basic or Visual C++ could use a DLL written in Borland C++ or Delphi. COM achieved this flexibility by imposing a binary standard with which components had to comply. Under this standard, components communicated with each other via interfaces only through the mediation of COM Services. To get around the problem of DLL symbols, COM identified interfaces via **Globally Unique Identifiers** (GUIDs), huge numbers recognized by all COM-compliant components and stored in the system registry. Initially, the development of COM components was a black art that only hardcore Visual C++ programmers could master, but vendors who recognized the financial incentive soon added the ability to create COM components to their environments too, and then other programmers, such as Visual Basic programmers could create COM components as well. COM was the foundation for a family of related technologies, including ActiveX controls and OLE automation.

COM+

To be used effectively in enterprise applications, COM components had to have certain abilities, such as the ability to authenticate the identity of clients, the ability to pool resources, the ability to commit or rollback related jobs atomically, and the ability to communicate with each other when distributed across different machines. To save COM developers the trouble of developing their own implementations of these abilities, Microsoft provided DCOM and later MTS. The term "COM+" refers to COM components that employ the kind of useful, out-of-the-box functionality provided by services such as DCOM and MTS. Although a couple of articles in *Microsoft Developers Journal* in 1999 used COM+ to refer to a prophesied technology sounding eerily like .NET, Microsoft has since recanted, and now COM+ and .NET refer to completely different technologies. .NET is .NET whereas COM+ is an extension to COM.

DCOM was an RPC (Remote Procedure Call) protocol for communications between distributed COM components. With it, a client application made requests to "proxy" classes on its local machine, allowing the proxy classes to invisibly relay the requests to remote "stub" classes installed elsewhere and to receive the results returned from those remote classes. Because the calling client remained blissfully ignorant of the actual location of the class performing the requested work, DCOM was said to achieve location transparency. To make DCOM development easier, development environments such as Visual Basic could automatically generate a component's proxy and stub classes for installation on the client and server machines, respectively. The disadvantages of DCOM are that it cannot easily cross firewalls and is restricted to certain network protocols. Unlike DCOM components, .NET components use non-proprietary, platform-independent XML to communicate with other components anywhere on the Web. The application of XML used by .NET components for this purpose is called **SOAP** (**Simple Object Access Protocol**).

Often, the remote server classes called by DCOM ran inside a separate process provided by Microsoft Transaction Server (MTS). To use MTS, component programmers placed special MTS hooks inside their components, compiled the components, and placed the components inside MTS as packages. When clients requested an instance of a component inside a package, MTS ensured that a dedicated process was created for that package, instantiated the requested component inside that process, and applied whatever transaction, pooling, and security abilities that the original developer requested of MTS. In a way, MTS served the same sort of managerial role for COM components that the .NET runtime serves for .NET components.

As its name implies, MTS gave components the ability to treat units of related work as transactions, where if all the constituent parts of the workload succeed then the whole transaction succeeds, whereas if any constituent work unit fails, the entire transaction is rolled back and the original settings and conditions are restored. The role of MTS is to manage this whole process silently and efficiently.

In addition to transactions, MTS provided two other valuable services.

❑ It conserved memory resources. It did this by retaining objects in memory after they were released by the clients that originally instantiated them. When another client requested an instance of the same class, MTS would hand the client a reference to the retained object. By passing the same object reference from client to client, MTS eliminated the processor overhead required to instantiate a fresh object from scratch, and prevented memory from being eaten up by thousands of requests for the same object. This last bit of behavior was particular useful in the context of web servers.

❑ It allowed component developers to equip their components with security mechanisms for authenticating the identities of client code. By selecting one of several authentication levels, developers could ensure that unauthorized persons would not misuse their components as a means to wreak havoc on the host system.

Originally a Windows NT Server add-on available from the Option Pack CD, MTS has now become a core part of the Windows 2000 operating system under a new name COM+. COM+ isn't just MTS, but includes COM and a host of other services, and comes under the umbrella term **COM+ Services**. In addition to the features first introduced with MTS, COM+ Services offers new functionality that will prove invaluable to enterprise component developers. Message queuing, which originated as MSMQ at around the same time as MTS, allows clients and servers to communicate asynchronously and thus absorbs the impact of periodic server inaccessibility. The Event Service provides a publisher-subscriber mechanism so that server classes can asynchronously communicate event occurrences to multiple clients. The Load Balancing Service dynamically instantiates requested objects on whichever machine, in a cluster of servers, has the most available resources.

.NET Components

Although you can use a utility program to quickly generate COM wrappers for .NET components, bare .NET components can't be registered with COM+ Services because they comply with a different standard than COM's binary one. The Common Language Specification delineates the requirements to which languages must adhere in order to be classified as .NET-compliant, and part of the CLS addresses the format of the components that .NET languages produce. Specifically, component classes produced with a .NET language must restrict the datatypes of their input and output arguments to a specified set and must follow one of several visibility options.

Unlike COM components, .NET components, which are also known as **assemblies**, don't have to be entered into the system registry. The purpose of COM registration was to record component information in a central location so that COM Services would know where to find it, but .NET assembly files encapsulate their own information in special sections known as **manifests**. For an assembly to be available to a client application, it needs only be within that client application's folder. When the application is executed, the .NET runtime can search the directories for assemblies and then interrogate the assembly's manifest in order to determine what classes the assembly provides. In terms of simplicity of deployment, .NET assembly DLLs are similar to pre-COM DLLs, and they have been termed "portable executables". As you may have inferred, it's possible for different versions of the same assembly to co-exist peaceably on a single machine. Conversely, if you want several applications to share the same assembly DLL, you can place that DLL in a special folder under the system's Windows folder. This new deployment scheme of DLLs, which does not require registration, promises to deliver developers from frustrating hours of DLL Hell.

Creating an assembly component with a .NET language such as C# is a lot like creating an ActiveX server component with VB6; you simply create a new class library project, add classes to the project, and compile it. The development environment does the dirty work of generating the necessary plumbing code that the runtime requires. You don't have to worry about GUIDs, IUnknown interfaces, or ATL macros. Similarly, because the .NET runtime maintains garbage collection externally, the assembly components that you create don't have to maintain their own reference counts. In short, it's easier to create .NET assemblies.

In the face of .NET, COM is going to be different in the future from what it is today. References to COM as "classic COM" imply that .NET assemblies are the way forward for future component development. However, the development investments in COM+ Services and the reliance of current applications on COM components suggest that COM may be around for a long time, if not forever. Perhaps most developers will write .NET assemblies, and a hardcore few for whom speed and control are primary concerns will continue to code COM. At this point, no one really knows. Microsoft itself may be waiting to see how well .NET catches on.

Until this uncertainty is resolved, Microsoft provides a couple of tools for using .NET assemblies and COM components together. The Type Library Importer program (TLBIMP.EXE) creates .NET wrappers for COM components so that new .NET applications can make use of legacy COM code. With this tool, you could migrate an existing thick-client application to a .NET browser-based version by wrapping the application's COM business objects inside .NET assemblies and referencing the assemblies from the new .NET user interface. Another utility, the Type Library Exporter (TLBEXP.EXE), creates COM components that wrap .NET assemblies. With this, you can migrate existing applications to .NET via a piecemeal approach, gradually replacing existing COM components with their .NET equivalents. Such a project might be a good way for a programming team to get their feet wet with .NET development before embarking on a completely .NET endeavor.

The enterprise functionality afforded by COM+ Services is considerable. It would require many man-years to develop client authentication, object pooling, transaction enforcement, and message queuing from scratch. So that the benefits of COM+ Services may be realized, .NET developers may wind up using attributes to generate COM wrappers for a good many of their .NET components. Alternatively, .NET programmers can access much of the COM+ functionality from classes in the .NET base class library.

The .NET Base Classes

As mentioned earlier, .NET supplies a library of base classes that developers can use to implement applications quickly. Developers can use them by simply instantiating them and invoking their methods or by developing derived classes that extend their functionality. For example, the WinForm designer allows developers to graphically develop a class that extends the built-in `System.WinForm` class with additional data members (controls).

Currently, the Web is transitioning away from a network for serving HTML documents to web browsers and towards a globally-distributed application consisting of millions of objects living on different platforms and negotiating with each other for information using SOAP.

`System` is the root of the .NET base class namespace. It defines a set of data types recognized by all .NET-compliant languages. Among other types, this set includes a dedicated Boolean type, a string type, a decimal type for financial computations, and a group of integer types ranging from 8 to 64 bits in length. One type, the `object` type, is the type from which all other classes are derived. All .NET types are objects in that they have methods that can be called on them. Even an `int` for example, has a `Format` method that can be used to express its value in different base systems.

Data Type	Description	Value Type	Reference Type
bool	Dedicated Boolean type (true or false)	X	
byte	8-bit unsigned integer value	X	
char	Unicode (2-byte) character	X	
decimal	Monetary value	X	
double	floating-point value	X	
float	floating-point value	X	
int	32-bit signed integer value	X	
long	64-bit signed integer value	X	
object	Reference to an object		X
sbyte	8-bit signed integer value	X	
short	16-bit signed integer value	X	
string	Unicode (2-byte) b-string		X
struct	A composite data type that can contains value and reference types	X	
uint	32-bit unsigned integer value	X	
ulong	64-bit signed integer value	X	
ushort	16-bit signed integer value	X	

The base classes will be discussed in more detail in Chapter 7.

Now that we've introduced the most basic types defined in the System namespace, let's take a brief glance at other .NET objects in some of the namespaces within System, and the functionality that they provide.

❑ System.Math provides useful mathematical functions.

❑ System.Random creates a sequence of pseudo-random numbers. To use this class, you create a Random object, set its seed property, and collect numbers from repeated calls to the object's Next() method.

❑ System.Exception defines several exception classes, all of which derive from the Exception base class.

❑ System.Collections provides a number of collection classes (such as StringCollection), and a Dictionary class for storing instances of the object type. For developers who want to roll their own type-safe container classes, the ICollection, IDictionary, and IEnumerator interfaces are defined.

❑ System.IO provides classes for easy, abstracted access to the filesystem.

❑ System.Threading defines Timer, Mutex, and Thread objects for multithreading functionality.

❑ System.Diagnostics contains functionality for determining such runtime conditions as call stack depth. Assert and Log classes are aids to debugging.

The CLR Debugger

The .NET SDK provides an entire suite of utility programs for developers targeting the .NET platform. One of the most powerful of these is the **CLR debugger** (CORDBG.EXE). This tool allows you to attach to an executing .NET program, step through its code, examine its dependencies, and interrogate its objects and much, much more. In its simplest form, this debugger is a command line program with simple commands which can be abbreviated to one, two or three letters. Some useful commands are:

❑ b – to set a breakpoint

❑ de – to delete a breakpoint

❑ g – continue the current process

❑ h – display debugger command descriptions

❑ i – step into the next source line

❑ n – step over the next source line

❑ o – step out of the current function

❑ q – kill the current process and exit the debugger

❑ r – start a process for debugging

The true significance of the CLR debugger is that it can debug programs written in any .NET language. If you were working on a n-tier application, for example, the debugger would allow you to follow the application's thread-of-execution from a user interface written in VB.NET to a business layer coded in C# to a data access layer implemented in managed C++. Because it exposes its functionality through a documented interface, compiler vendors can use the debugger in the tools that they build to plug in to the VS.NET IDE.

Summary

This chapter explored .NET and how C# relates to it. We learned that .NET is a new Microsoft development platform that allows developers to quickly create web-ready applications in whatever programming languages they choose. We took a peek under the hood to see how .NET achieves its magic, and the technologies that went into it.

Now that we have some perspective on the .NET platform, it's time to narrow our focus to the true subject of this book: the C# programming language.

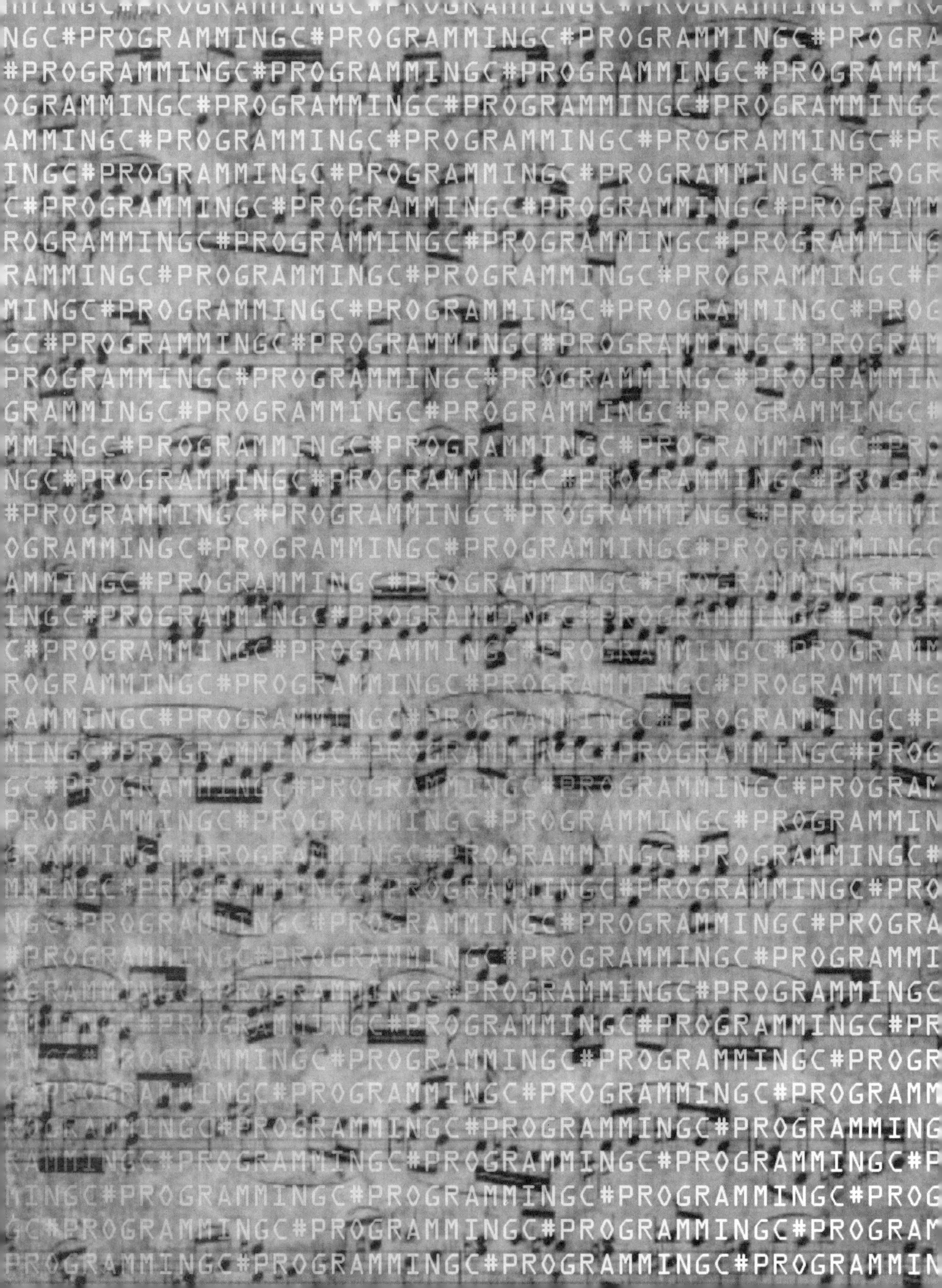
C#PROGRAMMING

2

Introduction to C#

What is C#?

This chapter will explore what C# is, what you can do with it, and how it relates to other languages. It concludes with a summary of C#'s major features, which will be further explained in the remainder of the book.

Let's begin by examining C#'s origins and ancestry.

The Development of C#

C and UNIX

The history of C# begins in the early 1970s, when Ken Thompson and Dennis Ritchie and their colleagues invented the C programming language and used it to write UNIX, a ground breaking operating system most notable for introducing the hierarchical file system.

By using simple, two-character text commands, a UNIX operator could create, copy, rename, delete, and traverse directories containing files. The commands could either be relative to the user's current working directory or absolute, in which case they were specified by a full path beginning at the file system's root. Obviously, UNIX had a tremendous influence on later operating systems such as DOS.

C allowed Thompson and Ritchie to concentrate more on UNIX and less on the tedious complexities of mainframe assembly language. As is often in the case in compiler development, the programmers first produced the core components of the C compiler and used these components to compile the rest of the compiler. C derived its name from Thompson and Ritchie's informal versioning scheme; it was the third in a series of experimental languages that they created.

C was inspired by BCPL, an earlier programming language that shared some of C's syntax but lacked definite data types. At once a low-level and a high-level language, C allows developers to reference memory locations via built-in primitives with pre-defined lengths (`int`, `float`, `double`, etc.), by user-defined types (`structs`), and by addresses (pointers).

C's flexible syntax makes it possible to declare a variable, initialize it, increment it, pass its value to a function, evaluate an expression with the function's return value, and enter a loop – all in a single line of code. A true programmer's programming language, C also includes powerful macros for linking files together, for defining global variables and functions, and for compiling different versions of the same files ("conditional compilation").

Because UNIX was implemented in C, it was portable to any platform with a C compiler, and UNIX initially shipped as C source code that the recipient had to compile before installing the resulting machine code on his mainframe. Even today, various Linux distributions provide the kernel's C source code so that developers can modify the kernel and thus produce their own private builds of the OS.

Expanding beyond UNIX, C proliferated throughout the programming world in scores of dialects targeting platforms both large and small. The American National Standards Institute ratified an ANSI C standard that dictates the data types, statements, and class libraries that a C implementation must support.

Although new object-oriented languages have stolen some of the spotlight from C, it's still a popular language for platforms for which efficiency is of the essence, such as embedded devices, and its low-level capabilities make it great for applications that need to directly address hardware.

Unfortunately, C is not perfect.

The power that C affords the programmer makes it easy for him to blunder. For example: just as C allows a developer to directly allocate memory, it also permits him to dereference this memory before he deallocates it, creating an unusable area in memory, a so-called memory leak. Other common C bugs include the mistaking of the assignment operator (=) for the Boolean equality operator (==), the failure to fit `switch...case` statements with requisite `break` clauses, and unintentionally `NULL` pointers. The effective use of C languages demands a degree of rigor that is difficult to achieve, particularly within corporate IT environments that demand periodic and punctual releases.

Even if C code is technically correct, it can be difficult to read. C's capacity for concision can prove an irresistible lure to coders who want to be considered clever by their peers. With C, such hotshots can crank out tiny programs that work effectively but are completely inscrutable to the unlucky maintenance programmers who inherit them.

C++ Modernizes C

In the early 1980's, Bjarne Stroustrup's "C with Classes", later known as C++, modernized C by enriching its facilities for abstract data types (ADTs). Implementation and interface inheritance and polymorphism are a couple of the idioms that a skillful C++ developer can use to realize such object-oriented benefits as modifiability, comprehensibility, and re-usability. Stroustrup's intent was to marry Simula67's object facilities with C's low-level efficiency. Stroustrup's achievement was a powerful, modern language applicable to a wide variety of problems. Like its predecessor, C++ took the programming world by storm.

C++ was improved by the introduction of the Standard Template Library, commonly known as the STL. For a generation of C++ programmers, the implementation of low-level data types such as strings, hashes, and linked lists was a rite of passage on which they cut their coding teeth. The STL introduced standard, optimized implementations of these ADTs and the algorithms (such as sorts) that can be performed on them. Small objects known as iterators or smart pointers allow the C++ programmer to loop through the STL's `Lists`, `Sets`, `Arrays`, and `Maps` using a common API. Because the ADTs in the STL are type generic, that is they can be used as container classes for objects of any type. Incidentally, the influence of the STL can be seen in the .NET base class library, and Microsoft has reported that future releases of C# will have facilities for generic code.

Despite it being object-oriented, and the convenience of the STL, C++ has its problems.

Veteran programmers often have a difficult time migrating from C to C++ because effective C++ programming requires a completely new mindset. A structured programming language, C is about functions that manipulate bits of data and pass those bits back and forth between them. An object-oriented language, C++ is about objects that encapsulate data and perform services at each other's request while hiding the complex details of how those services are performed. In order to build new million-line applications that took advantage of tremendous hardware advances, software engineers had to stop thinking of programs as huge monolithic blocks and instead regard them as complexes of smaller, discrete, cooperating subsystems. For many developers, this change was tough.

Although there have been many successful systems developed in C++ (such as the bulk of the United States' long distance telephone call routing services) there have been many failed projects that lacked the design or competency that a successful C++ project requires. Object-oriented software design is hard and requires practice. In the hands of an inexperienced or hurried developer, C++ is said to provide "enough ammunition to shoot yourself in the foot".

C at Microsoft

With Windows C, Microsoft applied a language originally designed for a procedural, mainframe OS to a real-time, microcomputer operating system that asynchronously receives events from a keyboard and mouse. Originally, the Windows OS and the programs for it were all coded in C. Nearly hundred lines of C code were required just to put a window up on the screen.

To write a Windows C program, you first created complicated `structs` that set the values for all the program's windows. Next, you equipped these window `structs` with special `WndProc functions` that were called by the operating system when the windows received messages, such as a mouse click or a key presses, from the operating system's message pump. The windows within an application were nested hierarchically, and child windows could either process their messages themselves or bubble up their messages to parent windows higher up in the hierarchy. Although the operating system provided stock child windows such as textboxes and buttons, the process of writing a Windows program in C was a painful, unforgiving one, and slight changes to the user interface could entail major overhauls of underlying code.

Even developers who mastered this event-driven programming model still had to contend with the sheer mind-boggling size of the Windows API. By Windows 95, it had swollen to several thousand function calls. It seemed that there was a function for everything – if only you knew where to find it! The developers best at programming Windows were those who had grown up with it because they had had sufficient time to absorb the incremental additions to the API that each new version of Windows introduced. A Microsoft newcomer struggling to learn a later version of Windows felt like an archaeologist attempting to excavate a mysterious city and uncovering layer after layer of confusing complexity.

C++ at Microsoft

One way in which Microsoft attempted to make Windows programming easier was by moving to object-oriented programming and C++. This move was not as difficult as you might imagine because Microsoft had taken a very object-oriented approach to C; to create windows, buttons, controls, and other entities, you stamped out `structs` in memory, received handles to those `structs`, and passed those handles to associated functions. It wasn't hard to glue the `structs` and their associated functions together inside C++ objects.

Microsoft wrapped the C-based Windows API in a thin layer of objects first called AFX but eventually renamed MFC (Microsoft Foundation Classes). Unfortunately, MFC, along with the ATL (Application Template Library), made Windows programming only a little less daunting. Even with C++, Windows programming was the domain of an elite group of top professionals, most of whom had been fortunate enough to get in early on the Windows programming game and thus keep pace with its snowballing complexity.

For a long time, Microsoft's Visual C++ compiler faced stiff competition from C++ compilers marketed by Borland. VC++ finally pulled ahead with the introduction of project wizards, applications that cranked out skeletal versions of the most popular VC++ project types: MFC applications, COM components, and ActiveX controls. These wizards did the dirty work, providing all of the necessary plumbing code necessary to get something up on the screen. Thus, with these later versions of VC++, programmers didn't have to start projects from scratch. Unfortunately, if a developer wanted to make serious modifications to the skeleton project that a wizard produced, he had to wade through a morass of Microsoft constants and macros. As Microsoft representatives have stated in print, VC++'s wizards appealed to the fantasies of mortal programmers who wanted to be C++ gurus. Windows programming still wasn't easy.

Visual Basic's Simplicity

In 1990, Microsoft introduced Visual Basic. With Visual Basic, Microsoft made Windows programming easier by applying BASIC, the language for beginners, to GUI development. The first versions of Visual Basic were a lot of fun, but flaky and restrictive. By Version 4, VB was no longer a toy, but a tool with which it was feasible to develop full-featured, industrial-strength applications. By version 6, Microsoft had provided VB with facilities for creating ActiveX controls and COM components.

The major breakthrough, which C# inherits, was VB's approach to user interface design. Instead of writing windows classes and `WndProc` code, developers dragged controls onto `Form` objects graphically, used a Properties Window to set a few values for those controls, and wrote just a little code to handle the events that those controls could generate. VB filled a niche and achieved a groundswell of developer support, as indicated by the plethora of VB books, magazines, web sites, and devoted fans.

Sun Creates Java

While Microsoft continued to refine the development environment targeting the Windows operating system, Sun Microsystems sought a single environment that would target multiple platforms. According to the popular legend, Sun provided a team of its best developers with a house, some videogames, and the instruction to "come up with something neat". The Java programming language was the neat thing that they came up with.

Java's most significant characteristic is the platform independence to which it aspires. Programs written in Java are compiled not to machine code, but instead to an intermediate language or **bytecode** that can be executed on *any* computer equipped with a suitable interpreter program (the Java runtime). Because the Java runtime is in charge of executing Java programs, it can guard system resources, reclaim unused memory, and thwart malicious code. Originally designed to program consumer electronic devices, Java first achieved popularity as a means of adding pizzazz and interactivity to Web pages. Java's motto was "write once, run anywhere". Amusingly, victims of the first failed Java projects satirized this statement, quipping "write once, *debug everywhere*".

As Java gained popularity, Microsoft released its own flavor of the Java language, Visual J++. Anders Hejlsberg, who went on to develop C#, was the leader of the Visual J++ effort. Although developers could use J++ to develop platform independent code, J++ also allowed platform-specific calls to the Windows API. Opponents claimed that such platform-specific code violated the intent of Java and resulted in bytecode that was not pure. Under legal fire from Sun, Microsoft quietly began to focus their development efforts on other products.

Microsoft .NET

One of Java's motivators was the World Wide Web. Everyone wants to transform the Web from a network for delivering HTML documents into a global application of distributed components running on different platforms and dynamically negotiating with each other for information. Unfortunately, getting all the computers in the world to talk to each other is no simple task.

Sun's approach was to encourage everyone to use the same language (Java). Unfortunately, this is a hard sell, no matter how good the language might be. Microsoft's approach was to develop different languages like VB and VC++ and blend them together in composite architectures using DCOM. The problem with *this* scheme is that it requires a skill set beyond the ability of the average developer, necessitates a lot of plumbing code, restricts the platform to Windows, and leads to deployment nightmares.

Today, Microsoft unveils an alternative strategy for bringing the development and Web worlds together and online: .NET. Because all .NET languages compile to a common bytecode, a developer can program in whichever language he wants and share his handiwork with developers using other .NET languages. Because .NET provides a runtime like that of Java, .NET code can execute safely and efficiently. Because .NET languages produce Web-ready XML, .NET components can communicate across the Internet with complete location transparency.

Under .NET, VB receives a major overhaul and C++ receives new keywords and extensions for interacting with the runtime. C# is the brand new language that .NET introduces. It combines the power of C++ with the productivity of VB and the elegance of Java.

C# and Other Languages

As you probably have inferred, the concept of the ideal programming language is a dynamic one that evolves over time. After reading this book, you may agree with the author that C# is better suited than any other existing language for an environment in which productivity, the Internet, and code-reuse are overriding concerns.

C# and Java

There's no doubt that passages of C# code can bear striking resemblances to functionally-equivalent passages of Java code. Both languages, for example, promote `one-stop coding`, the grouping of a classes, interfaces and implementation together in one file so that developers can edit the code more easily. C# and Java also handles objects in much the same way: via references rather than via pointers.

C# retains more of C++'s powerful features. For example, C# uses operator overloading (though not to the extent that C++ does) and type-safe enumerations, features that Java completely dispensed with. Furthermore, the C# compiler has an option to automatically produce XML-formatted code documentation using a special comment syntax – more on that in Chapter 6.

More significantly, C# makes better strategic sense for most organizations. Migrating to Java is an expensive undertaking requiring new hires, retraining, and a period of experimentation while everyone comes up to speed. With .NET's language interoperability, developers attracted to C# can work alongside other developers who prefer to work in older, more familiar tongues. Organizations that decide to standardize on C# can do so gradually, under the advice of their more advanced developers who make the leap first.

The one edge that Java has over C# is platform independence. In theory, the same Java bytecode that executes on one platform can execute on any other platform that is equipped with a Java virtual machine. For months now, developers have been excitedly speculating as to whether Microsoft will release CLR runtimes for platforms other than Windows. Doing so would endow C# and the other .NET languages with the platform independence that Java now enjoys. Microsoft has kept studiously quiet about this matter.

Although cynics make much of the syntactical similarities between Java and C#, they tend to ignore more fundamental parallels between the Java virtual machine and the Common Language Runtime. Both are in charge of interpreting bytecode. Both relegate memory re-allocation to a dedicated garbage collector component. Both are in charge of authenticating code before it is executed, and can restrict executing clients to a toolbox of operating system services that cannot compromise system security. Additionally, some of the classes and namespaces inside the .NET class library are eerily similar to classes and namespaces in the Java class library. The `Math` class that both platforms provide is the most obvious example.

C# and VB.NET

The differences between VB6 and VB.NET are dramatic. Justice demands that C# be compared to each version separately.

C# borrows VB6's approach to form design; in both languages, developers build user interfaces by dragging controls from a toolbox, dropping them onto forms, and writing event handlers for them. C# exploits this process to great effect, applying it not only to the development of user interfaces but to the composition of business objects as well. This is the only real similarity between C# and VB6, because VB6's object capabilities don't compare to those of C#. VB6, for instance, supports neither parameterized constructors nor implementation inheritance.

The next version of VB, formerly called VB7 but now called VB.NET, beefs up VB's object facilities, but this version of VB looks like C# with different keywords! In fact, sites on the web have shown that the same source code that will compile with the VB compiler will compile with the C# compiler after the global replacement of a few keywords. VB has certainly changed *a lot*: parameterized constructors and implementation inheritance are now included and more concise operators are present in VB.NET. There's a new syntax for declaring object properties as well.

Disturbingly, certain VB statements will mean different things in VB.NET than they did in VB6. In short, these statements will be more C-like. Consider the following statement as an example:

```
Dim strFirstName, strLastName as String
```

In VB6, only `strLastName` would be typed as a `String` and `strFirstName` would be typed as a `Variant`. In VB.NET, both `strFirstName` and `strLastName` will be `Strings`. This sort of compound variable declaration has been available from C for years.

Here's another example of the inconsistencies between VB6 and the coming VB.NET. This one involves what are termed short-circuiting conditionals. Take a look at this code:

```
If (A() And B()) Then
    Call C()
End If
```

Assume that the call to function A returns a value of False. Under VB6, the call to function B would still occur, even though False value returned by A dooms the Boolean conditional (And) joining the calls to A and B to failure. Under VB7, the False value returned by function A would cause the comparison to "short-circuit", terminating the statement early without ever activating function B. Here, VB.NET demonstrates more C-like behavior than VB6 did.

Despite VB's new features and behaviors, it is not quite as powerful as C#. C#'s most striking advantage over VB.NET is its capacity to contain embedded blocks of fast, efficient C++ code. In other words, you could use pointers to access an array, for example. This would still be compiled to IL, but as it's unsafe it would be faster, as C# wouldn't be checking for array boundaries. Another significant plus for C# is the ease with which it can make calls to the Windows API. The question is, will developers view VB.NET's shortcomings as being important?

Right now, it's still unclear how many developers will like C# and how many will favor VB. The letter "C" scares a lot of people, many of whom have had bad experiences with the arbitrary obtuseness of Windows programming in C and C++. Name recognition, loyalty, and fear of the unknown may perpetuate VB for a long time to come, although the author suspects that a sizable constituency of the VB camp can be expected to defect to C# right off the bat.

Of course, there's an outside chance that VB.NET's new object-oriented features will satisfy VB programmers for a while, making them reluctant to poke about in a brand new language like C#. Could VB.NET quash C#, making it a stillborn language, which though a good idea, never really gets off the ground? The amount of hype surrounding C#, Microsoft's decision to standardize on C# as their language for new development efforts, and the integral relationship between C# and the .NET platform make this last outcome seem highly unlikely. There's simply too much push for C# to go completely under.

It may be that, as time goes on, VB and C# will converge. Perhaps computer languages evolve in much the same way that human languages do – as a confluence of dialects – and that future compilers can understand source code incorporating elements from both C# and VB.NET. Right now, it's anyone's guess.

If you are a VB programmer who does not yet use classes, learn VB.NET first. In doing so, you can concentrate on mastering important object-oriented concepts and leave the memorization of a new set of keywords until later. If you are a VB6 programmer skilled in object-oriented techniques, consider whether C#'s advantages are enough to make you change. Keep in mind that the transition to VB.NET may not be a piece of cake even if you are skilled in VB6, and that C# has the aesthetic advantage of a lean, consistent syntax drawn on a clean slate.

C# and C++

As their names suggest, C# and C++ are related. In fact, you can rightly think of C# as a simpler, safer, and more productive subset of C++.

An example of C#'s simplicity is its *one-stop coding* approach to code maintenance. In C++, it's a constant challenge to keep class declarations in header (.h) files matched up with their implementations in server (.cpp) files. C# sidesteps this problem by encapsulating each class' definition and implementation into one code block in a single C# (.cs) file. Of course, some C++ programmers opted for this pragmatic strategy all along, but at the cost of foisting an unconventional approach on later developers who inherited their code. C# makes this simple approach the rule rather than the exception.

Another example of C#'s *simplicity* is the way that it resolves dependencies on external components. C++ required that you mention referenced components in two places: 1) in #include statements in the client project's source code, and 2) in the client project's references list. To use a .NET server component from a C# client, you only need to add a reference to the component with the Add Reference menu, or the Solution Explorer. There's no need to #include a header file. Thus, in its simple approach to external dependencies, C# is more like VB6 than C++.

In addition to being simpler than C++, C# is also *safer* – for both the developer and the execution environment. C# is safer for the developer in that it makes it more difficult to write buggy code. Examples of this safety include the elimination of bug-prone idioms such as preprocessor macros and fall-through `switch...case` statements, and the compiler's insistence that variables be initialized before their values are referenced. C# is safer for the development environment in that its elimination of pointers and its reliance on built-in garbage collection make memory leaks a thing of the past.

C# is *more productive* than C++ in that it adopts of the toolbox/control/form method of building GUI applications, that makes user interface design a snap. Also, C#'s compatibility with the .NET base classes provides it with a rich library of pre-existing functionality that developers can quickly plug together into new applications. When developing re-usable components, C# programmers simply implement classes and compile them, without having to worry about `IUnknown` interfaces, GUIDs, and messy ATL templates.

Since C# and C++ are so similar, readers might benefit from a list detailing some of the major differences between them:

❑ C# prohibits pointers. In C#, objects are manipulated strictly via references. Consequently, the indirection operator (`->`) has been eliminated from C#. If you want to use pointers, you can do so only within `unsafe` blocks, where the code is a subset of C++ rather than C#.

❑ C# uses a different, simpler syntax for arrays.

❑ To reduce bugs, C# eliminates preprocessor macros, though it retains other useful preprocessor commands, including those that enable conditional compilation.

❑ In C# `switch...case` statements control cannot accidentally "fall through" from one activated `case` clause to those below it. Fall-through occurs only where the `case` clause contains no code, in which case the fall-through is almost certain to be intended.

❑ C# demands that variables be initialized before they are referenced.

❑ C# limits inheritance to encourage the development of good class hierarchies. Specifically, a class can inherit as many interfaces as it needs to, but can only inherit functionality from one parent class.

Many of the restrictions imposed by C# are meant to discourage bad coding practices. In general, the more committed to good coding practices the C++ programmer is, the easier he will find the transition to C#.

C# and Managed C++

If you are a C++ programmer who wants the benefits of the Common Language Runtime without the language restrictions imposed by C#, you can create **managed C++** programs. Although managed C++ programs can make use of the garbage collector, the .NET base classes, and language interoperability, they can use unsafe features such as pointers without segregating these idioms into `unsafe` code blocks.

Microsoft promotes managed C++ as a way to gradually migrate large, legacy C++ applications to the .NET platform. Using a special set of keywords that extend the C++ language, C++ programmers can make C++ source code .NET-compliant without making a lot of changes. For instance, by prefixing existing C++ class definitions with simple keywords, a C++ developer can indicate to the compiler that the classes should now run in the context of the CLR. Conversely, C++ extensions can also be used to reference .NET components from C++ code. By applying managed extensions to C++ classes selectively, you can create executables that contain both managed and unmanaged code.

C# and JScript

JScript is another language that can be used to program .NET. Its syntax is much like C's, though simpler. At the time of this writing, JScript can only be used for server-side scripting and to control web browsers via client-side code. In other words, it's not yet possible to author WinForm applications, components, and other .NET projects with JScript.

Basically, JScript is Microsoft's answer to JavaScript, the scripting language used to perform client-side dynamic HTML in Netscape Navigator. Unlike VBScript, JScript is recognized by both Netscape Navigator and Internet Explorer. Often, web developers use JScript to validate fields in HTML <FORM> elements and to implement roll-overs, those web browser images that change when you pass the mouse pointer over them. JavaScript and JScript have nothing to do with Java.

Some developers use JScript to do the server-side scripting. A special setting in the Internet Services Administrator applet allows you to determine whether the server-side scripting tags indicate blocks of JScript or blocks of VBScript. Of course, under .NET, you can also code ASP.NET pages with C# or VB, or other third party languages.

Like C#, JScript inherits a concise and elegant syntax from C.

Unlike C#, JScript is weakly-typed (although JScript.NET also supports strong typing); all JScript variables are declared with the keyword `var` and can be implicitly converted from one kind of value to another. Furthermore, JScript takes a rather unusual approach to the creation and manipulation of objects. Instead of creating class definitions and using them to stamp out objects, you create functions that assign values to the `this` variable, thus approximating constructor functions. Because of this strange approach, the use of objects in JScript has remained something of a black art. JScript is another example of a hybrid language that has gradually been embellished to meet the increasing demands of its developers.

Because C# is cleaner and more powerful than JScript, most C-oriented developers will probably choose C# over JScript for server-side applications. However, because JScript is recognized by both Netscape and Microsoft browsers, JScript may be used in the development of client-side web controls, which we'll talk about in the next section.

What Can I Do with C#?

Thanks to .NET's language interoperability, a single solution can combine projects written in different .NET languages. For example, one data access solution might consist of a Windows application written in VB.NET that uses business objects written in C# that call data access objects coded in managed C++. Because these projects all reference the same `Exception` class defined in the .NET base class library, errors raised in the data access could be passed up through each of the projects, across languages, to be logged and/or presented to the user. Similarly, because these projects all reference the same .NET debugger, you can use VS.NET to step through the entire solution, following the thread-of-execution from one project to another.

Let's take a moment to examine the different kinds of .NET projects and how they relate to each other. The process for creating these .NET projects is much the same regardless of the language with which you choose to implement them, so programmers using languages other than C# can benefit from reading this section. As we look at these project types, we'll mention the role each plays in n-tier, distributed architectures.

Console Applications

The simplest of all .NET projects, console projects derive their name from the character-only, graphics-free terminal consoles that connected users to the mainframe systems of yesteryear. A console program executes entirely in a DOS command window. Fast to develop but visually unappealing, console projects are useful for creating driver programs for components that you are testing.

The main body of a console project consists of a class definition containing a function that matches this signature:

```
public static void Main(string[] args)
```

This function serves as the program's entry point. When the program is invoked, the operating system delivers any command line argument to it through the `args` array. (As you may already know, the `static` modifier makes the function a class method rather than an instance method, so that it can be invoked on its own, without the creation of an instance of the class.)

During execution, console applications rely on the `Read`, `ReadLine`, `Write`, and `WriteLine` methods of the `System.Console` object for input and output.

Although you could use a console project to create a primitive user interface for an n-tier application, such a user interface would seem very unattractive to modern computer users accustomed to flashy GUIs. As stated earlier, the most common use of console applications is testing other components.

Creating console applications is a great way to start learning C#. You don't have to have Visual Studio in order to do so; all that's required is the C# compiler that is freely available from Microsoft. We'll talk more about using the C# compiler later in this chapter.

Windows Applications

A WinForm project looks and feels like a *traditional* Windows application such as Microsoft Word. When executed, a WinForm program displays windows that a user interacts with by manipulating various list box, button, and text box controls. Windows applications require installation on clients' machines.

You can use WinForm projects as interfaces for distributed applications, or as stand-alone programs. The upside of a WinForm project is its simplicity and the "slickness" of its interface; the downside of a WinForm project is its troublesome installation and upgrades. Microsoft promotes WebForms rather than WinForms as the user interface strategy of the future. There is more on WinForms in Chapter 8.

Windows Controls

.NET wraps up the basic Windows control types and presents them in the VS.NET tool box so that you can drop them onto WinForms. However, in case you need specialized functionality beyond that provided by the intrinsic controls, .NET allows you to roll your own. If you've ever used VB6 or VC++ to create an ActiveX control, you have a head start on learning to create custom windows controls for use with .NET. The process, and the issues that you have to address, are very much the same.

ASP.NET Projects

Because browser-based applications run on web servers and use clients' web browsers for user interfaces, they are inexpensive to install, upgrade, and maintain. If a change needs to be made, it needs only be made at one location – on the server. The next time users browse to the application's site, they will reap the rewards of the improvement.

Active Server Pages (ASP) is a popular Microsoft technology for creating browser-based applications. An ASP application consisted of a series of ASP pages stored together in a folder on a web server. Each page was an .asp file containing blocks of HTML mixed with blocks of server-side VBScript or JScript. When a browser requested an ASP page, the server delivered the HTML in the page to the requesting browser and processed the chunks of server-side script that it encountered as it served the document up. Thus, in the blocks of server-side script, ASP pages could invoke business objects to fetch data from the database or to perform other services, creating dynamic pages with changing content.

ASP.NET promises to significantly enhance the performance of ASP by allowing developers to create pages that are compiled rather than interpreted. That's right; instead of using JScript or VBScript to code pages that are re-interpreted each time they are requested, you can use full-fledged .NET languages (including C#) to code pages that compile to IL. The first time that such an ASP.NET page is requested, the ASP.NET code is translated to a .cs (or a .vb) file which is then compiled. The Just-in-Time compiler then converts the resulting IL to native code, caching it in case the page is requested again. Obviously, this new approach means that ASP.NET pages will render much faster than ASP pages ever did. We will cover this in more detail in Chapter 13.

Web Controls

Like regular Windows controls, Web controls are depicted as icons in Visual Studio.NET's toolbox. When a developer drags a web control's icon from the toolbox onto a WebForm, an XML tag corresponding to that web control is added to the HTML page that the WebForm represents. When a remote browser requests an HTML page, the web server ascertains the requesting browser's type and transforms the XML tag into a hunk of HTML and JScript that the browser will understand. Thus, a web control is an abstraction for a chunk of HTML and JScript.

To create a web control, you simply create a .NET component that implements a particular interface. To use a web control from within a WebForm project, you must create a reference to that control from the control tab of the IDE's References dialog.

VS.NET ships with web controls that implement calendars, grids, and hyperlinks. Experts predict that a cottage industry of third-party web control vendors will probably emerge.

Visual Studio.NET is explained in more detail in the next chapter.

Web Services

WebForm projects interact with human beings through browser interfaces, but Web Service projects provide information to other applications and components.

To put it simply, a web service is a class with a web front end. An ASP.NET page associated with the class allows other classes to call methods on the class from across the Internet. The format of the requests, and the format of any return values is the SOAP protocol. In the World Wide Web envisioned by Microsoft, web services all over the world will provide client applications with all kinds of dynamic information, from stock market quotes to weather reports.

The beauty of a web service is the ease of its creation. The developer simply opens a new web service project, adds classes, and implements them. At compilation, the compiler does the dirty work of creating an ASP page for accepting the SOAP requests and activating the object.

Web services are discussed in Chapter 14.

.NET Components

A component is a compiled library of classes that can be referenced and used by other programs. In the past, creating a Windows COM component with a C-style language was an arduous task involving interfaces, GUIDs, and lots of boilerplate code. Now, .NET makes component-creation a simple matter in any language:

- ❑ Open a new component project.
- ❑ Add classes to the project and implement them.
- ❑ Compile the project to a DLL.

As we said in Chapter 1, a compiled .NET component is called an assembly, and contains a manifest, an embedded chunk of metadata that describes its classes and interfaces. To avail an assembly to a client, you simply copy the assembly to the client's folder. Because a client can dynamically obtain information about an assembly from the assembly's manifest, there's no need to enter assemblies into the system registry. Handily, different versions of the same component with the same name can exist side-by-side on the same machine as long as they are in different folders. For this reason, assemblies are sometimes said to be "application private".

.NET plays well with traditional COM components. The SDK provides programs that generate COM proxies for .NET assemblies and .NET proxies for COM components. From `unsafe` blocks in C# code, you can manipulate COM components in the traditional way, using their `IUnknown`-derived interfaces. From C++, you can directly manipulate .NET components using managed extensions.

.NET components are discussed in Chapter 10 on assemblies and manifests.

Compiling and Running C#

The C# compiler currently ships with the .NET beta. The Visual Studio beta allows you to invoke it graphically from the IDE. You can download the .NET beta from the Microsoft website and invoke it from the command line or from one of the shareware editors that have been specially created for it.

To get the compiler, browse to `http://msdn.microsoft.com/downloads/default.asp` and download the.NET beta. It's 86MB, so be prepared to wait.

The compiler's behavior is controlled using command line arguments.

Here's a list of all the command line arguments:

Command Line Argument	Description
@	@response_file gives the name of a file which contains more compiler options - just as if the text in the file was input on the command line.
/?	This displays a list of compiler options on the screen.
/addmodule	Used to add in metadata from DLLs into the project.
/baseaddress	State the preferred address base to load a DLL into.
/bugreport	Outputs debug information into a file.

Command Line Argument	Description
/checked	States that integer arithmetic, that hasn't been specified as checked or unchecked in the code, and overflows the allowed range of the data type will produce a run-time exception.
/codepage	Decided which code page will be used for the source files.
/debug	Outputs debugging information to a .pdb file. .
/define	This is the same as the #define preprocessor directive.
/doc	Outputs the XML comments present in your code into a file.
/fullpaths	Any files that the compiler displays (for example in debugging information) will give the full path to the file.
/help	Same as /?.
/incremental	Lets you compile only those files that have changed since the last compilation.
/linkresource	Lets you link in a .NET resource.
/main	Lets you specify the class containing the Main() method - useful in that it allows you to specify which class to load first if you have more than one class with a Main() method.
/nologo	Stops the sign-on banner and messages being displayed.
/nooutput	Compile but do not create an output file - useful for checking for any compiler warnings.
/nostdlib	Stops the standard library (mscorlib.dll) from being imported.
/nowarn	Stops the compiler from generating specified warnings.
/optimize	Tells the compiler whether or not it should optimize the code.
/out	Specify the output file - discussed below.
/recurse	Search child subdirectories and compile all files found.
/reference	Imports manifest data into your project.
/resource	Specify that a .NET resource should be embedded in the output file.
/target	Or /t. Specifies what type of file to output - this is covered below.
/unsafe	Allows code containing the unsafe keyword to compile.
/warn	Or /w. Set the level of warnings the compiler outputs, 0 is no warnings, 4 gives the most detail.
/warnaserror	Promotes warnings to errors, so any code which gives a warning won't compile.

Command Line Argument	Description
/win32icon	Lets you define how the executable will appear in the Windows Explorer by specifying a .ico file.
/win32res	Specify that a Win32 resource should be inserted into the output file.

The /out: argument indicates the name of the output file. The /w argument allows you to set the compiler's warning level. Most importantly, the /t: argument allows you to indicate the type of output file that should be generated – a simple EXE, a DLL or a Windows EXE. A fourth type of output file, a module, is a .NET component with the manifest left out so that the file can be combined with other module files to form a single assembly.

Command Line Argument	Output Indicated by the Argument
/t:exe	An .exe file (a Console application)
/t:library	A component with a manifest
/t:module	A component without a manifest
/t:winexe	A Windows application program

Now we'll see how to compile a simple C# console application. If the name of the C# source code file is Whassup.cs, the proper command would be:

```
csc Whassup.cs /t:exe /out:Whassup.exe
```

As /t:exe and /out:Whassup.exe are the default compiler settings these can be left out, therefore the simplest command you can issue is:

```
csc Whassup.cs
```

When you tire of typing in commands, check out the shareware and third-party C# editors. Some of the better ones not only automatically invoke the compiler, but provide syntax coloring and automatic indentation as well. A free trial of one of the most popular third-party editors, Antechinus, is available at www.c-point.com.

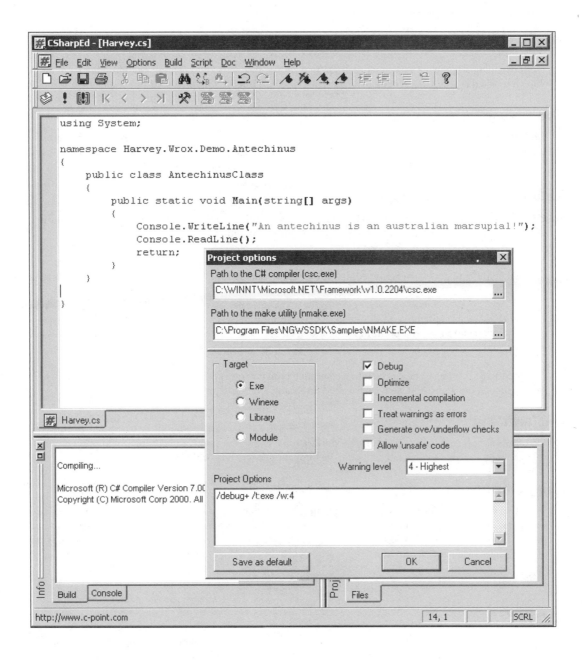

The C# Language

To conclude this chapter, we'll present you with a very broad overview of the C# language. Later chapters will explain these concepts in greater detail.

Data types

Understanding a language's treatment of data types is the first step towards understanding the language. After you've finished reading this section on data types, you can refer to Chapter 4 for more specific information.

The Object Type

All C# types are said to inherit from the `object` type. This means that if a function takes an `object` as an input argument, you can pass a variable of any type to that function. Thus, the `object` type allows you to do late binding. It's similar to the `variant` type in VB6 or to a void pointer in C++.

Value and Reference Types

C# types can be divided into two categories: value types and reference types. These categories differ in where they are stored in memory and in how assignment operations affect them.

Value types are allocated on the stack. When you assign one instance of a value type to another instance of the value type, you get two separate copies of the same value in memory. `int` and `double` are examples of value types.

Reference types are allocated on the heap. An assignment between two instances of a reference type results in two references that point at a single object. All user-defined classes are reference types as are `string` and `object`.

The process of turning a value type into a reference type is known as boxing. The process of turning a reference type back into a value type is called unboxing.

Declarations

C# allows simple and compound variable declarations. For safety's sake, the compiler will prevent you from referencing a variable's value before you have explicitly assigned an initial value to it.

Enumerations

With C#, you can define an enumeration, an integer type that only accepts values from a user-specified set. Enumerations make your code more readable because they allow you to refer to integer values by intuitive names. Enumerations make you code more correct because they allow the compiler to catch the assignment of meaningless values. C# provides the `enum` keyword for creating enumerations.

```
public enum OrdinalType { first=1, second=2, third=3 }
```

Arrays

C# supports single and multidimensional arrays using a syntax not unlike that of C or C++. You can define an array's size at when you declare it or leave the size undefined and define it later.

```
int[] intArray;
intArray=new int[5];
```

Operators

C#'s operators are just what you'd expect from a C-style language. The following table lists a few of the most common ones. For a more detailed examination of C#'s operators, see Chapter 4.

Operator	Meaning
,	Separates clauses in a compound statement.
&&	A logical AND
||	A logical OR
!	Logical NOT
&	A bitwise AND
|	A bitwise OR

Flow Control

This section addresses the primary means of controlling flow in a C# program: conditional statements, loops, and functions. Flow control is addressed at length in Chapter 4.

Conditionals

C# supports if...else and switch...case statements. The ternary operator form of the if...else statement is legal; in other words you can write a = b<c ? b : c instead of if (b<c) a=b; else a=c;. To aid readability for those used to other C-style languages, you should follow each case clause in a switch...case statement with a break; statement, although fall-through to the next case clause occurs only when the clause contains no code.

Loops

C# supports for, while and do...while loops. Additionally, C# provides the foreach loop for iterating through items in collections.

Classes

C#'s greatest asset is its rich facilities for implementing object-oriented designs. C# makes it easy to specify every aspect of a class: its visibility, its lifetime, its data members, and how it relates to other data types. For a more in-depth examination of the ideas presented here, see Chapters 5 and 6.

Accessibility

One of the primary goals of object-oriented programming is data hiding; you want only certain details of your classes to be visible to the outside world. C# provides a set of access modifiers for determining the visibility of your classes' properties and methods. These modifiers include private, protected and public.

Lifetime

C# permits you to equip a class with multiple, parameterized constructors. It provides a special syntax for invoking the constructors of parent classes from their child classes.

In C#, as in the other .NET languages, you can't rely on destructor functions executing as soon as the object is de-referenced. Because of this uncertain timing, and because of certain inefficiencies in the CLR's garbage collector, C# classes shouldn't rely on `finalize` functions to do a lot of work.

Data Members

Like VB6, C# provides a dedicated syntax for defining class properties. Unlike VB6, this syntax centralizes a property's read and write aspects into a single block of code so that the property code is more maintainable.

Indexers are special properties that expose arrays inside classes. You can use an indexer to make an array read-only or write-only or to validate values before they are placed inside the array.

Methods

You define C# methods in the same way that you define C or C++ methods. However, C# introduces a couple of new keywords for controlling how input arguments behave.

The `ref` keyword does just what you'd think it does – it specifies an input argument as being by reference. Changes that the method makes to the value of the input argument are visible from outside the method.

Earlier, I mentioned that C# requires you to initialize a variable before you reference its value. This can be inconvenient when you're defining a variable to be passed by reference to a method. If you prefix a method's input argument with the `out` keyword, you don't have to initialize variables that you pass to the method through that argument.

Inheritance

C# permits implementation and interface inheritance, and in a way that promotes the development of robust class hierarchies. Specifically, a class can inherit as many interfaces as it wants to, but can inherit *implementation* from only one parent class. This restriction is in line with the thinking of leading object-oriented developers.

An abstract class is a one that cannot be instantiated; its only purpose is to supply an interface and default functionality that child classes can inherit. C# provides an explicit keyword for marking classes as abstract.

Classes prefaced with the `sealed` keyword cannot be used as parent classes.

Operator Overloading

C# lets you define what the various operators (such as +)mean in the context of your classes. By doing so, you can allow clients to use your classes in intuitive ways. For instance, by overloading the addition (+) operator for a hypothetical `Matrix` class, you could allow clients to invoke the class's addition functionality in a way that makes sense.

```
//Clumsy, without overloaded operators.
Matrix matrixX;
matrixX=matrixY.Add(matrixZ);

//Intuitive, with overloaded operators.
Matrix matrixC=matrixA + matrixB;
```

Reflection

With reflection, a C# program can dynamically ascertain a late-bound object's underlying type. Once this type has been determined, reflection allows other information to be gathered as well, including the type's properties and methods. Using attributes, a programmer can attach metadata to classes and to class members.

For more information on attributes and reflection, see Chapter 6.

Interoperability

Another of C#'s features is its ability to interoperate with other programming languages and APIs.

COM Interoperability

Microsoft designed .NET in such a way that organizations could move to it gradually, integrating legacy COM components with newer .NET pieces. There are several ways of using COM components and .NET components together. These ways include creating .NET wrappers for COM components and invoking COM interfaces directly from C# code.

For the dirty details, see Chapter 11.

Invoking the Windows API

Invoking the Windows API from C# is a lot like invoking the Windows API from VB6. You just reference the proper DLL and define a wrapper function for the desired call. To reference the DLL, you have to use an attribute.

```
//This imports a Win32 API function so that it can be
//called from the .NET environment.
[sysimport(dll="user32.dll")]
private static extern int MessageBoxA(int hWnd, string
                         Message, string Caption, int Type);
```

For more information, see Chapter 11.

Structured Error Handling

Like VB.NET, C# promotes a structured approach to error handling. This structured approach involves the use of several kinds of code blocks.

If code inside a `try` block encounters an error or an anomalous condition, it throws an `Exception` object. At this point, the thread of execution leaves the `try` block and enters a `catch` block, where the properties of the `Exception` object are interrogated and appropriate action is taken. Finally, code inside the `finally` block is executed. Because the `finally` block is invoked whether or not an `Exception` was thrown, it's the ideal place to put clean up code. To learn more about structured error handling, see Chapter 4.

Because the various .NET languages all share the same `Exception` object, errors can be thrown back through components written in different languages.

The Preprocessor

C#'s preprocessor does away with the macros that introduced so many bugs into C and C++ programs. Preprocessor commands for conditional compilation are still supported, though: #define, #if, and #endif. Other preprocessor commands allow you to divide your code into collapsible and expandable regions for easy viewing, and to control the line numbering scheme that the compiler uses when reporting errors.

The C# preprocessor is one of the topics covered in Chapter 6.

Summary

C# is a new programming language uniquely suited for environments in which productivity, power, and the Internet are important. It has its roots in C, C++, Java, and, to a limited degree, Visual Basic.

Developers can use C# to create different kinds of projects: Console applications, Windows applications, ASP.NET applications, .NET components, and Web Services. These projects can be fitted together to implement n-tier, distributed applications.

Subsequent chapters will discuss the ideas presented here in greater detail.

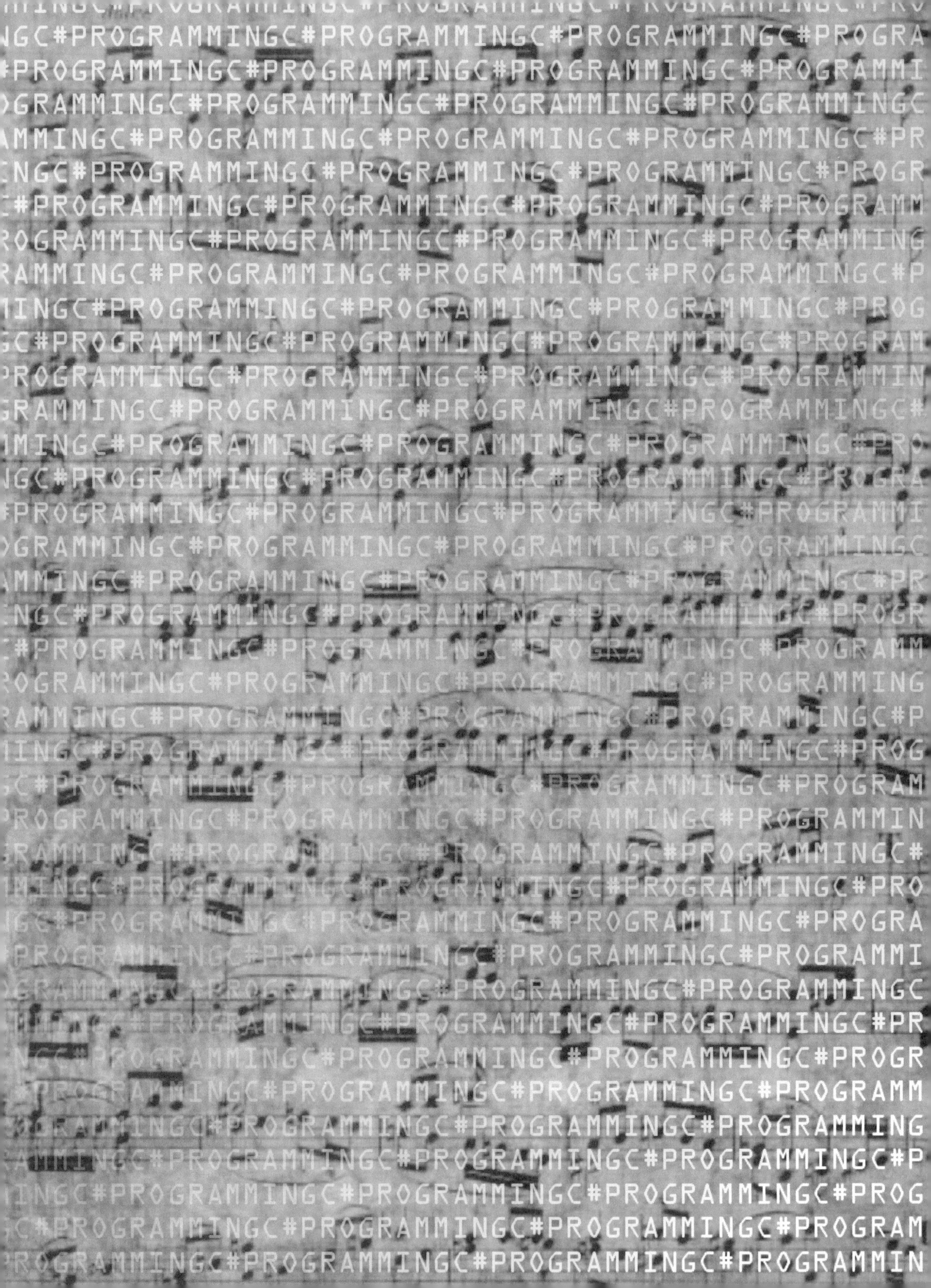
C#PROGRAMMING

3

A Tour of VS.NET

Microsoft's forthcoming Visual Studio.NET is a truly *integrated* development environment. With it, the folks at Redmond have fulfilled their long-standing promise to provide a single code editor common to all programming languages. Plus, there's an XML editor, an HTML editor, a SQL Server interface, a designer for building server-side components graphically, and a Server Explorer for monitoring remote machines. In short, Visual Studio.NET centralizes *everything* that you need to build distributed applications.

We'll begin our tour of VS.NET by examining its various windows. Next, we'll walk through some of the more common VS.NET tasks. Finally, we'll conclude with a look at some of the ways to customize VS.NET for greater productivity.

One word of caution from your tour guide: remember that this book was written using the Beta 1 version of the VS.NET software. Your version may have some differences.

The Start Page

The first window we'll look at isn't really a window at all; it's the HTML-formatted Start page, and it's shown within the same tabbed window frame as the other VS.NET windows.

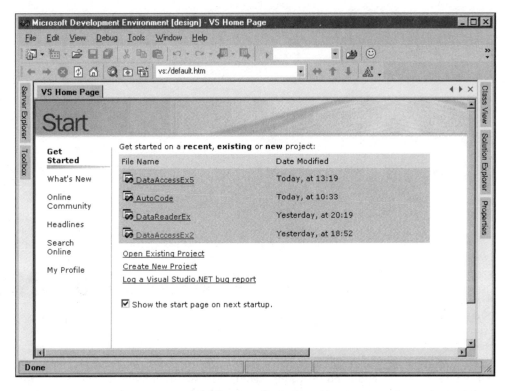

As its name implies, the Start page is an HTML document. Being the first thing that you see when you start up Visual Studio, the Start page has links to the last few projects on which you've worked, a link to a Visual Studio News site (you'll have to have an Internet connection for that), and a link for creating user profiles that customize the appearance and behavior of the IDE. We'll talk more about user profiles in the section on customization.

As the Start page demonstrates, VS.NET has a web browser integrated right into it. A menu bar above and to the left of the browser window has all the typical browser buttons– a box for a URL, a Refresh button, a Home button, a Stop button, Forwards and Backwards buttons, and a button for displaying a Favorites folder, but of course, to be able to employ web functionality, you'll need a connection to the Internet.

Overview of the VS.NET IDE

Tabbed and Auto-Hide Windows

To conserve screen real estate, the VS.NET IDE (Integrated Development Environment) uses a couple of interesting techniques. The first trick is to use tabbed windows, the practice of layering several windows on top of each other, and exposing a row of tabs above or below them so that you can select a single window and move it to the top of the stack. The second trick, auto-hide, shows windows on an as-needed basis, displaying them fully only when you drag your mouse pointer over them and collapsing them again to the edge of the screen when the pointer is removed.

Some of the windows that we'll look at use these techniques. If you really want to get the most out of your screen space and it doesn't bother you too much for windows to be constantly popping out and hiding again, you can make *all* the IDE's windows into auto-hide windows by setting the Auto Hide All option on the Window menu.

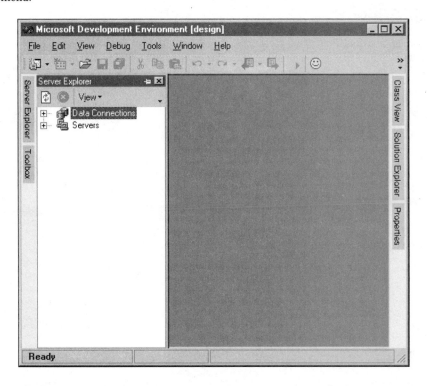

The Solution Explorer

The Solution Explorer presents a hierarchical list of all the files on which you are working. Files are grouped into projects, and several projects form a solution. A typical solution might consist of several component projects, and a user interface (WinForm or WebForm) project that references them. In such a solution, the name of the WinForm project would be **bolded**, indicating that it is the start-up project, i.e. the point at which execution should begin when you start debugging. To mark a project as start-up, right-click on its name and select Set as Start Up from the resulting menu.

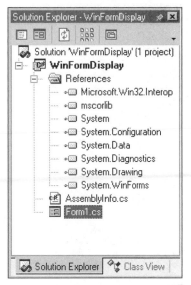

VS.NET has inherited the functionality of the late, not-so-great Visual InterDev. When you work on a web project, the ASP and HTML files comprising that project are listed in the Solution Explorer, right beside your C# or VB code files.

The Class View

As its names implies, the Class View presents a logical view of your work using an Explorer-like tree view of the your classes, methods, and properties.

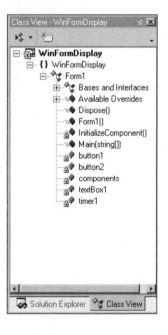

The Properties Window

You may remember the Properties window from the Visual Studio 6 IDE. In that environment, the Properties window was used to view and set property attributes of controls, classes, and projects. In the VS.NET, the Properties window's responsibilities have been expanded. In addition to providing details about controls, files, and projects, the Properties window can display information about machines monitored in the Server Explorer.

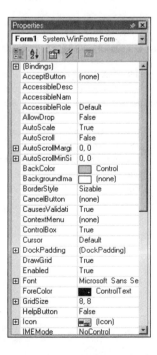

Using the Properties window couldn't be any easier. You can select a control or class simply by clicking on it, and then the Properties window will show a list of properties and values appropriate to the item that you selected. The incorporated drop-down boxes also allow you to quickly set properties by choosing from a list of appropriate values.

The Toolbox

When hidden, this window is a thin strip just big enough for the label: Toolbox. When you move your cursor over this strip, it expands into a toolbox of goodies that you can drag-and-drop onto the user interfaces that you design.

These goodies, or controls as they are more formally known, are divided up into several categories indicating the kinds of user interfaces that they target: WinForm controls, HTML controls, WebForm controls, etc. To open a control category, click on the gray divider bearing the category's name. It will snap open, expanding vertically to fill the toolbox with the controls inside it.

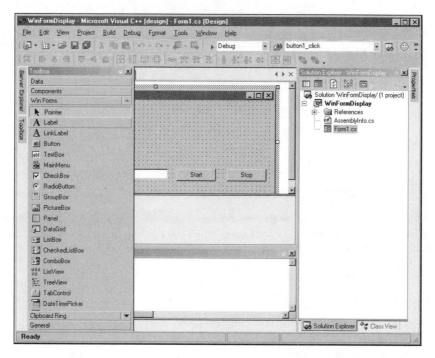

If you examine the status bar at the top of the toolbox window carefully, you'll notice the thin white outline of a pushpin. By clicking on this pin at the top right of the window, you can pin the toolbox window open. This makes it easier to drag several controls at a time from the toolbox onto a form. When you're done, you can click on the pin again. The window is now unpinned, and will fold itself away neatly when you move the mouse pointer away. All the windows that can be auto-hidden have pins.

The Server Explorer

Applications created with Visual Studio can consist of many discrete components on separate machines communicating across a network. With the Server Explorer, you can monitor and manage the machines involved in your application without leaving the comfort of the Visual Studio IDE.

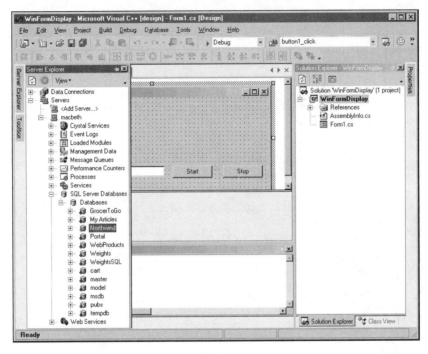

Located beside the Toolbox, the Server Explorer presents each server as a node in a hierarchical tree. Each server node has sub-nodes representing it attributes. When you double-click on an attribute, Server Explorer displays detailed information about it. These attributes include the following

- ❏ Services (you can start and stop them)

- ❏ Processes (you can kill and prioritize them)

- ❏ SQL Databases (you can do *virtually* anything with them)

- ❏ Performance Counters

- ❏ Message Queues

- ❏ Event Logs

You have to register a server before Server Explorer can monitor it. Registration is accomplished by clicking on a node labeled Add Server, and then providing the resulting pop-up box with the relevant connection information, e.g. username, password, IP address, etc. Once you have entered all of the required information, click OK, and a node for the newly registered server will then be added to the tree.

In addition to servers, the Server Explorer also maintains a list of Data Connections that represent the different databases used by your application. Through a data connection, you can edit tables, views, and stored procedures. Server Explorer lets you connect to databases using all of the popular access engines, including SQL Server and Oracle. You create a data connection in Server Explorer in much the same way that you register a server: by clicking an Add node, and providing the necessary security information to a dialog. Server Explorer centralizes control over all the servers involved in a solution.

Creating Projects

Projects and Solutions

One of the challenges of enterprise development is organizing the multitude of files that a single enterprise application can sometimes contain. To meet this challenge, VS.NET presents the files in a development effort as a hierarchical tree consisting of a single solution node with several child projects.

In practical terms, a project is a group of files that will be compiled together into one executable file or a single component. A group of co-operating projects is referred to as a solution because it solves a problem that users have. You can think of solutions as applications in progress, and of projects as components within the application. In other words, a single solution can consist of several projects. A solution that avails database information across a network, for instance, could consist of one project that creates the component that accesses the database, another that creates the component that enforces the business rules, and another that contains the WinForm files that present the retrieved information to the users.

Wizards and Project Types

One of the reasons for Visual C++'s popularity was its AppWizards. When invoked, an AppWizard would walk the developer through several windows of options, collecting information about the kind of project that the developer wanted to create. At the end of this process, the AppWizard would spit out a brand-new, empty project matching the developer's specifications. Although the project wouldn't actually *do* anything, it would be compilable, and consequently could serve as a good foundation upon which the developer could build his own product.

Visual Studio inherits VC++'s AppWizard concept. Although most of the AppWizards provided with the Beta 1 version of VS.NET don't collect any information from the user, they do create compilable, modifiable projects. There are AppWizards for every kind of project in every kind of language: Console applications, WinForm applications, ASP.NET applications, class libraries, and web services. To create a new project, you simply select New from the File menu, and then in the New Project dialog that pops up, indicate the kind of project that you want to create, and then go to work. ToDo comments inside the wizard-generated files indicate places where you can begin adding code.

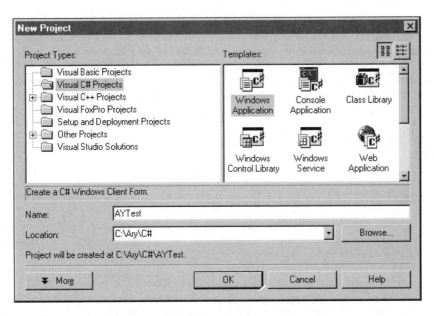

In addition to the project types mentioned above, VS.NET provides wizards for generating a couple of other types as well. First, there are AppWizards for installation projects. Second, and more significantly, there are Enterprise Frameworks. These AppWizards crank out entire solutions with separate projects for the data access, business object, and presentation layers of n-tiered applications. Unfortunately, in the Beta 1 version of VS.NET, the code produced in these projects is rather bare, but hopefully this feature will be retained and strengthened in future versions.

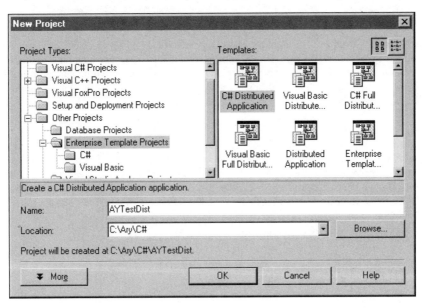

Writing Code

When you start a new project you will undoubtedly want to start writing code. This section leads you through the editing facilities that VS.NET provides for you.

The Code Window

This window has two complimentary ways of presenting your project as it is being created: the code aspect and the designer aspect. For certain tasks, such as the composition of WinForm user interfaces, VS.NET supplies designer windows that speed the tasks up by providing a graphical user interface in a similar way to the VB6 developer environment. As you use a graphical designer to design a form, or even more impressively, a server-side object, the designer modifies your code to reflect the changes you make. You can then see the modifications that have been made by flipping back over to the code aspect of this window. The design window looks like this.

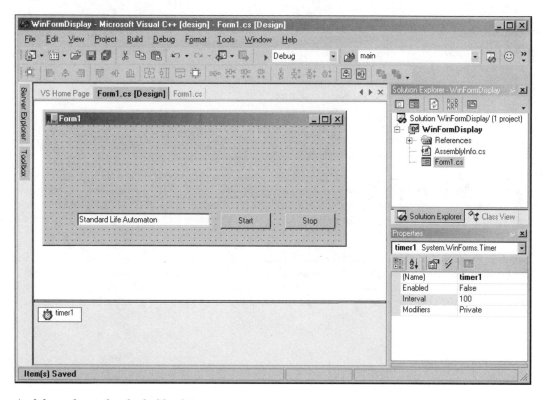

And the code window looks like this:

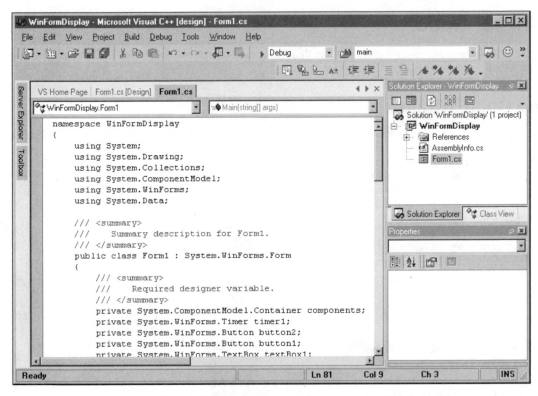

One designer that plugs into the code window merits special attention: the WebForm Designer. Using a wide selection of controls, the WebForm Designer makes the creation of DHTML interfaces into a simple matter of "drag and drop". This innovation is significant because it reduces the number of skills required in order to develop browser-based web applications. Now that the necessary skills-set has been reduced, you can bet that more and more development projects will be browser-based.

Two drop-down list boxes at the top of the code window allow you to move very quickly through your code. The left-hand box lists the classes that have been defined in your code. The right-hand box lists the methods and data members of the class and controls used by the class (such as buttons and list boxes) and their event handlers. Selecting any items from these lists positions the cursor on the first line of the method indicated.

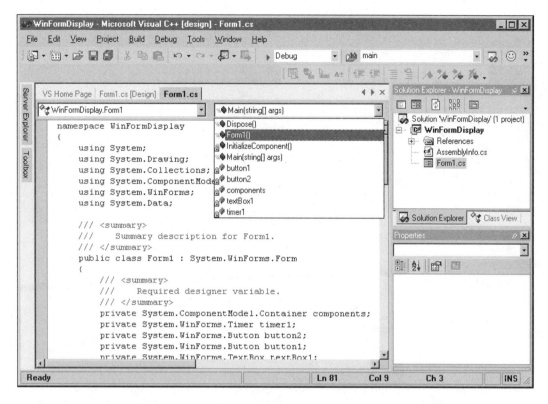

As you open new code files for editing, the IDE adds new tabbed windows to the code window. You can move back and forth between various files by clicking on their tabs. Incidentally, before you can rename a file that's open, you have to close it first. You can do this by bringing the tab to the top of the stack, and then clicking the X near the top of the code window.

Code Collapsing

Another useful function is "code collapsing". This function enables you to expand and collapse indented sections of code, so that you can more easily see which sections are nested where. If enabled, this function operates in much the same way as you would expand and collapse the tree structure in a Windows Explorer, by expanding and collapse folder nodes using the + and − icons located on the tree. This function may already be operating in your code window (if it is in operation, there will be a thin gray vertical line on the left-hand side of your code window, with small boxes containing + or − signs denoting whether a given node is expanded or not). In the version of VS.NET available at the time of writing this book, the only way to turn this option off is to use the Edit menu, then select Outlining, and then from the subsequent options, Stop Outlining. If you wish to enable this function, using the menu path Edit | Outlining | Collapse to Definitions will switch the function on. The tree will then appear in its fully collapsed state, whereupon you can then expand and collapse nodes to suit your preferences.

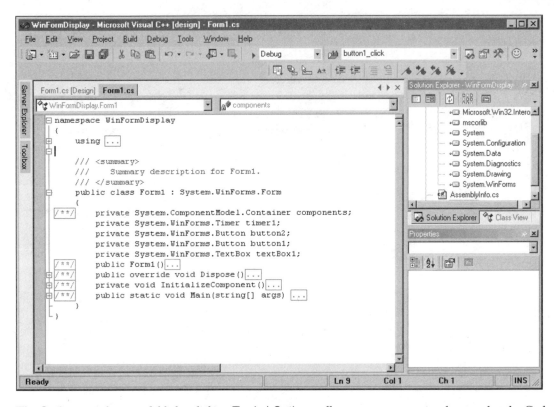

The Options window, available by clicking Tools I Options, allows you to customize the way that the Code Editor displays code (for instance font, font-size, font-color, indentation, etc). You can also set different values for keywords, syntax errors, and comments. This feature is great for alleviating eyestrain by upsizing fonts and avoiding boredom by periodically changing the colors around. We're discussing these windows in order of relative significance, so we'll talk more about the Options window later.

Now let's look at a group of two tabbed-windows that, by default, share the upper-right corner of the VS IDE. These windows work together to provide different views of your work. They'll seem familiar to users of Visual Studio 6.

Intellisense

Before cool code editors like Visual Studio were available, one of the hardest things about coding multi-file, object-oriented projects was remembering the exact syntax of methods on server objects in other files. It was easy to create a compile-time error by leaving out an argument in a function call. With Intellisense, it's virtually impossible to make such errors. When you type the name of an object followed by the indirection operator," . ", Intellisense pops up a list of methods that can be called on that object. Instead of typing out the full method name and possibly making a spelling error, you simply select the method that you want and hit *Enter*.

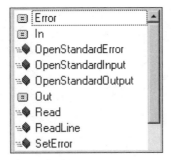

Intellisense then adds the method call to the code in the code window. Similarly, when you open the function's argument list by typing an open parenthesis, " (", Intellisense displays a floating window detailing the proper input argument types, ensuring that you get that portion of the method invocation correct as well.

```
Console.WriteLine ("Average                    {0}", t.avg(t.num1,t.num2));
Console.WriteLine (
 ▲1 of 18▼  void Console.WriteLine (string format, object[] arg)
 format: Formatting string.
```

As you enter words into the code window, the IDE sorts theses words into various categories and colors, each word according to the category into which it falls. Keywords, identifiers, operators, and literals receive different colors. If a word that you type is colored differently than you expected it to be, then something's wrong; you may have made a spelling error, for instance. The colors of these categories are configurable from the Options window, just in case you get bored with them.

Context-sensitive help is one of the best-kept secrets of Microsoft IDEs. If you're unsure about the syntax or purpose of a word in your code, you can simply highlight that word and press *F1*. The IDE will then launch the Help file and scroll to an article that is appropriate to the word that's stumping you.

Finally, the IDE performs some cursory syntax checking of your code even before you compile it. After you enter a line of malformed code, the IDE will indicate the offensive portion of the line by underlining it with a small (by default, red) squiggle.

```
Console.WriteLine ("Average                    {0}", t.avg(t.num1,t.num2));
Console.WriteLine ("Have a nice day
```

The Object Browser

As one of the most useful tools in the Visual Studio IDE, the Object Browser is a centralized source for information about all of the components associated with a solution (both the components referenced by the solution, and components defined therein).

When you start up the Object Browser, the left frame consists of a list of the .NET components installed on your machine. When you select a component from this list, the node opens up and you see a list of the objects contained within the component. You can then select an object to view a list of classes. Finally, double-clicking on the class name will cause the public methods and properties exposed by the selected class to be displayed in the frame on the right, as follows:

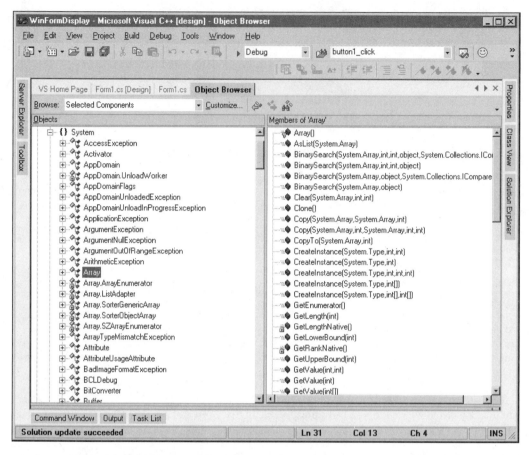

The **Object Browser** displays components as they are seen by client code: only the public properties and methods are shown. Before you release a component that you've built, it's a good idea to look at it through the **Object Browser** just to ensure that you've used the access modifier keywords (public, private, protected, internal) correctly so that clients will see only as much of the class interface as they need to.

Referencing Components and Controls

As you develop applications with VS.NET, you'll sometimes want to use components that aren't in the default namespace or controls that aren't normally in the toolbox.

To make an external component available to a project, you have to reference that component from within the project. You may have noticed a **References** node that appears beneath each project node in the **Solution Explorer**. If you expand this node, you'll find default references to the `System` namespace. To add new references, right-click on the **References** node and select **Add Reference** from the menu that pops up. You'll then be presented with a dialog box that allows you to browse through the file system to the assembly DLL providing the component that you want to use in your project. After you locate the DLL, select it, and close the dialog box. A reference to the components provided by the DLL will then appear under the project's **References** node. Once you've added a reference to a component to your project, you can investigate the classes, methods, and properties supplied by that component using the **Object Browser**. Through Intellisense, the IDE will make coding with the component easy.

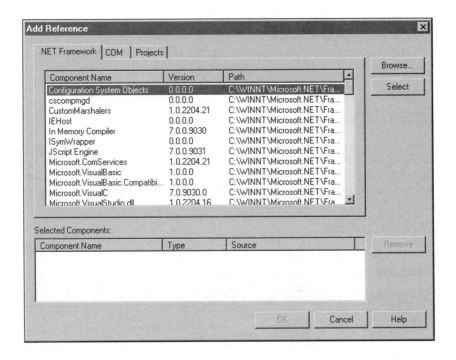

Referencing External Controls

There is a similar process for adding external controls to the IDE's toolbox. From the Tools menu, select Customize Toolbox. A dialog box will allow you to browse to an .OCX file containing the new control.

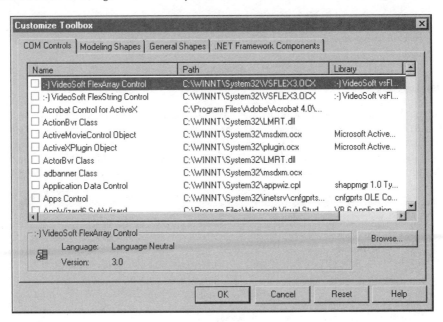

Many people confuse references with the namespaces listed after C#'s `using` keyword. The purpose of those keywords is abbreviation; they provide developers with the ability to refer to a class by its shortened, relative name rather than by its full namespace. For example, `using System` allows a developer to create instances of `int`s and not `System.Int32`s. Also, references perform the necessary task of linking in external files at compile time.

Compiling Code

When you come to compile code (or debug code, as we shall see later on) several other windows pop up at the bottom of the screen. There are several ways to build your projects. One is to elect the Build option from the Build menu. Another is to press the blue arrow icon in the middle of the top toolbar. The difference between the two is that the first builds the project only and the second builds and runs it in one step.

The Output Window

When you build a solution, the compiler displays errors, warnings, and success messages in the Output window.

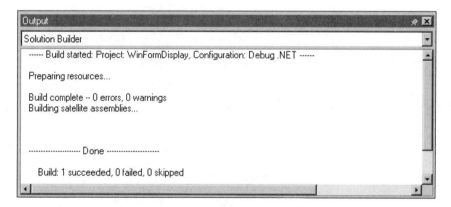

The Task List

Located on a tab beside the Output window, the Task List maintains a to-do list for the developer. When a project fails to compile, any associated errors appear in the Task List automatically, along with their associated filenames and line numbers. Clicking one of these listed errors causes the offending code to be displayed in the Code window. By clicking on the empty, top line in the Task List, a developer can add his own task explicitly, to serve as a reminder that something needs to be done before compilation occurs.

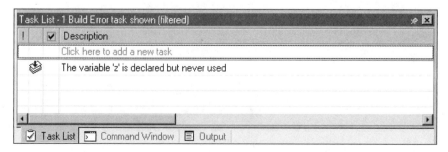

Interestingly, by using the `ToDo` comment, a VB or C# programmer can insert reminders into the Task List without leaving the Code window. This allows him to continue coding without having to break his train of thought.

Debugging Code

Effective debugging involves more than just executing your code to determine whether it delivers the expected results. Sometimes, in testing, code will produce the right output for the wrong reason, and such code is likely to eventually fail. So that you can see *how* your code returns what it returns, VS.NET allows you to step through the code using the debugger, thereby observing its execution line-by-line.

Before you can step through your code, you need a debug version of it. Unlike purely executable code, debug code has hooks compiled inside. These hooks allow the IDE to attach the debugger to the code, watch what's going on, and control the thread of execution. When the IDE creates a debug version of your component or executable, it creates a sister file with a `.pdb` extension. Files with this extension provide supplemental information about your code to the debugger.

A small list box at the top of the IDE allows you to determine whether the Build option generates a debug or an executable version of the code that you're authoring. The list box comes with two built-in sets of Build options, or configurations: Debug and Release. Obviously, you'll want to use the Debug configuration while you test your code, and switch over to the Release configuration when you want to make a production version. You can expect the Release version of your code to run a bit faster.

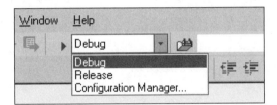

If you want to, you can create your own configurations. When you do so, you determine whether or not the symbolic debug information needed by the debugger is embedded in compiled code. Once you've selected a configuration with debug information, you're ready to step through your code. You can start by clicking on the Start button at the top of the IDE. A blue triangle that points to the right – the Start button – has Break, Pause, and Stop buttons beside it.

You can pause the executing program by clicking the Break button. In response, the IDE will scroll the code window to the next statement that is to be executed and highlight it. The IDE is now in debug mode, and you have free reign to investigate the program. Although it will do so in response to the Break button, a program will also enter debug mode when a runtime error occurs or when it comes to a line that you marked as a breakpoint before execution began (shown as a red dot in the left margin next to the line of code at which execution stops). One time-saving approach to debugging involves stepping through the code line by line until an error is encountered, fixing the error, setting a breakpoint on it, and then re-running the program, allowing it to breeze through the statements that have already been verified. When you get to the corrected line where you set the breakpoint, you can commence single-statement stepping again.

When you're in debug mode, you can set the instruction counter to any statement within the function being executed. By pressing the *F10* key, you can advance the program one line. By pressing *F11*, you can step into a function that is called. By positioning the cursor on a different line and pressing *Ctrl+Shift+F10*, you can jump the thread of execution forwards or backwards several lines, skipping the statements between the last statement executed and the new one. If you take a few moments to memorize the keys associated with these actions, you'll soon be able to step through your code with speed and ease.

In addition to moving the instruction counter around (the yellow arrow that moves up and down the left margin of the code window), you can examine the values of variables in the code. The quickest way to do this involves "auto-data tips"; while in debug mode, hover your mouse pointer over the variable that you're investigating; the IDE will then momentarily display that variable's value in a tiny window just above it. If you want to monitor the value of a variable as it changes from line to line, you can put a watch on this variable by highlighting it in the code editor and dragging it to the Watch window, which will dynamically display the variable and its changing value. If the need arises, you can interact with the executing program by explicitly setting the values of variables from the command line prompt of the Command window. The Watch and Command windows will be explained shortly.

```
Class1.cs

Numbers.Test                                          Main(string[] args)

        else
        {
            Console.WriteLine("You must supply two numbers");
            return 0;
        }

        Console.WriteLine ("Addition:          {0}", t.add(t.num1,t.num2));
        Console.WriteLine ("Subtraction:       {0}", t.subt(t.num1,t.num2));
        Console.WriteLine ("Multiplication:    {0}", t.mult(t.num1,t.num2));
        try
            {
                Console.WriteLine ("Division (no rem)  {0}", t.div(t.num1,t.num2));
                Console.WriteLine ("Decimal devision   {0}", t.double_div(t.num1,t.num2))
                Console.WriteLine ("Remainder          {0}", t.get_remainder(t.num1,t.nu
            }
        catch
            {
                Console.WriteLine ("Denominator zero: Cannot do division");
```

Also, VS.NET will allow you to step through code in ASP.NET pages in the same way that you can step through code in other VS.NET projects. The IDE will even step from project to project, allowing you to follow the thread of execution from an ASP.NET page to a component that it calls and back out again to the page. Even better, by adding a `trace` command to the top of an ASP.NET page, you can instruct Internet Information Server to append to the end of each ASP.NET page that it delivers a complete report profiling the performance of the page's code.

```
<%@ Page Language="C#" Trace=True %>
```

Incidentally, the advanced developers among you will be interested to know that you can modify the debugger so that it steps not only by line, but by statement or instruction as well.

Debugger Windows

There are many other windows that you can use when the debugger is invoked, some of which are only accessible when it is running, (the Disassembly and Memory windows, for example).

The Command Window

You can call this window up without the debugger running from the View | Other Windows list, but you would mainly use it while debugging. It is useful when the debugger has paused at a breakpoint or error, since the Command Window allows you to set or read the value of any of the variables currently in scope. The question mark (?) is shorthand for "Debug.Print".

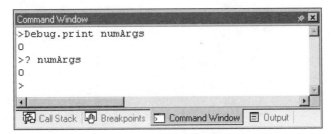

The Command Window allows you to assign and invoke text-based aliases for menu items. To see a complete list of the built-in aliases, type in `alias` at the Command window's command prompt and hit *Enter*.

The Watch Window

The following four windows usually appear on the left side when they are called up by the debugger. The Watch window, the Locals window, the Autos window, and the This window are similar in appearance and purpose. Let's take a brief look at these windows to learn how they differ. Like many of the debugging windows, they are only available from the Windows sub-menu of the Debug menu, while the debugger is running.

The Watch window lets you monitor the values of selected variables as you step through code with the debugger. If you want to watch a variable, simply highlight the variable name in the code window and drag it to the Watch window. Hey presto! You've just created a watch. As each line of code is executed, the IDE refreshes the values displayed for the watch.

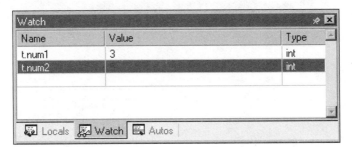

The Locals Window

The Locals window is like the Watch window in that it displays the values of variables as you debug code. However, the Locals window automatically lists the values of all variables in the current scope; you don't have to go to the trouble of adding them yourself. As such, the Locals window is a very handy tool. It doesn't get enough press.

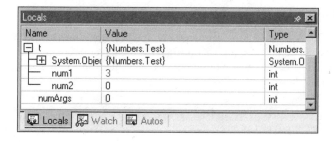

The Autos Window

The Autos window displays variables used in the current statement (that is the one that is to be executed) and the previous statement (the one just executed).

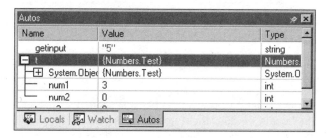

The This Window

The This window shows the values of the data members of the object that is currently in scope.

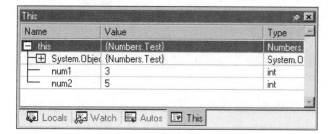

The Call Stack Window

The next two windows appear on the right side when the debugger is invoked and, like the windows just described, are only available from the Windows sub-menu of the Debug menu. You might notice that the Output and Command windows move across as the debugging IDE arranges itself. We've discussed both of these already. However, we have not mentioned the Call Stack and Breakpoints windows.

As programs execute, the call stack grows as functions call sub-functions, and shrinks as functions return. The Call Stack window offers a graphical representation of the call stack to which you can refer as you debug your programs:

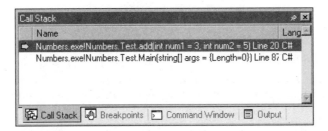

The Breakpoints Window

This lists the breakpoints that have been set for the project and you can control the setting and removing of breakpoints from this window.

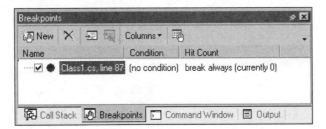

The following windows can also be loaded into the debugging environment, though by default they appear over the code window and not in the already crowded panes at the bottom left and bottom right.

The Disassembly Window

As you know, source code is compiled into machine code that the computer can actually execute. Because source code is at a higher level of abstraction than machine code is, one source code statement can translate into several machine code commands. As a personal favorite of the author, the Disassembly window provides a glimpse into the compilation process, and allows you to evaluate the efficiency of your programs at the machine language level. As you step through the source code lines of your program, this window displays the machine code commands produced by each source code line.

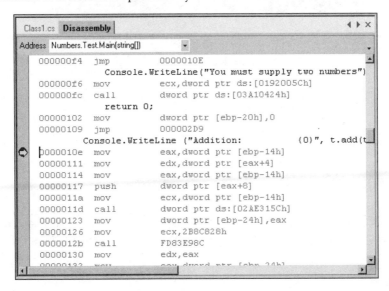

Fortunately, the machine code commands are displayed with assembly language mnemonics. All those 1's and 0's would be very hard to read!

The Memory Window

As its name implies, this window displays the contents of addresses in memory. A column on the left-hand side of the window lists the addresses. Columns to the right of this column represent the bytes stored at each respective address.

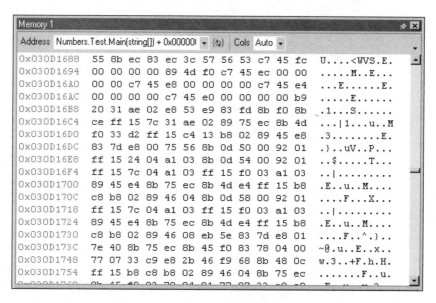

You can scan forwards and backwards in memory by simply dragging the vertical scrollbar alongside the window, or by typing an address directly into the textbox just beneath the window's title bar.

Customizing VS.NET

As with any good IDE, VS.NET's user interface can be customized to suit your personal needs and wishes. There are several features that we'll look at in this section:

❑ Custom Profiles

❑ Filtered Help

❑ Options Window

❑ Custom Toolbars

Custom Profiles

Microsoft wants MS.NET to be a unifying platform in which developers using different languages can work together to achieve incredible results. So that everyone will feel at home in Visual Studio, Microsoft has endowed it with the ability to assume the look and feel of older, more familiar IDEs, including VB6 and Visual InterDev.

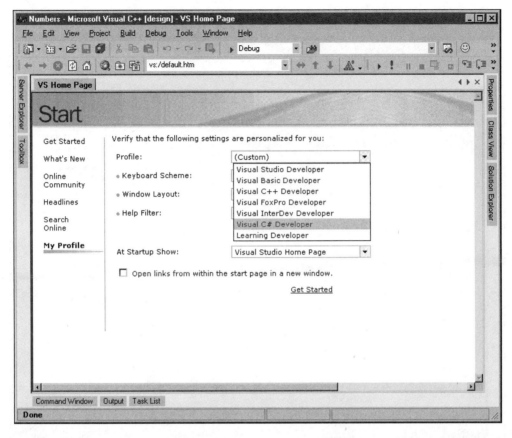

These custom profiles are available from the My Profile link on the Start page. Clicking this link will reveal another page with a list of the profiles that are available. After you make a choice, the IDE will assume the look and feel of the environment that you've selected, and will retain it until you select another.

Filtered Help

Tired of doing a search in MSDN library and getting back 250 references about Visual FoxPro? With VS.NET's filtered help, you won't have that problem any longer. Like custom profiles, filtered help is available from the Start page. A drop-down menu near the top of the page allows you to limit the reference materials that the Help window brings up. Categories that you may choose from include:

❑ Unfiltered, Visual Studio Documentation

❑ .NET Framework SDK Documentation

❑ Visual Basic Documentation

❑ Visual C++ Documentation

❑ C# Documentation

❑ Visual FoxPro Documentation

❑ Visual Studio Macro Documentation

The filtered help option that you choose will now appear in the start page next to the Help Filter label:

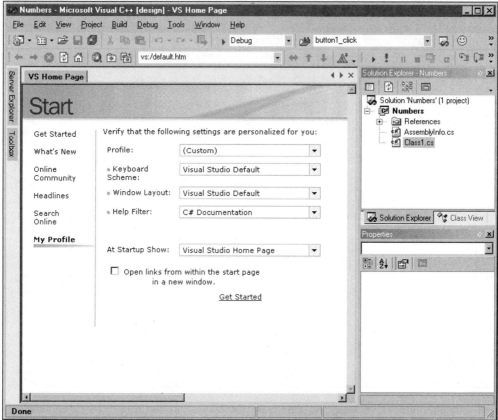

The Options Window

We've already seen that the Options window (Tools | Options from the menu bar) allows us to select different fonts and colors for the code editor. It also allows us to do much more than that. By using the Options window, a developer can also determine how the IDE *behaves*:

❑   For your comfort, you can make the environment work as either an SDI (single-document interface) or MDI (multiple-document interface) application. Similarly, you can determine whether requested Help files are displayed within the Visual Studio IDE or outside, in a separate application.

❑   You can determine what the environment displays at start up – among the choices are the Start page, the last project worked on, the Open Project dialog, or the New Project dialog.

❑   You can assign keyboard shortcuts for any selections from any of the IDE menus.

❑   You can configure Dynamic Help. Dynamic Help, shown on a tab behind the Properties window, contains quick links to help files in several categories: Actions, Training, Help, Miscellaneous, and Samples. The Options window allows you to restrict Dynamic Help to the categories that you really need.

❑ Most significantly, you can determine how the IDE implements source code control. Different behaviors make sense in different development situations; an independent developer, for example, might want to get all files at check out whereas a member of a development team might want to specify only certain ones. The Options window allows you to set such versioning behaviors discretely, and also provides several profiles for setting them en masse: Independent Developer, Team Development, Custom, and Visual SourceSafe.

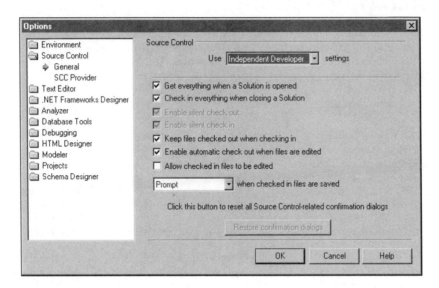

Custom Toolbars

Customizing toolbars is a very simple way to make VS.NET a bit more homely. You can add new options to existing toolbars, or create your own personal toolbars and fill them with the options you most commonly use.

From the main menu bar, select Tools | Toolbars. You'll be presented with a tabbed dialog box. The second tab on this dialog lists the various menus in the IDE. Highlighting a menu's name causes a box to fill with the options available from that menu. Once you've located an option that you want on a toolbar, it's a simple matter to drag the option's icon across the screen, from the dialog box to the toolbar on which you want the option to appear. When you've positioned the dragged icon at a location in which it can be dropped, the cursor will change to an I-beam shape. At that point, you can release the mouse button and the icon will snap into place on the toolbar.

To create your own toolbar, launch the Toolbar dialog again. Locate the New button on the dialog's Toolbar tab and click it. After answering the prompt for the new toolbar's name, it will appear as a small window floating on top of the IDE. To add options to your toolbar, drag them from the Toolbar dialog to your new toolbar in the manner described previously.

Other VS.NET Features

Visual Studio is a well-planned piece of software. The windows, the menus, the menu items, the editors, and even the debugger are all exposed as objects with documented properties and methods, and developers can address these objects in code to extend the functionality of the IDE. There are two basic approaches to doing this: macros and add-ins. We'll discuss macros first because they are simple.

The Macro Explorer

Macros provide a way of automating dull, repetitive tasks. For example, at the press of a button, a macro could preface all the source code files in an application with time-stamped header comments and save the files to disk. Another macro might automate a development team's daily build process by checking files out of SourceSafe, compiling them into the necessary components, and deploying the components to the test server.

VS.NET's approach to macros is elegant. A dedicated window, the Macro Explorer, lists all of the macros that you've created. Clicking on a macro's name executes it and right-clicking on the macro's icon enables you to edit it. There's an automated way of creating this source code, as the following example demonstrates.

After you've added a new, empty macro to the Macro Explorer, right-click on it. From the menu that pops up, select Set as Recording Project. Then, select Tools | Macros | Record Temporary Macro. A small macro Recorder window with Pause, Stop, and Cancel buttons will appear, indicating that you are recording a macro. Use the mouse pointer to go through the steps that you want the macro to automate, selecting menu options, opening files, etc. When you're done, click the Stop button on the Macro Recording window and flip back to the Macro Explorer.

When all is done, your new macro will appear in the Macro Explorer.

Now look at the code node under the macro. Something amazing has occurred; the IDE has translated the actions in your recording into VB statements! Your mouse clicks, menu selections, and file openings were stored by the IDE as code that you can now execute by double-clicking on the macro node in the Macro Explorer.

```
Option Strict Off

Imports EnvDTE
```

```
Public Module RecordingModule

    Sub LastTemporaryMacro()
        DTE.ActiveDocument.Selection.Text = "Console.WriteLine("""
    End Sub
End Module
```

This automated approach to macro creation is convenient, but sometimes you may want to create macros that perform actions too complex to represent via recordings. On those occasions, you could go the more time-consuming route of typing code directly into the **Macro Editor**. For efficiency, you could create the initial skeleton of a macro with a recording, and then touch-up the finer details with some hand-written code.

*Beware, the Beta 1 version of the **Macro Editor** is very slow.*

VS.NET provides a couple of shortcuts for getting at your macros quickly, and the **Options** window allows you to assign hot keys to your macros. However, typing m in the **Command** window displays a drop-down list of menus; scroll down to the macro that you want, press *Enter*, and the macro will then be executed.

The Add-In Manager

Add-ins are a more sophisticated way of extending VS.NET. Distributed as DLLs, they integrate seamlessly into the IDE, adding new options to the menus and new buttons to the command bars.

Numerous third-party vendors offered add-ins for previous versions of Visual Studio. These add-ins could automatically add event handlers to your code, analyze your projects' dependencies, spell-check your comments, and perform other useful work. After an add-in DLL is installed on your machine, you activate the add-in from the **Add-In Manager** under the **Tools** menu. At that point, the new functionality supplied by the add-in appears in your IDE. If ever you tire of an add-in, you can de-activate it from the **Add-In Manager** and all of its options will disappear from the IDE.

Architecturally, an add-in is just a component that meets a couple of requirements. First, so that the IDE can communicate with the component, one class in the component must implement the `IDTExtensibility2` interface. This interface provides methods that are executed when the component is activated and de-activated via the **Add-In Manager**. Second, once compiled, the component must be listed in a special area in the system registry so that the **Add-In Manager** can offer it to VS.NET users.

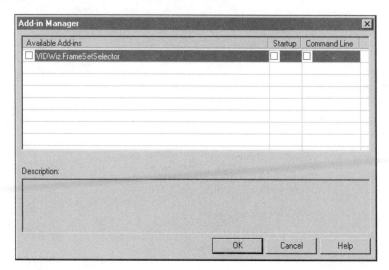

Editing HTML, XML, and CSS

VS.NET provides built-in HTML, XML, and CSS editors. The HTML editor will feel familiar to anyone who has used Microsoft Front Page or Visual InterDev. Basically, it ushers HTML authoring into the age of WYSIWYG editors. It enables you to create HTML pages graphically, by dragging controls from a toolbox to a blank page, leaving the dirty work of writing the supporting HTML code to the editor. If you want to tweak the HTML yourself, you can do so by flipping from the design view to an HTML view of the document.

The XML editor encourages you to write well-formed XML. As you enter opening XML tags into the document, the editor stores them in memory. As you start to close the tag, the editor uses the stored tags to suggest closing tags to you, via a drop-down list box, similar in style to that of Intellisense.

The CSS editor is a lot like that which came with Visual InterDev. It reduces the development of CSS stylesheets to a simple matter of selecting options in a dialog box.

Summary

This chapter has provided a tour of VS.NET, the development environment for the new MS.NET platform. In it, we examined the components of the environment, looked at some of the common tasks that those components can be used to accomplish, and explored how the IDE's object model can be automated to extend Visual Studio's functionality.

Dedicate some time at the beginning of each programming session to learning a new feature of the IDE. Hours of frustrating guesswork can often be avoided by applying Visual Studio's powerful tools to gain insight into difficult problems. Also, as your ability to interact with the IDE increases you'll be able to dedicate more of your thoughts to programming and fewer of them to getting around in the environment. When the tools and the keystrokes for activating those tools become second-nature to you, you'll be able to code for extended periods without breaking your train of thought, and uninterrupted concentration is the programmer's greatest strength.

We'll have ample opportunity to hone our VS.NET skill in the next chapters, which bring the focus back to C# development.

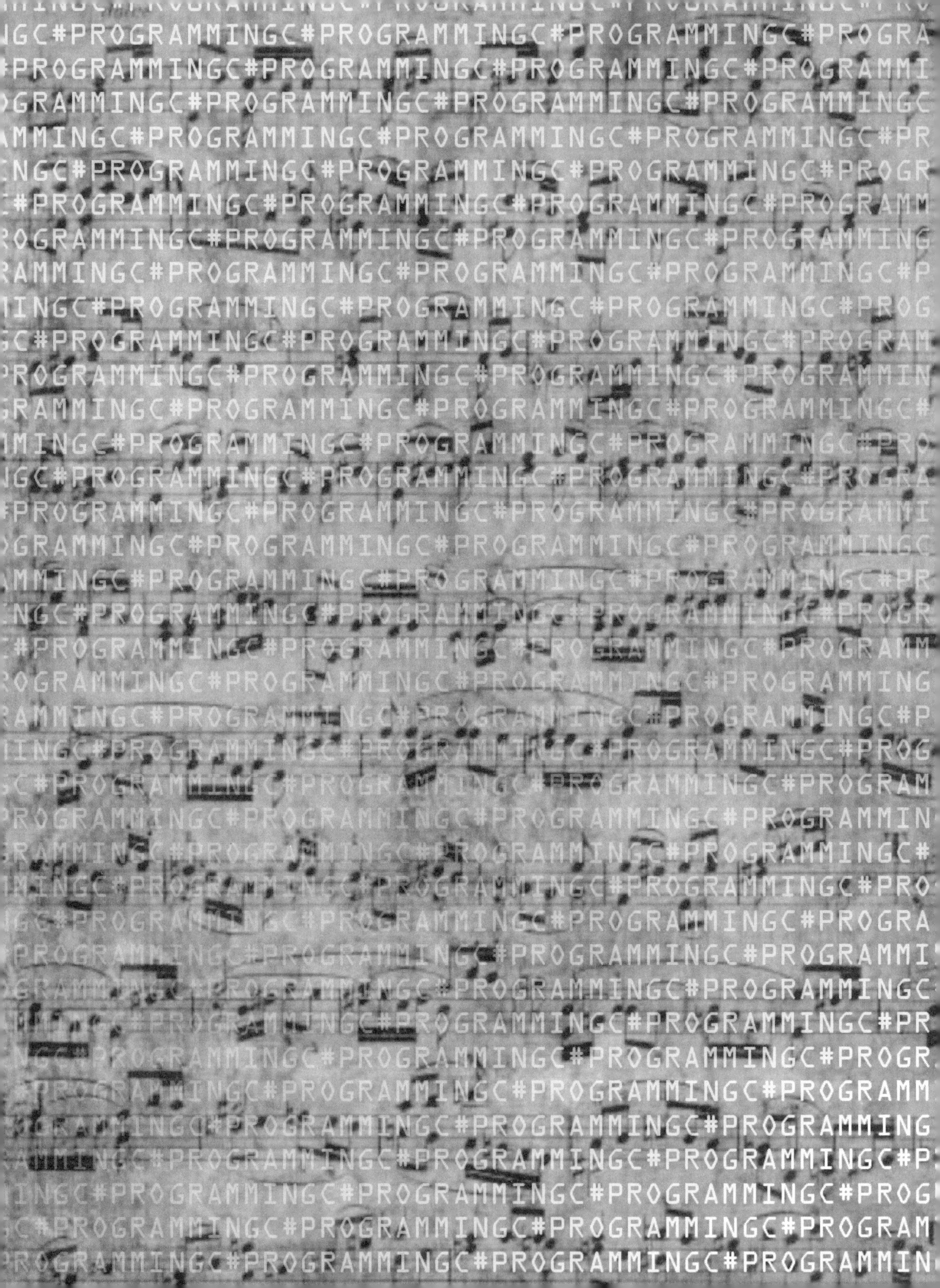
C#PROGRAMMING

4

C# Syntax

In this, the first of three chapters on the core of the C# language, we're going to cover the basic syntax elements. The second chapter is going to look at the OO-specific features of C#, while the third chapter will concentrate on advanced topics.

While just about everyone who reads this is going to be new to the C# language, I've assumed that you do have some basic knowledge of OO, at least to the level of what classes are. If you're very new to OO programming, this may be a good point to go and review some basic material on how OO programming works. A useful introduction to objects for the VB programmer can be found in "Beginning Visual Basic 6 Objects", published by Wrox Press, ISBN 1-861001-72-X.

Since C# has so many similarities to both Java and C++, I'll use some special paragraphs in the text to point out special features of interest to C++ and Java programmers. If you don't use either of those languages, feel free to ignore them!

Start At the Beginning...

It is traditional that the first program you write in a new language is one which prints "Hello world!" to the console. I've no desire to break with tradition, so here you are:

```
using System;
// Here's a Hello World program in C#
class Hello
{
    public static int Main()
    {
        Console.WriteLine("Hello world!");
```

```
        return 0;
    }
}
```

You can type this code into Notepad (or another text editor), and save it into a file with a .cs extension, which is the default extension for C#. Note that C# is case-sensitive, so you have to type everything with the correct case. If you haven't come from a C or C++ background this may cause you some initial problems. Once you've done this, compile it by using the csc command from the command line:

```
csc hello.cs
```

This will produce you an executable file called hello.exe, which you can run from the command-line just like any other executable:

```
C:\WINNT\System32\cmd.exe                                        _ □ x
Microsoft Windows 2000 [Version 5.00.2195]
(C) Copyright 1985-2000 Microsoft Corp.

C:\>cd\dotNet book

C:\dotNET Book>csc hello.cs
Microsoft (R) Visual C# Compiler Version 7.00.9030 [CLR version 1.00.2204.21]
Copyright (C) Microsoft Corp 2000. All rights reserved.

C:\dotNET Book>hello
Hello world!

C:\dotNET Book>
```

C++ Note
C# compiles straight from source code to executable, with no object files. Note that the Main() function is capitalized, and must be declared as returning int or void.

Java Note
Even though C# uses a bytecode system like Java, the output from compilation is an executable file.

And that's all there is to writing and compiling a C# program! But before we move on to look at all the language features, let's examine the program for a few minutes and point out a few salient features.

First, note that all the code occurs within class Hello, because C# is like Java, in that all code must be part of a class, and there are no global functions or variables. The program also contains a function (or 'method' in C# jargon) called Main(); this is the method where the program starts executing, and every C# application has to have exactly one. If you have either zero or more than one Main() in a program, you can expect compiler errors.

Comments are started by two slashes and continue to the end of the line, and it is also possible to use the C-style commenting convention where comments start with the `/*` characters and are terminated with `*/`. These comments can occur within a line, and can also span more than one line.

We use the `Console.WriteLine()` function to write a string to the screen. `Console` is an object whose job is to handle screen and keyboard I/O, and `WriteLine()` is a method which writes a single line complete with the newline character.

All the I/O in C# is part of the system library, rather than being part of the language itself. This means that in order to do any I/O, we have to tell the compiler to reference the appropriate library, and this is done using the `using` directive, which tells the compiler to look in the `System` library for unknown classes. System is actually a namespace, a concept which we'll explain later on; for now, think of it as similar to a library.

C++ Note
`using` isn't the same as `#include` at all, because it doesn't result in any code being included. All it does is tell the compiler where it can look for unresolved class names.

Java Note
`using` is very similar in concept to Java's `import` keyword.

Types

C# has two distinct groups of data types, called **value types** and **reference types**. Value types are designed to map onto things which can be considered as dumb(ish) values (or wrappers around values). A good example of a value type might be a type that represents a point on a graph, and which simply encapsulates a pair of X and Y values. Value types therefore include:

- ❑ the simple types (int, char, etc)
- ❑ structs
- ❑ enums

We'll look at the simple types here, while `structs` and `enums` will be described in Chapter 5. Reference types include all the others, namely classes, interfaces, delegates and arrays. In OO terms, value types are those where state dominates, while reference types are those where behavior dominates. From the programmer's point of view the main difference between them is that value types directly contain their data, while reference types are accessed indirectly using *reference variables* that point to the object.

C++ Note
C# supports the use of pointers, but only in 'unsafe' code where the garbage collection mechanism doesn't operate.

Java and C++ Note
All types in C# – value and reference – inherit from the `object` superclass.

Predefined Types

The following table shows the predefined value types.

Name	Description
sbyte	8-bit signed integer
short	16-bit signed integer
int	32-bit signed integer
long	64-bit signed integer
byte	8-bit unsigned integer
ushort	16-bit unsigned integer
uint	32-bit unsigned integer
ulong	64-bit unsigned integer
float	Single-precision floating point
double	Double-precision floating point
bool	Boolean value
char	Unicode character
decimal	Precise decimal with 28 significant digits

C# is directly built upon the .NET base classes (discussed in Chapter 7), and .NET defines all the data types that are supported by the .NET languages. This means that all these C# types are synonyms for the underlying system types, so that int is a synonym for System.Int32, for example. Although you can use the underlying .NET types, it is recommended that you stick to the C# names for clarity.

Numeric literals are declared as you'd expect from a C-type language. Floating point values are double by default, and you can use F to denote single precision (i.e. 12.7F). U can be used to denote unsigned literals, and L longs. The precise decimal type is denoted by an M suffix, as in 12.77M.

```
int n = 3;
double d = 12345.67;
float f = 12.7F;
decimal dc = 100000.0M;
```

C++ Note

All these types have fixed sizes, and will be the same size on any system. This removes some of the problems traditionally associated with porting C and C++ code between architectures, and is pretty vital for writing distributed applications.

Java Note

You can choose between signed and unsigned integer types. If you choose unsigned, you obviously get extra magnitude because the sign bit can be used.

C# provides you with two predefined reference types – `object` and `string`. All other classes are based on `object`, even if they don't claim inheritance from any other class.

Java Note

The C# `object` class is very similar to Java's `Object`. It acts as an ultimate superclass, and supplies several basic methods whose names and function will be quite familiar.

Operators

The table below lists all the operators supported by C#:

Category	Operators
Arithmetic	+ - * / %
Logical	& | ! ^ ~ && ||
String concatenation	+
Increment and decrement	++ --
Bit shifting	<< >>
Comparison	== != < > <= >=
Assignment	= += -= *= /= %= &= |= ^= <<= >>=
Member access	.
Indexing	[]
Cast	()
Conditional	?:
Delegate operations	+ -
Object creation	new
Type information	is sizeof typeof
Overflow exception control	checked unchecked
Indirection and address	* -> [] &

The vast majority of these will be familiar to the Java and C/C++ programmer, and those which may be unfamiliar (delegate operations, overflow control) will be mentioned in due course. For those who aren't familiar with those languages, here are a few notes on some common operators:

❑ % (known as the modulus operator) gives the remainder on division.

❑ & and | perform bitwise AND and OR operations, while ~ and ^ are bitwise NOT and XOR.

❑ && and || perform Boolean 'and' and 'or' operations and ! is the Boolean 'not' operator.

❑ << and >> perform left and right bit shifts on integer types.

❑ ++ and -- are used to increment and decrement numeric types. The operators can be put either before or after the variable they affect. If put before the variable (the prefix version), the variable's value is changed before it is used in the expression; if put after the variable (the postfix version), the variable is used in the expression and then its value is changed.

❑ += and the other compound assignment operators are shorthand, so that a+=n means the same as a=a+n, a/=n means the same as a=a/n, and so on.

❑ ?: is the ternary conditional operator, and is used to choose between two alternatives depending on whether the value of an expression is true or false, e.g. (x>3) ? 5 : 7, which results in the value 5 if x is greater than 3, and 7 if it is not.

❑ Note that = is used for assignment, and == is used to test for equality. Mixing these up, by writing a=b where you mean a==b and vice-versa, is a common cause of errors in C++.

❑ new is used to create objects.

❑ sizeof lets you find the size of an object or type in bytes, so that sizeof(decimal) returns you the value 16, because decimals are 16 bytes in size.

❑ is and typeof are involved with finding the type of an object at run-time

❑ checked and unchecked are used to control how the compiler deals with overflow conditions in arithmetic calculations.

Precedence follows a logical pattern, as shown in the following table. The operators with highest precedence are at the top of the table:

Group	Operators
	() . [] x++ x-- new typeof sizeof checked unchecked
Unary	+ - ! ~ ++x --x and casts
Multiplication	* / %
Addition	+ -
Shifting	<< >>
Relational	< > >= <= is
Equality	== !=
Bitwise AND	&
Bitwise XOR	^

Group	Operators
Bitwise OR	`|`
Boolean AND	`&&`
Boolean OR	`||`
Conditional	`?:`
Assignment	`= *= etc`

These operators have been provided to work with the predefined types, and it is possible to make them work with other types that you invent by defining your own versions of many of these operators, a process known as *operator overloading*, which we cover in Chapter 5

Everything Is an Object

OO languages tend to have a problem when it comes to representing the primitive types such as integers and characters, because while it is useful and consistent to treat everything as objects, this isn't very efficient. Languages have tended to solve this in two ways, either by having the primitive types as special cases (as in Java and C++), which makes for an inconsistent type system, or by having everything as an integer (as in Smalltalk and Lisp), in which case efficiency suffers.

C# takes a third approach, in that primitive types can be treated as objects as and when necessary. There are several consequences of this, such as the fact that basic value types can be used in containers that expect objects without any need for conversion. A second is that since all types are objects (and hence derived from `object`), we can call object methods directly on them, like this:

```
int n = 3;
string s = n.ToString();  // call object.ToString()
```

Java Note
This is in contrast to Java, where the basic types have no object-like behavior at all, and need to be explicitly converted to and from object wrapper types.

Value types can be converted to objects by *boxing* them (wrapping them in an object 'box') and back again by *unboxing* them. We'll have more to say about this in the next chapter when we talk about objects.

Variable Creation and Initialization

How variables are declared and initialized depends on whether they are reference or value types. Value types can be directly declared and referenced, as shown in the examples below:

```
int n;              // uninitialized int
long l = 327;       // initialized long
float f = 3.13F;    // float initialized from single-precision literal
```

As with C++ and Java, local variables (declared on the stack) aren't initialized to anything.
Reference types, on the other hand, are created in two parts: the reference variable, and then the object itself. The code below shows how to create a string reference:

```
// create a reference to a string
string s;
```

The variable s is a reference variable that can point to a string–think of a pointer in C++ or an object reference in Visual Basic. At this point the reference is uninitialized – it isn't referring to anything – and we need to make it refer to an object before we can use it. Trying to use an uninitialized reference will quite possibly give you a compiler warning, and will crash your code at run-time.

C++ Note

If you think of reference variables as being similar to pointers, you won't be too far wrong. You have to create the 'pointer' variable, and make it refer to something, but you don't have to dereference it when you use it.

Objects are created using the new keyword, which returns a reference to the newly created object. We'll have more to say about object creation in the next chapter.

```
// create a new string and store the reference
string s = new string("abc");
```

Note that this code only illustrates how you create object references in C#. For the string object, you don't need to use new as the syntax string s = "abc" is preferred and you will get a compiler warning if you use the above syntax.

C++ Note

You can only create objects in C# using the new keyword. There's no way to create stack-based objects, as all objects are accessed by reference.

The fact that references are used to point to objects means that it is quite legal (and reasonable) to have two references pointing to the same object, as shown here:

```
// create a new string and store the reference
string s = "abc";
string s2;
s2 = s;    // s2 and s refer to the same object
```

Because of this behavior, you also have to be careful when comparing references, since the == and != operators compare the reference, not the content of the objects. Supposing we have a fictitious 'name' class that stores employee names. We can create two instances that contain the same value, but a comparison will fail because the two references point to different objects – they aren't 'equal'.

```
public void TestNames()
{
    // create a new string and store the reference
    name n1 = new name("fred smith");
    name n2 = new name("fred smith");
    if (n1 == n2)
        Console.WriteLine("This shouldn't happen!");
    else
        Console.WriteLine("Objects aren't equal...");
}
```

So what do you do when you do want to compare object content? You use the `Equals()` method which all classes inherit from the `object` superclass, and which we'll explain in the next chapter.

The only exception to this rule is the string class, where the `==` and `!=` operators have been overloaded to provide content comparison.

```
using System;
class Test
{
    public static int Main()
    {
        // create a new string and store the reference
        string s = "abc";
        string s2 = "abc";
        if (s == s2)
            Console.WriteLine("Strings are equal");
        else
            Console.WriteLine("This shouldn't happen!");

        return 0;
    }
}
```

This may make for an inconsistent set of operations, but it may make programming string comparisons more intuitive for some programmers.

A Word about Characters

C# has the basic `char` value type and the `string` reference type, both of which use 16-bit Unicode characters. The Unicode wide-character encoding has become the standard for languages that are used for web programming, because the Unicode character encoding is large enough to hold a wide variety of national character sets.

> *Don't confuse character set and character encoding. A character set is what you see on the screen, while an encoding is a way of representing it in memory. There are many possible encodings for any character set.*

A `char` is an unsigned 16-bit integer, and as such can hold the 65535 values which form the Unicode character space. Character literals can be written in several forms:

❑ as a quoted character, `'A'`

❑ as a hexadecimal value, `\x002D`

❑ as an `int` with a cast, `(char)32`

❑ as a Unicode value, `\u002D`

String literals can be written in two forms, quoted and @-quoted. Quoted string literals are simply enclosed in double quotes, and support the normal range of C-style escape sequences, such as `\n` for newline and `\t` for tab. If you put an `'@'` in front, it turns into an @-quoted string where escape sequences are not processed, making it rather more convenient for expressing path names.

```
"quoted string"
@"c:\temp\newfile"      // escape sequences not expanded
"c:\\temp\\newfile"     // use '\\' to get a literal backslash
```

Constants

A variable can be made unmodifiable by using the `const` keyword. If a variable is declared as `const`, it must be initialized since, by definition, a constant can't have its value changed later.

```
const int i;            // error! You must provide a value
const int i = 3;        // OK
```

A const variable can be initialised using an expression, but this expression must be one which can be evaluated by the compiler.

```
const int m = 10;
const int n = m * 4;    // OK - compiler knows value of m
int p = 3;              // non-const value
const int q = p + 4;    // error
```

Memory Management

C# implements an automatic memory management scheme similar to the one used in Java. Objects are always accessed through reference variables, so if all references to an object have gone out of scope there's no way that it can be accessed by anyone. The Common Language Runtime implements a garbage collector which looks for orphan objects and reclaims their memory, thus freeing the programmer from the need to manually manage memory allocation and deallocation.

Note that you can't tell exactly when an object is going to be garbage collected, since the collection mechanism runs when it feels a need to reclaim some memory. This means that objects might not be reclaimed until some time after the last reference to them has gone. We'll have more to say on this topic when we come to talk about object destruction in the next chapter.

Arrays

C++ Note:
Arrays in C# work very differently to their C++ counterparts!

Arrays in C# are objects in their own right, accessed through a reference variable. The following code shows how to declare references to `int` arrays:

```
int[] arr;          // declare int array reference
int[] arr2, arr3;   // declare two array references
```

Note that the type is `int[]` ('reference to `int` array'), and that this type declaration applies to all variables in the statement. You don't put any value in the square brackets because you're not declaring the array itself here, just a reference to it.

> **Java Note**
>
> The square brackets have to appear immediately after the type in C#. The alternative C-style declaration allowed in Java won't work here.

Once you've declared the array reference, you can construct the array itself:

```
int[] arr;                 // declare the array reference
arr = new int[25];         // create a 25 element int array
```

We use new just the same as we do for any other object, and the size of the array we want is specified in square brackets after the type. This size is fixed, and can't be changed afterwards; if you need a dynamic array, consider using one of the collection classes defined in the `System.Collections` namespace.

Once you've created an array you can access its elements, using the zero-based addressing scheme which originated in C. This means that the valid subscripts for a 25-element array run from `[0]` through to `[24]`, and any attempt to access an element outside those bounds will result in a runtime error.

```
using System;
class Test
{
    public static int Main()
    {
        int[] arr = new int[25];    // declare 25 element int array
        arr[0] = 1;                 // first element
        arr[24] = 10;               // last element
        arr[25] = 12;               // error!

        return 0;
    }
}
```

How do you give initial values to your array elements? Apart from the obvious – assigning them one by one, as in the code above – you can also provide a list of initial values in braces:

```
int[] arr = new int[] { 1,2,3,4 } ;
// which can be shortened to...
int[] arr = { 1,2,3,4 };
```

Note that if you do this, you don't have to provide a size for the array as the compiler can work it out for itself.

Multidimensional Arrays

C# supports two types of multidimensional arrays – *rectangular* and *jagged*. In rectangular arrays, as their name implies, every row is the same length. A jagged array, on the other hand, is simply an array of one-dimensional arrays, each of which can be of a different length if desired.

The following code shows how to declare and initialize rectangular arrays.

```
using System;
class Test
```

```
    {
        public static int Main()
        {
            int[,] arr2;            // 2D rectangular array of ints
            arr2 = new int[5,5];    // create 5-by-5 array

            for (int i=0; i<5; i++)
                for (int j=0; j<5; j++)
                    arr2[i,j] = i*j;

            // create a 2D array with implied size of 3-by-2
            int[,] arr3 = new int[,]{
                    {1,2},          // first row
                    {4,5},          // second row
                    {7,8}           // third row
                };

            // write out some elements
            Console.WriteLine("{0}", arr2[2,2]);
            Console.WriteLine("{0}", arr3[1,1]);

            return 0;
        }
    }
```

As you can see, the syntax for initializing multidimensional arrays is a simple extension of the single dimension case, although using nested curly brackets. You may have noticed the '{0}' in the WriteLine() method call – the string represents the output format, and markers such as '{0}' show where to substitute the arguments, with '{0}' representing the first argument, '{1}' the second, and so on. This is explained more fully towards the end of the chapter, where we discuss I/O.

The syntax for declaring jagged arrays is different. A jagged array is an array of 1D arrays (each of which can be of a different length), and this means that you have to declare the jagged array itself plus each of the 1D arrays which makes it up. An example should make it clear:

```
using System;
class Test
{
    public static int Main()
    {
        int[][] arr4;               // 2D jagged array of ints
        int[][][] arr5;             // 3D jagged array of ints

        arr4 = new int[4][];        // four rows in this array
        arr4[0] = new int[5];       // first row has 5 elements
        arr4[1] = new int[3];       // second row has 3 elements
        arr4[2] = new int[4];       // third row has 4 elements
        arr4[3] = new int[10];      // last row has 10 elements
        arr4[1][1] = 3;             // assign an element

        arr5 = new int[2][][];      // create 3D array
        arr5[0] = new int[3][];
        arr5[0][0] = new int[3];
        arr5[0][1] = new int[4];    // ...and so on

        return 0;
    }
}
```

Notice the difference in the way you access the two types of array. With rectangular arrays all indices are within one set of square brackets, while for jagged arrays each element is within its own square brackets.

Statements

A C# program is structured into classes, which contain methods, and these in turn are made up of statements. As is common in C-type languages, statements are free format, can run over more than one line without any need for continuation characters, and are terminated with a semicolon.

Statements may be arranged into blocks, a block simply being a sequence of statements enclosed in curly brackets. Each of the statements in a block is executed in turn:

```
{
    x = 0;              // these statements are inside a
    y = 2;              // block
}
```

In common with all the C-type languages, a block can be used wherever a single statement is expected. To illustrate this, consider the definition of an `if` statement:

```
if (boolean-expression)
    statement;
```

The `if` expects to control a single statement, so if we want to associate more than one statement with an `if`, we have to enclose them in a block, like this:

```
if (x == 0)
{
    y = 4;
    x = 7;
}
```

If we miss out the curly brackets, you'll have code which looks like this:

```
if (x == 0)
    y = 4;
    x = 7;
```

But it will execute like this:

```
if (x == 0)
    y = 4;          // this line is executed if x equals 0
x = 7;              // this line is always executed
```

For this reason, many programmers always put the curly brackets in, even when there's only a single line in the block.

A statement may have a label associated with it. Normally labeled statements are used in `switch` statements, but in C# they can also be used as the destination for a `goto` operation. You can see an example of a label used with a `goto` in the next section.

Program Control

In this section we're going to look at the selection and looping statements supported by C#.

The goto Statement

Let's get this one out of the way right at the start. Microsoft have, for reasons of their own, included a fully-working `goto` in C#. It works the same way that it does in C/C++, taking a reference to a label elsewhere in the code:

```
goto label;
    // intervening code
label:
    // more code here
```

Needless to say, no one is going to use this in a fully structured OO language, right? However, it turns out that there's one place where you may well need to use it, and that's to jump between cases in a `switch` statement.

The C# compiler will also check for some cases of `goto` abuse, such as trying to jump into a block, but it still isn't recommended for general use.

C++ Note

C# is far less strict than C++ in some areas, and will let you declare variables between `goto` and `label`.

The if Statement

The `if` statement is very similar to the one found in C++ and Java. A statement or block of statements is executed if the expression in round brackets evaluates to true. The `if` can optionally be followed by one or more `else if`'s, and/or an optional `else`.

```
if (x == 0)
    Console.WriteLine("X is zero");
else if (x < 0)
{
    Console.WriteLine("X is negative");
    x = 0;
}
else
    Console.WriteLine("X is positive");
```

C++ Note

The expression in an `if` statement must resolve to a `bool` value. The link with C has finally been broken, and you can no longer use integers.

The for Statement

The `for` statement is the first of four iteration statements that C# supports.

C++ and Java Note
Yes, four iteration constructs rather than three. We've got the familiar `for`, `do` and `while` loops, plus a new one which has come from Visual Basic, `foreach`.

A `for` statement is driven by three expressions in parentheses – an initializer expression, a condition expression, and an iterator expression:

```
for (initializer; condition; iterator)
    statement;
```

The initializer expression lets you declare a variable local to the loop and set its value, and can be used to count the number of times the loop is executed. The condition expression is commonly used to test that expression, and the iterator expression provides a place where you can increment the value of the loop control variable. An example will show how it works:

```
for (int i=0; i<10; i++)
    Console.WriteLine(...);
```

The initializer expression declares an `int` and sets it value to zero; note that the `i` variable is local to the loop. Each time around the loop, the `int` is incremented, and the loop continues while its value is less than 10. The increment expression is executed at the end of each iteration, and the condition is checked at the beginning; this means that it is possible for a loop not to execute at all, since the condition may fail at the top of the very first iteration:

```
int i = 0;
// Loop won't execute at all
for (; i>0; i++)
    Console.WriteLine(...);
```

This example shows another property of the `for` loop – you don't have to include any of the expressions, provided that you do the work yourself elsewhere in the code. In this case we've declared and initialized the loop control variable outside the loop, so we don't need to put anything in the initialization expression.

Missing out all three expressions is one way of obtaining an infinite loop:

```
for(;;)
{
    // endless loop
}
```

The break and continue Keywords

The `break` and `continue` statements can be used to control iteration. The `break` statement will exit from the immediately enclosing `for`, `do`, `while`, `foreach`, or `switch` statement, as shown below:

```
for (int j=0; j<10; j++)
{
    for (int i=0; ; i++)
    {
        // Terminate when i==10
        if (i == 10) break;
            Console.WriteLine(...);
    }
    // break comes to here
}
```

The continue statement works with iteration statements, and will terminate the current iteration, causing a jump to the end of the block forming the body of the loop:

```
for (int i=1; i<20; i++)
{
    // Only write out even numbers
    if (i%2 == 1) continue;
        Console.WriteLine(...);
}
```

Java Note
C# doesn't support the labeled break, so that jumping out of nested loops can be messy.

The do And while Statements

The do and while statements are very similar to one another, both looping until a Boolean expression evaluates to false. As the code example shows, the only difference between them is that the body of a do loop will always execute once, while a while loop may execute zero times.

```
int n = 0;
// while loop may execute zero times
while (n < 10)
{
    // do something
    n++;    // increment the counter
}

int m = 0;
do {
    // some code goes here...
} while (m > 0);
```

The foreach Statement

This statement lets you iterate over the elements in arrays and collections, and is very similar to Visual Basic's For Each construct. Here's a simple example to show how it is used:

```
int[] arr1 = new int[] {1,2,3,4,5};
foreach (int i in arr1) {
    Console.WriteLine("Value is {0}", i);
}
```

When applied to an array, the content of the `foreach` loop is repeated for each element in the array.

C# arrays are collection classes, since they're based on the underlying `System.Array` base class, and the same mechanism applies to collections. This means that `foreach` is simple to use with the collections provided in the `System.Collections` namespace, such as `List` and `HashTable`.

If you want to use `foreach` with your own collections, you need to design them correctly, and we'll cover how to do this in Chapter 6.

The switch Statement

The `switch` statement is, again, very similar to the one found in other C-type languages. It selects between alternatives based upon the value of a `switch` expression:

```
switch (n)
{
case 0:
    Console.WriteLine("X is 0");
    break;
case 1:
    Console.WriteLine("X is 1");
    break;
default:
    Console.WriteLine("X is neither 0 nor 1");
    break;
}
```

If the value of n is zero, control transfers to the `case 0` label. If the value is one, it transfers to `case 1`, and otherwise it transfers to the optional `default` label. `break` shows that you're finished with this case, and jumps out of the `switch` statement. Note that the `break` isn't necessary with the default case, because it is the last one in the `switch`, but many programmers will put it in anyway, as it helps guard against future editing introducing errors.

C++ and Java Note
There are quite a few differences hiding here to catch the unwary, the major one being that you no longer fall through from case to case if you omit the break *and* there's code in the case. You'll get a compiler error instead, and have to use a `goto` to jump to the next case. If you have adjacent case labels (i.e. no code in the case) then you can fall through. Note that the `goto` mechanism lets you jump forward and back between cases.

The switch expression must be an integer type (including `char`) or a `string`. This means that we can write code like this:

```
switch (name)
{
case "Jim":
    Console.WriteLine("It's Jim!");
    break;
case "Jon":
    Console.WriteLine("It's Jon!");
    break;
```

```
    default:
       Console.WriteLine("Must be someone else...");
       break;
    }
```

The case labels have to be constants, which means you *can't* write code like this:

```
switch (n)
{
case m:                     // Use whatever value m has at runtime
    Console.WriteLine("Can't do this");
    break;
...
}
```

If you want to 'fall through' from one case to the next, it isn't enough to simply omit the break; you have to use a goto to signal your intention to the compiler, as shown in the next example. This is done so that you won't introduce an error by inadvertently omitting a break. Note that you don't have to do this if the cases don't contain any code.

```
using System;

public class Test
{
    public static int Main()
    {
        string s = "abAcdEefgjIk";

        // Loop over each character in the string
        for (int i=0; i<s.Length; i++)
        {
            switch (s[i])
            {
            case 'a':
            case 'A':
                Console.WriteLine("A found");
                break;
            case 'e':
                Console.Write("Lower-case ");
                goto case 'E';
            case 'E':
                Console.WriteLine("E found");
                break;
            }
        }
    }
    return 0;
}
```

In the example, we're declaring a string containing a selection of upper and lower-case letters. We use a for loop to iterate over all the characters one-by-one; note the use of the Length member to find out how long the string is, and the use of square brackets to access individual characters of the string as if it was an array. In the first two cases we're simply counting upper and lower-case A's as the same thing, so we declare two case labels next to one another. The fact that there's no code between the first and second case labels means that we can drop through from the first to the second without having to do anything. For the E's, on the other hand, we're counting upper and lower-case letters separately. When we get a lower-case E, we want to execute the first case (to print 'Lower-case') and then drop through to the second case to print 'E found'. C# requires us to use a goto to tell the compiler that we mean to drop through.

Calling Methods

Defining and calling methods in C# closely follows the C++/Java model. This means that every method has to have a declaration that follows the pattern below, where the items in square brackets are optional:

```
[modifiers] return-type method-name([parameter-list])
```

Every method has to have a return type; if the method doesn't return a value, its return type is void. A method may not take any parameters, in which case the method name is followed by empty parentheses.

The method's return type may be preceded by one or more modifiers. If there are more than one, they are separated by whitespace. We'll talk about the method modifiers in the next chapter, when we come to talk about classes.

This method declaration is followed by a method body, which takes the form of a code block (i.e. statements contained in curly brackets). The example below shows the definition of a method square, which takes a float value and returns its square:

```
double square(float n)
{
   return n*n;
}
```

You call a method by using its name, supplying any necessary arguments, and saving the return value away. Here's an example:

```
using System;

public class CallIt
{
   public static int Main()
   {
      // Call Square(), passing in 3.0
      double d = Square(3.0F);
      Console.WriteLine(d);
      return 0;
   }

   static double Square(float n)
   {
      return n*n;
   }
}
```

Note how all these methods are declared within the class, because you can't have any code outside a class in C#. Note also how the method is declared with the static keyword. This is simply done here so that we can show how to call the method without getting into the complication of creating objects. Static members and how they relate to classes are discussed in the next chapter.

As in C++ and Java, you're free to ignore the return value if you don't need it (although in this example it is hard to see why you'd want to!)

```
square(3.0F);     // ignore return value
```

Note how the argument is passed through as 3.0F, showing that it is to be passed as a float rather than the default double floating point type.

Precisely how the arguments are passed through to a method depends on whether they are of a value or reference type.

If an argument to a method is a value type, it is passed (as you might expect) by value, which means that a copy of the argument is passed to the function. In the code fragment below, an int is passed to the function, and the change made to the local copy inside the function doesn't affect the value of the original argument.

```
int n = 3;

// value of n is 3 before the call

someFunc(n);

// n is still 3 after the call
...
void someFunc(int m)
{
    // change the value from 3 to 4
    m = 4;
}
```

If value types are passed by value, then it won't surprise you to learn that reference types are passed by reference. This means that what gets passed around is a reference to the real object, and this means that any changes you make in the method will affect the real object itself. There's no copying involved.

```
myObject.value = 3;       // value is 3 before the call

someFunc(myObject);       // pass over a reference to myObject

// value is 4 after the call
...
void someFunc(SomeThing obj)
{
    // change the value from 3 to 4
    obj.value = 4;
}
```

What if you want to pass a value type into a method and modify it? C# provides two ways of doing this using the ref and out keywords.

Marking a parameter as ref means that any modifications you make to its value will persist, just as if it was a reference type.

```
void refMethod(ref int n)
{
    n += 3;
}
...
int p = 3;
refMethod(ref p);      // value of p will be changed
```

Note the use of `ref int` as the parameter type, and the use of the `ref` keyword in the method call to tell the compiler to pass by reference rather than by value.

If you don't assign a value to p before making the call, the compiler will give you an error about using an uninitialised variable.

C++ Note

Because C# checks for uninitialized variables and gives an error at compile time if they are used, it is much less likely that you'll forget to initialize variables and get completely unpredictable output and bugs as the result.

If it is intended that the method is going to assign a value to the parameter, as opposed to modifying its existing value, then an `out` parameter should be used.

```
void outMethod(out int n)
{
    n = 3;
}
...
int p;                  // uninitialised
outMethod(out p);       // value of p will be set
```

C++ Note

C# doesn't support either default or anonymous arguments, but it does have method overloading...

Method Overloading

Like Java and C++, C# allows you to declare more than one method with the same name. This practice is called **overloading**, and we'll see numerous examples when we cover classes in the next chapter.

Overloaded functions must differ in the number and/or type of arguments they take, and this enables the compiler to tell which one should be called by the arguments that have been provided in the call. Here are two overloaded methods:

```
long square(int n)
{
    return n*n;
}
double square(float n)
{
    return n*n;
}
```

Both are called `square`, but one takes an `int` as an argument, while the second takes a `float`. This means that the compiler can tell which version to call, depending on whether an `int` or a `float` has been passed as an argument:

```
long l = square(3);         // int version
double d = square(3.0F);    // float version
```

Note that the return type doesn't play any part in the overload resolution, since it is always possible to call a function without using the return value.

```
long square(int n)
{
    return n*n;
}
int square(int n)
{
    return n*n;
}
square(3);     // won't work - which to use?
```

Handling Errors

C# supports exceptions in very much the same way as Java and C++. The following few paragraphs describe how exceptions work, for the benefit of those who may not have met them before. If you're a C++ or Java programmer, you can skip through these fairly quickly.

In many languages errors are reported by setting a return value and relying on the caller to check and act upon it:

```
bool aFunc()
{
    ...
    // check for error
    if (val < 0)
        return false;
    else
        return true;
}
```

There are two problems with this. Firstly, the caller may choose to ignore the status which is sent back, and secondly the caller may not even bother to collect the status, since it is legal to call any function in C# and not bother with the return value:

```
aFunc();       // don't get the return value
```

Exceptions solve both these problems and more. They are useful for three main reasons:

1. They can't be ignored. If calling code doesn't handle an exception, it causes program termination.

2. They don't have to be handled at the point the error occurred. This makes them very suitable for library or system code, which can signal an error and leave you to handle it.

3. They can be used when passing back a return value can't be used. For example, we've seen that arrays are objects, and we know how many elements they contain. What happens if you try to access element 15 of a 10-element array? The array object can't give you a return value, so it throws an exception.

To signal an error, you *throw* an exception using a `throw` statement:

```
void aFunc()
{
    ...
    // check for error
    if (val < 0)
    {
        throw new System.Exception();
      // never gets here
    }
}
```

When an exception is thrown, normal execution stops and the runtime goes off looking for a handler. This means that if there's any code in a block after a throw, it can never be executed.

An exception is tagged with an object reference which identifies the type of error which has occurred. In C#, what you throw has to be a `System.Exception` object, or something derived from `System.Exception`.

C++ Note
Unlike in C++, you can't throw any type in C#. The thrown value has to be a reference to a `System.Exception` object (or derived class).

If a handler can't be found in the same method, the runtime mechanism goes back up the call stack, looking for handlers. If it gets back to the top level (i.e. the `Main()` method of an application) without finding one, the program will terminate. This makes it easy for a library or system routine to throw an exception way down in the code and make it the responsibility of the client to catch it.

Exceptions are handled by using `try...catch` statements. Code which may give rise to exceptions is enclosed in a `try` block, which is followed by one or more `catch` blocks:

```
public void ThrowException()
{
...

    try
    {
        // Code that might raise a runtime exception
    }
    catch(System.Exception e)
    {
        // Code that will be executed if an exception occurred
        Console.WriteLine("Exception occurred: " + e);
    }

    //We'll get here after the handler has been executed

}
```

The `catch` block is only executed if an exception occurs during execution of code within the `try` block; if nothing occurs, the handler is skipped. Once an exception has occurred, execution of the `try` block is finished. There's nothing to stop you looping round to before the `try` and having another go, but you can't jump back into the `try` block and carry on from where you left off.

If you know – or suspect – that more than one kind of exception may occur during execution of a `try` block, you can chain `catch` blocks together and they'll be checked in order to see which one (if any) is going to handle the exception. You can see an example of this a little further down, when we discuss the exception classes.

Note that the Beta 1 of the .NET framework includes built in exception handlers for common exception types such as the divide-by-zero exception. For example if you run this code, without `try...catch` blocks:

```
double a = 15.0;
double b = 0.0;
double result = a/b;

Console.WriteLine("Result is {0}", result);
```

you will get this output:

Result is Infinity

Putting the third line in the above code in a `try` block and adding a `catch` block makes no difference in this case.

C++ and Java Note
You have to order your catch blocks correctly in C#. If you code a `catch Derived.From.System.Exception)` block after a `catch(System.Exception)` block you'll get a compiler error, because the second catch will never be reached.

A `catch` block which will catch any exception is called a general `catch` clause. These blocks don't specify an exception variable, and can be written like this:

```
try
{
    // code which may fail
}
catch
{
    // handle error
}
```

This is rather a last-resort kind of error handler and shouldn't be used very often, because you lose the information that came with the exception, so you don't know what went wrong.

C++ Note
General `catch` clauses are equivalent to `catch(...)`

And finally...

A try block can also have a finally block associated with it. If a finally block exists, it will be executed before the try block is completed, and after any possible exceptions are caught in the catch clauses. This will happen no matter how control leaves the try, whether it is due to normal termination, to an exception occurring, a break or continue (or goto) statement, or a return. The following pseudo-code shows how this might work in practice:

```csharp
public void ReadFile()
{
    try
    {
        // code which may fail
    }
    finally
    {
        // close the file
    }
}
```

A finally block can occur with or without catch blocks. Note that it is an error to transfer control out of a finally block using break, continue, return or goto. If an exception occurs during execution of a finally block, it is passed to the enclosing try; if another exception was being processed at this point, it will be lost.

Exception Classes

There are a number of exception classes provided in C#, all of which inherit from the System.Exception class. Common exception classes that you may meet when writing application code are summarized in the following table:

Exception Class	Cause
SystemException	A failed run-time check; used as a base class for other exceptions
AccessException	Failure to access a type member, such as a method or field
ArgumentException	An argument to a method was invalid
ArgumentNullException	A null argument was passed to a method that doesn't accept it
ArgumentOutOfRangeException	Argument value is out of range
ArithmeticException	Arithmetic over- or underflow has occurred
ArrayTypeMismatchException	Attempt to store the wrong type of object in an array
BadImageFormatException	Image is in the wrong format
CoreException	Base class for exceptions thrown by the runtime

Table continued on following page

Exception Class	Cause
DivideByZeroException	An attempt was made to divide by zero
FormatException	The format of an argument is wrong
IndexOutOfRangeException	An array index is out of bounds
InvalidCastException	An attempt was made to cast to an invalid class
InvalidOperationException	A method was called at an invalid time
MissingMemberException	An invalid version of a DLL was accessed
NotFiniteNumberException	A number is not valid
NotSupportedException	Indicates that a method is not implemented by a class
NullReferenceException	Attempt to use an unassigned reference
OutOfMemoryException	Not enough memory to continue execution
StackOverflowException	A stack has overflowed

Java Note

CoreException is C#'s equivalent of Error, and you are not expected to handle it. There is also no division of exceptions into checked and runtime.

When catching these, remember that some of them inherit from others (e.g. an OutOfMemoryException is derived from SystemException, which is in turn derived from Exception), and if you're going to catch at different levels in the hierarchy, you need to get them in the right order:

```
try
{
    // code which may fail
}
catch (OutOfMemoryException e)
{
    // this one must come first
}
catch (SystemException se)
{
    // this one must come second, as it can't hide the first one
}
```

You can make up your own exception classes by deriving from one of these, typically System.Exception.

checked and unchecked

Two operators, checked and unchecked, can be used to control overflow checking for arithmetic operations and conversion of integer types. If an operation is checked, an exception will be thrown if overflow occurs; if it is unchecked, the overflowing bits will be silently discarded.

```
public void CheckIt(int a, int b)
{
    try
    {
        int result1 = checked(a * b);
        Console.WriteLine("Checked value is {0}", result1);
    }
    catch(System.OverflowException soe)
    {
        Console.WriteLine("Exception occurred: " + soe);
    }

    // this won't throw an exception
    int result2 = unchecked(a * b);
    Console.WriteLine("Unchecked value is {0}", result2);
}
```

Depending on the values passed in, the result may overflow an int. If this is the case, the checked expression will result in an exception being thrown, while the unchecked expression will simply lose bits. So, if you run the above code with a and b taking the values 50000 and 60000 respectively (which when multiplied will easily exceed the maximum value for an int, you will get output like this:

```
Exception occurred: System.OverflowException: An exception of type
System.OverflowException was thrown.
   at Test.CheckIt(Int32 a, Int32 b)
Unchecked value is −1294967296
```

If you don't use either, the result you get will tend to depend on other factors, such as compiler options. As well as using the two operators to check expressions, the checked and unchecked keywords can be applied to statements:

```
checked                    // all operations are checked
{
    largeNumber * largeNumber;
    number2 + number3;
}
```

Console I/O

We've already seen simple use of the Console.WriteLine() method to produce text output. In this section we'll look in a little more detail at the console I/O classes.

Console I/O is provided by the System.Console class, which gives you access to the standard input, standard output, and standard error streams.

Object	Represents
Console.In	Standard input
Console.Out	Standard output
Console.Error	Standard error

The standard input stream gets character input, by default from the keyboard although this can be redirected to obtain input from a file. The standard output stream writes to the screen by default, but can be redirected to a file. The standard error stream is like `Console.Out`, in that it usually displays output to the screen. The reason for having two output streams is that it lets you write normal output to `Console.Out` and error messages to `Console.Error`, so that if you got an error when standard output is being redirected to a file, you'll still see it on the screen.

Console Input

`Console.In` has two methods for obtaining input. `Read()` returns a single character as an `int`, or -1 if no more characters are available. `ReadLine()` returns a string containing the next line of input, or `null` if no more lines are available.

```
for(;;)
{
    string s = Console.In.ReadLine();
    if (s == null) break;
    // use string...
}
```

Or to use a more C-like way of coding:

```
string s;
while((s = Console.In.ReadLine()) != null)
{
    // use string...
}
```

Note that `Console.In.ReadLine()` and `Console.ReadLine()` are equivalent.

Console Output

`Console.Out` has two matching methods for writing output. `Write()` outputs one or more values without a newline character, while `WriteLine()` does the same but appends a newline.

`Write()` and `WriteLine()` have numerous overloads, so that you can easily output many different types of data. There is one for each of the basic types (such as `short` and `long`) and for string, plus several for producing formatted output.

If you want to produce formatted output, you use a version of `WriteLine()` which takes a string containing a format and a variable number of objects:

```
Console.Out.WriteLine(format, object1, ...)
```

Note the `Console.Out.WriteLine()` and `Console.WriteLine()` are equivalent.

C++ Note
C# doesn't support variable argument lists in the way C and C++ do. See Chapter 6 for details on how it works.

Formats contain both static text, plus markers which show where items from the argument list are to be substituted, and how they are to be formatted. In its simplest form a marker is a number in curly brackets, the number showing which argument is to be substituted:

```
"The value is {0}"      // use the first argument
"{0} plus {1} = {2}"    // use the first three arguments
```

The more general form of a format looks like this:

```
{N[,M][:FormatString]}
```

As we've already seen, 'N' is the zero-based number of the argument to be substituted, and it can be followed by an integer specifying a field width. If the field width value is negative the value will be left-justified within the field; if positive, right-justified.

```
{1}                     // output the second argument
{0,-8}                  // output the first argument, left justified
// in a field eight characters wide
```

These can optionally be followed by a formatting specification, which consists of a character and optionally a precision specifier.

```
{1:D7}                  // output the second argument as an integer,
                        // field width of 7, padded with zeros
{0:E4}                  // output in exponent notation with four
                        // decimal places
```

The table below shows the list of format characters. Note that although I've given them in uppercase, they can be specified in either upper or lowercase.

Format Character	Description	Notes
C	Locale-specific currency formatting	
D	Integer, with optional zero padding	If a precision specifier is given, e.g. {0:D5}, the output will be padded with leading zeros
E	Scientific	The precision specifier sets the number of decimal places, which is 6 by default. There is always one figure before the decimal point.
F	Fixed-point	The precision specifier controls the number of decimal places. Zero is acceptable.
G	General	Uses E or F formatting, depending on which is the most compact.
N	Number	Produces a value with embedded commas, e.g. 32,767.44
X	Hexadecimal	The precision specifier can be used to pad with leading zeros

As well as these formatting characters, you can also use placeholder characters to map out formats. Here's an example:

```
Console.WriteLine("{0:00000}", 123);
```

The output from this will be 00123, because the format outputs a digit wherever one is available, and outputs a zero where there isn't one.

Namespaces

As our final topic in this chapter, we'll take a look at namespaces, a feature of .NET that is heavily used in the .NET class library that underlies C#.

C++ Note
Namespaces in C# are similar to C++ namespaces, in that they're used to provide another level of scoping for classes, but they have extra functionality.

Java Note
Namespaces in C# are similar to packages in Java, but the components of the namespace name do not have to map onto directories. There is still special access between classes in a namespace.

Namespaces provide a way to group classes, by providing an extra level of naming beyond the class name. For example, if we had several classes to do with banking, we could wrap them in a namespace like this:

```
namespace Bank
{
    public class Account
    {
    ...
    }
    public class Teller
    {
    ...
    }
}
```

We can see that the definition of the Bank namespace wraps the definition of the Account and Teller classes.

What advantage does this give you? Firstly, it gives you a way to organise your classes, so that related classes are bound together in a namespace. The second advantage is that it helps in large applications, where different classes may be provided by different people, different teams or even different organizations. Avoiding name clashes in large applications can be quite a headache, and in the past developers have resorted to arcane naming conventions to ensure uniqueness for their class names.

This problem is greatly helped by the fact that namespaces can also be hierarchical, with namespace names being composed of several parts separated by dots. If we had a number of different namespaces to do with financial matters, we could name them like this:

```
namespace Finance.Bank
{
    ...
}
namespace Finance.InsuranceCo
{
    ...
}
```

When building large applications, or producing classes for others to use, multi-level namespace names can prove very useful in avoiding naming problems.

There are two ways to refer to these classes in code. The first is to use the fully qualified name, like this:

```
Finance.Bank.Account ba = new Finance.Bank.Account();
```

The reference to `Account` is completely unambiguous, but it will get rather wearing having to type `Finance.Bank.Account` every time we want to refer to the `Account` class. In order to avoid this, we can use a using directive, which is a way of importing all the names defined in a namespace into the current scope, so that they don't have to be fully qualified.

```
// import all the names from Finance.Bank
using Finance.Bank;
...
// Use Account without qualification
// ba is a Finance.Bank.Account
Account ba = new Account();
```

Note that you have to import the exact package you want; if we want to use `Finance.Bank` and `Finance.InsuranceCo`, we have to import both of them.

You can also provide aliases for namespaces and classes with using. Suppose that both `Finance.Bank` and `Finance.InsuranceCo` contain a class called `Account`. If we want to use both `Accounts` without tedious qualification, we can define aliases like this:

```
using BankAccount = Finance.Bank.Account;
using InsuranceAccount = Finance.InsuranceCo.Account;
```

We can now simply create `BankAccount` and `InsuranceAccount` objects, and the compiler will know which classes we mean.

Java Note
You can't import a single class in C#, but the whole package.

There is more on namespaces in Chapter 7.

Namespaces and Assemblies

The basic element of packaging in .NET is the **assembly**. Traditionally, code has been compiled up and built into EXE or DLL files, and these were the units of distribution and execution.

In .NET, languages compile down to Intermediate Language (IL), and an assembly consists of the IL code, metadata that describes what is in the assembly, and any other files that the application needs to run, such as graphics and sound files. On Windows systems, assemblies can be physically housed in EXEs or DLLs, but since assemblies are regarded as logical rather than physical collections, one assembly can be split across more than one physical file.

There is often a correspondence between namespaces and assemblies, so that the classes in the Finance.Bank namespace would be built into an assembly called Finance.Bank.dll. This isn't mandatory in any way, and the classes in the System namespaces are housed in a DLL called mscorlib.dll, but it will help to identify the content of an assembly if you use a suitable naming convention based on namespaces.

In order to create an assembly with a particular name, you can use the /out option on the compiler command line to set the name of the output file:

```
csc BankStuff.cs /t:library /out:Finance.Bank.dll
```

Assemblies are covered in more detail in Chapter 10.

Summary

In this chapter we've looked at the basic syntax of C#, and we've seen that it is very similar in many ways to both C++ and Java, but has tried to overcome some of the shortcomings of both languages.

The main features we've covered are:

- ❑ All C# programs must have a Main() method.
- ❑ C# types are based on the underlying language-independent .NET types.
- ❑ The 16-bit Unicode encoding is used for characters.
- ❑ Exceptions provide an efficient and safe way of handling program errors.
- ❑ Namespaces are used to group classes into hierarchies.
- ❑ Namespaces are often related to assemblies.

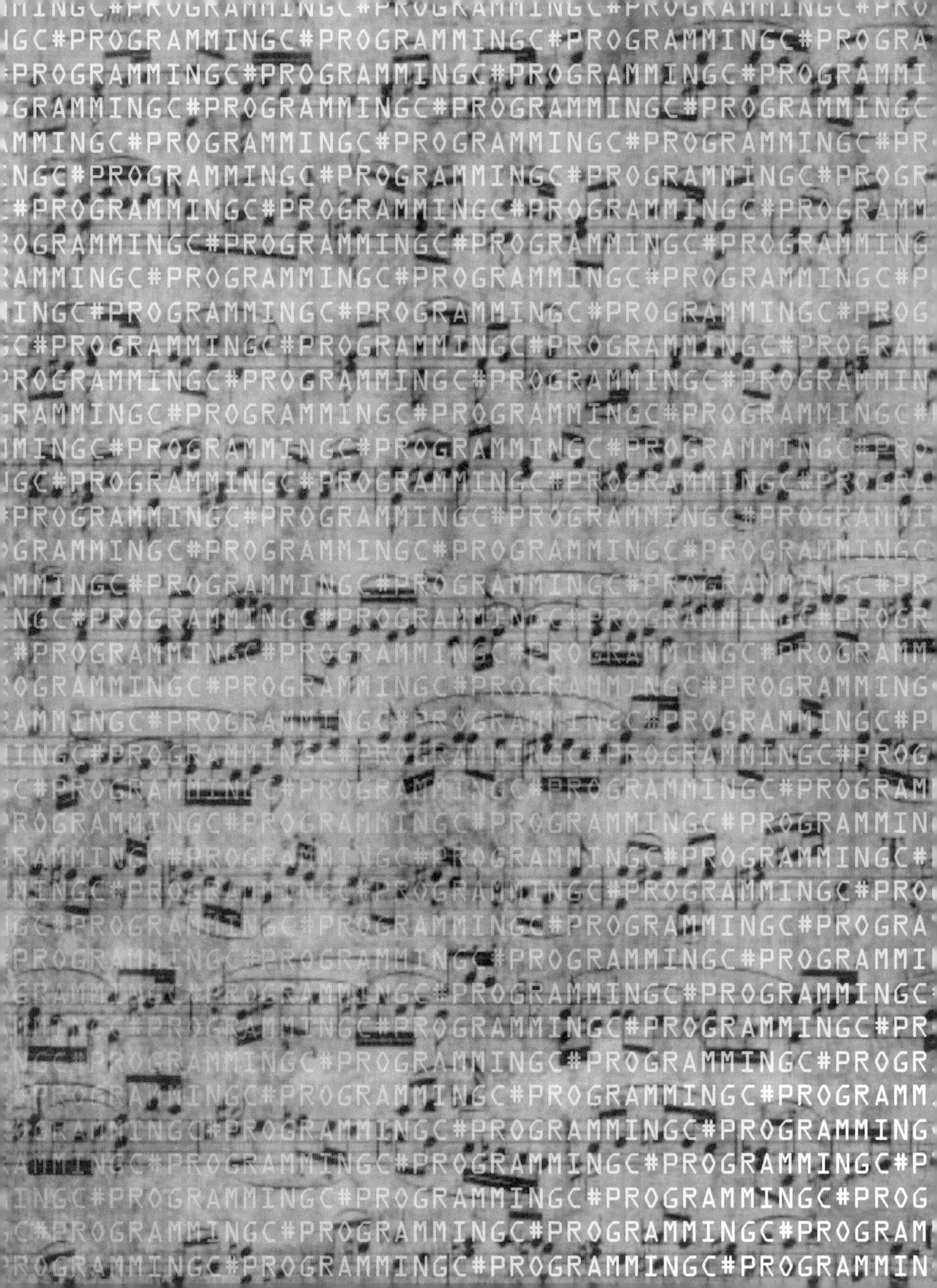
C#PROGRAMMING

5

Object-Oriented Programming

This chapter is going to introduce some of the object-oriented (OO) features of the C# language, starting with simple compound data types in the form of structs and enumerations, and moving onto classes and inheritance.

C++ and Java programmers will find that there are considerable similarities between C# and their languages, but they'll also find a lot of new – and some changed – features in addition.

Structs

A struct in C# is simply a composite data type, consisting of a number of elements (or **members**) of other types, and defined using the struct keyword:

```
// A struct called Point

struct Point
{
    public int x;
    public int y;
}
```

Structs are intended to be used to declare simple composite data types, as in the example above, and because of this they are value types. This means that they're directly created on the stack, and they are not accessed through references.

C++ Note

In C# struct member access is the same as class member access, so you need to specify `public` if you want typical struct behavior. The fundamental difference between structs and classes in C# is that structs are value types. Like C++, structs in C# can have all the features of classes, including constructors and other methods.

The variables which make up a struct are called its members (and are also often referred to as 'fields' in C#), and can be accessed using a simple dot notation:

```
Point p1;          // Declare a Point

p1.x = 10;         // Set the x member of p1
p1.y = 10;         // Set the y member of p1

Console.WriteLine("{0},{1}", p1.x, p1.y);
```

It is quite possible to nest references to structs, and you can use the dot notation to access all levels within the nested structure:

```
struct Inner
{
    public int a;
    public int b;
}

struct Outer
{
    public Inner i;
    public int x;
}

Outer o;
o.i.a = 3;         // assign to the a member of the i member of o
o.x = 4;           // assign to the x member of o
```

You can also declare structs nested inside other structs:

```
struct Outer
{
    public struct Inner
    {
        public int a;
        public int b;
    }
    public Inner i;
    public int x;
}
```

In this case, the members of `Inner` will be accessed in exactly the same way as in the previous example. Suppose we want to use the `Inner` struct on its own; that might not be a very common thing to want to do, but it is possible, as the following example shows:

```
using System;

public class Test
{
    public static int Main()
    {
        Outer o;
        o.x = 4;

        // The Inner struct is a member of Outer, so it needs to be
        // declared as such
        Outer.Inner i;
        i.a = 3;
        return 0;
    }
}

struct Outer
{
    public struct Inner
    {
        public int a;
        public int b;
    }
    public int x;
}
```

Enumerations

An enumeration is a data type consisting of a set of named integer constants:

```
enum Weekday {Mon, Tue, Wed, Thu, Fri, Sat, Sun};
```

Each of the named constants has a value, which by default starts at zero and increases by one for each succeeding member. So, in the example above, Mon has the value 0, Tue is 1, and so on. You can give explicit values to any or all of the constants; any that you don't specify get a value one more than the preceding constant:

```
enum Error {FileNotFound=100, AccessDenied=200, UnknownError=500};
```

The default type of the constants is int; if you wish to, you can declare enumerations which use other integral types:

```
enum Weekday : short {Mon, Tue, Wed, Thu, Fri, Sat, Sun };
```

You can use the byte, sbyte, short, ushort, int, uint, long, and ulong types as the base types for enumerations.

Classes

The concept of the class is at the heart of OO programming. We've seen that structs are compound data types; classes are an extension to this idea, in that you can add methods along with the data. This isn't the place for a wide-ranging discussion of OO programming, but I'll just quickly list a few of the principal advantages:

❏   'Black-box' development and testing. OO programming lets you bind data and functionality (in the form of methods) together into classes. Access constraints make some functionality available to users of the class, while other parts are for internal use only. When done properly, this results in the creation of software 'black boxes' that can be independently developed and tested.

❏   Reusability. Classes can be designed so that they have minimal dependency on the rest of the program, and such classes can be taken and used elsewhere.

❏   Robustness. If all access to the data which makes up the state of an object is via methods, they can ensure that the user does nothing which will compromise the integrity of the object.

This example shows a very simple implementation of a class that represents a bank account:

```
public class Account
{
    private double balance;              // a data member

    public bool Deposit(double amt)
    {
        // deposit cash
        balance += amt;

        return true;
    }

    public bool Withdraw(double amt)
    {
        // withdraw cash
        if (balance-amt < 0.0)
            return false;
        else
            balance -= amt;

        return true;
    }

    public double QueryBalance()
    {
        return balance;
    }
}
```

The first thing to note is the use of the `class` keyword when defining the class. Classes and structs are very similar, but the use of `class` tells the compiler that this is a reference type, rather than a value type. It also gives a hint to users that `Account` contains some functionality, and isn't simply a container for other data types.

> **C++ Note**
>
> Note that in C# you don't need (and mustn't have!) a semicolon at the end of the class definition.

The `Account` class consists of declarations of data members – in this case only the balance – and definitions of methods. Note that all the declarations and definitions take place between the opening and closing curly brackets.

> **C++ Note**
>
> Like Java, C# doesn't separate class definition from implementation. Classes are defined and implemented in the same place, so there's no place for header files.

Class methods are invoked using exactly the same dot notation as we've used for accessing the members of structs.

```
// Create an account
Account a1 = new Account();

// Deposit and withdraw
a1.Deposit(5000.0);
a1.Withdraw(1000.0);
```

You may be wondering what value the balance has immediately after we've created the account, but before we deposit any money. The answer here is 'zero', because unlike in C++, data members in C# classes are set to sensible default values, zero for numeric types, false for Booleans, and null for references.

You'll notice that methods and data members are qualified by either the `public` or `private` access modifiers. The `private` modifier means that a method or data member is not accessible to any code outside the class. In effect, it can't be accessed outside the opening and closing parentheses that bracket the class content. `public`, on the other hand, means that anyone can use the member. We can also see `public` applied to the class itself, which means that this class can be used from anywhere.

There are two other access modifiers, which we'll discuss later on.

You can see the advantage to this approach in our simple class. We really don't want users being able to modify the account balance arbitrarily, so we make it private, and only grant indirect access to it through the `Deposit()` and `Withdraw()` members. In this way, we can make sure that access to the balance is controlled and data integrity is maintained.

```
public bool Deposit(double amt)
{
    // Can't deposit negative amounts!
    if (amt < 0.0)
        return false;
    else {
        balance += amt;
        return true;
    }
}
```

Although C# will let you have public and private data members, as a general point of good OO design always make data members private and grant access to them through methods, so that you can control what happens to the data in your objects.

The `QueryBalance()` method is simply used to return the value of the `balance` member. Since `balance` is a value type, a copy of it will be returned to the caller; in this way we let them *see* the value without being able to modify it. A method like `QueryBalance()` that returns the value of a member is commonly called an **accessor** method.

Constant and Read-only Members

The `const` modifier can be used to declare constant members of classes:

```
public class Account
{
    public const string sortCode = "12-00-23";
    ...
}
```

One problem you may encounter is that the values of `const` members are calculated at compile time, so you can't use `const` to define a member whose value can't be set in this way. To get round this, C# has provided the `readonly` modifier, which specifies that the member can have its value set once only, and afterwards is read-only. In the example below, we're setting the sort code to the string value passed into the constructor.

```
public class Account
{
    public readonly string sortCode;

    public Account(string code)
    {
        sortCode = code;
    }
}
```

The *this* Reference

A class method is always called in the context of some object. In the example below, `Deposit()` is being called for `a1`, so it is `a1`'s balance which will be modified.

```
a1.Deposit(5000.0);
```

This association is done automatically by the compiler, and you need never be aware within a method which object's data members are being referenced.

```
public bool Deposit(double amt)
{
    if (amt < 0.0)
        return false;
    else {
        balance += amt;    // this time, it's a1's balance
```

```
        return true;
    }
}
```

Supposing you wanted for some reason to know which object has called the method. You can get at this via the keyword `this`, which is a reference to the object that called the method. It's quite common to use this to disambiguate local and class variables that have the same name, as shown here, where `this.x` refers to the member of class `Point`, and `x` refers to the argument of the `SetX()` method:

```
public class Point
{
    int x;
    int y;

    public void SetX(int x)
    {
        this.x = x;
    }
    ...
}
```

Constructors and Destructors

A constructor is a method which is called when an object of a class type is constructed, and it is usually used for initialization. A constructor method has several characteristics:

❑   It has the same name as the class.

❑   It has no return type.

❑   It doesn't return any value.

You can use overloading to create several constructors for a class; which one will get called depends on the arguments you give to `new`.

```
using System;

public class Account
{
    private double balance;          // a data member

    public Account()
    {
        // if no opening balance given, explicitly set it to zero
        balance = 0.0;
    }

    public Account(double amt)
    {
        // set up the opening balance
        balance = amt;
    }
```

```
      // Method code omitted for clarity
      public bool Deposit(double amt)...
      public bool Withdraw(double amt)...
      public double QueryBalance()...

}

public class Test
{
   public static int Main()
   {
      Account a1 = new Account();        // use no-argument constructor
      Account a2 = new Account(3000.0); // use double constructor

      return 0;
   }
}
```

We can see that the example code is creating two `Account` objects. The first call to `Account()` has no arguments, so the compiler selects the constructor which takes no arguments. Likewise, the second call to `Account()` is passed a `double`, so the compiler selects the constructor that takes a `double`.

C++ and Java Note
If you don't specify any constructors or destructors for a class, C# doesn't provide any defaults.

Constructors are usually `public`, but can also be `private` or `protected` (which relates to inheritance, and is discussed later in the chapter). If a constructor is `private`, it means that objects of that class type can't be created, and the class can't be used as a base class for inheritance.

Structs can also have constructors and methods, although they cannot have parameterless constructors.

Destructors

A destructor also called a finalizer is in may ways the opposite to a constructor, in that it is a method called when an object is reclaimed by the garbage collector.

C++ Note
Destructors in C# are *not* the same as in C++, and are used much less frequently. Read this section carefully!

Java Note
C# destructors are very similar to Java's `finalize()` method, and have all the same disadvantages.

The following example code shows the syntax used for a destructor:

```
public class Test
{
    private int n;         // a data member

    public Test()
    {
        n = 0;
    }

    ~Test()
    {
        // tidy up
    }
}
```

The name of a class destructor is the class name preceded by a tilde (~). They are always public, and like constructors they have no return type. They also take no arguments, so there can only ever be one for a class.

Note that structs cannot have destructors.

I said above that a destructor is called when an object is destroyed, and it is worth taking a minute to explain just how this works. Like Java, C# manages dynamically allocated memory for you, and uses a **garbage collector**, running on a separate thread, to reclaim the memory for unused objects. An object becomes unused when the last reference to it disappears, so that it can no longer be accessed. Such objects are candidates for garbage collection, and the process of calling the destructor when an object is reclaimed is called **finalization**.

The problem is that you can't tell when an object is going to be reclaimed by the garbage collector, because the C# runtime schedules garbage collections when it feels they're necessary (e.g. when memory is getting short). In fact, it is possible that your destructor will never get called at all, because when a program exits the runtime it doesn't automatically call object destructors, in order to speed up program shutdown. As a final kicker, you also can't tell the order in which destructors will be called.

For these reasons it is recommended that you don't do anything significant in destructors. If you do need to ensure that some clean-up operation is done at a particular point – such as updating a database record or closing a file – then implement a method which users of your class will call explicitly. Microsoft recommend that these methods are called `Close()` if the object can be reopened, or if closing is a natural term to use (such as closing a file), and `Dispose()` if the object is not to be used again. This technique is used by many of the .NET Framework classes.

Note that it is possible to influence the behavior of the garbage collector, using `System.GC.Collect()` to request a collection and `System.GC.RequestFinalizeOnShutdown()` to ask the garbage collector to execute all destructors on exit.

Static Members

Some methods and data members really belong to the class as a whole rather than to any individual instance. For example, in our `Account` class the balance is unique to each instance, but the interest rate applies to every `Account` object equally, and such methods and data members are called **static** members.

```
public class Account
{
    private double balance;
    private static double interestRate;        // a static data member

    public bool Deposit(double amt)
    {
        // deposit cash
    }

    ...
}
```

Each `Account` object has equal access to the `interestRate` member, so all will share the same value.

Since static data members belong to the class and not to any one member, it follows that they will exist regardless of whether any instances of the class exist.

We're used to interacting with methods and data members in the context of an object, but how do we interact with members which belong to a class? Static methods are methods which belong to a class, and are commonly used to interact with static data members. So we can define get and set methods for interacting with the interest rate like this:

```
public class Account
{
    private double balance;
    private static double interestRate;      // a static data member

    public static bool SetInterestRate(double amt)
    {
        // error checking omitted...

        interestRate = amt;
        return true;
    }

    public static double GetInterestRate()
    {
        return interestRate;
    }

    ...
}
```

To use a static method, call it using the class name rather than an object reference:

```
Account.SetInterestRate(5.5);

double int = Account.GetInterestRate();
```

C++ Note
In C#, static members must be accessed through a class name. You can't also access them via an object, as you can in C++.

Constructors are used to set or calculate the initial values for object data members, and there is an equivalent mechanism that can be used for static members, called the **static constructor**.

```
public class Account
{
    private double balance;
    private static double interestRate;      // a static data member

    static Account()
    {
        // calculate interest rate here
    }
```

You can see from the example code that a static constructor is coded up like a constructor, with the addition of the `static` keyword. Note also that there's no access modifier on static constructors, and there's also no such thing as a static destructor.

Inheritance

The principle of inheritance is one of the fundamentals of OO, giving us the ability to *derive* new classes from ones that have already been written. Inheritance may be used in order to set up a relationship between two classes; if we say that `Car` inherits from `Vehicle`, then we're saying that there's a relationship between `Car` and `Vehicle`, and this allows us to use our class in certain ways, as we'll see shortly.

When a class inherits from a parent (or **base class**), it also inherits the members of that base class, and that allows us to build on and extend existing classes. By inheriting members, we mean that the derived class has its own copy of the base class data members, and it is possible to call the methods of the base class on the derived object.

Here's an example showing how we could derive a new class from `Account`:

```
public class CheckAccount : Account
{
}
```

Note the ': Account', which sets up the inheritance relationship. That's all you need to do to set up inheritance, and if we left it there, we'd effectively have two classes with different names but exactly the same behavior, since `CheckAccount` has inherited all the members of `Account`, and hasn't added any functionality of its own.

Here's how we could use the derived class:

```
// Create a check account
CheckAccount s1 = new CheckAccount();

// Deposit and withdraw
s1.Deposit(5000.0);
s1.Withdraw(2000.0);
```

> **C++ Note**
>
> C# only allows single inheritance. Interfaces, discussed later in this chapter, can be used when you need to inherit from multiple base types, but there's no multiple code inheritance.

Using Base Class References

Once we've derived a class such as `CheckAccount`, we can access it through a reference to its base class, like this:

```
// Create a check account
CheckAccount s1 = new CheckAccount();

// Refer to it through a base class reference
Account a1 = s1;
```

We now have two references to our `CheckAccount` object, one of type `CheckAccount` and one of type `Account`. Why does it work, and why might we ever want to do this? It works because a `CheckAccount` really *is* an `Account`: it contains all the fields and supports all the methods that `Account` does, and while it may have added some extra functionality, we can still call all the `Account` methods on it, and they'll work.

It turns out that you use this technique a surprising amount in OO programming. Inheritance and polymorphism let us create hierarchies of classes, and treat objects belonging to the hierarchy as either similar (they're all `Accounts`) or different (this one is a `CheckAccount`) depending on our current needs. We can hold a list of all our different account objects, referring to them by `Account` references, and then call `QueryBalance()` on each one. We don't need to know at that point what type of account each object represents, because all we want to use is behavior common to all accounts. We'll see this technique being used again when we discuss virtual functions, later in the chapter.

Accessing Base Class Members

You may want to call a method in a class' base class from time to time. Since C# only lets you inherit from a single base class, you can do this using the `base` keyword without having to specify the actual name of the base class since the compiler can work out which one it is.

For example, the `Account` class has no idea about what constitutes a valid withdrawal, so it leaves the decision to its derived classes:

```
public class Account
{
    private double balance;              // a data member

    // The base class makes no decision on whether the withdrawal
    // is valid
    public bool Withdraw(double amt)
    {
        balance -= amount;
        return true;
    }
```

```
      . . .
   }
```

Derived classes decide whether a withdrawal is allowed, and then call the base class method.

```
public class CheckAccount : Account
{
   public bool Withdraw(double amt)
   {
      if (amt <= base.QueryBalance()) {
         return base.Withdraw(amt);
      else
         return false;
   }
   . . .
}
```

Note that you don't have to do this for all base class methods, but only ones where you want to modify the functionality in some way.

Java Note
`base` is in many ways the equivalent of Java's `super` keyword.

Protected Access

Classes derived from `Account` can call the `Account.Withdraw()` method to cause a withdrawal to take place, but we certainly don't want just anyone to be able to do this. C# provides a third level of access control, `protected`, which limits access to the defining class itself and to any classes derived from it.

```
public class Account
{
   private double balance;              // a data member

   protected bool Withdraw(double amt)
   {
      balance -= amount;
   }
   . . .
}
```

We can now call `Account.Withdraw()` from `CheckAccount`, but not from any other class that is unrelated to `Account`.

Internal Access for .NET Assemblies

As we saw at the end of the last chapter, the assembly is the basic unit of packaging in C#, and there is a special access modifier that controls access to, and within, assemblies. If the `internal` modifier is applied to a class or a member, then that class or member is only usable by other classes in the same assembly. See Chapter 10 for a fuller discussion on assemblies.

Calling Base Class Constructors

We've seen that when an object is created its constructor is called. If the class has a base class, the base class constructor is also called, and so on up the chain until we run out of base classes.

If the base class has a constructor that takes no arguments – known as a **default constructor** – then the compiler can arrange for it to be called automatically. But what if the base class constructor takes arguments? How do they get passed along? The answer is that you have to do it in your derived class constructors, as the following example shows:

```
public class CheckAccount : Account
{
    public CheckAccount(double amt) : base(amt)
    {
        // don't do a lot here
    }
    ...
}
```

Here, if a CheckAccount is created with a double being passed in to the constructor, that double is passed on to the base class constructor. The compiler sees base(amt) as meaning, "Pass amt through to the base class constructor which takes one double as an argument." In this case, Account has a suitable constructor, so the compiler can find and use it.

The base class constructor is called before the derived class constructor code (if any) is executed. This means that constructor code actually gets executed from the top downwards, with the most-derived class code being executed last.

Note also that we've only implemented the CheckAccount constructor in order to pass the data over to Account. This is quite common practice.

Casting

C++ Note
Casting in C# is much safer than in C++, and doesn't need to be discouraged as much!

We've seen that it is quite safe (and very common) to refer to derived classes through base class references. What if we have a base class reference to Account and want to get our CheckAccount reference back?

```
Account acc = new CheckAccount();
...
CheckAccount chk = acc;        // Error!
```

The problem here is that acc could hold a reference to any type of object derived from Account, and not just a CheckAccount object, and we could end up with a CheckAccount reference pointing to a DepositAccount object.

The solution is to use a cast, like this:

```
Account acc = new CheckAccount();
...
CheckAccount chk = (CheckAccount)acc;        // OK
```

We're effectively saying to the compiler, See what type of object `acc` is referring to, and if it is a `CheckAccount` give me back a reference.

What will happen if it isn't? In that case you'll get a `System.InvalidCastException` thrown at run-time.

There are also a host of methods provided in the .NET class libraries to help you convert to and from various types. For instance, most of the .NET types (such as `System.Double`) have a static `FromString()` method that tries to convert a string into their particular type:

```
public class Test
{
    public static int Main()
    {
        double d = Double.FromString("123.45");
        Console.WriteLine("{0}", d);

        return 0;
    }
}
```

If the conversion works, the double value will be assigned to `d`. If it fails, a `System.FormatException` will be thrown. Classes may also support other conversion methods where appropriate, such as `ToBoolean()` and `ToChar()`.

Virtual Functions

One of the properties of inheritance is that we can use a derived class object through a base class reference, like this:

```
// Create a savings account
Account s1 = new CheckAccount();

// Deposit and withdraw
s1.Deposit(15000.0);
s1.Withdraw(2000.0);
```

As I've already mentioned, this works because a `CheckAccount` *is* an `Account`, so we can do everything to a `CheckAccount` that we can to the base class. In this case, we're simply calling the `Deposit()` and `Withdraw()` methods that `CheckAccount` inherits from `Account`.

Suppose, though, that we want to provide `CheckAccount` with its own version of `Withdraw()`, because `CheckAccounts` can have an overdraft limit. We can code one up quite easily:

```
public class CheckAccount : Account
{
    private double overdraftLimit = 500.0;
```

```
  . . .

  public bool Withdraw(double amt)
  {
     // allow withdrawal if enough cash in account...
     if (balance-amt >= overdraftLimit)
     {
        base.Withdraw(amt);
        return true;
     }
     else
        return false;
  }
  . . .
}
```

There's a problem with this, though, if we try to use our new version through an `Account` reference, as the compiler will insist on calling the one from `Account`, rather than the one from `CheckAccount`. This problem arises because the compiler has to decide which method to call, so it looks at the reference `s1`, sees that it is of type `Account`, and so calls the `Account.Withdraw()` method.

The problem is due to the fact that a reference to a base class such as `Account` actually has two types – what it was declared as, called its **static type**, and what it is actually referring to now, often called its **dynamic type**. As it is, the compiler is using the reference's static type to resolve the call, and that is leading it to call `Account.Withdraw()`. What we'd like it to do is to use the reference's dynamic type instead, and this can be done by using the virtual function mechanism.

A **virtual function** is one where the decision on exactly which method to call is delayed until run-time, allowing the dynamic type of the reference to be used. You declare a function as virtual by using the `virtual` modifier in the base class:

```
public class Account
{
   . . .

   public virtual bool Withdraw(double amt)
   {
      ...
   }
}
```

When you override a virtual function in a derived class, you use the `override` keyword to signal that you are overriding a virtual function:

```
public class CheckAccount : Account
{
   . . .

   public override bool Withdraw(double amt)
   {
      ...
   }
}
```

C++ Note

You must use the `override` keyword in C# when you're overriding a virtual function. The virtual keyword is only valid in the class which defines the top of the virtual tree. Making this distinction between the original and overriding methods helps to prevent accidental overriding.

Now `CheckAccount.Withdraw()` will be called, regardless of whether we call it through an `Account` or `CheckAccount` reference.

This ability to call objects of derived classes through base class references and get the correct methods executed at run time is called **polymorphism**, and is an extremely valuable technique for writing good OO code.

Hiding Base Class Methods

If you don't declare a method to be virtual but still override it in a derived class, the derived method is said to *hide* the base class version. The C# compiler will warn you if you do this without using the `new` modifier:

```
public class CheckAccount : Account
{
    ...

    public new bool Withdraw(double amt)
    {
    ...
    }
}
```

The new method won't take part in the virtual function mechanism, so if I access a `CheckAccount` object using an `Account` reference, I'll get the `Account` method called:

```
Account s1 = new CheckAccount();

// These call Account's deposit and withdraw methods, even though
// we're referencing a CheckAccount object
s1.Deposit(15000.0);
s1.Withdraw(2000.0);
```

Abstract Classes and Methods

Taking our bank account example a little further, we could imagine ending up with a number of different account types (`CheckAccount`, `SavingsAccount`, `HighInterestSavingsAccount`), all derived from the base `Account` class. It becomes evident at this point that the `Account` class is simply a base from which the others derive, and which is not useful on its own. In fact, we might not *want* anyone to create `Account` objects, but only objects of one of the derived classes, and we can do this by making the `Account` class **abstract**.

If a class definition is qualified by the `abstract` modifier, it means that no-one can directly create objects of that type.

125

```
public abstract class Account
{
    ...
}
```

Although we can't create objects of type `Account`, we can still use references to `Account` to refer to derived objects.

```
// Try to create an account
Account s1 = new Account();            // Error!

// Create a savings account
Account s1 = new CheckAccount();       // OK
```

We can also create abstract methods. In the `Account` class, we've provided a default implementation of `Withdraw()` which derived classes override in order to provide specific checks. What happens if the writer of a derived class forgets to provide an overriding version of `Withdraw()` in his or her class? In that case the derived class inherits `Withdraw()` from `Account`, which isn't quite what is intended.

By marking the `Withdraw()` method as abstract in `Account`, we ensure that derived classes have to implement it if they aren't also to be considered abstract.

```
public abstract class Account
{
    ...
    public abstract bool Withdraw(double amt);
    ...
}
```

Abstract methods are implicitly virtual, since derived classes have to override them, and they don't contain any implementation, so there's no method body.

C++ Note
Abstract methods are similar to pure virtual functions, but C# abstract methods can't have implementations.

Java Note
The presence of an abstract method in a class doesn't implicitly make the class abstract. You have to use the abstract modifier on the class as well.

Preventing Derivation

You may have reasons – arising from design or security factors – for not wanting anyone to use a class as a base class for their own derived classes. If that's the case, you can mark the class as **sealed**.

```
public sealed class XX
{
    ...
}
```

Any attempt to derive from this class will result in a compiler error. It should be obvious that `sealed` and `abstract` are mutually exclusive modifiers for a class, since the one prevents inheritance while the other mandates it.

The Object Class

Rather confusingly, C# has two classes called `object` and `Object`. The object-with-a-small-O class is a C# type, and is equivalent in some ways to Visual Basic's `Variant`, in that you can use it to store references to other kinds of objects. See the discussion below on boxing for more details.

However, here we're looking at the other `Object` class, `System.Object` in the .NET Framework base classes. This class is important because all other .NET (and hence C#) data types inherit from it, even if they don't specifically say so. Unlike Java and C++, this even includes the simple, built-in value classes such as `int` and `long`.

This means that there are certain methods which all types inherit, and which can provide useful functionality. The `Object` class has four methods, the first three of which you'll quite often need to override in your own derived classes. These four are:

- `ToString()`
- `Equals()`
- `GetHashCode()`
- `GetType()`

The `ToString()` method returns a string which represents the object in some way. By default it simply returns the name of the class, but you'll frequently want to override it for your own classes. For most value types it is pretty obvious what this will represent. For example, a `Person` class could use `ToString()` to return the name of the `Person` represented by this object:

```
public class Person
{
    String name;
    ...
    public override string ToString()
    {
        return name;
    }
}
```

Note the use of the `override` method qualifier, because we want this to be treated as a virtual function.

`Equals()` is a very important method, and is used to compare the content of objects. Because C# uses a system of object references, the `==` operator normally compares references:

```
if (r1 == r2) ...
```

The code above evaluates to `true` if `r1` and `r2` are referring to the same object.

> **C++ Note**
>
> Think of comparing pointers...

What if I want to test whether object content is the same?

```
Name n1 = new Name("Fred");
Name n2 = new Name("Fred");

if (n1 == n2) ...
```

In this case the test returns `false`, because n1 and n2 are different objects. C# provides the `Equals()` method to let you compare object content. The default implementation of `Equals()` is equivalent to ==, but any class can override it to implement its own custom object comparison:

```
public class Name
{
    private String nm;
    ...
    public override bool Equals(object o)
    {
        return (nm == ((Name)o).nm);
    }
    ...
}
```

Note that because `Equals()` is inherited from the top-level `Object` class, its argument is the most general thing possible, an `object`. This means that we need to cast it to a `Name` before we can access any members of the `Name` class. If the cast fails, you'll get a `System.InvalidCastException` thrown, which you'll have to handle.

We can then code up the comparison correctly:

```
Name n1 = new Name("Fred");
Name n2 = new Name("Fred");
Name n3 = n2;              // n2 and n3 point to the same object

if (n1 == n2) ...          // false
if (n2 == n3) ...          // true
if (n1.Equals(n2)) ...     // true
if (n2.Equals(n3)) ...     // true
```

The next method, `GetHashCode()`, returns a hash code which identifies an object, and has to be considered along with `Equals()`. A hash code is an integer key, calculated in a way that makes it unlikely that two objects will end up with the same code. These codes can be stored in a hash table, and it can make searching for particular objects very efficient.

`GetHashCode()` is related to `Equals()` in that objects which are 'equal' according to `Equals()` must return the same hash code. This means that in most cases if you override `Equals()` you'll also need to provide your own version of `GetHashCode()`. What would you return as a hash code? If there's a unique integer value associated with your objects (such as a bank account number) then use that. If there isn't a unique integer, you could make one up out of the hash codes for other members of the object:

```
public override int GetHashCode()
{
    return (name.GetHashCode() + address.GetHashCode() + birthday.GetHashCode();
}
```

Finally, there's GetType(), which lets you obtain type information about an object, returning you a type object which you can query. We discuss this further in the next chapter.

Boxing and Unboxing

I said in the previous chapter that 'all types are objects', and that this applied to the simple built-in types so that you can write apparently outrageous things such as:

```
string s = 10.ToString();
```

The way that C# does this is through a piece of sleight-of-hand known as **boxing**.

When the compiler finds a value type where it needs a reference type, it creates an object 'box' into which it places the value of the value type. It'll do this automatically when necessary, but we can also do it manually:

```
int n = 4;

// Create a box to hold n
object obj = n;
```

If we want to extract the int we can unbox it by using it on the right-hand side of an assignment:

```
int n = 4;

// Create a box to hold n
object obj = n;

// Unbox it
int m = (int)obj;
```

Note that we need to use a cast here, because obj could be referring to any kind of object. The compiler will check that obj does contain an int, and give an error if it doesn't.

Operator Overloading

Like C++, C# supports the idea of operator overloading, meaning that operators can be defined to work with classes where it makes sense.

As an example, consider a Currency class. It would be useful (and intuitive) in code if we could simply add two Currency objects using the '+' operator, rather than having to use an add() method:

```
Currency a, b, c;
...
c = a.add(b);        // call a member method
c = a + b;           // more intuitive
```

Operator overloading lets us define a new '+' operator that works with `Currency` objects; we're overloading the '+' symbol, in the same way that a function name can be overloaded.

The principle is the same as in C++, although the set of operators that can be overloaded is smaller in C#.

Operators	Overloading Behavior
`+ - ! ~ ++ -- true false`	Unary operators can be overloaded
`+ - * / % &	^ << >>`	Binary operators can be overloaded
`== != < > <= >=`	Logical operators can be overloaded
`&& ||`	Can't be overloaded
`[] ()`	Can't be overloaded
`+= -=` etc.	Can't be overloaded
`= . ?: -> new is sizeof typeof`	Can't be overloaded

Note the following points:

❑ `&&` and `||` can't be directly overloaded, but are evaluated using `&` and `|` which can.

❑ `[]` can't be overloaded, and you're supposed to use indexers instead.

❑ `()` can't be overloaded. Instead, define new conversion operators.

❑ Compound assignment operators can't be overloaded. This is because they are always decomposed so that `+=` is evaluated as a `+` followed by an `=`.

❑ Logical operators must be overloaded in pairs, so `==` and `!=` must be done together.

C++ Note
You can't separately overload the prefix and postfix versions of the `++` and `--` operators.

Here's an example of overloading some operators in our `Currency` class:

```
public class Currency
{
    double val;

    public Currency(double val)
    {
        this.val = val;
    }

    public static Currency operator+(Currency lhs, Currency rhs)
    {
        return (new Currency(lhs.val + rhs.val));
    }

    public static bool operator==(Currency lhs, Currency rhs)
```

```
   {
      return (lhs.val == rhs.val);
   }

   public static bool operator!=(Currency lhs, Currency rhs)
   {
      return (lhs.val != rhs.val);
   }
}
```

Note that all the operator overload functions have the name `operator` plus the operator symbol, so we get `operator+`, `operator==`, and so on. Furthermore, all operator overloads are static methods of the class. Note also how if we want `operator==` the compiler will force us to define `operator!=` as well.

Interfaces

An interface in C# is a reference type, similar to a class, but which contains only abstract members.

Java Note
C# interfaces are very similar to Java interfaces, and work in very much the same way.

C++ Note
An interface in C# can be considered very similar to a C++ abstract base class which contains only pure virtual functions. There's never any implementation in a C# interface.

A typical interface might look like this:

```
interface IPrintable
{
   void Print();
}
```

There are a couple of things to note about this definition. An interface looks like a class definition, but its only purpose is to define a set of methods, and not to implement them. For this reason, the interface definition only includes the definitions of methods, and no implementation code. Interfaces can only contain methods, properties (covered later in this chapter), plus things called events and indexers, which we'll explain in the next chapter. They can't contain constants, fields (private data members), constructors and destructors, or any type of static member. If you think back to our discussion on abstract classes, you may realize that an interface is very similar to an abstract class that contains only abstract methods.

Note that all the members of an interface are public by definition, and the compiler will give you an error if you try to specify any other modifiers on interface members.

If you haven't come across the concept of interfaces before, you may be wondering quite how much use something so limited is. In short, the answer is "very useful", but before we explain why, let's see how you use them.

In order to use an interface you inherit from it, just as you would from a class. The difference between inheriting from a class and inheriting from an interface is that you have to implement all the members defined in the interface:

```
interface ICame
{
    void Come();
}

public class Test : ICame
{
    public void Come() {
        // implementation of method
    }

    // rest of class...
}
```

The compiler will enforce this, so you'll get a compilation error if you don't implement a Come() method. Note that I've started the interface name with an 'I'; this is not required, and is simply a naming convention which has been inherited from Microsoft COM, and can be useful to help separate interfaces from classes.

What advantages does using interfaces give you? There are two main ones. C# doesn't support multiple inheritance, but interfaces can be used to give some semblance of multiple inheritance because although you can only inherit from one class, you can inherit from (or 'implement') as many interfaces as you like.

```
interface ICame
{
    void Come();
}

interface ISaw
{
    void Look();
}

public class Test : ICame, ISaw
{
    public void Come()
    {
        // implementation of method
    }

    public void Look()
    {
        // implementation of method
    }

    // rest of class...
}
```

The second, and more important use for interfaces is to describe behavior. In the example above, class Test inherits from and implements the ICame and ISaw interfaces (and an IConquered interface if you so wish). This means that by the usual rules of inheritance a Test object can be considered to be an instance of both ICame and ISaw, and that means that we can pass a Test object where one of the interface types is specified:

```
void func(ICame ic)        // method takes an ICame
{
    ic.Come();             // call object's Come() method
}

...

Test t = new Test();       // create a Test object
func(t);                   // pass it to the method
```

The method doesn't care exactly what kind of object it is passed, as long as it implements the methods of the ICame interface. Since the method is thinking of the object in terms of ICame, it can only call methods defined in ICame, and not any others defined as part of Test.

This idea of *interface-based programming* is powerful. It lets us design functionality by specifying the members of an interface. As a concrete example, in a banking application we may want to implement a mechanism so that an object can be notified when the interest rate changes. As the overall architects of the system, we could design an interface like this:

```
interface INotify
{
    void RateChange(double newRate);
}
```

We could use it in the interest rate mechanism like so:

```
// Rate has changed!
foreach (INotify obj in notifyArray)
{
    obj.RateChange(rateNow);
}
```

Other developers within the team would construct objects which inherit from (and thus implement) the INotify interface. They'd then call some suitable method to register their interest, so that they'll get a callback when the interest rate changes:

```
public class FinancialInstrument : INotify
{
    double interestRate;

    public void RateChange(double r)
    {
        interestRate = r;
    }

    public FinancialInstrument()
    {
        // Tell the bank we want to know about rate changes
        bank.Advise(this);
        ...
    }
    ...
}
```

133

Note that the first part of the application – the definition of INotify and the notification loop – can be written first, and the other classes can be implemented long after the code has been compiled. As long as the classes which call Advise() implement INotify, it doesn't matter exactly what they are.

```
public void Advise(INotify observer)
{
    // Add observer to list
}
```

We're implementing notifications using interfaces as an example, but if you're doing this for real in C#, you'll tend to use the built-in event mechanism, which we discuss later on in the chapter.

Properties

It is considered bad programming practice to give users of a class public access to data members, because of the implications for integrity. For this reason it is very common practice in OO languages to give access to data members via "get and set" (or **accessor**) methods, like this:

```
public class Test
{
    private int val;

    public void setVal(int v)
    {
        // do any checking you need, then...
        val = v;
    }

    public int getVal()
    {
        return val;
    }
}
```

This is a reasonable way to give access to members, but suffers from two drawbacks: firstly, you have to code the accessor methods up manually, and secondly, users have to remember (or figure out) that they have to use these accessor methods to work with data members.

C# has this idea of accessing data members through get and set code built into the language, in the form of **properties**. The difference between using get/set methods and properties is that to a user, using a property looks like they're getting direct access to the data, whereas in fact the compiler is mapping the call onto the get/set methods. This idea—mapping data access onto get/set methods—was pioneered in Visual Basic, and is one of the VB ideas that has been borrowed by C#.

Here's how we could rewrite the code above to use a property:

```
public class Test
{
    private int val;
```

```
    public int Val
    {
       get
       {
          return val;
       }
       set
       {
          val = value;
       }
    }
}
```

The class now implements a single property called `Val`, of type `int`, which we can manipulate using the `get` and `set` clauses. Note how the `set` clause makes use of the special variable `value`, which represents the value passed in from the user. The type of `value` is determined by the type of the property.

We could use the property just as we would use a public data member:

```
Test t = new Test();

t.Val = 10;
int n = t.Val;
```

You can omit either the `set` or `get` clause if you want to model a read-only or (more rarely) a write-only property.

Properties provide a useful way to handle access to data members, but they can be much more powerful than that. First, you don't have to return the value of a variable in a `get` clause, but can use any code you like to calculate or obtain the value of the property. This means that properties don't have to be tied to a data member, but can represent dynamic data. Second, properties are inherited, and you can use the `abstract` and `virtual` modifiers with them, so that derived classes can be required to implement their own versions of property methods. Third, the `static` modifier can be used to create properties that belong to classes as opposed to individual objects.

Indexers

Indexers are an elaboration of properties, and are used where you want to access some class property by index, in an array-like manner. They are useful in cases where a class is a container for other objects.

C++ Note
Indexers are roughly equivalent to the overloaded `[]` operator.

The syntax used for writing indexers may look a little strange:

```
public class Test
{
```

```
    public static int Main()
    {
        IndexTest it = new IndexTest();

        Console.WriteLine("index 1 is {0}", it[1]);
        return 0;
    }
}

public class IndexTest
{
    double[] values;

    public IndexTest ()
    {
        // set up array of values
        values = new double[] { 1.1, 3.3, 5.5, 7.7, 9.9 };
    }

    public double this[int index]
    {
        get
        {
            // do some error checking
            if (index<0 || index>=values.Length)
                throw new ArgumentOutOfRangeException();

            return values[index];
        }
        set
        {
            values[index] = value;
        }
    }
}
```

Indexers are declared using the this[] syntax. The return type determines what will be returned, in this case a double. The parameter in square brackets is used as the index; in this example we've used an int, but there's no need for it to be numeric. You could easily index a class on a string or even another object type.

You can overload indexers by giving them different parameter types, and it is possible to have indexers with more than one parameter, allowing you to create objects that act as multidimensional arrays.

Delegates

We've already seen how interfaces can be used to specify behavior, which is then implemented by one or more classes. Delegates are similar, but they provide a 'template' for a single method, rather than a number of related methods, as is common with interfaces.

As with interfaces, then, a delegate defines a function without implementing it, and another class then provides an implementation. As an example, consider a class which wishes to let callers perform an arithmetic operation on two integers:

```
public class ArithTest
{
    int n,m;

    public delegate int ArithOp(int a, int b);

    ...

    public int DoOp(ArithOp ar)
    {
        return ar(n,m);
    }
}
```

The class first declares a delegate called `ArithOp`, which is a template for a method that takes two `int`s and returns an `int`.

The `DoOp()` method takes an `ArithOp` delegate as an argument, passes it the two `int` arguments, and returns the result. In effect, a delegate is a reference to a method rather than a data member, and it enables you to pass round method references and execute them.

C++ Note
You may be thinking that delegates sound like function pointers, and you'd be correct. The difference is that C# delegates are much safer than function pointers, due to their type-safety.

How do we call the `DoOp()` method? First, we need to define the methods that are going to be called to do the actual operations:

```
public class DoTest
{
    public static int AddOp(int a, int b)
    {
        return a+b;
    }

    public static int SubOp(int a, int b)
    {
        return a-b;
    }
}
```

These are simply two functions whose signatures (in other words, the return type, and the number and type of arguments) match that of the delegate. Note that they have to be `static`, because they need to belong to the class rather than to an object. Next, we have to create the delegates themselves:

```
public class DoTest
{
    public static int AddOp(int a, int b)
    {
        return a+b;
    }
```

```
public static int SubOp(int a, int b)
{
    return a-b;
}

public static int Main(String[] args)
{
    ArithTest.ArithOp add = new ArithTest.ArithOp(AddOp);
    ArithTest.ArithOp sub = new ArithTest.ArithOp(SubOp);

    return 0;
}
}
```

We create delegate objects, passing in the name of method to be used. You can now see where the name 'delegate' comes from, because the delegate object will simply delegate the actual processing to the method we pass it.

Having created these two objects, we can now use them:

```
public static int Main(String[] args)
{
    ArithTest.ArithOp add = new ArithTest.ArithOp(AddOp);
    ArithTest.ArithOp sub = new ArithTest.ArithOp(SubOp);

    ArithTest at = new ArithTest();

    int resultOne = at.DoOp(add);
    int resultTwo = at.DoOp(sub);

    return 0;
}
```

We execute the DoOp() method, passing in a reference to the delegate objects we've created. Within DoOp() itself, the delegate gets called, and it simply hands the processing on to the AddOp() and SubOp() methods. Here's the entire code for the example, so you can see how it all fits together:

```
public class DoTest
{
    public static int AddOp(int a, int b)
    {
        return a+b;
    }

    public static int SubOp(int a, int b)
    {
        return a-b;
    }

    public static int Main(String[] args)
    {
```

```
        ArithTest.ArithOp add = new ArithTest.ArithOp(AddOp);
        ArithTest.ArithOp sub = new ArithTest.ArithOp(SubOp);

        ArithTest at = new ArithTest();

        int resultOne = at.DoOp(add);
        int resultTwo = at.DoOp(sub);
        return 0;
    }
}

public class ArithTest
{
    public delegate int ArithOp(int a, int b);

    public int DoOp(ArithOp ar)
    {
        int n=4, m=3;

        return ar(n,m);
    }
}
```

Events

Anyone who has done GUI programming will be familiar with the idea of events, where an object tells interested parties that something significant has occurred. Examples might include a button object telling its parent form that it has been pressed, or a list box telling other controls that its selection has changed. C# takes the idea of events out of the GUI world, so that now any class can *publish* a set of events, to which other objects can *subscribe* at run time. This means that you can, for example, code up a FileSystem class which will notify interested parties whenever files are added or deleted, or a database table class which can notify observers when its contents have been changed.

Events in C# are based on delegates, with the originator defining one or more callback functions. A callback function, as traditional Windows programmers will know, is a function which one piece of code defines and another implements; in other words, one piece of code says, "If you implement a function which looks like this, I can call it". A class that wants to use events defines callback functions as delegates, and the listening object then implements them. Once again, an example will be the easiest way to show how it works. Suppose that in our banking application we want various objects in the system to be able to obtain information on interest rate changes.

We can add a class called RateWatcher which gets data on various interest rates from some external source, and a RateWatcher object can notify other objects in the banking system when an interest rate changes. In our case we'll use a class called RateObserver so we can show simply how events are set up, but we could just as easily add the code to the Account class. We'll use the classes like this:

```
public static int Main(String[] args)
{
    // Create a RateWatcher object
    RateWatcher rw = new RateWatcher();
```

```
    // Create an observer object
    RateObserver obs = new RateObserver(rw);

    return 0;
}
```

The `RateWatcher` is created and starts monitoring the interest rates. We then create a `RateObserver`, passing it a reference to the watcher object. The `RateObserver` tells the `RateWatcher` that it is interested in being notified, and so its callback method will get called whenever the `RateWatcher` detects that the interest rate has changed.

The delegate method that is used for the notification takes two arguments. The first is a reference to the object that has originated the notification, and the second contains any data which needs to be passed as part of the notification process. In our example, we'll want to pass over the name of the rate (such as "base" for the base rate) and the new value. This information is passed in the second argument as a reference to a class derived from the system class `EventArgs`:

```
class RateInfo : EventArgs
{
    public readonly string rateName;        // name of interest rate
    public readonly double newRate;         // new rate value

    public RateInfo(string name, double rate)
    {
        rateName = name;
        newRate = rate;
    }
}
```

A `RateInfo` object simply holds the name of a rate and the new value for the rate. Since these are only used once in the notification call, we can use read-only properties to fix the values.

We're now in a position to implement the `RateWatcher` class itself. The first task is to define the delegate that will be used for callbacks. As I mentioned above, event delegates take two arguments, one representing the sender object, and the second the data passed with the event:

```
class RateWatcher
{
    public delegate void RateChange(object sender, RateInfo info);
}
```

We then add to our class a reference to an event object:

```
class RateWatcher
{
    public delegate void RateChange(object sender, RateInfo info);

    public event RateChange OnRateChange;
}
```

This line defines an event object of type `RateChange`, called `OnRateChange`. We don't implement this object – we only declare a public reference to it. Clients will create the delegate object and attach it to our reference, so that when we use the event object we are calling back to them.

The final part of `RateWatcher` is the notification method, which calls back to the client:

```
class RateWatcher
{
    public delegate void RateChange(object sender, RateInfo info);

    public event RateChange OnRateChange;

    public void Notify(string name, double newval)
    {
        if (OnRateChange != null)
        {
            RateInfo r = new RateInfo(name, newval);
            OnRateChange(this, r);
        }
    }
}
```

If the event reference is `null`, then no one has registered with us. If it isn't `null`, we create a `RateInfo` object to hold the event data, and then use the delegate to call back to the client.

Now we need to implement the client, in the form of the `RateObserver` class:

```
class RateObserver
{
    // Reference to the watcher we're working with
    RateWatcher wr;

    public RateObserver(RateWatcher r)
    {
        // Save the watcher reference away
        wr = r;
    }

    // The callback method
    public void RateHasChanged(object sender, RateInfo info)
    {
        Console.WriteLine("Rate '{0}' has new value {1}",
                        info.rateName, info.newRate);
    }
}
```

First, we implement the constructor to store away the reference we're passed. We also implement the delegate in the form of the `RateHasChanged` method, which takes the two arguments that were defined in `RateWatcher`. This method just gets the name of the rate and the new value from the `RateInfo` object, and writes them to the command window.

The final piece of the jigsaw is to link our callback method to the event reference in the watcher object:

```
class RateObserver
{
    // Reference to the watcher we're working with
    RateWatcher wr;
```

```
public RateObserver(RateWatcher r)
{
    // Save the watcher reference away
    wr = r;

    // Set up the delegate
    wr.OnRateChange += new RateWatcher.RateChange(RateHasChanged);
}

// The callback method
public void RateHasChanged(object sender, RateInfo info)
{
    Console.WriteLine("Rate '{0}' has new value {1}",
                            info.rateName,info.newRate);

}
}
```

Using standard delegate syntax, we create a RateWatcher.RateChange delegate, passing it a reference to our callback method, and save it to the public OnRateChange member of the watcher. You may have spotted the '+=' being used in this assignment – this is a very useful property of delegates and allows you to chain delegate references together. Thus, if two clients register themselves with the same RateWatcher, their delegates will get concatenated, and when OnRateChange is called in the watcher, both callback methods will get called one after the other. And so you can see how it all fits together, here's the entire program. It's got one modification, in that we pass a name over to the RateObserver objects when we create them:

```
namespace Event
{
using System;

public class TestEvent
{
    public TestEvent()
    {
    }

    public static int Main(string[] args)
    {
        // Create a RateWatcher...
        RateWatcher rw = new RateWatcher();

        // Create a couple of objects to notify, and pass references
        // to the watcher over
        RateObserver obs = new RateObserver("One",rw);
        RateObserver obs2 = new RateObserver("Two",rw);

        // Do the notification
        rw.Notify("base", 5.7);

        return 0;
    }
}
```

```csharp
// This is the class that wants to be notified when a rate changes
class RateObserver {
   RateWatcher watcher;
   string myName;

   // The constructor takes a ratewatcher object, which is going to
   // notify this RateObserver
   public RateObserver(string name, RateWatcher r) {
      myName = name;

      // Save the watcher reference
      watcher = r;

      // Tell it about our notification method
      watcher.OnRateChangeHandler +=
            new RateWatcher.RateChangeHandler(RateHasChanged);
   }

   // Define the notification method
   public void RateHasChanged(object sender, RateInfo info) {
      Console.WriteLine("{0}: Rate '{1}' has changed to {2}",
         myName,info.rateName, info.newRate);
   }
}

// This class watches the rates, and uses Notify() to notify
// observers when the rate changes.
class RateWatcher {
   // Here's the delegate that defines the method observers
   // must implement
   public delegate void RateChangeHandler(object sender,

 RateInfo info);

   // Declare an event called OnRateChangeHandler, of
   // type RateChangeHandler
   public event RateChangeHandler OnRateChangeHandler;

   // Call this method to notify observers that something
   // has occurred
   public void Notify(string name, double val) {
      RateInfo r = new RateInfo(name, val);
      if (OnRateChangeHandler != null)
         OnRateChangeHandler(this, r);
   }
}

// This class holds the notification information
class RateInfo : EventArgs {
   // private name and rate members
   public readonly string rateName;
   public readonly double newRate;

   // construct the info object
   public RateInfo(string name, double rate) {
```

```
        rateName = name;
        newRate = rate;
    }
}
}
```

Summary

This chapter has shown how C# implements OO features. Many of the basic elements are similar to their counterparts in C++ and Java, but there are significant differences, such as delegates and events.

Here are the main features we've looked at in this chapter:

- ❑ C# supports structs and enums.

- ❑ Structs are similar to classes, but are value types whereas classes are reference types.

- ❑ Classes consist of methods and data. Both can be public or private, but data ought to be private.

- ❑ Properties let you define get and set methods for accessing data members.

- ❑ C# supports inheritance, but only single inheritance is supported.

- ❑ All classes are ultimately derived from the object class.

- ❑ Virtual methods are used to implement polymorphism.

- ❑ Interfaces are used to define functionality without implementation.

- ❑ Interfaces can be used to provide some of the features of multiple inheritance.

- ❑ Indexers are useful for classes that manage collections, and let you retrieve data using an array-like notation.

- ❑ Delegates provide an OO-based analog of function pointers.

- ❑ Events let objects notify clients of interesting happenings.

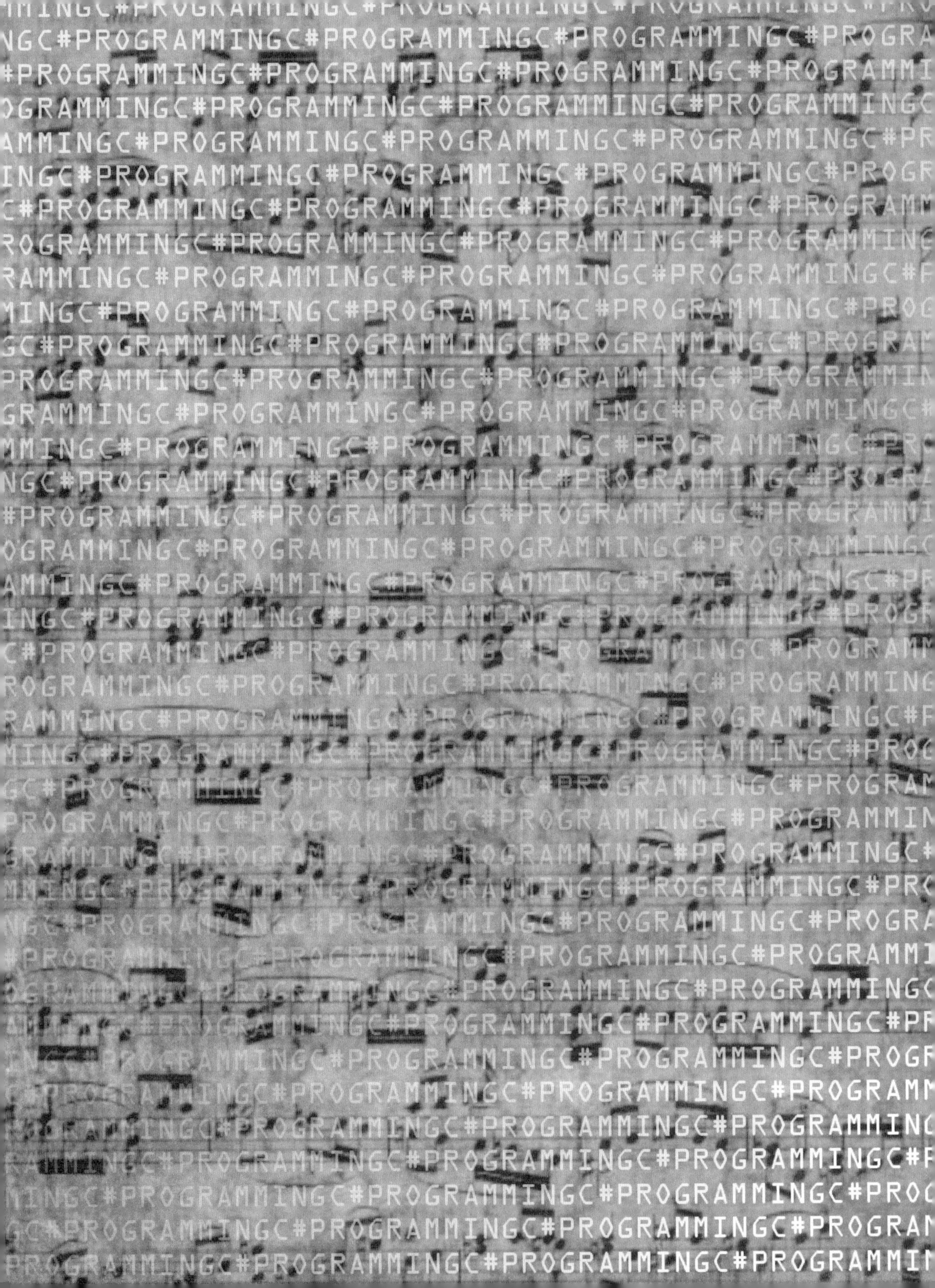
C#PROGRAMMING

6

Advanced C# Concepts

Chapters 4 and 5 gave you the basics for doing a lot with C#. Indeed, what we've already covered may suffice for 90% or more of your programming needs. There will be times, though, when you'll want to do some more advanced things with the language, using features that may not be encountered on a daily basis. This chapter will introduce several of these features:

- ❑ Some advanced features of classes, including:
  - Variable argument lists
  - Implicit and explicit type conversions
  - Implementing collections
  - Reflection
  - Dynamic invocation
- ❑ The C# Preprocessor
- ❑ Defining and using attributes
- ❑ Using unsafe code

Finally, we will introduce C#'s built-in documentation feature, which lets you add comments to the code that can be saved out as XML-formatted text files just by using an appropriate compiler switch.

More About Classes

We covered the basics of using classes and object-oriented programming in the previous chapter, so we'll start off this chapter by looking at some of the more advanced features that C# provides for working with classes.

Variable Argument Lists

In C#, we can define methods that can be called with variable numbers of arguments, and in this section we'll show how it can be done. The key to handling variable argument lists lies in the fact that all objects can be referred to via an `object` reference.

Variable argument lists are implemented using the `params` keyword together with a reference to an array object:

```
public class Test
{
    public static int Main()
    {
        AFunc(1,2,"abc");
        return 0;
    }

    public static void AFunc(params object[] args)
    {
        // Get the number of arguments; the '0' indicates that
        // we want to retrieve the number of elements in the first
        // dimension of the args array.
        int numArgs = args.GetLength(0);
        Console.WriteLine("Number of args is {0}", numArgs);
    }
}
```

The method is passed an array of `object` references, and we can use the array's `GetLength()` method to find out how many references it contains. As an aside, using `GetLength()` like this allows us to find out how many command-line arguments have been passed in the `Main(string[] args)` method.

How does it work? The first thing to note is that if the compiler can find a method whose argument list matches those in the method call, then it will use that overload and no variable argument list will be generated.

If the compiler can't find an overload of the method that matches the argument list but it *does* find a version with the `params` keyword, it will use that one and automatically build an `object` array to hold the arguments, boxing value types as necessary. So the call above is equivalent to coding:

```
object[] o = new object[3];
o[0] = 2;
o[1] = 2;
o[2] = "abc";

obj.AFunc(o);
```

Note that in this example we've used an array of `object` references, but you can use any type you like. If you do want to use `object` and don't know exactly what you're going to get passed, you'll probably want to use reflection – see below – to find out the details about what the array references.

Because the compiler has to do extra work in creating the array and populating the elements, it is more efficient to provide overloads for versions of methods that you know you'll need. For example, if you know you're going to need the (`int`, `int`, `string`) version of a method as above, it is more efficient to provide this as an overload as well as the variable argument list version.

User-Defined Conversions

User-defined conversions let us define operators for a class to convert objects to and from other types. This is often done for value types, and other classes that are wrappers around some single value. As an example, you may want to define an operator for a string class that can convert to and from arrays of `chars`.

C++ Note
These are very similar to C++ type conversion operators.

As a practical example, we'll use the `Currency` class we built in the previous chapter. This class is basically a wrapper around a `double` value, with some extra information and functionality added in, and we'll add operators to convert `Currency` objects to and from `doubles`.

Here's how the class looks with the two new operators added:

```
public class Currency
{
    private double val;        // the amount

    public Currency(double amt)
    {
        val = amt;
    }

    public static explicit operator Currency(double val)
    {
        Currency c = new Currency(val);
        return c;
    }

    public static implicit operator double(Currency c)
    {
        return c.val;
    }
}
```

The first thing to note about these conversion operators is that they are always implemented as static methods. The name of the operator is the type being converted *to*, and the single parameter is the type being converted *from* (this argument must be a value parameter, not an `out` or reference parameter). So, in the above example, the first conversion is from `double` to `Currency`, and the second is from `Currency` to `double`.

You'll notice that these methods are qualified by the `explicit` and `implicit` modifiers, which determine in what context a conversion will be done. If an operator is qualified with `explicit`, it means that a cast has to be used to apply the conversion, as in:

```
Currency c1 = (Currency)12.4;
```

Implicit conversions can be used whenever the compiler needs to do a cast:

```
double d = c1;
```

Which should you choose? It's very important to remember that implicit conversions can take place without the programmer realizing it, so you should be very careful to ensure that nothing could go wrong and present the programmer with an unpleasant surprise. This means that implicit conversions shouldn't throw exceptions, and shouldn't be able to lose any data. If you can't guarantee this, make your conversion explicit so that programmers know when they're using it.

Overloaded operators and conversions can be made to work usefully together. In the previous chapter, we defined operators for our `Currency` class, such as the '+' operator:

```
public static Currency operator+(Currency lhs, Currency rhs)
{
    return (new Currency (lhs.val + rhs.val));
}
```

Now that we've defined conversion operators, we can write code like this:

```
Currency c1 = c2 + (Currency)12.4;
```

The conversion operator will convert the `double` into a `Currency` before invoking the '+' method. We need the cast because the conversion is an explicit one; if we recoded to make the double-to-Currency conversion implicit, we could do away with the cast.

Implementing Collections

We saw in the previous chapter how indexers can be implemented on a class that represents a collection, so that data can be accessed using the array (`[]`) notation. We can extend this idea to allow a collection class to work with C#'s `foreach` statement, using a pair of interfaces called `IEnumerable` and `IEnumerator`.

Here's what the `IEnumerable` interface looks:

```
public interface IEnumerable
{
    IEnumerator GetEnumerator();
}
```

Any class which wants to be used with `foreach` has to implement this interface, which C# and VB will use to ask for an enumerator object.

An enumerator object is one that implements the `IEnumerator` interface:

```
public interface IEnumerator
{
    bool MoveNext();
    object Current { get; }
    void Reset();
}
```

Note the form of the `Current` member, which shows how to specify a read-only property in an interface. Any class which wants to implement this interface will have to provide this read-only property.

As far as the members are concerned, `MoveNext()` moves to the next item in the collection, returning `true` until it reaches the end, when it returns `false`. The `Current` property retrieves the value currently being pointed to by the enumerator. Note that, since the initial position of the enumerator is *before* the first element, clients need to call `MoveNext()` before using `Current`, else an exception should be thrown by the implementation. `Reset()`, as you might expect, resets the enumerator back to its initial state.

It is easy to see how C# can use an object that implements this interface in a `foreach` statement, using `MoveNext()` to iterate over the collection, and `Current` to fetch each element.

The example program below uses a class called `StringCollection`, which manages a collection of strings. The `Main()` method simply creates a `StringCollection` object and iterates over its content using `foreach`:

```
namespace enumerate
{
using System;
using System.Collections;

public class Test
{
    public Test()
    {
    }

    public static int Main(string[] args)
    {
        StringCollection sc = new StringCollection();

        foreach (string s in sc)
            Console.WriteLine(s);

        return 0;
    }
}
}
```

Note that we need to access the `System.Collections` namespace in order to be able to use the `IEnumerable` and `IEnumerator` interfaces, because that's where they're defined.

Now let's see how we define `StringCollection`. For the sake of simplicity, the class manages a static set of strings, but it could easily be extended to store strings provided by clients. The class itself derives from `IEnumerable`, and so implements `GetEnumerator()`, returning a reference to a new `Enumerator` object.

`Enumerator` is a separate class, nested within `StringCollection`, that implements `IEnumerator`. It is nested within `StringCollection` because it is part of that class, and there's no need for anyone else to be able to access it. You may wonder why we make it a separate class, and don't implement `IEnumerator` directly on `StringCollection`. If `IEnumerator` were implemented directly on `StringCollection`, each `StringCollection` object would only be able to support one iterator. If we have it as a separate inner class, then each request for an iterator results in a new `Enumerator` object being created.

Here's the code for the `StringCollection` class:

```csharp
public class StringCollection : IEnumerable
{
    // Set up some test data strings
    private string[] ss = new string[] {
        "one", "two", "three", "four" };

    public StringCollection()
    {
    }

    // The GetEnumerator method returns a new Enumerator
    // object
    public virtual IEnumerator GetEnumerator()
    {
        return new Enumerator(this);
    }

    // The nested Enumerator class
    private class Enumerator :    IEnumerator
    {
        // pos holds the current position of the enumerator
        private int pos;

        // coll is a reference to the object we're working with
        private StringCollection coll;

        public Enumerator(StringCollection sc)
        {
            // Save the reference, and set the position to denote
            // an invalid position
            coll = sc;
            pos = -1;
        }

        // IEnumerator methods

        // Move to the next object
        public bool MoveNext()
        {
            // If we haven't reached the end, return true, otherwise
```

```
                    // set the position to invalid, and return false.
                    pos++;
                    if (pos < 4)
                        return true;
                    else {
                        pos = -1;
                        return false;
                    }
                }

                // Return the current object
                public object Current
                {
                    get
                    {
                        // If the position is invalid, throw an exception;
                        // otherwise return the element
                        if (pos == -1)
                            throw new InvalidOperationException();

                        return coll.ss[pos];
                    }
                }

                // Reset the position
                public void Reset()
                {
                    pos = -1;
                }
            }
        }
```

Reflection

Reflection is the ability to find out information about objects at run-time. C++ has this to a limited extent, in that you can use RTTI (Runtime Type Information) to find out an object's class, but in C# (and the other .NET languages) this is taken much further, so that you can find out details of an object's methods, and even create one dynamically at runtime.

Java Note
Reflection in C# is very similar to reflection in Java.

Reflection is a powerful mechanism, but it is also a very complex topic, with the `System.Reflection` namespace containing nearly forty classes and interfaces, so we'll just give an idea of what you can do with it in this section.

The starting point for much of your use of reflection will be using the `typeof` operator or `GetType()` method to get a `Type` object. The `Type` class is the root of the reflection information for an object, and can be used to obtain all the metadata for an object.

To show how reflection works and how to use it, we'll use this simple class:

```
namespace Reflect
{
    using System;
    public class Test
    {
        private int n;
        private string s;

        public Test(int a)
        {
            n = a;
        }

        public int AMethod(int m)
        {
            return m*m;
        }

        public string S
        {
            get
            {
                return s;
            }
            set
            {
                s = value;
            }
        }
    }
}
```

It's got one method, one data member, one property, and one constructor, which is enough to let us see how to use reflection with a typical class.

A `Type` object can be retrieved using the `GetType()` method or the `typeof` operator, depending on whether you are using a class name or an object reference.

```
namespace Reflect
{
using System;
    public class Test
    {
        // rest of class definition...

        public static int Main(string[] args)
        {
            Type type1 = typeof(Test);

            Test t1 = new Test(0);
            Type type2 = t1.GetType();

            Console.WriteLine("Type of t1 is {0}", type2);

            return 0;
        }
    }
}
```

The output from this piece of code will be:

Type of t1 is Reflect.Test

This shows that the `ToString()` method for the `Type` class returns the name of the class that this object represents. What can you do with a `Type` object once you've got it? Find out just about anything you want about a class or object, as the following list of properties and methods shows. Since the `Type` class has over 100 members, you'll appreciate that this only a partial list:

Name	Description
GetFields()	Returns an array of `FieldInfo` objects describing the fields in the class.
GetMethods()	Returns an array of `MethodInfo` objects describing the methods of the class.
GetConstructors()	Returns all the constructors for an object.
GetInterfaces()	Gets all the interfaces implemented by the type.
GetMembers()	Gets all the members (fields, methods, events, etc) of the current type.
InvokeMember()	Invokes a member of the current type.
BaseType	Gets a `Type` object for the type's immediate base type.
IsAbstract	Returns `true` if the type is abstract.
IsClass	Returns `true` if the type is a class (i.e. not a value type or an interface).
IsEnum	Returns `true` if the type is an enum.
IsNestedPublic	Returns `true` if a type is nested within another and is public.
Namespace	Retrieves the namespace of the type.

If we want to get a list of the methods supported by a class, we can use the `GetMethods()` method:

```
namespace Reflect
{
    using System;
    using System.Reflection;

    public class Test
    {
        // rest of class definition...

        public static int Main(string[] args)
        {
            Type type1 = typeof(Test);

            MethodInfo[] minf = type1.GetMethods();
            foreach(MethodInfo m in minf)
                Console.WriteLine(m);
```

```
        return 0;
      }
    }
  }
```

Note that the .NET security mechanism will only allow a class to obtain the public members of another class, unless it has been given `ReflectionSecurity` permission.

For our test class, this is the output I get:

Int32 GetHashCode()
Boolean Equals(System.Object)
System.String ToString()
Int32 AMethod(Int32)
System.String get_S()
Void set_S(System.String)
Int32 Main(System.String[])
System.Type GetType()

We can see that `MethodInfo.ToString()` returns the signature of the method, but using .NET base types rather than their C# wrappers. It is also evident that the listing includes all the methods defined in `Test`, plus all those it has inherited from `Object`.

You may be wondering where the information on the constructor is. It doesn't appear in the method list, because a constructor isn't a normal method, and there's another member of `Type`, `GetConstructors()`, which is used to retrieve constructor information. In this case, if we add these lines to our `Main(string[] args)` method:

```
ConstructorInfo[] cinf = type1.GetConstructors();
foreach(ConstructorInfo c in cinf)
    Console.WriteLine(c);
```

... we will get an extra line in the output describing the constructor:

Void .ctor(Int32)

We can drill down further if we want, using the members of the `MethodInfo` class to obtain more information about each method. This example uses only a couple of the thirty-odd members of `MethodInfo`:

```
public static int Main(string[] args)
{
    Type type1 = typeof(Test);

    MethodInfo[] minf = type1.GetMethods();
    foreach(MethodInfo m in minf)
    {
        // Print out the method name and whether it is public
        Console.WriteLine("Name: " + m.Name + "," +
            ((m.IsPublic) ? " public" : "") +
```

```
            ((m.IsVirtual) ? " virtual" : "")
        );

        // Get the list of parameters and print out the type and
        // name of each one
        ParameterInfo[] pi = m.GetParameters();
        foreach(ParameterInfo p in pi)
            Console.WriteLine("   " + p.ParameterType +
                                        " " + p.Name);

    }
    return 0;
}
```

We've added code to retrieve the method name, and use two of the class properties to tell us whether the method is public, and whether it is also virtual. This produces the following output:

```
Name: GetHashCode, public virtual
Name: Equals, public virtual
  System.Object obj
Name: ToString, public virtual
Name: AMethod, public
  Int32 m
Name: get_S, public
Name: set_S, public
 System.String value
Name: Main, public
 System.String[] args
Name: GetType, public
```

That's probably enough to give you a flavor of how you can use the members of the Type class to find out about how a class is constructed.

Dynamic Creation and Invocation

One very useful feature related to reflection is the ability to create objects dynamically and call methods on them. You can specify which class you want using a Type object, or by giving the name of an assembly and a class as strings, so this even makes it possible to get the name of a class from the user and create an object of the appropriate type. You can then interact with the new object just as if you'd created it with new, and use reflection to find out just what you're dealing with and what it can do.

Here's an example of how it works. The code below creates an instance of our Test class, and invokes AMethod on the object:

```
public static int Main(string[] args)
{
    Type type1 = typeof(Test);

    // Instantiate the Test object,
    // passing in the value 1 to the constructor
    object[] ctorParams = new object[] {1};
    object obj = Activator.CreateInstance(type1, ctorParams);
```

```
        // Invoke AMethod, passing in the parameter 3
        object[] methodParams = new object[] {3};
        int res = (int)type1.InvokeMember("AMethod",
                        BindingFlags.Default |
                        BindingFlags.InvokeMethod,
                        null, obj, methodParams);

        Console.WriteLine(
            "The result of calling AMethod on {0} was {1}",
            type1.Name, res);

        return 0;
    }
```

When run, the program outputs:

The result of calling AMethod on Test was 9

How does it work? The `System.Activator` class is the class which dynamically creates objects for us via its `CreateInstance()` member. We provide it with information about the type of object we want to create – via a `Type` object in this case – and arguments for the constructor, in the form of an `object` array. If creation succeeds, you get back an `object` reference to the newly created object.

> *Note for COM programmers – you can create COM objects using*
> `Activator.CreateInstance()` *too, as you might expect. We will look at this use of the*
> `CreateInstance()` *method in Chapter 11.*

The `InvokeMember()` method of `Type` can be used to invoke methods dynamically on objects. It takes a number of parameters, and anyone who has looked at COM's `IDispatch` interface will notice certain similarities here. The method takes the name of the method as a string, flags which tell the method what we're doing (in this case, invoking a method as opposed to getting or setting a property), a reference to a `Binder` object (which we're not using), and finally the object itself and an array of parameters which will be passed to the invoked method.

> *A `Binder` object can be used to control the invocation process, for example to select the specific version of an overloaded method to invoke, or to convert the method's arguments to the necessary type.*

The result of invoking the method is returned from `InvokeMember()` as an object reference, which we cast to an `int` to unbox it.

The Preprocessor

The C# compiler supports C-style preprocessing directives in order to provide a conditional compilation mechanism. These directives are processed before the source code is compiled, and provide a means for us to prevent or enable the compilation of specific blocks of code (for example, code which is only used in debug builds, and which we want to omit from the release builds).

The `#define` and `#undef` directives are used to define and undefine preprocessor identifiers; we can use these to tell the preprocessor whether specific blocks of code are to be compiled, according to whether a particular identifier has been defined.

```
#define someName
#undef someOtherName
```

Identifier naming conventions follow those for C# variables. It isn't an error to #undef a name more than once. Note that, like in C++, a preprocessing directive must be the first non-whitespace token on a line. In addition, the #define directive must be placed before any 'real' code, including the using declarations.

The preprocessor #if mechanism can be used to conditionally include or omit blocks of code:

```
#define someName

#if someName
    // include this
#endif
```

Blocks of code are delimited by #if and #endif, and will be included if the appropriate identifier has been defined.

The #elif and #else keywords provide an if...else if...else mechanism:

```
#define someName

#if someName
    // include this
#elif someOtherName
    // include that
#else
// include the other
#endif
```

You can nest #ifs inside one another:

```
#define someName

#if someName
    #if someOtherName
        // include this
    #endif
#endif
```

Since we can use logical operators with #if, the above code is equivalent to:

```
#define someName

#if someName && someOtherName
    // include this
#endif
```

We can use the !, ==, !=, &&, and || operators with #if. This means that we can write code such as:

```
#if someName == true
```

... to test whether a symbol is defined. This is exactly the same thing as simply writing #if someName.

#warning and #error

These two preprocessor control lines will cause a warning or an error to be raised at compile time:

```
#if someName && someOtherName
    #error Can't have someName and someOtherName defined together!
#endif
```

#line

The #line directive can be used to alter the file name and line number information which is output by the compiler in warnings and error messages. It isn't very likely to be used in application code.

#region

The #region directive can be used to mark blocks of text with a comment for other developers. The end of each #region block is marked by an #endregion directive. These blocks can be expanded and collapsed when using Visual Studio.NET's outlining feature. The code in the following screenshot uses a #region block to mark off a couple of methods which were generated by Visual Studio in an ASP.NET page:

```
/**/public class WebForm2 : System.Web.UI.Page
    {
    #region code generated by VS.NET
    public WebForm2()
    {
        Page.Init += new System.EventHandler(Page_Init);
    }

    protected void Page_Load(object sender, EventArgs e)
    {
        if (!IsPostBack)
        {
            //
            // Evals true first time browser hits the page
            //
        }
    }
    #endregion

    protected void Page_Init(object sender, EventArgs e)...
/**/private void InitializeComponent()...
    }
}
```

Note that #region blocks may not overlap with #if blocks. Also, each #endregion directive terminates the region that was opened immediately before this one, even if we follow it with the name of a different region. This means that it is also impossible to have overlapping #region blocks.

Attributes

In most programming languages, all information has to come from the code, and the forms of information that we can express are fixed, or at best extensible through limited mechanisms, such as macros.

In all .NET languages, attributes are items of declarative information that can be declared by the programmer and attached to elements in your code, whether they are classes, methods, data members, or properties. Once you've associated an attribute with an entity in your code, it can be queried at runtime by anyone making use of your class, using reflection.

Attributes are implemented by attribute classes. A number of standard attributes are provided with C#, and we'll see shortly how it is possible to write your own. Most of the standard attributes are used to provide data to allow C# code to work with unmanaged (and most often COM) code. The following table lists some of the most commonly used standard attributes, and those who have had any experience with using IDL for COM programming will recognize several of them:

Attribute Name	Description
attributeusage	Used to determine what elements an attribute can be applied to.
conditional	Conditionally includes a method in a class.
obsolete	Marks an entity as obsolete; the compiler will give a warning or error if it is used.
guid	Specifies a GUID for the class or interface.
in	Indicates that a parameter is passed from caller to method.
out	Indicates that a parameter is passed from the method back to the caller.
returnshresult	Method returns a COM HRESULT.
serializable	Marks a class or struct as serializable.
nonserialized	Marks a data member or property as being transient.

Using Attributes

Attributes are places in square brackets on the line before the element (method, class, etc.) which they describe. As an example, here's how we would use one of the standard attributes that controls conditional inclusion of methods in a class:

```
public class Test
{
    [conditional("DEBUGGING")]
    public void TraceOutput()
    {
        Console.WriteLine("Some trace output...");
    }
}
```

Here, the `conditional` attribute takes the name of a preprocessor symbol `DEBUGGING` as its argument; if that symbol is defined, the method `TraceOutput` and all calls to it are included in the compilation. If the symbol isn't defined, then all traces of `TraceOutput` are omitted from the compiled code.

Here's how we could use our conditional method in code:

```
#define DEBUGGING

using System;

public class Test
{
    [conditional("DEBUGGING")]
    public void TraceOutput()
    {
        Console.WriteLine("Some trace output...");
    }

    public static int Main(string[] args)
    {
        Test t = new Test();

        Console.WriteLine("Some ordinary output");

        // If DEBUGGING is not defined, the following line will be
        // ignored, and no exception will be thrown.
        t.TraceOutput();

        Console.WriteLine("Some ordinary output");

        return 0;
    }
}
```

We define the preprocessor symbol at the start of the file, and that means that both the definition and the call will be compiled. If we run the code as listed above, we will see output like this:

Some ordinary output
Some trace output...
Some ordinary output

However, if we remove or comment out the definition of `DEBUGGING`, or replace the #define directive with #undef, we will see this output:

Some ordinary output
Some ordinary output

There are a few restrictions on methods that can be used with the `conditional` attribute, the main one being that they can only have a `void` return type. This effectively prevents such methods being used in expressions, where it would be impossible to selectively discard calls. For example, suppose we had an expression `t.foo() + t.bar()`, where the `bar()` method was marked as conditional. If this method weren't included when the class was compiled, it would be impossible to evaluate the expression. This restriction is designed to prevent code being broken in this way.

Writing Custom Attributes

The first step to writing your own attributes is to create an attribute class, which inherits from `System.Attribute`:

```
using System;

[attributeusage(AttributeTargets.Class)]
public class IsDrawingPlugin : System.Attribute
{
}
```

This attribute, `IsDrawingPlugin`, is going to be used to mark classes that are plug-ins for a mythical drawing program. The first thing to note is that the attribute class itself has an attribute, `attributeusage`. This is really a meta-attribute, in that it is an attribute that applies to attributes!

The `attributeusage` attribute is used to determine which elements in a program this attribute can be applied to, and in this case we can apply it to classes. The `AttributeTargets` enumeration contains methods which let us tie down pretty well exactly what we want our attributes to be used on, but we can use `AttributeTargets.All` if we're not fussy.

The above definition isn't complete, because attribute classes must have at least one public constructor. Since our attribute has no data associated with it, the constructor is very simple indeed, and our completed simple attribute would therefore look like this:

```
using System;

[attributeusage(AttributeTargets.Class)]
public class IsDrawingPlugin : System.Attribute
{
    public IsDrawingPlugin()
    {
    }
}
```

We would compile this class as part of an assembly, and have the assembly available when we want to use it. In client code, we'd use it on a class like this:

```
[IsDrawingPlugin]
public class Plugin
{
}
```

For a more complex example that uses arguments, consider an attribute that can be used to attach information about who writes a particular class:

```
using System;

[attributeusage(AttributeTargets.Class)]
public class AuthorInfo : System.Attribute
{
    private string name;
```

```
    public AuthorInfo(string name)
    {
        this.name = name;
    }
}
```

In this case we're using `AttributeTargets.Class` to restrict this attribute to use on classes only.

Attributes take two kinds of parameters, known as *positional* and *named*. Positional parameters are used as arguments to constructors, and must be specified every time the attribute is used, so you use them for data that is central to the operation of the attribute. The string `name` in the example above is a positional parameter.

Named parameters are represented by a non-static data member or property in the attribute class. They are optional, and if used, they are identified by their name. We can add optional `Date` and `Comment` named parameters to our class like this:

```
using System;

[attributeusage(AttributeTargets.All)]
public class AuthorInfo : System.Attribute
{
    private string name;
    private string date;
    private string comment;

    public AuthorInfo(string name)
    {
        this.name = name;
    }

    public string Name
    {
        get
        {
            return name;
        }
    }

    public string Date
    {
        get
        {
            return date;
        }
        set
        {
            date = value;
        }
    }

    public string Comment
    {
```

```
        get
        {
            return comment;
        }
        set
        {
            comment = value;
        }
    }
}
```

We've only added a get property for the name, because that's set via the constructor. We could use the positional and named parameters like this in code:

```
[AuthorInfo("julian")]
[AuthorInfo("julian", Date="27/10/00")]
[AuthorInfo("julian", Date="27/10/00", Comment="First revision")]
```

The first version just uses the one positional parameter, which has to be included in all uses of this attribute. The second and third use one and both of the named attributes respectively. To use the attribute, you simply include it at the top of a class definition:

```
[IsDrawingPlugin, AuthorInfo("julian", Date="27/10/00",
                        Comment="First revision")]
public class Plugin
{
    ...
}
```

Note that only a subset of the .NET types can be used for attribute parameters, as shown in the following list:

- bool, byte, char, double, float, int, long, short, and string
- object
- System.Type
- A public enum
- Arrays of the above

Using Reflection with Attributes

You can use reflection on objects that you create to find out about the attributes they support, using the Type.GetCustomAttributes() method:

```
public class Test
{
    public static int Main(string[] args)
    {
        Type t = typeof(Plugin);
```

```
        bool blnPlugin = false;

        object[] attribs = t.GetCustomAttributes();
        foreach (object o in attribs)
        {
            if (o.GetType().Equals(typeof(IsDrawingPlugin)))
            {

                Console.WriteLine("Supports IsDrawingPlugin attribute");
                blnPlugin = true;
            }
        }

        if (blnPlugin == false)
            Console.WriteLine("Not a plugin");

        return 0;
    }
}
```

We start by getting a `Type` object that represents the class we want to test, and then call its `GetCustomAttributes()` method to retrieve an array of objects, each of which represents an instance of an attribute class. We use a flag, `blnPlugin`, to indicate whether the `IsDrawingPlugin` attribute is supported, and initialize this flag to `false`. We can then walk through this collection using `foreach`, testing the type of each member to see whether it is an `IsDrawingPlugin` object. If it is, then the class supports that attribute and we report the fact and set `blnPlugin` to `true`. Notice that we use `Equals()` when comparing types, because we're dealing with references to `Type` objects. If `blnPlugin` is still `false` when the `foreach` loop has finished, we know that the attribute isn't supported, and report this.

Using an attribute class that has parameters is simply a matter of accessing the members of the attribute object. Note how we need to cast the `object` reference into an `AuthorInfo` reference in order to access its members:

```
using System;
using System.Reflection;

public class Test
{
    public static int Main(string[] args)
    {
        Type t = typeof(Plugin);

        bool blnAuthorInfo = false;
        bool blnPlugin = false;

        object[] attribs = t.GetCustomAttributes();
        foreach (object o in attribs)
        {
            if (o.GetType().Equals(typeof(IsDrawingPlugin)))
            {
                Console.WriteLine("Supports IsDrawingPlugin attribute");
```

```
            blnPlugin = true;
        }
        if (o.GetType().Equals(typeof(AuthorInfo)))
        {
            Console.WriteLine(
                "Class has AuthorInfo attribute, name={0}, date={1}",
                ((AuthorInfo)o).Name, ((AuthorInfo)o).Date);
            blnAuthorInfo = true;
        }
    }

    if (blnPlugin == false)
        Console.WriteLine("Not a plugin");

    if (blnAuthorInfo == false)
        Console.WriteLine("Class doesn't have AuthorInfo");
    return 0;
    }
}
```

Unsafe Code

By this point, C++ programmers may be thinking that, while they can see the advantages of garbage collection and accessing variables via references, they still miss pointers and being able to directly manipulate memory.

C#, in attempting to marry the best features of both C++ and Java, provides a way to let programmers use pointers just as we would in C or C++, but to do so in a way that doesn't conflict with the operation of the GC. In effect, C# lets us write code which runs outside the control of the memory management mechanism. This code is called **unsafe**, because there's a possibility that you can introduce all the problems that pointers and direct memory access bring with them.

Why would you want to do this, and step outside the safe memory management provided for you by C#? There are several possible reasons. Firstly, there's efficiency – using references to access objects imparts an extra layer of indirection, and the GC mechanism itself must add its own overheads. For certain critical blocks of code, you may want to be as efficient as possible, and using pointers may give you that edge.

Secondly, you may want to import some C or C++ code into C# that uses pointers, and you don't want to have to convert the pointers to references. Thirdly, you may want to use a system call or COM interface method which requires a pointer as an argument. And lastly, some C and C++ programmers may simply like using pointers from time to time!

Blocks of code where you want to work outside the control of the GC and use pointers have to be marked as 'unsafe', which tells both the runtime and anyone reading the code what you're doing. You can mark blocks of code or whole methods as unsafe:

```
public class Test
{
    ...
    unsafe public void DoSomething()
```

```
    {
        ...
    }

    public void DoSomethingElse()
    {
        unsafe {
            // do something unsafe in here
        }
    }
}
```

Pointers in C#

For anyone who may not have come across C-style pointers before, here's a brief explanation. We access objects in C# using references, and this means that whenever we use an object we're actually dealing with two entities – the reference, and the object to which it refers. Only the reference knows the actual address of the object and that address isn't accessible to users, so the GC can move the object around in memory, and provided it fixes up the reference, users will be none the wiser.

A pointer, on the other hand, is a variable that holds an address; this address is the value of the pointer variable, it is visible and may be modified by the user. So using pointers means that you're directly playing with memory addresses, and here's where the problems start. As far as the GC is concerned, pointers are bad news, because it can no longer move objects around as it wishes. Pointers are also inherently unsafe, because they rely on correct values being used for the addresses they hold; if a bad value gets assigned to a pointer, it can end up accessing incorrect memory locations, resulting in possible memory corruption or programs crashing. Indeed, it is estimated that the majority of bugs in C and C++ code result from pointers, which is one of the reasons why Java doesn't support them, and why C# handles them specially.

Pointer variables are declared using the '*' notation:

```
int* pi;        // pointer to an int
char* pch;      // pointer to a char
```

Pointer variables have to be typed, so that `int*` declares a 'pointer to `int`', and can only be used to hold the address of an `int`. If you try to make it hold the address of any other type, the compiler will complain.

It is very common to use pointers to access arrays, using the pointer to access the address of each element in turn as we move through the array:

```
public static int Main(string[] args)
{
    unsafe
    {
        int[] myArray = { 1, 2, 4, 9 };        // int array reference

        // Make pi point to the array object somehow...
        // we'll see how shortly
```

```
    {
        for (int i=0; i<myArray.Length; i++)
            Console.WriteLine("Element {0} is {1}", i, *(pi+i));
    }
    return 0;
    }
}
```

Once we've got the pointer pointing at the array object, we can access the elements in the array. The '*' operator is used to **dereference** the pointer, returning us the value stored at the address the pointer holds. If the pointer holds the address of the start of the array, *pi will return the value of the first item.

We can use our loop counter i in conjunction with the pointer to access the address of the next array element. Pointer variables can only be declared and used within unsafe blocks, because the GC has to be warned about them.

I've already said that the use of object references means that the GC can move the actual objects around in memory as it wishes. If we want to use pointers, the objects we want to reference obviously mustn't be moved around by the GC while we're using them, and C# provides the fixed keyword to tell the GC not move an object while it is being referenced by a pointer. Using fixed to stop the GC from moving an object is known as **pinning** the object:

```
unsafe public void DoSomething(int[] ar)
{
    fixed (int* pa = ar) {
        // use pa
    }
}
```

This method is passed a reference to a normal managed int array object. We use fixed to get an int* pointer to the start of the actual object in memory, so that the address of the object ar is stored in the pointer variable pa. We can then use pa within the fixed block to access the elements of the array. And of course, while we're using pa in this block, the GC won't touch the object referred to through ar. When we exit from the fixed block, the pointer goes out of scope, and the GC can then take control of the object once more.

> *Note that using fixed also prevents us from modifying the pointer itself. This is why, in our previous example, we used* *(pi+i) *to iterate through the array, rather than, for example,* *pi++.

Note that you don't need to use fixed for value types, because they're allocated on the stack, so the GC isn't going to move those around. That means that we can do traditional C-style manipulation of value types via pointers, the only proviso being that the pointers must be declared in an unsafe block.

```
unsafe public void UsePoint(Point p)
{
    Point* pp = &p;
    Console.WriteLine("p is ({0},{1})", pp->x, pp->y);
}
```

When using value types, we need to use the & operator to take the address of the variable and assign it to the pointer. Once we have a pointer to the value type, we can use the -> operator to access its members. This operator is used to access members through a pointer, in the same way that the period (.) is used to access members through a reference.

XML Documentation

Our final topic in this chapter covers C#'s documentation facilities. Java programmers will be familiar with `javadoc`, an application which processes special tags in Java source code, and produces HTML pages as its output. The idea, based on the web documentation system invented by Donald Knuth, is that you write the code documentation at the very best time – as you're writing the code. You can then automatically generate the documentation from the code, and it should be easy to keep code and documentation up to date.

C#'s version is different to `javadoc` in two main ways. Firstly, it is processed by the compiler and not by a separate tool, and secondly, it generates XML rather than HTML. The reason for generating XML is that it is relatively easy to apply an XSL stylesheet to XML in order to generate HTML, but because XML tags mark up content rather than presentation, you can also use the documentation for purposes other than just display.

> *For a very comprehensive discussion of XML, check out Professional XML, ISBN 1-81003-11-0, published by Wrox Press.*

Text that is to be processed into XML documentation is provided in special comments that use three slashes (`///`) instead of the normal two. These will be treated as normal comments by the compiler, unless you use the `/doc:filename` compiler option to tell it to generate the XML. The following command line will compile the `myclass.cs` file, and place the generated XML into `myclass.xml`:

```
csc /doc:myclass.xml myclass.cs
```

The compiler also supports a set of documentation tags that you can use within XML comments. Some of these are simply standard tags to which you'll have to attach your own meaning when you process the XML, but a few of them are processed by the compiler. You can also make up and use your own XML tags in order to extend the set.

Tag	Description
`<c>`	Marks text within a line up as code, e.g. `<c>code</c>`.
`<code>`	Marks multiple lines as code.
`<example>`	Marks up a code example.
`<exception>`	Documents an exception class.
`<list>`	Inserts a list into documentation. Uses `<listheader>` and `<item>` tags.
`<param>`	Marks up a method parameter.
`<paramref>`	Indicates that a word is a method parameter.
`<permission>`	Documents access to a member.
`<remarks>`	Adds a description for a member.
`<returns>`	Documents the return value for a method.

Tag	Description
<see>	Provides a cross-reference to another member.
<seealso>	Provides a 'see also' section in a description.
<summary>	Provides a short description of an object.
<value>	Describes a property.

The compiler will check <param> and <paramref> tags to make sure that the parameters you're using do actually exist, and it also processes the <see> and <seealso> tags to make sure that the entities named in the cross-reference exist, and expands them to put in their full names (including class and namespace).

XML Documentation in Visual Studio

In Visual Studio.NET, <summary>...</summary> tags will be added automatically around our comment if we type three slashes at the start of a line. Visual Studio will also add context-specific elements; for example, it will examine the parameters for a method and add the requisite <param> elements when we type three slashes on the line before a method's signature:

```
public class Test
{
    /// <summary>
    /// |
    /// </summary>
    /// <param name="args"> </param>
    public static int Main(string[] args)
    {
```

To generate the documentation files from these comments, select the Build Comment Web Pages option from the Tools menu. A dialog will be displaying asking whether we want to generate files for the entire solution or just for a particular project, and will prompt us for the folder in which the files should be placed. If we elect to generate files for the entire solution, Visual Studio will create a "start page" bearing the name of the solution and listing the constituent projects as hyperlinks. For each project documented, a subfolder will be created, and this subfolder will contain HTML pages particular to the project.

When we browse to a project's page, we are presented with an Explorer-style view of the project. Clicking on one of the classes listed as hyperlinks in the left pane causes the right pane to fill with information particular to the class. Clicking on the one of the links in the right pane "drills down" to provide detailed information about a particular class method or property:

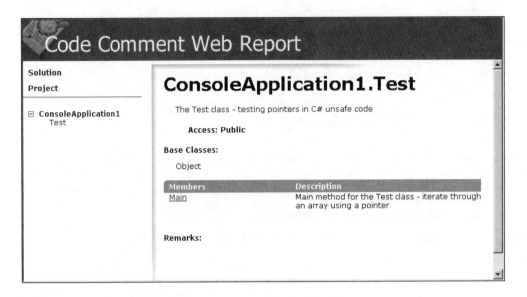

Documenting the StringCollection Class

To show you how to use this documentation feature, here's the `StringCollection` class marked up using the XML documentation tags. If you're using the Visual Studio editor, typing the third slash on a comment will put in a skeleton summary block for you. If you're using some other editor (such as Notepad), you'll have to type all the XML in yourself.

```
/// <summary>
/// The StringCollection class implements a collection class
/// that can be used with foreach
/// <see>IEnumerable</see>
/// </summary>
public class StringCollection : IEnumerable
{
    /// <summary>
    /// Test data strings for use with this class
    /// </summary>
    private string[] ss = new string[] {
        "one", "two", "three", "four" };

    /// <summary>
    /// The default constructor
    /// </summary>
    public StringCollection()
    {
    }

    /// <summary>
    /// GetEnumerator creates a new Enumerator object
    /// </summary>
    /// <returns>The IEnumerator interface on an enumeration
    /// object</returns>
    public virtual IEnumerator GetEnumerator()
    {
        return new Enumerator(this);
    }
```

```csharp
/// <summary>
/// The nested Enumerator class
/// </summary>
private class Enumerator :    IEnumerator
{
    /// <summary>
    /// pos holds the current position of the enumerator
    /// </summary>
    private int pos;

    /// <summary>
    /// coll is a reference to the object we're working with
    /// </summary>
    private StringCollection coll;

    /// <summary>
    /// Constructor for the Enumerator class. Save the
    /// reference, and set the position to denote an
    /// invalid position
    /// </summary>
    /// <param name="sc">The StringCollection object to be
    /// enumerated</param>
    public Enumerator(StringCollection sc)
    {
        coll = sc;
        pos = -1;
    }

    /// <summary>
    /// Move to the next object. If we haven't reached the end,
    /// return true, otherwise set the position to invalid, and
    /// return false.
    /// </summary>
    public bool MoveNext()
    {
        pos++;
        if (pos < 4)
            return true;
        else {
            pos = -1;
            return false;
        }
    }

    /// <summary>
    /// Return the current object. If the position is
    /// invalid throw an exception, otherwise return the element
    /// </summary>
    public object Current
    {
        get
        {
            if (pos == -1)
                throw new InvalidOperationException();

            return coll.ss[pos];
        }
    }

    /// <summary>
    /// Reset the position
    /// </summary>
```

```
        public void Reset()
        {
            pos = -1;
        }
    }
}
```

You can see that classes and methods are documented by placing the XML comments immediately before the class or method concerned. `<summary>` tags are used for the bulk of the documentation, with others inserted to add emphasis as necessary.

Here's an extract from the XML file that's produced:

```
<?xml version="1.0"?>
<doc>
    <assembly>
        <name>StringProject</name>
    </assembly>
    <members>
        <member name="T:enumerate.StringCollection">
            <summary>
                The StringCollection class implements a collection class
                that can be used with foreach
                <see>IEnumerable</see>
            </summary>
        </member>
        <member name="F:enumerate.StringCollection.ss">
            <summary>
                Test data strings to use with this class
            </summary>
        </member>
        <member name="M:enumerate.StringCollection.#ctor">
            <summary>
                Default constructor
            </summary>
        </member>
        ...
    </members>
</doc>
```

This is a standard XML file built from nested tags. All the members of the assembly are denoted by `<member>` tags, and you can see how the compiler has added the full name of the member as a `name` attribute. The `T`, `F`, and `M` prefixes denote types, fields, and members respectively.

At the time of writing, there are no tools for processing this XML into documentation, and it is necessary for you to provide your own XSL stylesheet file to render the XML as HTML. The following simple stylesheet can be used to display the summary information for each member of an assembly in an HTML table in IE5.5:

```
<?xml version="1.0" encoding="UTF-8" ?>
<xsl:stylesheet xmlns:xsl="http://www.w3.org/TR/WD-xsl">

<xsl:template match="/">
    <HTML><BODY>
        <h1>Formatted XML output</h1>
        <hr/>
        <h3>
            Project name:  <xsl:value-of select="doc/assembly/name" />.cs
```

```
            </h3>
            <TABLE border="2">
                <THEAD><h3>Members</h3></THEAD>
                <TBODY>
                    <TR>
                        <TD><B>Member</B></TD>
                        <TD><B>Summary</B>
                        </TD><TD><B>See also</B></TD>
                    </TR>
                    <xsl:for-each select="doc/members/member">
                        <TR>
                            <TD><xsl:value-of select="@name" /></TD>
                            <TD><xsl:value-of select="summary/text()" /></TD>
                            <TD><xsl:value-of select="summary/see/text()" />
                                <FONT color="white">#</FONT>
                            </TD>
                        </TR>
                    </xsl:for-each>
                </TBODY>
            </TABLE>
        </BODY></HTML>
    </xsl:template>
</xsl:stylesheet>
```

When we view the `StringCollection` XML file using this stylesheet, we will see a basic, but nicely formatted table:

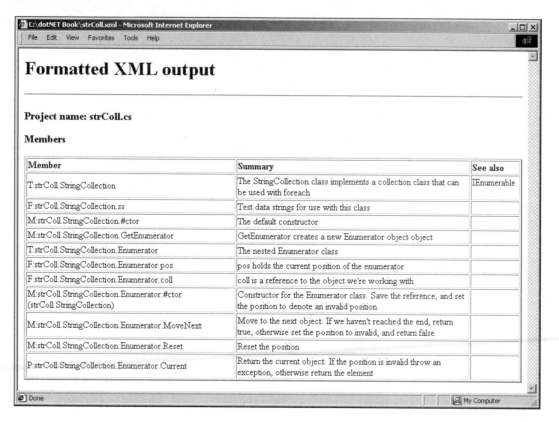

```
 C:\dotNET Book\strColl.xml - Microsoft Internet Explorer              _□×
 File   Edit   View   Favorites   Tools   Help
```

Formatted XML output

Project name: strColl.cs

Members

Member	Summary	See also
T:strColl.StringCollection	The StringCollection class implements a collection class that can be used with foreach	IEnumerable
F:strColl.StringCollection.ss	Test data strings for use with this class	
M:strColl.StringCollection.#ctor	The default constructor	
M:strColl.StringCollection.GetEnumerator	GetEnumerator creates a new Enumerator object object	
T:strColl.StringCollection.Enumerator	The nested Enumerator class	
F:strColl.StringCollection.Enumerator.pos	pos holds the current position of the enumerator	
F:strColl.StringCollection.Enumerator.coll	coll is a reference to the object we're working with	
M:strColl.StringCollection.Enumerator.#ctor (strColl.StringCollection)	Constructor for the Enumerator class. Save the reference, and set the position to denote an invalid position	
M:strColl.StringCollection.Enumerator.MoveNext	Move to the next object. If we haven't reached the end, return true, otherwise set the position to invalid, and return false.	
M:strColl.StringCollection.Enumerator.Reset	Reset the position	
P:strColl.StringCollection.Enumerator.Current	Return the current object. If the position is invalid throw an exception, otherwise return the element	

```
 Done                                                    My Computer
```

Summary

In this chapter we've seen some of the more advanced features of C#. In particular:

❑   The System.Reflection namespace provides a mechanism to find out about the structure of classes dynamically at run-time. It also allows for dynamic creation of objects, and invocation of their methods.

❑   Attributes let us attach metadata to objects in a way which lies outside normal C# syntax. The attributes of a class can be queried at run-time, and custom attributes can be written.

❑   C# has a preprocessor that provides a subset of the functionality provided by the traditional C preprocessor. This is mainly used for conditional compilation, and macros aren't supported.

❑   Pointers and memory manipulation can be used with 'unsafe' code blocks. Objects can be referenced by address within these blocks, and the garbage collector won't move them around.

❑   Special comments within the text can be used to produce XML documentation.

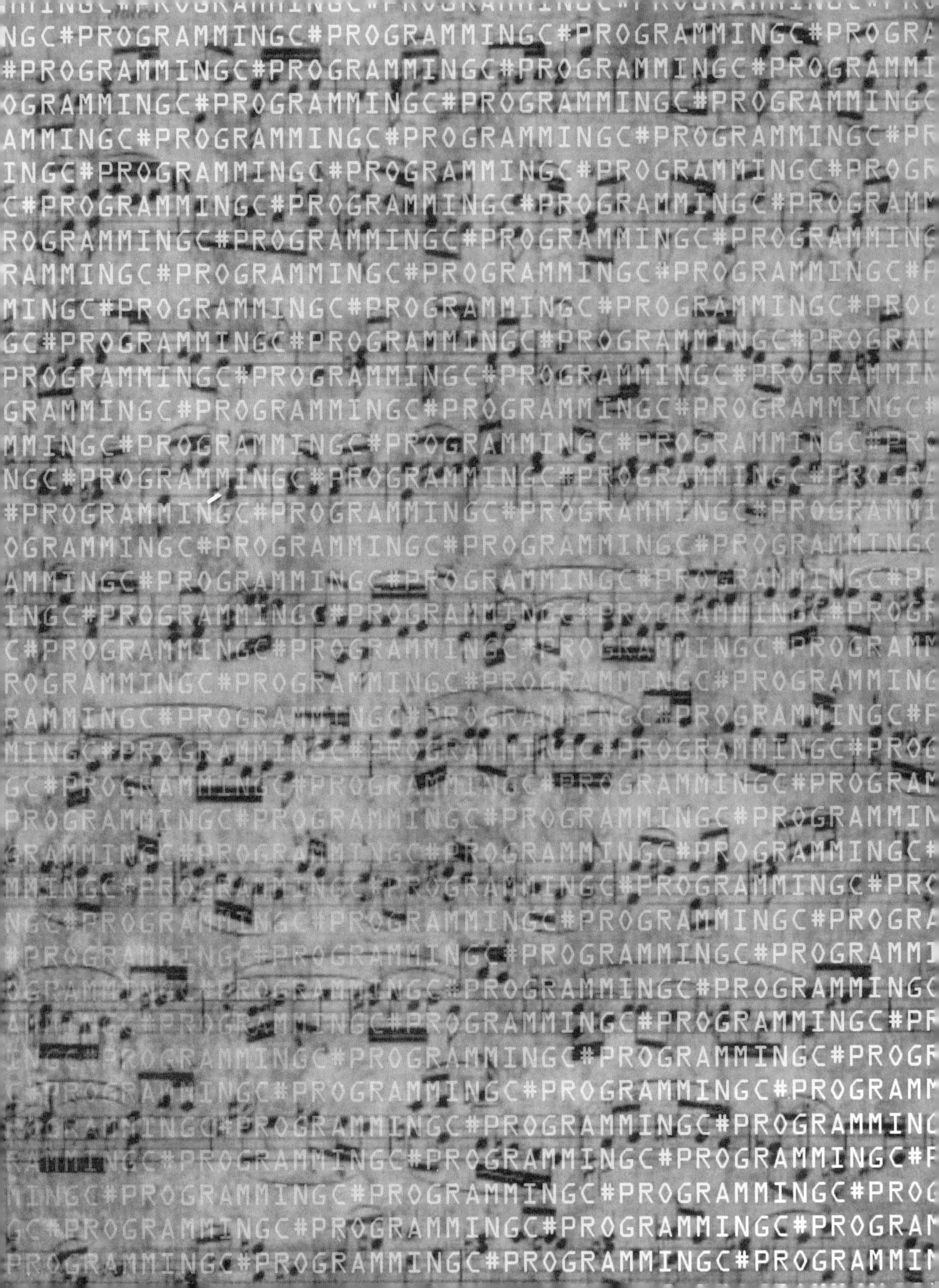
C#PROGRAMMING

7

Namespaces and the Base Classes

In this chapter we're going to look at the base classes – the vast number of .NET classes that Microsoft has written for you, and also namespaces – the system by which classes are grouped together.

A significant part of the power of the .NET framework comes from the base classes supplied by Microsoft as part of the .NET framework. These classes are all callable from C# and provide the kind of basic functionality that is needed by many applications to perform, amongst other things, basic system, Windows, and file handling tasks. To a large extent the .NET base classes can be seen as replacing the previous Win32 API and a large number of MS-supplied COM components. The base classes are simpler to use, and you can easily derive from them to provide your own specialist classes. You can also use the base classes from any .NET-aware language (calling Win32 API functions from VB was possible but not easy). The types of purposes you can use the base classes to do include:

- ❑ String handling
- ❑ Arrays, lists, maps etc.
- ❑ Accessing files and the file system
- ❑ Accessing the registry
- ❑ Security
- ❑ Windowing
- ❑ Windows messages
- ❑ Connecting to other computers and to the Internet

❑   Drawing

❑   Directory Access

❑   Database Access

You can see from the above list that besides giving access to basic Windows operations, the base classes define many useful data types, including strings and collections of data.

The base classes are not, of course, only available to C# programs – they can equally well be accessed from VB, C++ or any other .NET-compliant or (by use of some wrapper objects) COM-aware language, but we will concentrate on C# here.

The aim of this chapter is to give you an overview of the kinds of things you can do using the base classes and how to perform certain common operations. Clearly the scope of the base classes is so vast that we cannot give any kind of comprehensive guide in one chapter – instead we are going to pick on a few common programming tasks and present sample code to demonstrate how you can easily execute those tasks. However we will also show you how you can use the WinCV tool which is supplied with the .NET SDK to explore the base classes for yourself.

The tasks we're going to cover in this chapter include:

❑   Manipulating dates and times

❑   Navigating the file system

❑   Reading and writing to files

❑   Copying, Moving and Deleting files

❑   Connecting to the Internet

❑   Accessing the registry

❑   Mathematical functions

Note that we are not covering windowing or data access in this chapter. These areas are important enough to warrant chapters in their own right and are respectively covered in Chapters 8 and 9.

Before we do that though, we need to switch topics for a while and understand how namespaces work in C#, since you need to be able to use and reference namespaces in order to be able to access the base classes.

Namespaces

A **namespace** can be seen as a container for some classes in much the same way that a folder on your file system contains files. Namespaces are needed because there are a lot of .NET classes. Microsoft has written many thousands of base classes, and any reasonably large application will define many more. By putting the classes into namespaces we can group related classes together, and also avoid the risk of name collisions: If your company happens to define a class that has the same name as the class written by another organization, and there were no namespaces, there would be no way for a compiler to figure out which class a program is actually referring to. With namespaces, there isn't a problem because the two classes will be placed in different namespaces, which compares with, say, the Windows files system where files with the same name can be contained in different folders.

It is also possible for namespaces to contain other namespaces, just as folders on your file system can contain other folders as well as files.

When Visual Studio generates your projects, it automatically puts your classes in a namespace. Say for example you use the developer environment to create a C# Windows Application project called MyProject. If you do this and look at the code generated for you, you'll see something like this.

```
namespace MyProject
{
using System;
using System.Drawing;
using System.Collections;
using System.ComponentModel;
using System.WinForms;
using System.Data;
```

There's two C# keywords here that we need to understand: namespace and using. We'll look at namespace first then examine what using does.

The initial namespace command indicates that everything following the opening curly brace is part of a namespace called MyProject. Later on in the file, a class called Form1 is declared.

```
public class Form1 : System.WinForms.Form
```

Because this class has been declared inside the namespace, its 'real' name is not Form1 but MyProject.Form1, and any other code outside this namespace must refer to it as such. This name is correctly known as its **fully-qualified name**. Notice that in the above line, Form1 is derived from a class called Form. This class is defined inside the namespace WinForms, which in turn is defined inside the namespace System (recall we mentioned earlier that it is possible for namespaces to contain other namespaces). This code sample refers to the Form class using its fully qualified name.

Now we'll have a look at the purpose of the using command in the above code. It's basically a way of avoiding having to write fully-qualified names everywhere, since the fully-qualified names can get quite long and make your code hard to read. For example if we consider the line

```
using System.WinForms;
```

This line declares that I may later in the code use classes from the System.WinForms namespace, without indicating the fully-qualified name – and the same applied for every other namespace mentioned in a using command. For example consider the line of code, also generated by the developer environment

```
public class Form1 : System.WinForms.Form
```

Because of the earlier using command, we could equally well write this as

```
public class Form1 : Form
```

In this latter case the compiler will locate the class by searching all the namespaces that have been mentioned in a using command. If it finds a class named Form in more than one of these namespaces, it will generate a compilation error – in that case you would need to use the fully-qualified name in your source code.

Note that the only purpose of the `using` command in this context is to save you typing and make your code simpler. It doesn't, for example, cause any other code or libraries to be added to your project. If your code uses base classes or any other classes that are defined in libraries (recall in .NET these are stored in assemblies), you need to ensure separately that the compiler knows which assemblies to look in for the classes. If you are compiling from the Visual Studio developer environment, this is done through the project references, which are listed in the Solution Explorer window, as shown in this screenshot:

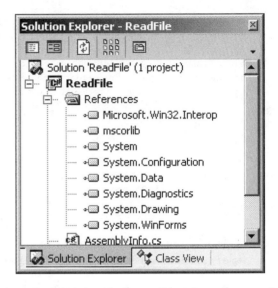

Some references are inserted automatically when your project is created – which ones depends on the type of project, and you can add others using the **Project | Add Reference** menu. The screenshot shows the situation for a newly created C# Windows Application. (Note that although it is assemblies rather than namespaces that are referenced, the solution explorer shows the namespaces that are found in these assemblies. A given assembly can contain more than one namespace and vice versa.)

If you are compiling from the command line then the assembly `mscorlib.dll`, which contains some of the most important base classes, is referenced implicitly. You will need to indicate any other assemblies to be referenced with the command line parameter `/r`, supplying the full file system path to the assembly. For example for the above project, the appropriate command is:

```
csc ReadFile.cs /r:c:\WinNT\Microsoft.NET\Framework\v1.0.2204\System.Drawing.dll
/r:c:\WinNT\Microsoft.NET\Framework\v1.0.2204\System.WinForms.dll
/r:c:\WinNT\Microsoft.NET\Framework\v1.0.2204\System.Data.dll
/r:c:\WinNT\Microsoft.NET\Framework\v1.0.2204\System.Diagnostics.dll
/r:c:\WinNT\Microsoft.NET\Framework\v1.0.2204\System.dll
/r:c:\WinNT\Microsoft.NET\Framework\v1.0.2204\Microsoft.Win32.Interop.dll
```

Now we've understood the concept of a namespace we can go on to look at the namespaces that contain the various base classes.

Using Aliases

If you have a very long namespace and you want to use it several times in your code, then you can substitute a short word for the long namespace name which you can refer to in the code as often as you want. The advantages of doing this are that the code becomes easier to read and maintain and it saves you typing out very long strings.

The syntax for declaring an alias is:

```
using Alias = Wrox.SampleCode.CSharpPreview.Examples;
```

and this sample code illustrates how you can use an alias:

```
namespace Wrox.SampleCode.CSharpPreview
{
    using System;
    using MathEx = Wrox.SampleCode.CSharpPreview.Examples;

    namespace ChBaseClasses
    {
        public class clsExample1
        {
            public static void Main()
            {
                MathEx.clsMath MyMathClass = new MathEx.clsMath();
                Console.WriteLine(MyMathClass.Add(3,4));
            }
        }
    }

    // The alias MathEx refers to this namespace
    namespace Examples
    {
        public class clsMath
        {
            public int Add(int x, int y)
            {
                int z = x + y;
                return (z);
            }
        }
    }
}
```

The Base Classes

As we've remarked there are a huge number of base classes, and there are also a large number of namespaces that contain these classes. We cannot hope to give comprehensive coverage in this chapter, but we'll give a quick summary of some of the more useful namespaces here.

Namespace	Classes Contained
System	Most fundamental classes that are frequently used. For example the class object, from which every other class is derived, is defined in System, as are the primitive data types int, string, double etc.
System.Reflection	Classes that allow examination of the metadata that describes assemblies, objects and types. Also used for COM Interoperability.
System.IO	Input and output, file handling etc.
System.Collections	Arrays, lists, linked lists, maps and other data structures.

Table continued on following page

Namespace	Classes Contained
`System.Web`	Classes that assist in the generation of web pages using ASP+
`System.Net`	Classes to make requests over the network and Internet
`System.Data`	ADO+ classes that make it easy to access data from relational databases and other data sources.
`System.WinForms`	Classes to display controls for standalone (as opposed to web) windows applications.
`Microsoft.Win32`	Functions that were previously accessible mainly through the Win32 API functions, such as registry access.

There are many more namespaces, and the best way to learn about them and the classes they contain is to explore them yourself – and Microsoft have provided a tool for just this purpose. That's what we'll look at next.

The WinCV Tool

WinCV is a class viewer tool, which can be used to examine the classes available in shared assemblies–including all the base classes. (A shared assembly is an assembly that has been marked for use by other applications – we'll cover shared assemblies in Chapter 10). For each class, it lists the methods, properties, events and fields using a C#-like syntax.

At the present time you start it by typing in `wincv` at the command prompt or clicking on the file in Windows Explorer. This gives you a basic window with two panes, as shown.

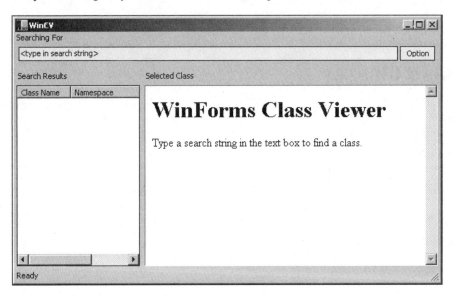

You then type in a search string that is contained in the class you are looking for in the **Searching For** box. For example if you want to find a class that handles dates, you might try typing in **Date** in this box. As you type, WinCV will display a list of classes that contain the string in question in their names:

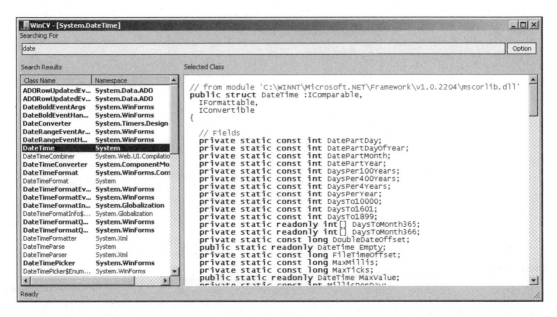

As this screenshot shows, there are a lot of classes whose name contains the string date – then it's just a question of scanning through the names to find the one that looks most suitable. The definition of the selected class is then displayed in the right hand pane. The left hand pane also indicates the namespace the class is contained in – you'll need this in order to be able to use that class in your C# code. In the case of DateTime, WinCV tells us that it is part of the System namespace, which means that the line

```
using System;
```

that is placed by the AppWizard by default in most C# projects will be sufficient to give us access to the class without explicitly indicating the namespace.

The right hand pane of WinCV tells us which assembly the class is defined in – the screenshot shows us that System.DateTime is defined in mscorlib.dll. This information is useful to indicate if we need to link in any assemblies when we compile, in order to have access to the class. Again, the above screenshot tells us that we are OK for the DateTime class, since it is defined in mscorlib.dll, which is, by default, referenced anyway.

Now we've laid the groundwork, the rest of this chapter is devoted to presenting a number of sample C# projects which are designed to illustrate how to carry out some common programming tasks that are made easy by the base classes.

About the Samples

Before we go through the samples in this chapter, we'll quickly go over how we are structuring them. Since in most cases all we want to do is perform a few operations such as writing to a file or accessing some registry keys then displaying the results, it would be simplest to provide console samples – that way we minimize the extraneous code. However in practice, very few Windows applications are written as console applications, and it would be nice to put the output in a more realistic environment. Accordingly, the samples will all be presented as Windows applications, based on a form that has a list box, as shown here.

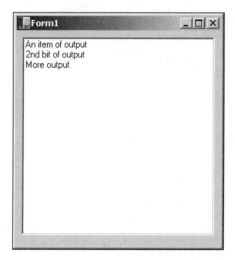

We haven't yet covered how to write Windows applications in C# – that's the subject of Chapter 8, but we'll give you just enough information here for you to understand how the samples are created.

Each project is created as a C# Windows application: So when we start up the Visual Studio developer environment and select New Project, we fill in the New Project dialog like this (though supplying our own name and path for the project).

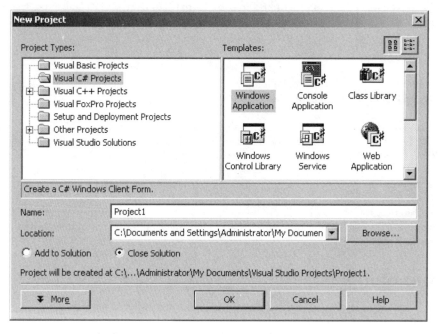

Once the project has been created, we use the Toolbox in the developer environment to place a List box on the form – by default this will be called `listBox1`. The List box is actually an instance of a C# object of type `ListBox`, from the `System.WinForms` namespace.

We then examine the code the wizard has generated for us and make the following changes (shown highlighted).

```
public class Form1 : System.WinForms.Form
{
    /// <summary>
    ///     Required designer variable
    /// </summary>
    private System.ComponentModel.Container components;
    private System.WinForms.ListBox listBox1;

    private int nItems=0;
    public void AddItem(string sItem)
    {
        object oItem = sItem;
        listBox1.InsertItem(nItems,oItem);
        ++nItems;
    }

    public Form1()
    {
        //
        // Required for Win Form Designer support
        //
        InitializeComponent();
        //
        // TODO: Add any constructor code after InitializeComponent call
        //

        AddItem("An item of output");
        AddItem("2nd bit of output");
        AddItem("More output");
    }
    ...
```

The code that we are adding is to the `Form1` class which represents the entire form (window) created when the program is run. We first add a member field, `nItems`, and a member function, `AddItem()`. These are to make it easier for us to add lines of text to the list box. This is normally done by using the member function, `InsertItem()` of the `ListBox` class. But in its simplest overload, this function takes two parameters – the zero-based index of where we wish to insert the item, and the item itself, passed as an object (`InsertItem()` will use the `ToString()` function to extract the string to be added). Since we wish to add each successive item to the end of the list box, this would require us to keep a count of how many items we have added. Our `AddItem()` function automates that process for us.

```
    private int nItems=0;
    public void AddItem(string sItem)
    {
        object oItem = sItem;
        listBox1.InsertItem(nItems,oItem);
        ++nItems;
    }
```

I should mention we could also add the items to the list box with the line of code

```
    listBox1.Items.Add(oItem);
```

though either way our function does marginally simplify the code.

We then actually add the items in the `Form1` constructor. In this case we have simply added three strings.

```
AddItem("An item of output");
AddItem("2nd bit of output");
AddItem("More output");
```

In all the subsequent samples these three lines will be replaced by the code to do whatever processing is required to illustrate the task in hand, followed by `AddItem()` calls to display the results. Each of the projects in this chapter were created in essentially the same way to the above example. Note however that in the following samples, we've also changed the name of the `Form1` class and the namespace that it appears in. The developer environment by default gives us a namespace that has the same name as the project, however Microsoft guidelines say that the namespace should start with the company name (which makes sense, as you would not have any name clashes with other company's classes). So for all the projects here we'll use the namespace `Wrox.BookSamples.CSharpPreview.ChBaseClasses`.

You should bear in mind when reading through the samples that some of the classes may be modified before the .NET SDK is finally released. Hence they will give you a good idea of how to carry out tasks, but some of the names or signatures of methods may be slightly different. Also in many cases there are several classes or methods whose functionality overlaps. Just because we've presented a certain way of doing something doesn't mean there won't be alternative ways of doing the same task.

Manipulating Dates and Times

Our first samples will demonstrate how to access the date-time functionality provided by the base classes. There are two classes of relevance here: `DateTime` and `TimeSpan`, both of which are in the `System` namespace. We start off by displaying the current date and time in various different formats, using this code:

```
namespace Wrox.SampleCode.CSharpPreview.ChBaseClasses
{
using System;
using System.Drawing;
using System.Collections;
using System.ComponentModel;
using System.WinForms;
using System.Data;

public class FormDisplayDateTimes : System.WinForms.Form
{
... as before

/// <summary>
///     Summary description for FormDisplayDateTimes.
/// </summary>
    public FormDisplayDateTimes()
    {
       //
       // Required for Win Form Designer support
       //
```

```
InitializeComponent();

//
// TODO: Add any constructor code after InitializeComponent call
//
DateTime dtCurrTime = DateTime.Now;
AddItem("Current Time is " + dtCurrTime.ToString());
AddItem("Year is " + dtCurrTime.Year.ToString());
AddItem("Month is " + dtCurrTime.Month.ToString());
AddItem("Day of month is " + dtCurrTime.Day.ToString());
AddItem("Day of week is " + dtCurrTime.DayOfWeek.ToString());
AddItem("Hour is " + dtCurrTime.Hour.ToString());
AddItem("Minute is " + dtCurrTime.Minute.ToString());
AddItem("Second is " + dtCurrTime.Second.ToString());
AddItem("Millisecond is " + dtCurrTime.Millisecond.ToString());
AddItem("ShortDateString is " + dtCurrTime.ToShortDateString());
AddItem("LongDateString is " + dtCurrTime.ToLongDateString());
AddItem("ShortTimeString is " + dtCurrTime.ToShortTimeString());
AddItem("LongTimeString is " + dtCurrTime.ToLongTimeString());
}
```

As explained earlier, we are adding our code to the constructor of the `FormDisplayDateTimes` class in our project. (`FormDisplayDateTimes` was `Form1` in the generated code but we've changed its name to a more meaningful class name.)

We first instantiate a variable `dtCurrTime` of class `DateTime`, and initialize it using the static property of the `DateTime` class, Now, which returns the current date and time. We then use various properties, fields and methods to extract portions of the current date and time. This code produces the following output:

Next we will create another sample, which we'll call the `FormTimeSpans` sample. This shows how to add and take the differences between date-times. This is where the `TimeSpan` class comes in. The `TimeSpan` class represents a difference between two date-times. The following sample takes a `DateTime`, initialized to 1 January 2000, 12 pm, adds an interval of 4 days 2 hours 15 minutes to it, and displays the results along with information about the times and timespan.

```
...

public class FormTimeSpans : System.WinForms.Form
{
... as before

    public FormTimeSpans()
    {
        //
        // Required for Win Form Designer support
        //
        InitializeComponent();

        //
        // TODO: Add any constructor code after InitializeComponent call
        //

        // constructor: TimeSpan(days, hours, minutes, seconds)
        TimeSpan Span = new TimeSpan(4,2,15,0);

        // initialize date to 1 Jan 2000, 12 pm
        // constructor: DateTime(year,month,day,hours,minutes,seconds,
        // milliseconds)
        DateTime dtOld = new DateTime(2000,1,1,12,0,0,0);

        DateTime dtNew = dtOld + Span;

        AddItem("Original date was " + dtOld.ToLongDateString() +
                "  " + dtOld.ToShortTimeString());
        AddItem("Adding time span of " + Span.ToString());
        AddItem("Result is " + dtNew.ToLongDateString() + "  " +
                dtNew.ToShortTimeString());
        AddItem("");
        AddItem("Time span broken down is:");
        AddItem("Days: " + Span.Days.ToString());
        AddItem("Hours: " + Span.Hours.ToString());
        AddItem("Minutes: " + Span.Minutes.ToString());
        AddItem("Seconds: " + Span.Seconds.ToString());
        AddItem("Milliseconds: " + Span.Milliseconds.ToString());
        AddItem("Ticks: " + Span.Ticks.ToString());
        AddItem("");
        AddItem("TicksPerSecond: " + TimeSpan.TicksPerSecond.ToString());
        AddItem("TicksPerHour: " + TimeSpan.TicksPerHour.ToString());

    }
```

In this sample we see the new operator being used to construct DateTime and TimeSpan instances of given value. Both these classes have several constructors with different numbers of parameters depending on how precisely you wish to specify the time. We add the span on to the time and display the results. In displaying the results we use the ToLongDateString() method of the DateTime class to get the date in plain English, but the ToShortTimeString() method to get the time (using ToLongTimeString() would give us milliseconds as well). We then use various properties of the TimeSpan class to show the days, hours, minutes, seconds, milliseconds and ticks. Ticks are the smallest unit allowed by the TimeSpan class and measure one ten-millionth of a second, as indicated by a couple of static fields that give conversion factors, which we also display.

The above code gives this output:

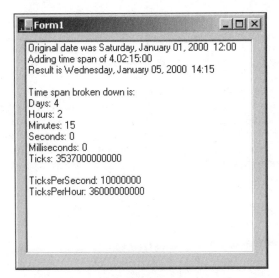

```
Form1                          _ □ ×
Original date was Saturday, January 01, 2000  12:00
Adding time span of 4.02:15:00
Result is Wednesday, January 05, 2000  14:15

Time span broken down is:
Days: 4
Hours: 2
Minutes: 15
Seconds: 0
Milliseconds: 0
Ticks: 3537000000000

TicksPerSecond: 10000000
TicksPerHour: 36000000000
```

File and Folder Operations

One of the most common things you'll need to do is access the file system, to read and write to files, to move or copy files around, or to explore folders to check what files are there. The .NET base classes include a number of classes that provide a rich set of functionality to do these tasks. These classes are contained in the System.IO namespace. Since the AppWizard doesn't add code to refer to this namespace by default, we add the line using System.IO near the top of the Form1.cs source file for all the samples in this section:

```
namespace Wrox.SampleCode.CSharpPreview.ChBaseClasses
{
using System;
using System.Drawing;
using System.Collections;
using System.ComponentModel;
using System.WinForms;
using System.Data;
using System.IO;
```

Note that (as you can find out from the WinCV tool) these classes are still defined in mscorlib.dll, so we don't need to add any files to the project references.

Finding Out Information About a File

Our first file operations sample, which we'll call FileInfo will demonstrate how to get information about a file, such as its last write time, and its size. To do this we use a class, System.IO.File. The code to obtain the information is as follows:

```
File f1 = new File("C:\\dotNET Book\\Ch8_ADO.doc");
AddItem("Connected to file : " + f1.Name);
```

```
            AddItem("In Folder: " + fl.Directory);
            AddItem("Full path: " + fl.FullName);
            AddItem("Is Directory: " + fl.IsDirectory.ToString());
            AddItem("Is File: " + fl.IsFile);
            AddItem("Last write time: " + fl.LastWriteTime.ToString());
            AddItem("Size in bytes: " + fl.Length);
```

This code should be fairly self-explanatory. We construct a `File` instance by supplying the full path name of the location of the file in the file system, and the `File` instance then refers to that file, and we can simply read off a number of properties of it. In this case I'm binding to the file for one of the other chapters of this book, the ADO+ chapter. Note that \ by itself is interpreted as the start of an escape sequence in strings in C#, so we need to use \\ to represent a single backslash in the pathname. You can also use an alternative syntax, in which the @ character precedes the string, which indicates that characters should not be escaped. Hence you would write:

```
        File fl = new File(@"C:\dotNET Book\Ch8_ADO.doc");
```

This code gives us this output.

In general you can use a `File` object to connect to either a file or a folder, although if you connect to a folder then attempting to access those properties that don't make sense for a folder (such as `Length` or `LastWriteTime`) will raise an exception.

Listing Files in a Folder

To explore the contents of a folder, we need another base class – in this case the class `Directory` also in the `System.IO` namespace. Note that the .NET base classes generally refer to folders as *directories* in class and method names. This corresponds to normal terminology on web sites and on Unix and Linux machines, as well as on Windows 3.1 when it was around, but can be confusing if you're used to Windows terminology, in which a folder is an item in the file system that contains files, and a directory is a more sophisticated complete information store (such as Active Directory). I'll continue to use the term folder in this chapter, in accordance with normal usage for the Windows file system.

The following code sample connects to the folder C:\dotNET Book and separately lists the files and folders in it.

```
Directory fl = new Directory("C:\\dotNET Book");
AddItem("Connected to folder: " + fl.Name);
AddItem("Full path: " + fl.FullName);
AddItem("Is Directory: " + fl.IsDirectory.ToString());
AddItem("Is File: " + fl.IsFile);

AddItem("");
AddItem("Files contained in this folder:");
File [] childfiles = fl.GetFiles();
foreach (File childfile in childfiles)
{
    AddItem("   " + childfile.Name);
}

AddItem("");
AddItem("Subfolders contained in this folder:");
Directory [] childfolders = fl.GetDirectories();
foreach (Directory childfolder in childfolders)
{
    AddItem("   " + childfolder.Name);
}
```

This code starts off by showing that the way of connecting to a folder is the same as for a file, and that the Directory and File classes both share the Boolean IsDirectory and IsFile properties, which can be used to distinguish what the object is if you are unsure. This means that you do not know what an object is, you can for example bind to it as a file, then use the IsDirectory property to check if it is actually a folder – and re-bind to it as a Directory if IsDirectory returns true. The resulting code would look something like this:

```
File fl = new File("C:\\DotNET Book");
if (fl.IsDirectory == true)
{
    fl = null;
    Directory dr = new Directory("C:\\DotNET Book");
    // process as directory
}
else
{
    // process as file
}
```

In the above code we next use a method, GetFiles() to retrieve a list of the files in the directory. This method returns an array of File instances, each one already bound to a file – so we can use a foreach loop to iterate through the array and carry out whatever processing we need to do on each file. The Directory class has another method, GetDirectories(), which works in exactly the same way as GetFiles(), but returns an array of Directory instances that refer to each subfolder. In both cases in the sample we use these methods to simply display the names of the files and folders.

This code produces this output on my computer:

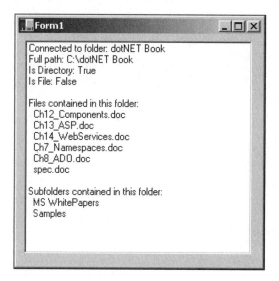

Copying and Deleting files

The next sample is the one in which we really get to have a bit of fun mucking about with the directory system. As usual, it's a Windows project in which we add the code to the form's constructor, though in this case there's no real output to display.

We start off by binding to the dotNET Book folder, and we create both a new empty file and a new empty subfolder there.

```
Directory f1 = new Directory("C:\\dotNET Book");
f1.CreateSubdirectory("SampleBackups");
f1.CreateFile("MyNewFile.txt");
```

We're not going to write anything to the file yet – we'll do that soon.

Next we bind to one of the files in the C:\dotNET Book folder, rename it and copy it:

```
File adofile = new File("C:\\dotNET Book\\Ch8_ADO.doc");
adofile.CopyTo("C:\\dotNET Book\\SampleBackups\\Ch8_Backup.doc");
```

Note that you should put the complete path in otherwise the file will be copied to the same directory as the executable.

Now we have a go at deleting things – first the file spec.doc, then the Samples folder.

```
File sparefile = new File("C:\\dotNET Book\\spec.doc");
sparefile.Delete();

Directory sparefolder = new Directory("C:\\dotNET Book\\Samples");
sparefolder.Delete(true);
```

The `File.Delete()` method doesn't take any parameters. The `Directory.Delete()` method has two overloads. One (which we haven't demonstrated here) takes no parameters and does a simple delete and the file or directory goes to the recycle bin. The other takes one parameter – a Boolean which indicates whether the delete operation is recursive, which in this case we've specified that it is. If we'd wanted the delete not to be recursive we'd have written:

```
sparefolder.Delete(false);
```

In that case if `sparefolder` contained subfolders an exception would be raised.

Reading Text Files

Reading files is quite simple, since Microsoft have provided a large number of classes that represent streams, which may be used to transfer data. Transferring data here can include such things as reading and writing to files, or downloading from the Internet, or simply moving data from one location to another using a stream.

The available classes are all derived from the class `System.IO.Stream`, which can represent any stream, and the various classes represent different specializations, for example streams that are specifically geared to reading or writing to files. In general, for the examples in this chapter that involve using streams, there are potentially a number of different ways to write the code, using any of several of the available stream objects. However, in this chapter we'll just present one way that you could perform each of the processes of reading and writing to text and binary files.

Reading text files is quite simple – for this we're going to use the `StreamReader` class. The `StreamReader` represents a stream specifically geared to reading text. We'll demonstrate the process with a sample that reads in and displays the contents of the `ReadMe.txt` file generated by the developer environment's AppWizard for our earlier `EnumFiles` sample. The code looks like this.

```
File fIn = new File
           ("C:\\dotNET Projects\\Namespaces\\EnumFiles\\ReadMe.txt");
StreamReader strm = fIn.OpenText();

// continue reading until end of file
string sLine;
do
{
   sLine = strm.ReadLine();
   AddItem(sLine);
}
while (sLine != null);
strm.Close();
```

We obtain a `StreamReader` instance using the `OpenText()` method of the `File` class. The `StreamReader` class contains several methods that either read or peek at differing amounts of data.

Peeking means looking ahead at the data, but without actually moving through the data. The best way to understand this is by imagining a pointer that indicates which bit of the file you are due to read next. If you read data, then the pointer will be moved to point at the byte following the last byte read, so the next read (or peek) will bring in the next block of data. If you peek at data, the pointer is not changed, so the next read (or peek) will retrieve the same data again.

The most useful method however for our purposes is ReadLine(), which reads as far as the next carriage return, returning the result in a string. If we have reached the end of the file, ReadLine() does **not** throw an exception, but simply returns a null reference – so we use this to test for the end of the file. Note that a null reference is not the same as an empty string. If we'd instead applied the condition

```
while (sLine != "");
```

to the do loop, the loop would have finished the moment we came to a blank line in the file, not at the end of the file. (StreamReader.ReadLine() returns the string without the trailing carriage return and line feed).

Running this sample produces this output, showing it's correctly read the ReadMe.Txt file:

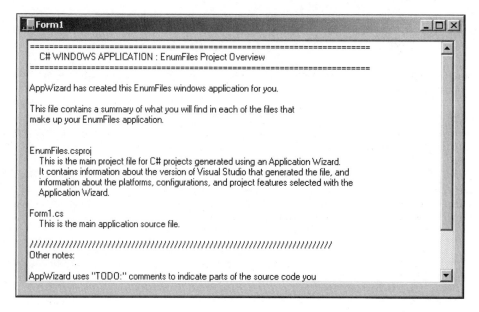

Writing Text Files

Writing text files follows similar principles to reading from them – in this case we use the StreamWriter class.

What makes writing text files even easier than reading them is that the method we use to write a line of text output followed by a carriage return-line feed, StreamWriter.WriteLine(), has a number of overloads so we don't necessarily need to pass it just text. It will accept a string, an object, a Boolean or several of the numeric types. This can be seen from this code sample, which writes out some text to the blank file we created earlier, MyNewFile.txt.

```
StreamWriter strm = new StreamWriter
    ("C:\\dotNET Book\\MyNewFile.txt", false);

strm.WriteLine("This is some text");
strm.WriteLine("Next lines are numbers");
strm.WriteLine(3);
strm.WriteLine(4.55);
```

```
        strm.WriteLine("And the next line is a boolean");
        strm.WriteLine(true);
        strm.Close();
```

The results of this can be seen in Notepad:

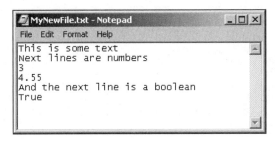

There are a number of overrides to the constructor of the StreamWriter. The constructor we have picked in our code sample is quite flexible, taking two parameters: the full name of the file, and a Boolean that indicates whether data should be appended to the file. If this is false then the contents of the file will be overwritten by the StreamWriter. In either case, the file will be opened if it already exists or created if it doesn't. This behavior can be customized by using other more complex constructors to the StreamWriter.

Reading Binary Files

Once we get to binary files we need to abandon the text-specific StreamReader and StreamWriter classes in place of a more general-purpose class. There are actually two classes that will do the job, System.IO.Stream and System.IO.FileStream. FileStream is designed specifically for reading and writing to files, while Stream is able to transmit data between files or other objects. The two classes work in very similar ways, and for the sake of demonstrating both of them, we'll use Stream for reading data and then use FileStream in the following sample which writes data to a file.

This sample demonstrates how to use the Stream class to read data. It opens a file and reads it, a byte at a time, each time displaying the numeric value of the byte read.

```
        File fl = new File("C:\\dotNET Book\\TestReader.txt");
        Stream strm = fl.OpenRead();
        int iNext;
        do
        {
            iNext = strm.ReadByte();
            if (iNext != -1)
                AddItem(iNext.ToString());
        }
        while (iNext != -1);
        strm.Close();
```

We obtain an instance of the Stream class by first instantiating a File object attached to the required file and calling its OpenRead() method. We then read through the file by calling the Stream.ReadByte() method. This method reads the next byte returning its value as an int. If we have reached the end of the file, then -1 is returned, but no exception is thrown – and it is this condition we use to test for the end of the file. Note that the Stream class also has a Read() method which can read a specified number of bytes in one go – I've chosen to use ReadByte() here as it leads to simpler code.

The file I've tested this code on looks like this – the first few letters of the alphabet followed by three carriage return-line feeds. Although the code will work on any file, I've demonstrated it on a text file because that makes it easier to see visually that the results are correct.

Running the code on this file produces the following:

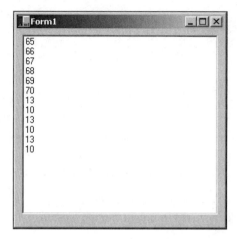

Writing Binary Files

Although we can use either the `Stream` or `FileStream` classes to perform this task, we'll use an instance of `FileStream` for this sample. This code writes out a short text file that contains the letters **FGHIJK** followed by a carriage return-line feed combination. Note that again although this code is capable of writing any data, we're using textual data in the sample so that we can easily use Notepad to check that the sample has worked.

The code looks like this

```
byte [] bytes = {70,71,72,73,74,75,13,10};
FileStream strm = new FileStream
    ("C:\\dotNET Book\\TestWriter.txt",
    FileMode.OpenOrCreate, FileAccess.Write);
foreach (byte bNext in bytes)
{
    strm.WriteByte(bNext);
}
strm.Close();
```

We first define an array of bytes that contains the data to be written to the file – in this case the ASCII codes of the characters. True binary data would have simply meant changing some of the values in this array to represent non-printable characters.

Next we instantiate a `FileStream` object. The constructor we use takes three parameters: the full pathname of the file, the mode we are using to open it and the access required. The mode and access merit more consideration –- they are enumerated values respectively taken from two further classes in the `System.IO` namespace: `FileMode` and `FileAccess`. The possible values these can take are all self-explanatory. In the case of the mode the possible values are `Append`, `Create`, `CreateNew`, `Open`, `OpenOrCreate` and `Truncate`. For the access they are `Read`, `ReadWrite` and `Write`.

Finally we use the `WriteByte` method of the `FileStream` object to write out each byte before closing the file. Again there is a `FileStream.Write` method, which can write out a number of bytes at a time and which you may prefer to use. We've stuck with `WriteByte` because it makes it clearer what is going on as we loop through the array.

And finally the test whether this code has worked: After running it, opening the new file with Notepad gives this:

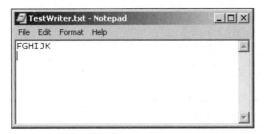

Browsing the Internet

Retrieving a file from the Internet really involves two processes: requesting the file, and reading it through a stream. We've already covered the latter process – the code to do it is essentially the same as our earlier sample to read text from a file using the `StreamReader` class. Loading and requesting the file is a little more complicated as it involves several new classes.

We're going to need a couple of classes concerned with web browsing: `HttpWebRequest`, `HttpWebResponse` and `WebRequestFactory`, which are all in the `System.Net` namespace. The assembly that defines this namespace is not by default loaded in C# projects so we need to add it to our references in the solution explorer. Recall we can do this by right-clicking on the **References** node in the explorer and selecting **Add Reference** from the context menu.

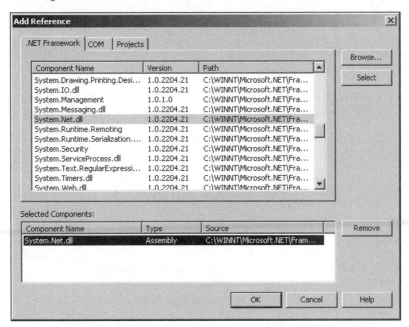

Next we add a couple of commands to refer to some new namespaces in the C# source file:

```
namespace WebRequest
{
using System;
using System.Drawing;
using System.Collections;
using System.ComponentModel;
using System.WinForms;
using System.Data;
using System.Net;
using System.IO;
using System.Text;
```

System.Net is for the web classes just mentioned, System.IO is because we will need to use a StreamReader, and System.Text provides a helper enumeration value used in constructing the StreamReader. These latter two classes are both in mscorlib.dll so no new references need to be added at compilation time.

Now we can proceed to the code needed to make our request to the web server and display the results:

```
HttpWebRequest webreq =
    (HttpWebRequest)WebRequestFactory.Create
    ("http://localhost/postinfo.html");
HttpWebResponse webresp =
    (HttpWebResponse)webreq.GetResponse();

StreamReader strm = new StreamReader(
    webresp.GetResponseStream(), Encoding.ASCII);
string sLine;
do
{
    sLine = strm.ReadLine();
    AddItem(sLine);
}
while (sLine != null);
strm.Close();
```

The request is made through an instance of the class HttpWebRequest. However, it is not possible to construct this instance directly – instead it needs to be constructed by a static method of another class, WebRequestFactory. The WebRequestFactory.Create() method is designed to create a general request for a given URL – in this case we pass the URL of one of the files created on the default web site on my local machine when IIS is installed – postinfo.html. Note that WebRequestFactory.Create() actually returns a reference to a WebRequest object, not an HttpWebRequest object, so we need to cast the return value. HttpWebRequest is derived from WebRequest – the latter class is more general-purpose and able to deal with requests using other protocols besides HTTP.

Once we have the HttpWebRequest instance, we actually make the request by calling its GetResponse() method. GetResponse() returns a WebResponse object, which encapsulates information returned by a web server in response to a request. In a similar manner to WebRequestFactory.Create(), the return value is a reference to a WebResponse rather than an HttpWebResponse, so we need to cast it to the required data type.

Once we have the `HttpWebResponse`, we simply need to obtain a `StreamReader` instance that we can use to retrieve the contents of the file. To do this we use a `StreamReader` constructor that takes two parameters: a more general stream and a value that indicates the encoding type. The stream is obtained from the `GetResponseStream()` method of the `HttpWebResponse` class, and the encoding type is `Encoding.ASCII`, an enumerated value from the `System.Text.Encoding` class, which indicates that this stream contains ASCII text data.

Although there are a lot of classes involved with this and hence a lot to take in, the actual code is still reasonably short and simple. Running this sample produces this result:

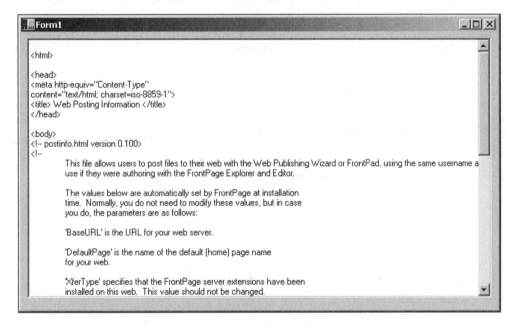

This indicates that the page has been successfully downloaded and displayed.

Accessing the Registry

In this section we'll present a code sample that enumerates registry keys and reads their values.

There are several classes used to access the registry, of which we will use two: `Registry`, and `RegistryKey`, both of which are in the `Microsoft.Win32` namespace. This namespace is defined in the same `mscorlib` assembly that contains the system namespace, so you have access to it without needing to add further references to your project. The remaining registry classes are concerned with security, which is beyond the scope of this chapter.

In order to access a given registry key using the base classes it is necessary to progressively navigate down the registry hierarchy to reach the key. We start off using the `Registry` class: This class contains static fields that allow access to any of the registry hives. The fields are named:

```
ClassesRoot
CurrentConfig
CurrentUser
```

```
DynData
LocalMachine
PerformanceData
Users
```

and are all of class `RegistryKey`. These hives should be familiar to most programmers, though we will comment that `PerformanceData` may be unfamiliar to some developers. This hive does exist, and is used to access performance counters, but it is not visible in Regedit. The `RegistryKey` class represents any given key in the registry and has methods to carry out all sorts of operations including accessing and enumerating subkeys, and reading and modifying values. Thus for example, to access the registry key at the top of the `ClassesRoot` hive, we would use the following:

```
RegistryKey hkcr = Registry.ClassesRoot;
```

and we would then be able to use the variable `hkcr` to perform operations on that key.

The sample, `RegEnumKeys`, binds to a registry key, enumerates its subkeys, and displays the name and all values of each subkey. The key we've chosen to bind to is the registry key whose subkeys contain details of all the ADSI providers installed on the computer, `HKLM/SOFTWARE/Microsoft/ADs/Providers`. When run, the sample gives this output on my machine:

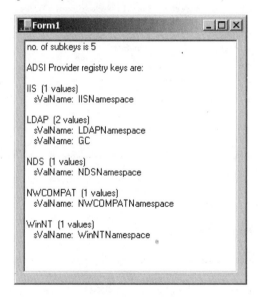

We first ensure that we can access the registry classes without giving full namespace names:

```
namespace Wrox.SampleCode.CSharpPreview.ChBaseClasses
{
using System;
using Microsoft.Win32;using System.Drawing;
using System.Collections;
using System.ComponentModel;
using System.WinForms;
using System.Data;
```

```
using System.IO;
```

As usual the action takes place in the constructor to the main form class which we've renamed
FormRegEnumKeys. We first need to navigate down to the required key. As mentioned earlier, we cannot
do this in one go, but have to progressively step down through the registry hierarchy. Note that the name
passed to the RegistryKey.OpenSubKey method is not case sensitive:

```
public FormRegEnumKeys()
{
    //
    // Required for Win Form Designer support
    //
    InitializeComponent();

    //
    // TODO: Add any constructor code after InitializeComponent call
    //
    RegistryKey hklm = Registry.LocalMachine;
    RegistryKey software = hklm.OpenSubKey("SOFTWARE");
    RegistryKey microsoft = software.OpenSubKey("Microsoft");
    RegistryKey ads = microsoft.OpenSubKey("ADS");
    RegistryKey prov = ads.OpenSubKey("Providers");
```

Now we can display the number of subkeys (corresponding in this case to the number of installed ADSI
providers), and start to enumerate over each of them in a foreach loop. The following code uses two
foreach loops, one to enumerate through the subkeys, and the other to enumerate through each value
associated with each subkey.

```
    AddItem("no. of subkeys is " + prov.SubKeyCount);
    AddItem("");
    AddItem("ADSI Provider registry keys are:");
    string [] sProvNames = prov.GetSubKeyNames();
    foreach (string sName in sProvNames)
    {
        RegistryKey provkey = prov.OpenSubKey(sName);
        AddItem("");
        AddItem(sName + "   (" +
            provkey.ValueCount.ToString() + " values)" );
        foreach (string sValName in provkey.GetValueNames())
        {
            AddItem("    sValName:   " +
                provkey.GetValue(sValName));
        }
    }
```

Mathematical Functions

Mathematical functions are included in the `Math` class, which is part of the `System` namespace. You don't therefore need to add any references to your project to make use of these functions.

The `Math` class basically contains a large number of static functions to perform operations such as calculating sines, logarithms etc. It also contains two static members, `E` and `PI`, which respectively return the values of the mathematical constants e and π. The class is quite basic: it contains all the important mathematical functions, but not much more. There is at present no support for, for example complex numbers or vector or matrix operations. Also the function names will probably annoy many mathematicians since their names often don't follow normal usage as far as case is concerned.

We'll demonstrate the use of this class with a simple application, `Math`, which displays the values of e and π and also the sines of angles between 0 and 90 degrees. The code that we add to the constructor to the main form class looks like this

```
AddItem("e is " + Math.E);
AddItem("pi is " + Math.PI);
AddItem("");
AddItem("sines of angles from 0 to 90 degrees:");

// display sines. Note we must convert from degrees to radians.
for (double theta=0 ; theta<90.1 ; theta+=22.5)
    AddItem("sin " + theta + " = " + Math.Sin(theta*Math.PI/180));
```

Note in this code that we need to convert degrees to radians by multiplying by $(\pi/180)$ since all the math trigonometric functions work in radians.

This code produces this output:

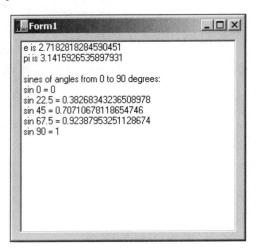

The main mathematical functions include the following:

Sin, Cos, Tan	sine, cosine and tangent of an angle in radians
Asin, Acos, Atan	Inverse trigonometric functions
Atan2	Inverse tangent, with x and y coordinates specified in order to find the angle of the vector between (0,0) and (x,y).
Sinh, Cosh, Tanh	Hyperbolic sine, cosine and tangent. Note that no corresponding inverse functions are provided.
Sqrt	square root
Pow	number raised to a given power
Exp	exponential
Log	natural (base e) logarithm
Log10	base 10 logarithm
Abs	absolute value of a number
Min	lower of two numbers
Max	higher of two numbers
Sign	whether a number is positive or negative

Note that these mathematical functions all take double as the parameter and return a double, apart from Abs, Max, Min and Sign, which returns 1, 0 or –1 – these functions make sense for any numeric type, for example it is equally valid to take the absolute value of an integer or a floating point value, and so Microsoft have provided overloaded functions that take different .NET numeric types.

Summary

In this chapter we've explained the concept of a namespace, and then gone on a quick tour of some of the functionality available via the .NET SDK base classes. Hopefully these examples will have shown you that the base classes make it very easy to carry out a lot of Windows tasks. Some of these tasks were previously only available via the Win32 SDK, which was not only conceptually harder to program with, but also made it difficult to carry out those tasks from any language other than C++. With the new base classes these tasks can be accomplished with ease from any .NET-aware or COM-aware language.

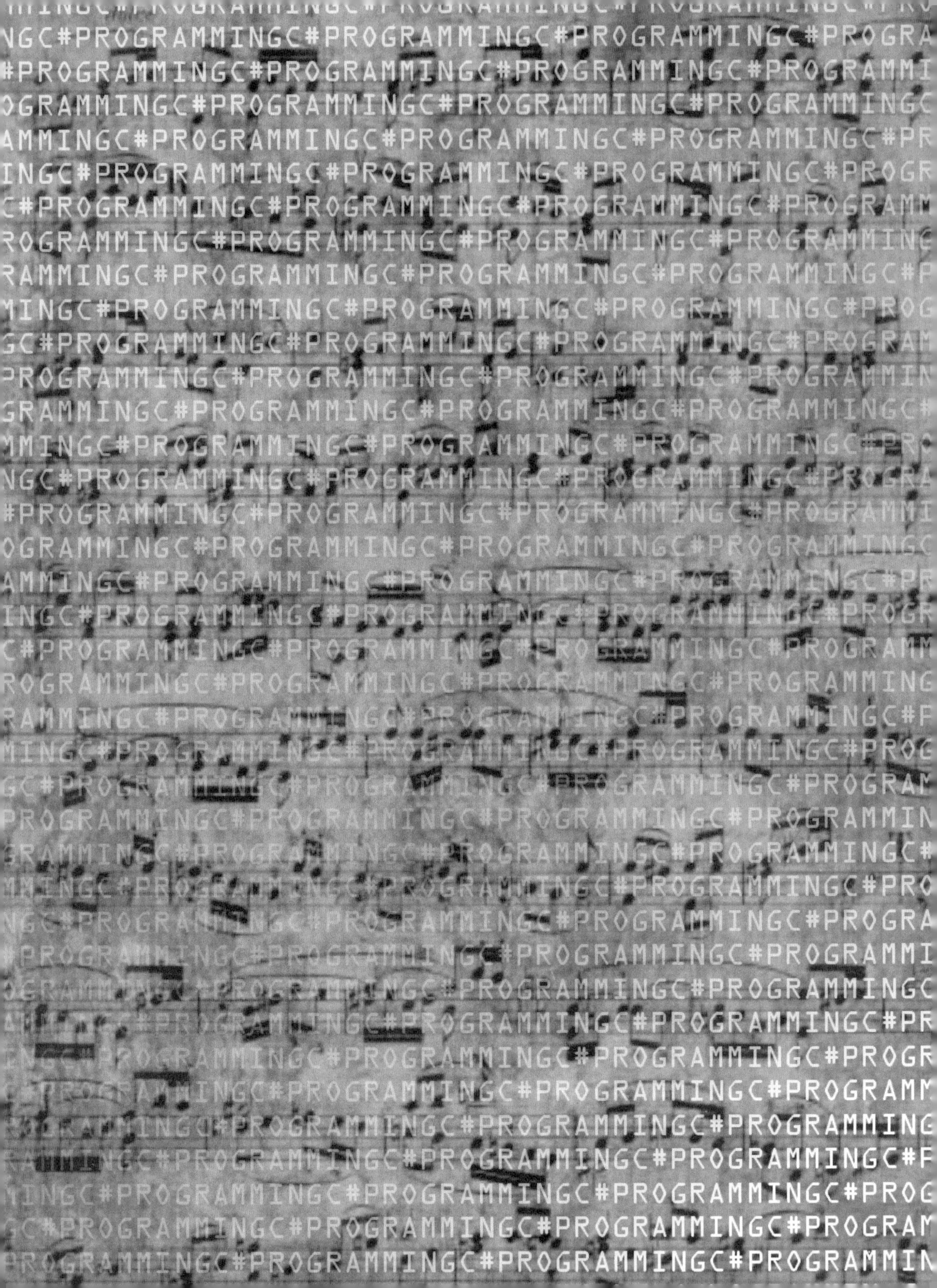
C#PROGRAMMING

8

Windows Applications

In the last chapter, we looked at some of the classes provided by the .NET Framework for some common programming tasks. In addition to this, .NET provides a library of classes and interfaces for the presentation tier of Windows applications – the `System.WinForms` namespace.

In this chapter we will look at how we can use the `WinForms` class library for **Rapid Application Development** (RAD) of Windows applications. By RAD I mean putting together applications quickly using classes as building blocks – it would take much longer to build such an application without a library like this. We'll start with a quick (command line compiled) example to illustrate the ease and economy that is inherent in building applications using WinForms. Next we will take a step back and look at what we mean by a "Windows application". In order to better understand the classes in the WinForms namespace, it is well worth looking at the concepts that are fundamental to Windows application programming in any language.

Once we've covered these concepts we will look at the tools that make constructing WinForms applications even easier, including the powerful VS.NET IDE. After this we'll take a more detailed look at the classes and interfaces provided in the WinForms namespace, through an example detailing the use of the more commonly used classes and discussing what else is available.

Finally, we'll look at application deployment, which involves getting our applications to users. This is important, as having a single "Setup" file is far simpler than copying individual files across to client hardware. Also, being able to compress the data required for installation and assemble many files into one big file is a definite advantage.

Simple WinForms Example

Let's dive straight in and look at a quick example, `HelloWinForms.cs`:

```
using System.WinForms;

public class frmHello : Form
{
    public static int Main(string[] args)
    {
        frmHello frmHelloApp = new frmHello();
        Application.Run(frmHelloApp);
        return 0;
    }

    public frmHello()
    {
        this.Text = "Hello WinForm World";
    }
}
```

Compile this code using:

csc /r:System.dll /r:System.WinForms.dll /r:System.Drawing.dll /r:Microsoft.Win32.Interop.dll
HelloWinForms.cs

(This assumes that the path to the .NET DLLs has been added to the CLASSPATH.)

And run the resultant file, `HelloWinForms.exe`, from the command line. You should see the following:

OK, so this is not the most exciting example in the world, but let's look at what we've achieved. Using some very simple code (which we'll analyze in a moment) we've created a fully functioning window on the desktop. If you play with this window you'll find that it functions exactly as you'd expect – you can resize it by dragging its borders, you can minimize it with the appropriate title bar button or menu, and you can close it, ending the application and returning control to your command prompt.

Let's break the code down line by line and see how it all works.

We start by using our standard `using` statement for the `WinForms` namespace:

```
using System.WinForms;
```

Note that this in itself doesn't give us the references we require to use the `WinForms` namespace. We also need to include references at compile time, using the `/reference` compiler option (`/r` for short), to import the types required:

```
csc /r:System.dll /r:System.WinForms.dll /r:System.Drawing.dll /r:Microsoft.Win32.Interop.dll
HelloWinForms.cs
```

Referencing types in this way requires the `.dll` suffix, as well as additional references to other namespaces that are used by the `WinForms` namespace. We'll see examples of where the `System.Drawing` and `Microsoft.Win32.Interop` libraries are necessary in our code later – they were only required for compilation, and we didn't use any of their types in our simple example.

In order to create our application we make a new class that inherits from one of the classes in the `WinForms` namespace: `Form`. `Form`, as we will see when we go on our tour of the `WinForms` namespace, is the fundamental class we'll almost always use to create Windows applications, and it contains all of the basic features required for a window – which is how our code could be made so compact:

```
public class frmHello : Form
{
```

We've called our new class `frmHello`, using a prefix to remind ourselves that the class is a form.

The next step is the entry point for our application (just like console applications, WinForms applications need an entry point). We can interpret command line arguments here in the same way as for console applications:

```
    public static int Main(string[] args)
    {
```

Our entry point `Main()` function needs to create an instance of our new `frmHello` class:

```
        frmHello frmHelloApp = new frmHello();
```

The next line tells our application to begin processing messages for the window that is created:

```
        Application.Run(frmHelloApp);
```

Note that omitting this line would still result in the window being displayed, but it will exit immediately. In effect, this line of code involves entering a message loop that continually and efficiently looks to see if there are any current unprocessed windows messages that are intended for `frmHelloApp` (such as mouse clicks in the form, key-presses when the form is in focus, etc.). If there are any messages that fit these criteria then they will be forwarded to the relevant message handlers in the form (which may involve further forwarding to contained objects like buttons, as we will see later). The loop will continue to do this until the form is terminated, at which point execution will continue with the following code:

```
        return 0;
    }
```

This ends our `Main()` function and therefore the application.

The rest of the code in our `frmHello` class is purely to add a small amount of customization to make things a bit more interesting. We are overriding the constructor for our class:

```
    public frmHello()
    {
```

and simply accessing the `Form.Text` property, which contains the title bar text for our form, modifying it for some visual feedback:

```
        this.Text = "Hello WinForm World";
```

The `this` keyword here refers to the instance of the `Form` class, `frmHello`. All that remains is to finish our code blocks:

```
    }
}
```

and we're done – a working Windows application with minimum effort.

This simple code forms the framework for most of the rest of the examples in this chapter. Even when we start to use the VS.NET interface later on, a quick look at the code will confirm that the essence of this example is preserved, however complex we make things.

Before we start doing this, though, let's take a look at Windows applications, to find out what we're hoping to achieve.

Windows Applications

The advent of WIMP (Windows Icons Mouse and Pointer) operating systems, such as Microsoft Windows, has brought about a great change in the way we write programs. A Windows application is one that merges seamlessly (we would hope) with the operating system it runs on, using standard styles for buttons, menus, etc. Only a few years ago, writing these applications required an in-depth knowledge of the nuts and bolts of the operating system, and being able to respond to mouse clicks or redraw sections of a window was tricky at best.

Tools quickly emerged to make life easier and hide many of the underlying processes. WinForms is the latest way of programming Windows applications, but it still uses many of the same concepts used by its predecessors (such as VB and MFC). The aim of this section is to whiz through the terminology we will be using in the rest of the chapter, much of which is standard when considering Windows applications (although some is WinForms specific).

Any Windows application will be contained in a window, which is piece of real estate on the desktop. In WinForms all windows are also called **forms**. The content of a window is made up of **controls**, such that forms are control **containers**. Typical controls include buttons, text boxes, drop down lists, menu bars, tool bars, status bars, and even static text labels. When users interact with controls, perhaps by clicking the mouse on a button, messages are generated by the operating system, and give rise to **events** being raised for individual controls. The controls handle these events in whatever way they are programmed to. Obviously, if we had to write the code for each and every possible event for every form and control in our application, things would get very tedious. As we have seen in the last section's simple example, though, much of the time we don't have to. We only need to write the code (**event handlers**) for events that are pertinent to our application; the WinForms classes themselves provide the rest of the code.

The creation process for windows applications is really a two-stage process. One part involves setting the properties of controls on forms, such as what text they contain, what color they are, how big they are, etc. The other part is defining the behavior of the controls and the event handlers for them.

There are many different types of forms that we might like to create. Other than simple forms, the most commonly used are **Single Document Interface** (SDI), **Multiple Document Interface** (MDI), and **dialogs**. Dialogs are the most simple and are often used for popping up messages that require simple acknowledgment, requesting small amounts of data, and reporting status. Often, dialogs will be **modal**, meaning that other windows making up the application they belong to are locked, and cannot be accessed until the dialog terminates. Non-modal dialogs are also possible, allowing the user to refer to information in other windows at the same time as dealing with the dialog.

SDI and MDI forms are used when applications work with multiple documents or files. SDI forms are capable of working with one document at a time, for example the simple Notepad Windows application that works with text documents. This doesn't always limit you to working on one document at a time, as many applications allow multiple instances to be open at the same time, each working with a separate document. These instances may even be linked behind the scenes, using the same business and data tier objects. MDI forms can work on many documents at the same time. Graphics applications are a good example of this, allowing many images to be worked on simultaneously. MDI applications function by containing child forms, which may be arranged in the main application form as the user sees fit. Typically, MDI applications have a <u>W</u>indow menu allowing the user to switch focus between documents, automatically arrange document windows, and so on.

In the next section we'll take a tour of the WinForms namespace, looking at the classes it contains before we start to use them in our code. We will see the controls that are provided for us for quick window application creation.

The WinForms Namespace

The `WinForms` namespace contains more than 300 entries. Because of this we can't hope to cover everything in one chapter, but we can look at the more commonly used items. Earlier on in the book we saw the WinForms class viewer. If we run this and type in the search string "WinForms", we will see a very long list – although to be fair this does include the `System.WinForms.ComponentModel`, `System.WinForms.ComponentModel.COM2Interop`, `System.WinForms.Design`, and `System.WinForms.PropertyGridInternal` namespaces, which we won't look at in detail here.

The entry for `System.WinForms.Form`, the class we used earlier, is also lengthy, as you can see by the size of the scroll bar on the right:

Again, this isn't the place to cover every method and parameter of every class in the namespace, so we'll just be looking at the common ones.

While we're on the subject of looking at namespaces, let's take a quick look at another tool supplied as one of the .NET samples: ClassView. When you unpack the samples, this ASP.NET application is found in the `Microsoft.Net\FrameworkSDK\Samples\ClsView` directory. Compile this, copy it to your web server, and fire it up in IE. You should see the following:

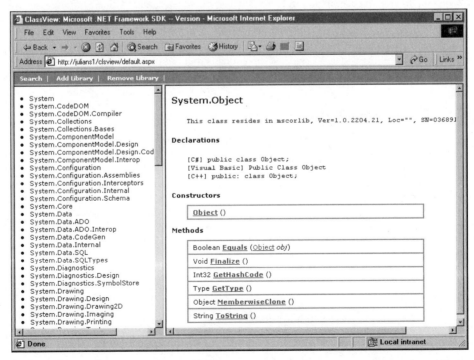

The pane on the left is a list of the .NET namespaces. Clicking on one of these expands its contents:

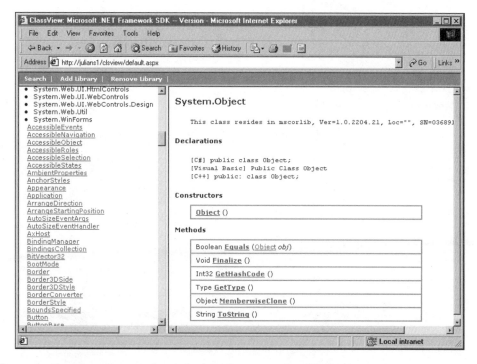

Clicking on a class then shows us the methods, properties, and fields for that class in the right hand pane:

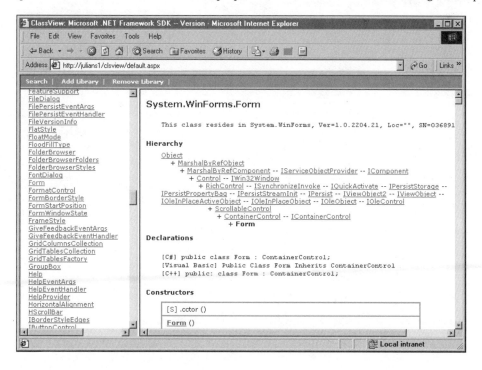

We can also follow the links in the right hand pane to find out further information about methods and types:

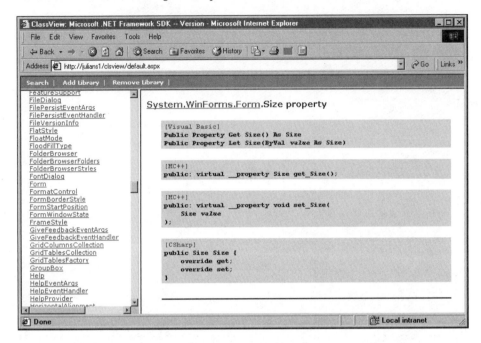

This is a useful quick reference tool when working with WinForms.

WinForms Controls

As we discussed earlier, controls are the main building block for windows applications. WinForms supplies the following control classes for us to use in our applications:

Button	CheckBox	CheckedListBox	ColorDialog
ComboBox	ContextMenu	DataGrid	DateTimePicker
DomainUpDown	FontDialog	GroupBox	HelpProvider
HScrollBar	ImageList	Label	LinkLabel
ListBox	ListView	MainMenu	MonthCalendar
NumericUpDown	OpenFileDialog	PageSetupDialog	Panel
PictureBox	PrintDialog	PrintPreview Control	PrintPreview Dialog
ProgressBar	PropertyGrid	RadioButton	RichTextBox
SaveFileDialog	Splitter	StatusBar	TabControl
TextBox	Timer	ToolBar	ToolTip
TrackBar	TrayIcon	TreeView	VScrollBar
ErrorProvider	DateTimeFormat	NumericFormat	

The names of many of these control classes are self-explanatory – such as `Button`, which is a standard Windows button – and many are basically the same as the standard VB controls. Others are more obscure, and many don't result in a visible object on the form. `SaveFileDialog`, for example, doesn't appear in the form that contains it, but allows you to call up a dialog box that contains all the functionality expected for browsing files and directories.

The best way to explain these controls is to use them, so they will be discussed as we do so throughout this chapter.

Creating WinForms Applications in VS.NET

As well as creating WinForms applications for command-line compilation, we can also create them through wizards and tools in the VS.NET IDE. This is definitely preferable and allows for much quicker development, as we will see.

Let's dive in and see this in action, explaining concepts as we go.

A Simple Application

To create a WinForms application using C# in VS.NET, we create a new project of type Visual C# Projects | Windows Application. Let's call this example `WFApp1`:

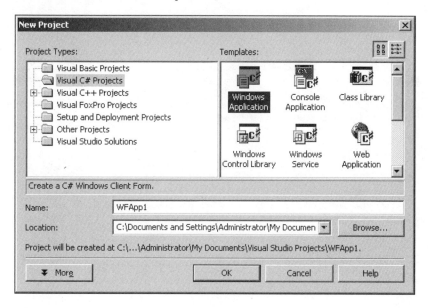

When the project has been created, we are presented with a design view of our form:

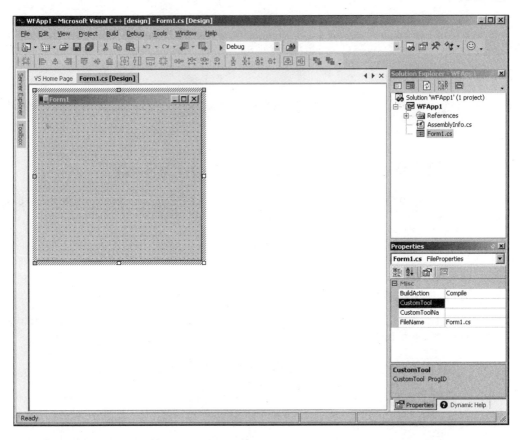

We can look at the code for this by right clicking on `Form1.cs` in the Solution Explorer window and selecting View Code. The code generated by default looks like this:

```
namespace WFApp1
{
using System;
using System.Drawing;
using System.Collections;
using System.ComponentModel;
using System.WinForms;
using System.Data;

/// <summary>
///     Summary description for Form1.
/// </summary>
public class Form1 : System.WinForms.Form
{
    /// <summary>
    ///     Required designer variable
    /// </summary>
    private System.ComponentModel.Container components;
```

```
    public Form1()
    {
       //
       // Required for Win Form Designer support
       //
       InitializeComponent();

       //
       // TODO: Add any constructor code after InitializeComponent call
       //
    }

    /// <summary>
    ///    Clean up any resources being used
    /// </summary>
    public override void Dispose()
    {
       base.Dispose();
       components.Dispose();
    }

    /// <summary>
    ///    Required method for Designer support - do not modify
    ///    the contents of this method with the code editor
    /// </summary>
    private void InitializeComponent()
    {
       this.components = new System.ComponentModel.Container();
       this.Size = new System.Drawing.Size(300,300);
    }
    /*
     * The main entry point for the application.
     *
     */
    public static void Main(string[] args)
    {
       Application.Run(new Form1());
    }
  }
}
```

There are a few additions when we compare this code with our earlier example, notably a few more namespaces, XML summary information, a new private member object, `components`, and an `InitializeComponent()` method, but otherwise the code is very similar to that which we saw earlier.

The additional `InitializeComponent()` method, as detailed in the code, allows you to use the WinForms designer test container to test your form, which we'll look at later in the chapter. Note also that the form initialization occurs here rather than in the constructor.

Adding Controls

The real power that VS.NET supplies is the ability to configure your form visually. Going back to the form display, if you hover your mouse pointer over the Toolbox pop-up toolbar, you'll see the following window:

217

This Toolbox window is essentially a palette of controls that we can place on our form, and will be familiar to those of you who have used, for example, Visual Basic. Let's try this out. Select the Button control and add it to your form by clicking on it (there are several options here – you can double click on the control, click once on the control then once on the form, or once on the control and drag an area on the form):

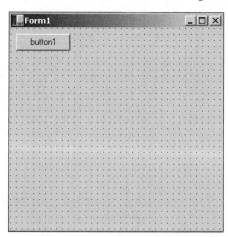

Now go back to the code for the form. You should find that some lines have been added:

```
public class Form1 : System.WinForms.Form
{
    /// <summary>
    ///     Required designer variable
    /// </summary>
    private System.ComponentModel.Container components;
    private System.WinForms.Button button1;
    ...
    private void InitializeComponent()
    {
        this.components = new System.ComponentModel.Container();
        this.button1 = new System.WinForms.Button();

        button1.Location = new System.Drawing.Point(8, 8);
        button1.Size = new System.Drawing.Size(75, 23);
        button1.TabIndex = 0;
        button1.Text = "button1";

        this.AutoScaleBaseSize = new System.Drawing.Size(5, 13);
        this.Text = "Form1";
        //@design this.TrayLargeIcon = true;
        //@design this.TrayHeight = 0;

        this.Controls.Add(button1);
    }
    ...
}
```

As you change the layout of your forms, the code required to generate them is kept up to date. This works the other way too; if you change the code then the design view will update to reflect the changes. You could, for example, remove all the code added above and end up with a buttonless form again. However, this isn't something you'll find yourself doing very much, as it's usually easier to use the form designer. Also, if you modify the code by hand you run the risk of entering invalid code, and will have to fiddle around before the form designer will allow you to make any more modifications.

As we've added a button, let's take a closer look at this particular control.

System.WinForms.Button

Like all controls, buttons are configurable via their properties. The easiest way to do this is via the Properties window in the VS.NET IDE. If you take a look at this, you'll see many self-explanatory properties, such as `BackColor` for the background color of the button, `Text` for the text to display on the button, `Location` for the position of the button on the form (expressed as a number of pixels across and down from the top left corner of the parent form), and so on. (Many of these properties are common to several controls, which makes life easier for us as new controls are easier to understand once we've used a few others.) The code added to the `InitializeComponent()` method simply sets the values for those properties that don't have default values, or where we don't want to use the default. If we change a property in the designer, the relevant code will be added to or modified in this method.

Let's make the button do something. To add the default event handler for a control we can just double-click on the control in the design view. Doing this for the button will add an event handler for clicking on the button, adding one line of code to `InitializeComponent()`:

```
        button1.Click += new System.EventHandler(this.button1_Click);
```

and one new method:

```
        protected void button1_Click(object sender, System.EventArgs e)
        {

        }
```

These lines are generated automatically, but it is up to you to fill in the code that is executed when the button is clicked, which will be contained in the currently empty button1_Click() method. The syntax of the method added is determined by the EventHandler delegate, and will be as shown above (more details on this later). Let's do something simple and change the text in the form title bar:

```
        protected void button1_Click(object sender, System.EventArgs e)
        {
            this.Text = "Form1 (button clicked)";
        }
```

If you run this code and click the button you should see the following:

Now we've added an event in this simple way, let's take a look at how we handle events in WinForms in more detail.

WinForms Event Handling

The Click field of the Button object allows us to register an event handler for the button control. We use the += operator to do this, and use the standard C# event handling syntax:

```
        button1.Click += new System.EventHandler(this.button1_Click);
```

This involves passing a System.EventHandler delegate object, which is initialized with the event handling method we want to use, in this case this.button1_Click(). The format of this method must have the following structure:

```
protected void button1_Click(object sender, System.EventArgs e)
```

All methods referred to by EventHandler objects use this form. They are protected void methods with the parameters as specified above.

The System.EventArgs object, e, contains any additional information that might be associated with the event. In the case of a button click event there is none.

The sender parameter contains the object that initiated the event, in this case the Button object. This can be useful if we use the same event handler for different controls. For example, we could add another button, button2, to our form and register it with the same event handler:

```
button2.Click += new System.EventHandler(this.button1_Click);
```

Alternatively, we could double click on the new button to add an event handler, remove the generated handler method, and modify the generated event handler registration. The method you use is up to you.

We could check to see which button was clicked by looking at sender:

```
protected void button1_Click(object sender, System.EventArgs e)
{
    if (sender == button1)
    {
        this.Text = "button1 clicked";
    }
    if (sender == button2)
    {
        this.Text = "button2 clicked";
    }
}
```

This code will result in the title bar text changing depending on which button was clicked.

All controls that have events use a similar syntax for registering event handlers, a field named according to the event. For example, list boxes have a SelectedIndexChanged field which also takes a System.EventHandler object specifying the method to handle the event.

The Form object also has a selection of events that can be handled. In fact, there are quite a lot of these! The easiest way to find them is to look at the **Events** list using the property viewer for your main form:

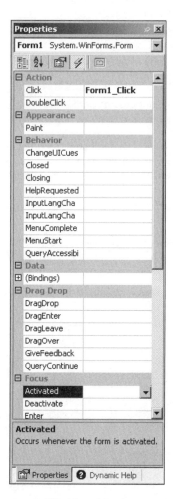

Making use of event handlers is a key part of building Windows applications, and this viewer can speed things up for us. We can use it to look at what events we can handle for each control, get a brief description of events we're unsure of, and even specify handlers by typing their names in here.

A More Advanced Application

Instead of stepping through all of the useful controls, methods, properties, events, etc. (which would, in all honesty, take up several lengthy chapters) let's look at a more advanced use of the `WinForms` namespace. By doing this we can point out the uses of a few more components and see where to look when we want to use others. This really is a namespace to play around with – there's a lot there, but it is often tricky to find!

The application we'll develop here is a Music Library SDI application, allowing you to create a list of music in your collection, where each entry consists of an artist, a title, and a format (such as CD). It will also be possible to save and load libraries.

Open a new project and call it **WFApp2**. The form layout is shown below, with each control named:

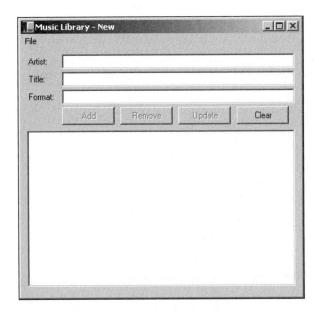

mainMenu1 contains a MenuItem called miFile, which in turn contains miNew, miOpen, miSave, miSeparator, and miQuit – all MenuItems. These can be added in the form designer by simply typing the relevant text into the spaces provided in the empty menu bar (although I took the additional step of renaming the objects created).

The two file dialogs, **openFileDialog1** and **saveFileDialog1**, are non-visual controls that encapsulate the functionality required to browse the file system and select files for opening or saving to. We'll use this to save and load music library files.

Let's quickly list the non-default properties for each of these controls, starting with the MenuItems:

MenuItem Name	Text
miFile	&File
miNew	&New
miOpen	&Open
miSave	&Save
miSeparator	-
miQuit	&Quit

The "&" character specifies that the character following it should be underlined, and used to speed selection via keyboard accelerators (by pressing Alt and the key corresponding with the underlined letter). Pressing Alt by itself will activate cause the relevant letter to be underlined in the display. Also, note that specifying the text "-" results in a horizontal bar dividing menu entries.

Next the TextBoxes:

TextBox Name	Text	Location	Size
txtArtist	""	56, 8	320, 20
txtTitle	""	56, 32	320, 20
txtFormat	""	56, 56	320, 20

The Buttons:

Button Name:	Text	Enabled	Location	Size
btnAdd	"Add"	False	56, 80	72, 24
btnRemove	"Remove"	False	136, 80	72, 24
btnUpdate	"Update"	False	216, 80	72, 24
btnClear	"Clear"	True	296, 80	72, 24

The Labels:

Label Name	Text	Location	Size
label1	"Artist:"	8, 12	48, 24
label2	"Title:"	8, 36	48, 24
label3	"Format:"	8, 60	48, 24

The ListBox:

ListBox Name	Location	Size
lstItems	8, 112	368, 212

And the file dialogs:

Dialog Name	Title	FileName	Filter
openFileDialog 1	"Open Music Library"	"*.mlib"	"Music Libraries[*.mlib]"
saveFileDialog 1	"Save Music Library"	"new.mli b"	"Music Libraries[*.mlib]"

Before we look at the code, let's discuss how the various controls will work.

The ListBox control will store a list of strings, which we'll add based on the content of the three TextBox controls. As all three entries are required for an item to be added to the list, the btnAdd button starts off disabled.

Once we have entries in the ListBox we will be able to select them. When we do this we'll copy the values into the three TextBoxes and enable the btnRemove button for removing items. If the content of the selected item is modified we'll also enable btnUpdate for changing the item.

btnClear will be enabled at all times and it lets us clear the contents of the three TextBox controls, and clear the selection in the ListBox.

The menu items allow us to clear the contents of the ListBox by selecting New, save and open files using Save and Load, and quit the application with Quit.

The first thing we'll add to the code is an event handler for the event that is raised when the content of the TextBox controls changes. Whenever this happens, we'll check to see if all the fields contain text. If they do, we'll enable the btnAdd button. If there is a selected item in the ListBox control and the fields change, we also know to enable btnUpdate. Finally, if any field is empty we'll disable btnUpdate and btnAdd.

First of all, let's register the event handlers. This requires the following three lines of code, which we should place in the form constructor (they'd work equally well in InitializeComponent(), but to be safe and avoid the designer removing them or placing them in odd positions we shouldn't add code like this there):

```
txtArtist.TextChanged += new System.EventHandler(this.DataChanged);
txtTitle.TextChanged += new System.EventHandler(this.DataChanged);
txtFormat.TextChanged += new System.EventHandler(this.DataChanged);
```

This registers DataChanged() for the TextChanged event for all three TextBox controls. The event handler code looks like this:

```
protected void DataChanged(object sender, System.EventArgs e)
{
    // Check to make sure that no TextBox fields are empty
    if ((txtArtist.Text != "") && (txtTitle.Text != "") &&
        (txtFormat.Text != ""))
    {
        if (btnAdd.Enabled == false)
        {
            // TextBoxes contain data, but Add button need enabling
            btnAdd.Enabled = true;
        }
        if ((btnUpdate.Enabled == false) && (lstItems.SelectedIndex != -1))
        {
            // TextBoxes contain modified data from existing record, so Update
            // button should be enabled
            btnUpdate.Enabled = true;
        }
    }
    else
    {
        if (btnAdd.Enabled == true)
        {
            // One or more TextBox is empty, so Add button needs disabling
            btnAdd.Enabled = false;
        }
        if (btnUpdate.Enabled == true)
```

```
        {
            // One or more TextBox is empty, so Add button needs disabling
            btnUpdate.Enabled = false;
        }
    }
}
```

We are using the `Button.Enabled` property to change the status of the buttons, and the `ListBox.SelectedIndex` property to see if an item is selected. A value of -1 reflects no selection, so that's what we check for.

Next, let's add the `OnClick` handler for `btnAdd`. To do this, we can either double click on the button or add the following code to the constructor:

```
btnAdd.Click += new System.EventHandler(this.btnAdd_Click);
```

And the following method:

```
protected void btnAdd_Click(object sender, System.EventArgs e)
{
    // Create entry string from TextBox contents
    string itmNew = new string(txtArtist.Text + ", " + txtTitle.Text + ", "
                        + txtFormat.Text);
    // Add new entry
    lstItems.Items.Add(itmNew);
    // Clear TextBoxes
    txtArtist.Text = "";
    txtTitle.Text = "";
    txtFormat.Text = "";
}
```

We create a new `string` object from the three `TextBox.Text` properties, separating them with commas, and add it to the `Items` collection of `lstItems`. While we're at it we clear the fields ready for the next item to be entered.

Once we have items in `lstItems` we will be able to select them, so let's add an event handler for the selection changed event of this control. We register the handler, `ItemChanged()` using:

```
lstItems.SelectedIndexChanged += new System.EventHandler(this.ItemChanged);
```

Then we add the method:

```
protected void ItemChanged(object sender, System.EventArgs e)
{
    // Check if an entry is selected
    if (lstItems.SelectedIndex != -1)
    {
        // Get data from entry
        string itmSelected = (string)lstItems.SelectedItem;
        char[] cSeparator = new char[] {','};
        string[] strFields = new string[] {};
        strFields = itmSelected.Split(cSeparator);
```

```
        // Place data in TextBoxes
        txtArtist.Text = strFields[0];
        txtTitle.Text = strFields[1].TrimStart(null);
        txtFormat.Text = strFields[2].TrimStart(null);

        // Enable Remove button and disable Update button
        btnRemove.Enabled = true;
        btnUpdate.Enabled = false;
    }
    else
    {
        Selection has been cleared, so clear TextBox fields
        txtArtist.Text = "";
        txtTitle.Text = "";
        txtFormat.Text = "";
        btnUpdate.Enabled = false;
        btnRemove.Enabled = false;
    }
}
```

If the selection is cleared and `lstItems.SelectedIndex` is -1, we clear the `TextBox` entries and disable `btnUpdate` and `btnRemove`. Otherwise, we copy the data into the three `TextBoxes` and enable the buttons. To get the data from the `string` object stored in the `ListBox` we use the `string.Split()` method, with `","` as a separator. This method returns a three-item array, each item being one of the three fields. We need to strip the white space from the beginning of the second and third fields, as some appears after the commas, which we can do using the `string.TrimStart()` method.

Note that this method stops us from including commas in any of our three fields, but other than that it works fine.

Now let's register our three other button event handlers:

```
        btnRemove.Click += new System.EventHandler(this.btnRemove_Click);
        btnUpdate.Click += new System.EventHandler(this.btnUpdate_Click);
        btnClear.Click += new System.EventHandler(this.btnClear_Click);
```

`btnRemove` just needs to call the `Remove()` method on the `Items` collection of the `ListBox`, passing it the index of the item to remove:

```
    protected void btnRemove_Click(object sender, System.EventArgs e)
    {
        // Remove selected entry
        lstItems.Items.Remove(lstItems.SelectedIndex);
        lstItems.SelectedIndex = -1;
    }
```

Once the item is removed we can clear the selection and `TextBox` fields by setting `lstItems.SelectedIndex` to -1.

`btnUpdate` replaces the `string` stored for the currently selected item in the list with a new one:

```
protected void btnUpdate_Click(object sender, System.EventArgs e)
{
    // Update selected entry with current TextBox contents
    lstItems.Items[lstItems.SelectedIndex] = new string(txtArtist.Text + ", "
        + txtTitle.Text + ", " + txtFormat.Text);
}
```

The last button, `btnClear`, can be used to clear the selection by simply setting the selected item index to -1 (which will also clear the three text fields):

```
protected void btnClear_Click(object sender, System.EventArgs e)
{
    // Clear selection and empty TextBox fields
    lstItems.SelectedIndex = -1;
}
```

We've now added everything we need for basic functionality. We can add items, remove them, and update them.

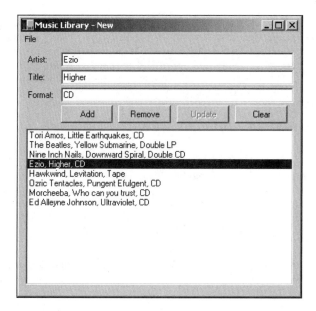

The only thing we can't do yet is save and load data. To do that we need to make use of our save and load dialogs, accessed through the File menu. While we're at it, we might as well register event handlers for all the menu items:

```
miNew.Click += new System.EventHandler(this.miNew_Click);
miOpen.Click += new System.EventHandler(this.miOpen_Click);
miSave.Click += new System.EventHandler(this.miSave_Click);
miQuit.Click += new System.EventHandler(this.miQuit_Click);
```

Let's quickly add the handlers for Quit and New:

```
protected void miQuit_Click(object sender, System.EventArgs e)
{
   // Close application
   this.Close();
}
protected void miNew_Click(object sender, System.EventArgs e)
{
   // Discard all data and begin new library
   lstItems.Items.Clear();
   lstItems.SelectedIndex = -1;
   this.Text = "Music Library - New";
}
```

`this.Close()` simply closes the application and `Items.Clear()` removes all items from the `ListBox`. We set the `this.Text` property to reflect a new document – we'll use this to display the filename of documents when we've implemented saving and loading.

The event handlers for the <u>O</u>pen and <u>S</u>ave menu items are surprisingly simple – all they need to do is call the `ShowDialog()` method on the two file dialog controls:

```
protected void miOpen_Click(object sender, System.EventArgs e)
{
   // Show dialog for opening files
   openFileDialog1.ShowDialog();
}
protected void miSave_Click(object sender, System.EventArgs e)
{
   // Show dialog for saving files
   saveFileDialog1.ShowDialog();
}
```

Note that we've already modified these file dialogs slightly by changing their properties earlier on. For example, we've specified the text to display in the title bars with the `Title` property.

Once this method is called, the dialog appears and allows the user to select a file. If a valid file is chosen and the **OK** button on the dialog is clicked, they raise an event. By adding event handlers for the events generated by the two dialogs, we know when to save and load data, and what filenames to use. Let's register handlers for the two events:

```
openFileDialog1.FileOk +=
   new System.ComponentModel.CancelEventHandler(this.openFileDialog1_FileOk);
saveFileDialog1.FileOk +=
   new System.ComponentModel.CancelEventHandler(this.saveFileDialog1_FileOk);
```

We'll start by saving data. We saw how to perform file IO earlier in the book. Here we'll just use simple text files:

```
protected void saveFileDialog1_FileOk(object sender,
                                      System.ComponentModel.CancelEventArgs e)
{
   // Create output stream to new file
   StreamWriter strmOutput = new StreamWriter(saveFileDialog1.FileName, false);
```

```
        // Cycle through entries
        for(int intItem = 0; intItem < lstItems.Items.Count; intItem++)
        {
            // Output each entry
            strmOutput.WriteLine(lstItems.Items[intItem]);
        }
        // Close file
        strmOutput.Close();
        // Update title bar
        this.Text = "Music Library - " + saveFileDialog1.FileName;
    }
```

Here we cycle through each string in the `ListBox` and use the `WriteLine()` method to save them to the file specified by `saveFileDialog1.FileName`. We also use this property to label the menu bar of the main form once the file is saved.

In order for the IO code to work we also need to add the following line of code to the top of our form:

```
using System.IO;
```

The code for opening lines is also quite simple:

```
    protected void openFileDialog1_FileOk(object sender,
                                    System.ComponentModel.CancelEventArgs e)
    {
        // Clear existing entries
        lstItems.Items.Clear();
        // Open input stream on file
        StreamReader strmInput = new StreamReader(openFileDialog1.FileName);
        string strItem;
        // Cycle through entries in data file
        do
        {
            strItem = strmInput.ReadLine();
            if ((strItem != null) && (strItem != ""))
            {
                // Add non-empty entry to ListBox
                lstItems.Items.Add(strItem);
            }
        }
        while (strItem != null);
        // Close file
        strmInput.Close();
        // Initialize display
        lstItems.Invalidate();
        lstItems.SelectedIndex = -1;
        this.Text = "Music Library - " + openFileDialog1.FileName;
        // Prepare default filename in save file dialog
        saveFileDialog1.FileName = openFileDialog1.FileName;
    }
```

We start by clearing any items in memory. Then we load the strings into `lstItems.Items`. We also perform some cursory checking on the data loaded. If any extra end-of-line characters occur, we could end up with empty strings, so we discard these (if an empty line is encountered then `ReadLine()` will return an empty string, so we just check for " ").

Once the data is loaded, we force the `ListBox` to redraw itself by **invalidating** it. This will result in the new data being displayed. We also make sure no item is selected, which has the added benefit of clearing the `TextBox` fields. We then update the title bar text and set the default filename in the save file dialog.

And that's all there is to it. Of course, there's a whole lot more we could add, even to this simple application. We could implement sorting on the fields, printing, a graphical toolbar, cut and paste functionality, saving as compressed data, and making the application an MDI one allowing editing of multiple libraries. All of this is possible with the WinForms namespace but, sadly, we can't fit everything in here.

One thing you might note here is the lack of error handling. This wouldn't be tricky to do, but for this example it made things clearer to stick to the essentials.

Deploying Windows Applications

Once we have created and tested our applications, the next stage is to get them to users. The .NET Framework simplifies things a bit for us here, as we don't have to worry about registering weird components on unknown systems – component assemblies are self-describing and no registry information is required. However, it would still not be an ideal solution to ask your users to copy files to their correct location, creating appropriate directories and adding shortcuts themselves.

Instead, VS.NET provides several **Setup and Deployment Projects**. These make it possible to assemble your program files, assemblies, and resources in a consistent way, and create an executable file to perform all the installation tasks you require.

Setup and Deployment Projects

The different types of projects are shown in the screenshot below:

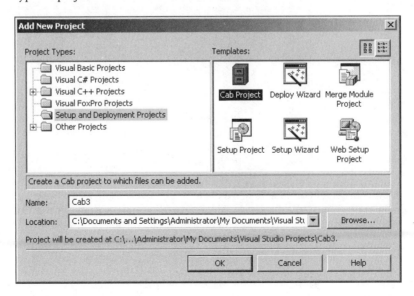

Since we are considering Windows applications here we'll ignore the Web Setup project. The other options are as follows:

- ❑ **CAB Project** – allows the creation of a compressed CAB archive file containing multiple smaller files. These can be used with the other types of project as resources if necessary.

- ❑ **Setup Project** – creates a setup file capable of automatically installing files and resources on target computers.

- ❑ **Merge Module Project** – when multiple projects use common files, it is often useful to make intermediate merge modules that can then be integrated into other setup and deployment projects.

- ❑ **Setup Wizard** – creates one of these other types of project with the aid of a wizard.

All of these can be added to the solution containing the project you want to deploy, allowing them to automatically extract relevant files.

Let's look at each of these in turn, creating setup projects for the WFApp2 Music Library project we created earlier in this chapter.

CAB Projects

If you add a CAB project to the solution containing WFApp2, let's say WFApp2CAB, you should see the following in the Solution Explorer window:

We can add files which will be stored in the CAB file to be generated using Add | Files... and Add | Project Output... from the context menu for this object. The first of these options allows us to add any file we like; the second is more interesting. Selecting this menu item brings up the following window:

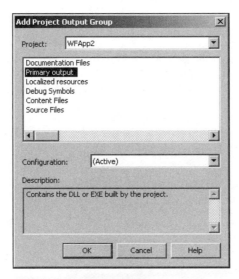

Here we can select files to be added to the CAB project from any of the other projects in the solution. The main list box here allows us to select:

❑ **Primary Executable Output** – the target executable from the selected project. For `WFApp2` this is `WFApp2.exe`.

❑ **Satellite Resource Files** – and additional resources required by the project, such as assemblies containing objects used by the executable.

❑ **Content Files** – additional external data sources.

❑ **Source Files** – the raw source code files that make up the project.

The configuration drop-down box allows us to select the build type for the files to add, such as Debug and Release. (Active) means to use whatever is currently selected in the project.

If we select the Primary Executable Output option and click OK, the Solution Explorer will reflect these changes:

The properties of this object allow us to further specify which files to exclude if multiple ones are made by the project, or which additional outputs to include.

Compiling the CAB project now will result in `WFApp2CAB.cab` being created. There are many tools that we can use to view the created contents of this file (WinZip, for example), which will contain both `WFApp2.exe` and a descriptive file, `WFApp2CAB.osd`. If we look at this descriptive file we find an XML document:

```
<?XML version="1.0" ENCODING='UTF-8'?>
<!DOCTYPE SOFTPKG SYSTEM "http://www.microsoft.com/standards/osd/osd.dtd">
<?XML::namespace href="http://www.microsoft.com/standards/osd/msicd.dtd"
as="MSICD"?>
<SOFTPKG NAME="WFApp2CAB" VERSION="1,0,0,0">
    <TITLE> WFApp2CAB </TITLE>
    <MSICD::NATIVECODE>
        <CODE NAME="WFApp2">
            <IMPLEMENTATION>
                <CODEBASE FILENAME="WFApp2.exe">
                </CODEBASE>
            </IMPLEMENTATION>
        </CODE>
    </MSICD::NATIVECODE>
</SOFTPKG>
```

This describes how the files in the CAB file fit in to the application for which they are intended. Other deployment projects can then make use of this information.

Setup Projects

Setup Projects are the richest form of deployment project, allowing many options all encapsulated in an MSI-type installation file.

Again, let's use the `WFApp2` project to demonstrate this, by adding a new deployment project to the solution called `WFApp2Setup`:

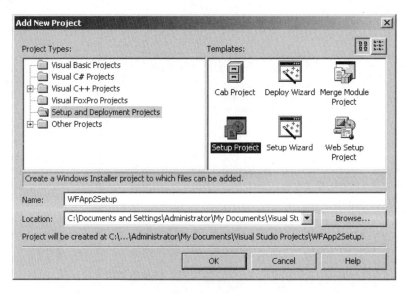

And here it is in Solution Explorer:

Again, we can use the context menu to add project output and files to this project, but this time we have two more options: Add | Merge Module... and Add | Component.... Merge modules, as we will discuss in more detail below, are really cut down versions of Setup Projects, creating files that can make up part of an installation, usually using files that are common to several other projects. We can ensure that our main project will work correctly by including vital components that it uses.

Let's add the output file by selecting Add|Project Output|Primary Output via the WFApp2Setup context menu, and also a demo music library file. If you haven't already created one, just make a couple of dummy entries using the Music Library application, save them as Example.mlib, and add this file using the context menu:

The configuration of the setup procedures can now be carried out. We can set various properties for the Setup Project, which we'll look at in context as we come to them. We can also specify information through the various pages accessible through the View context menu of the project. This contains the following menu items:

❑ **File System** – specifies the locations of installed files, which includes adding icons to the desktop and start menu, custom items in the Send To sub-menu, and more.

❑ **Registry** – specifies any registry entries that may be necessary.

❑ **File Types** – allows custom file types to be added to the system.

❑ **User Interface** – customizes the dialogs presented to the user during installation.

❑ **Custom Actions** – allows additional custom steps such as running specified EXE files during installation.

❑ **Launch Conditions** – conditions to check prior to installation, such as testing for the existence of dependent files, etc.

Let's look at the more important aspects of the pages that these menu options bring up, starting with the File System page. We won't look at the Custom Actions and Launch Conditions pages as these options are fairly advanced.

File System

Specifying install locations is performed through this page, which is a two-pane view with a directory tree on the left and a file view on the right:

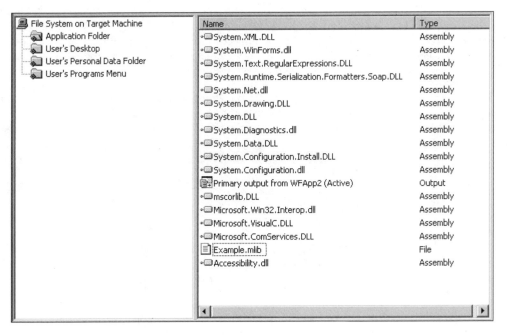

The files we've added so far have automatically been added to the Application Folder. This folder will be where the application runs from. If we select this folder we can look at its properties, the most important being `DefaultLocation`. By default, this will be `[ProgramFilesFolder]\[Manufacturer]\[ProductName]`. The first section of this specifies that files should be stored in the Program Files folder on the target system. The other two sections are properties of the project that we can modify.

The User's Desktop folder can be used to place a shortcut or other files on the desktop of the target machine. We can create a shortcut to our executable file by right clicking on it in the file pane, selecting the Create shortcut option, and dragging the created file to this folder. Similarly, we can place a shortcut in the Programs submenu of the Start menu by placing a shortcut file in the User's Programs Menu folder.

The User's Personal Data Folder can be used to place items in the My Documents folder of the installing user.

For this project, it makes sense to place a shortcut called Music Library on the desktop, an identical shortcut in a Music Library submenu of the Programs folder, and to move the Example.mlib file into a My Music Libraries subfolder of the My Documents folder:

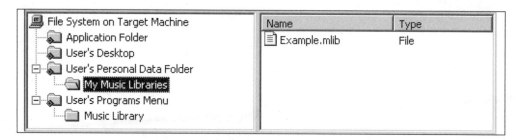

We can create new folders and add additional files using the context menu. If we try to add a folder from the root File System folder, we can add extra special folders:

Here we can specify install locations in many important places, such as the System folder, and so on.

We could also insert CAB files into the structure if our application was set up to make use of them.

Registry

This page allows us to add registry entries. It uses a similar view to the File System page, and works in much the same way. Note also that it will, by default, supply a typical destination for some keys, based on the `Manufacturer` property of the project:

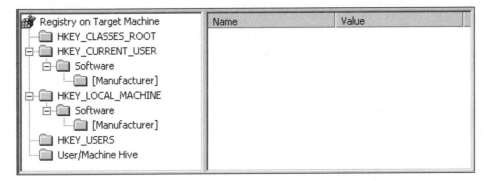

File Types

This page allows us to set up application specific file types to register on the target computer. The following screenshot shows one I've added for this project, a `.mlib` type for Music Library files:

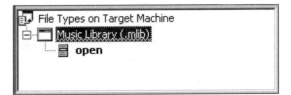

This type will need to be set up on the development machine to prevent VS.NET complaining.

User Interface

This page allows us to customize every stage of the install process. At its simplest level, this might involve changing the text and graphics to be used on each dialog. It is also possible to get more complex and import your own dialogs built from scratch.

The view of dialogs takes the form of a tree divided up into sections representing the stages of the installation process:

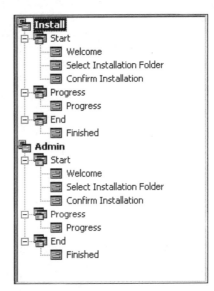

There is also a section for administration (the dialogs in the Admin branch above), which is needed if the user runs the setup file when the application is already installed. This will include uninstalling and repairing installation options.

Building the Project

When all options have been configured, we can build the project. This will result in a single file containing all the files in the project and specifying all the installation options. This file is ready to distribute.

Merge Module Projects

The next type of project we'll consider is a Merge Module Project. These are really cut down versions of setup projects and, as such, there isn't much to add to the description above. They are used when many projects have similar installations with common files. A single Merge Module can be used by multiple Setup projects, speeding delivery of applications.As an example, it would be possible to add a custom library of objects that you have created here. If you do this, you can add Merge Module files to individual Setup projects.

Setup Wizard

The pages of this wizard allow us to speed the construction of the other setup and deployment projects by initializing them appropriately. It also allows us to configure setting up applications on remote machines, over the Internet or an intranet. Basically, it allows you to automate common steps, such as specifying the output files to add from a project, additional files, and so on.

Summary

In this chapter we talked first about windows applications in the abstract and introduced important terminology, so as to make our aims clearer. We then moved through a substantial part of the content of the WinForms namespace, and saw how we can use it to construct Windows applications. As this is such a large library, it is impossible to cover everything in one chapter, so a fairly large example was used to show some possibilities.

Along the way we've taken a look at how we can use VS.NET to create WinForms applications, using many of the tools that it supplies through its interface to speed things up. The links between form editing and resultant code make this a particularly attractive option.

As well as covering Windows application development, we've also looked at ways to get the finished application to the user without requiring them to copy many files across manually. VS.NET provides tools to create setup and deployment projects with ease.

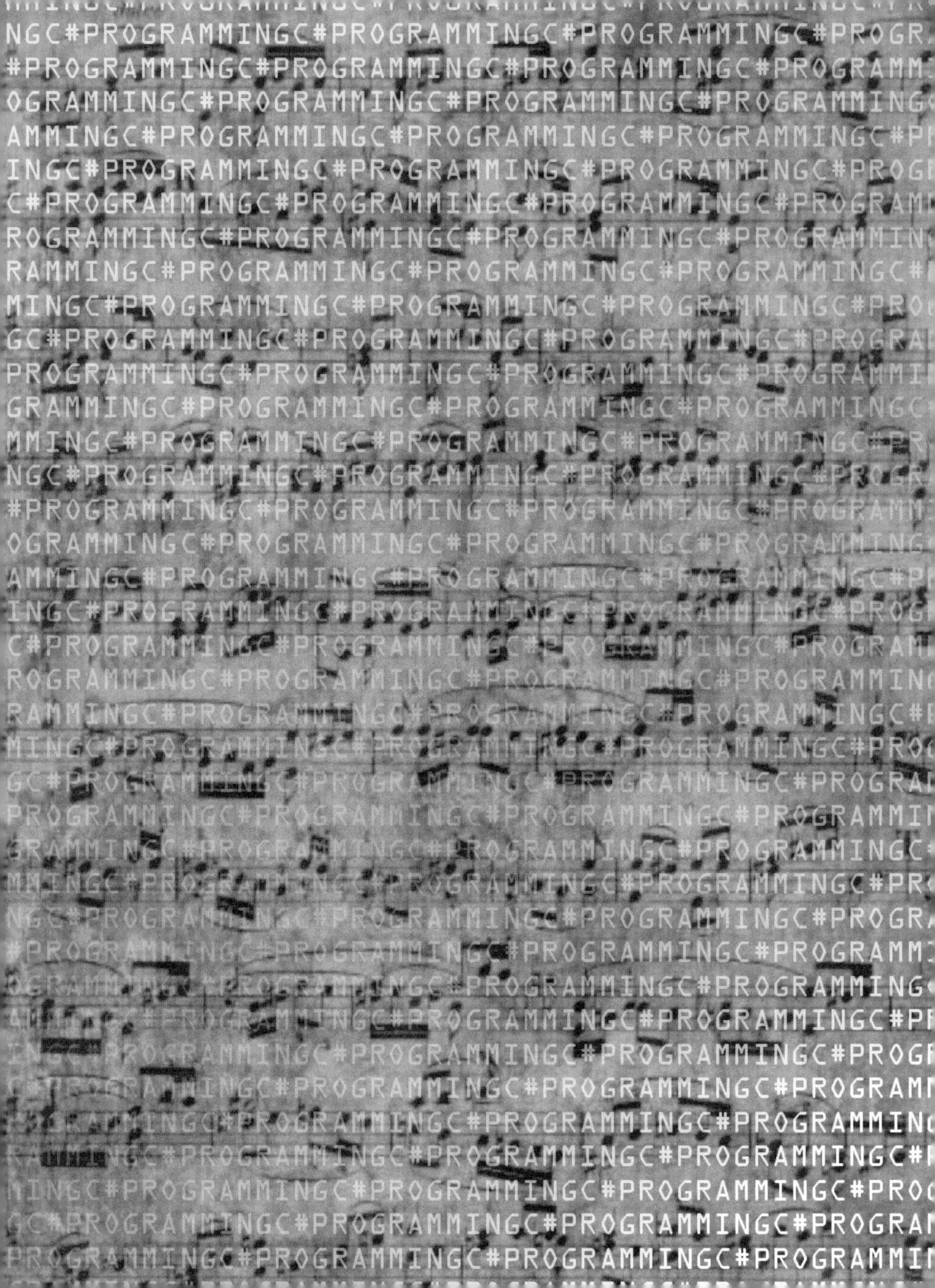
NGC#PROGRAMMINGC#PROGRAMMINGC#PROGRAMMINGC#PROGR
#PROGRAMMINGC#PROGRAMMINGC#PROGRAMMINGC#PROGRAMM
OGRAMMINGC#PROGRAMMINGC#PROGRAMMINGC#PROGRAMMING
AMMINGC#PROGRAMMINGC#PROGRAMMINGC#PROGRAMMINGC#P
INGC#PROGRAMMINGC#PROGRAMMINGC#PROGRAMMINGC#PROG
C#PROGRAMMINGC#PROGRAMMINGC#PROGRAMMINGC#PROGRAM
ROGRAMMINGC#PROGRAMMINGC#PROGRAMMINGC#PROGRAMMIN
RAMMINGC#PROGRAMMINGC#PROGRAMMINGC#PROGRAMMINGC#
MINGC#PROGRAMMINGC#PROGRAMMINGC#PROGRAMMINGC#PRO
GC#PROGRAMMINGC#PROGRAMMINGC#PROGRAMMINGC#PROGRA
PROGRAMMINGC#PROGRAMMINGC#PROGRAMMINGC#PROGRAMMI
GRAMMINGC#PROGRAMMINGC#PROGRAMMINGC#PROGRAMMINGC
MMINGC#PROGRAMMINGC#PROGRAMMINGC#PROGRAMMINGC#PR
NGC#PROGRAMMINGC#PROGRAMMINGC#PROGRAMMINGC#PROGR
#PROGRAMMINGC#PROGRAMMINGC#PROGRAMMINGC#PROGRAMM
OGRAMMINGC#PROGRAMMINGC#PROGRAMMINGC#PROGRAMMING
AMMINGC#PROGRAMMINGC#PROGRAMMINGC#PROGRAMMINGC#P
INGC#PROGRAMMINGC#PROGRAMMINGC#PROGRAMMINGC#PROG
C#PROGRAMMINGC#PROGRAMMINGC#PROGRAMMINGC#PROGRAM
ROGRAMMINGC#PROGRAMMINGC#PROGRAMMINGC#PROGRAMMIN
RAMMINGC#PROGRAMMINGC#PROGRAMMINGC#PROGRAMMINGC#
MINGC#PROGRAMMINGC#PROGRAMMINGC#PROGRAMMINGC#PRO
GC#PROGRAMMINGC#PROGRAMMINGC#PROGRAMMINGC#PROGRA
PROGRAMMINGC#PROGRAMMINGC#PROGRAMMINGC#PROGRAMMI
GRAMMINGC#PROGRAMMINGC#PROGRAMMINGC#PROGRAMMINGC
MMINGC#PROGRAMMINGC#PROGRAMMINGC#PROGRAMMINGC#PR
NGC#PROGRAMMINGC#PROGRAMMINGC#PROGRAMMINGC#PROGRA
#PROGRAMMINGC#PROGRAMMINGC#PROGRAMMINGC#PROGRAMMI
OGRAMMINGC#PROGRAMMINGC#PROGRAMMINGC#PROGRAMMING
AMMINGC#PROGRAMMINGC#PROGRAMMINGC#PROGRAMMINGC#P
INGC#PROGRAMMINGC#PROGRAMMINGC#PROGRAMMINGC#PROG
C#PROGRAMMINGC#PROGRAMMINGC#PROGRAMMINGC#PROGRAM
ROGRAMMINGC#PROGRAMMINGC#PROGRAMMINGC#PROGRAMMIN
RAMMINGC#PROGRAMMINGC#PROGRAMMINGC#PROGRAMMINGC#
MINGC#PROGRAMMINGC#PROGRAMMINGC#PROGRAMMINGC#PROG
GC#PROGRAMMINGC#PROGRAMMINGC#PROGRAMMINGC#PROGRA
PROGRAMMINGC#PROGRAMMINGC#PROGRAMMINGC#PROGRAMMI

9

ADO.NET

ADO.NET (ActiveX Data Objects .NET) is the set of classes that are used to access data sources within the .NET platform. The name ADO.NET implies that it is an evolution of the previous object model available for this purpose, ADO, but ADO.NET is more in the nature of a revolution. ADO.NET brings a completely new and improved object model, which is heavily based on using XML as the main format for transmitting data, and also makes it very easy to work with disconnected data. Compared to ADO, ADO.NET promises greater ease of programming, higher performance, improved scalability, less dependence on the peculiarities of each data source, and greater ability to interact with other platforms.

In this chapter we're going to show you how to use ADO.NET to access data in various data sources. We'll start off by providing an overview of the object model in ADO.NET and how this leads to the benefits just mentioned. We'll move on to look in more detail at the object you'll be using the most, the **DataSet** and **DataReader** objects, and at the **managed providers** which actually connect to the data sources, before presenting a number of samples that show how you can perform different tasks in ADO.NET.

How ADO.NET Works: The Object Model

ADO.NET can be schematically represented by this diagram:

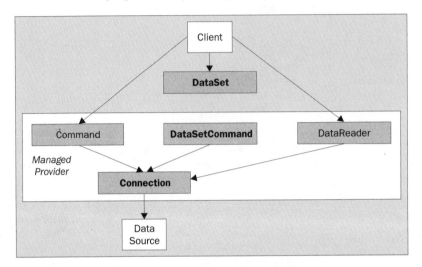

In this diagram the shaded boxes represent those objects that are a part of ADO.NET. Bold text indicates the most common way of getting data from the data source via the connection object, while the `Command` and `DataReader` objects represent alternative routes to the `connection` object.

If you've used ADO before, you'll know that the main object in ADO that allowed you to examine data was the `Recordset`. The `Recordset` was essentially a table of data – a set of rows and columns that you could move through. Although it was possible to create disconnected recordsets, ADO was designed more around recordsets that were connected – in other words, they would be in contact with the database, the connection being made via a `Connection` object. You could also issue commands to the database using a `Command` object.

With ADO.NET that has all changed. The fundamental object that holds data with ADO.NET is the **DataSet**. This is an instance of the .NET class `System.Data.DataSet`, and represents an in-memory copy of whatever part of the database you are interested in. It can even represent an entire database. It's not just a single table but rather a set of tables, along with data about the table structure – such as primary keys – and it contains all the relations between tables. The `DataSet` contains within itself a rich object model that allows access to the tables, rows, columns, relations embedded within it. And the emphasis is that the `DataSet` is a *disconnected* copy of the database, or part database. In working with data you will normally instantiate a `DataSet`, populate it from the database, then work on the `DataSet`. When you are ready to send your changes back to the data source, you do that in one go. The `DataSet` is quite intelligent; it is able, for example, to remember its previous state and make a note of any changes you have made to it and only those changes are sent to the database.

> *If you do need connected database access, and would prefer not to be caching large amounts of data, then there is an alternative object available, the `DataReader`, designed for sequential access, which we'll cover later in the chapter.*

With ADO, the `Recordset` would be able to talk to the database via the other ADO objects, whereas in ADO.NET the `DataSet` is an independent entity – a container that holds some data, and is not designed to talk to any data source. The role of communicating with the data source is played by **managed providers**. Each managed provider can be thought of as a set of objects that mediate between the `DataSet` and a data source. These objects internally take care of all the details of communication with a given data source, which means that the `DataSet` doesn't need to know anything about any data source – which in turn means it's easier to learn how to code up using the `DataSet` because there are no dependencies on the data source.

Each managed provider supplies its own set of objects for communicating with its data source – which might at first seem like a move away from the principle of universal data access. But it's not – it's more a move back towards the old idea of inheritance, in which a number of specialized objects that derive from the same abstract base class provide their own implementations of the same methods. The abstract base classes from which the main managed provider objects are derived from are:

- ❑ `System.Data.Internal.DataSetCommand`: Transfers data between the `DataSet` and data source. This object works at a very high level, able, for example, to populate the `DataSet` with complete tables in one go.

- ❑ `System.Data.Internal.DBConnection`: Similar to the `Connection` object in ADO, this maintains a connection with a data source

- ❑ `System.Data.Internal.DBCommand`: Again similar to the `Command` object in ADO, this allows you to send a command (for example SQL or a stored procedure) to a database.

- ❑ `System.Data.Internal.DBDataReader`: This object provides an alternative mechanism to the `DataSet` for reading data. It simply moves sequentially through records, one record at a time, in a similar manner to a `Recordset` of ADO with a forward-only, read-only cursor (sometimes known as the firehose cursor). It's available in case you do need that kind of access, since the `DataSet`, while being more scaleable in terms of database connections, can place high demands on bandwidth between the machine that runs your ADO.NET code and the database server.

And the idea is that although the object you call up will depend on which managed provider you are using (for example, `System.Data.SQL.SQLDataSetCommand` for the SQL provider, `System.Data.ADO.ADODataSetCommand` for the ADO provider) the methods of these two objects are the same. They effectively have the same interface, but different implementations.

The `DataSetCommand` objects automatically use both the appropriate connection and command objects internally to communicate with the data source, so you don't normally need to instantiate those explicitly, though you can do so if you wish.

Benefits of ADO.NET

We've seen in overall terms what the object model of ADO.NET is. It does have a different approach to data access from ADO, and we should stress that ADO is still a valid solution for data access. If you prefer to use connected recordsets you may find that ADO is more appropriate than ADO.NET. WIth that proviso, let's now have a look at why this model is so good, and what its benefits are.

Scalability

If you use the `DataSet` object rather than the `DataReader`, then ADO.NET is based on disconnected data access. This means that it only uses database connections for a short time. On many systems, the number of database connections is one of the biggest bottlenecks in terms of making a system scaleable, so for those systems built on ADO.NET are intrinsically highly scaleable. Obviously this won't be the case if the limiting factor on your system is bandwidth between the database server and the machine running the ADO.NET code, or the memory requirements on that machine.

Data Source Independence

With ADO, because the `Recordset` was intimately bound with the data source, the capabilities of the data source would impinge on the capabilities of the recordset in numerous different ways. Although in theory, ADO gave a way of accessing data that was independent of the data source, in practice you always needed a detailed knowledge of the capabilities of the data source if you wanted to be able to take full advantage of many of the features of the `Recordset`. With ADO.NET, the `DataSet` really *is* independent of the data source, which in theory should mean that if you swap data sources, you don't have as much learning to do to be able to use the new data source. The only change to your code will be that you'll instantiate objects from the managed provider you now wish to use, and change the connection string. This type of code modification, in which an instance of one class is replaced by an instance of a related class is something that will be very familiar to C++ programmers, but if you're moving to C# from VB you might find the concept a bit strange at first, since up to now VB hasn't used classes in that way. Be assured though, it is simpler than it sounds.

Interoperability

Because ADO.NET uses XML as its standard data transmission format, the software with which it is communicating the data does not need to be an ADO.NET component – or even based on the Windows platform. All that is required is that it is able to understand XML. And since XML is such a widely accepted standard, this means that your ADO.NET components can easily work with non-COM-aware or .NET-aware software on other platforms. Although later versions of ADO did also have support for XML, it was limited, and it was based on a rather clumsy schema that was designed specifically for recordsets rather than for general data transmission.

Strongly Typed Fields

In ADO the standard data type was the `Variant`. It had to be because that was the only data type scripting languages understood. But it meant not only that more memory was taken up storing the `Variants` but that the IntelliSense features of the various developer environments couldn't assist you with type information and the compiler couldn't pick up type mismatches, processing `Variants` was slower, and their use often encouraged sloppy programming techniques. With the .NET platform, that restriction is gone, and many ADO.NET objects are all strongly typed (although there are still method calls that use the generic `System.Object`).

Performance

Because ADO relied on COM marshalling for the transmission of data, a lot of processing time went into converting data between the types recognized in the database and the types that could be marshaled with COM. That's no longer really the case since transmission now occurs via XML.

Once more ADO.NET managed providers have been written, there will also be a separate performance benefit from the fact that code will no longer wrap around the native OLE DB providers, as was the case for ADO.

Firewalls

Because ADO.NET transmits data using XML, the data will be able to pass through most firewalls. Firewalls were a problem with ADO since they are most commonly configured to reject COM marshalling packets, which meant that ADO data couldn't get through them.

Now we've seen what advantages there are to ADO.NET, we'll go on to look at the object model inside the `DataSet` in more detail.

The DataSet

In this section we'll have a closer look at the `DataSet` and the hierarchy of objects contained by it. The overall architecture looks like this:

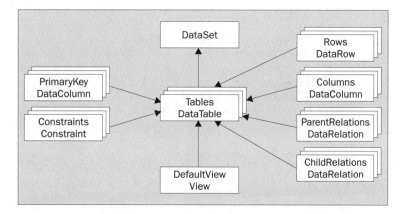

In this diagram, the top line in each box gives the name of the property that gives access to those objects, the second line names the class of that object – for example the `Rows` property of the `DataTable` object gives access to the collection of rows, with each row in the collection represented by an instance of the class `DataRow`. All classes in this diagram are in the `System.Data` namespace.

The objects are:

Class	Purpose
DataSet	Contains the entire set of data, possibly with multiple tables or even an entire database
DataTable	Contains the data for one table
DataRow	Contains all the values for one row of a table
DataColumn	Contains data about a column in a table – e.g. the name of the column, data type.
DataRelation	Contains details of a relationship between two columns
DataSetView	Details of a view of the table
Constraint	Details of a constraint that affects the values in a table

From this you should be able to see that the `DataSet` can essentially contain not only the data itself but all the information about the structure of a database needed to interpret and manipulate that data – and all arranged in a simple hierarchical object model.

We'll now have a look at the managed providers that are currently available, and then we'll be ready to go on to coding some examples.

The Managed Providers

In pre-.NET days, ADO was always to a large extent a wrapper around the (more complex) OLE DB objects. This meant that when you connected to a data source using ADO, it was actually OLE DB that was doing the work behind the scenes. By contrast, the ADO.NET objects by and large do not wrap around any other API. However we'll see that OLE DB still has a role to play for the time being, essentially for continuity purposes.

As we've mentioned earlier, a managed provider is a set of ADO.NET objects designed to allow you to connect to a particular data source. The idea is that between them they provide a universal mechanism to access any data source for which an ADO.NET provider exists. This works since all the objects expose the same base methods and properties, hiding the particular API needed to talk to a given source as well as any idiosyncrasies of that source. All you need to do is know which managed provider to call up. (Note however that if you wish you could write a managed provider that exposes additional methods and properties as well as the standard ones, but then clients would need to know about your provider in order to be able to use them).

At the present time there are two managed providers:

- ❑   The **SQL managed provider**, which connects to SQL Server version 7 onwards.

- ❑   The **ADO managed provider**, which connects to OLE DB objects.

If you use the SQL provider, you will use the `SQLDataSetCommand`, `SQLConnection`, `SQLCommand` and `SQLDataReader` objects, all from the `System.Data.SQL` namespace. Correspondingly for the ADO provider, you will call up the `ADODataSetCommand`, `ADOConnection`, `ADOCommand` and `ADODataReader` objects, all from the `System.Data.ADO` namespace.

You might be wondering what the ADO provider is there for. Well it's to solve this problem: Managed providers are not trivial to write, and as it's still very early days for ADO.NET, there aren't that many of them around yet – two to be precise. The situation is actually fairly similar to the early days of OLE DB, when there weren't too many OLE DB providers that had yet been written. At that time the solution Microsoft found was to write an OLE DB provider for ODBC, the data access technology that OLE DB was replacing. At a stroke this meant that you could use OLE DB to talk to any data source for which there was an ODBC provider. There was a slight overhead in having to go through two providers, but it meant people could start writing OLE DB/ADO clients and take advantage of all the new features of this new technology straight away. Then over time the more efficient native OLE DB providers started to appear.

Well the problem is similar and the solution Microsoft has gone for is the same. Microsoft has written a provider that lets you access any data source for which an OLE DB provider exists, which means an awful lot of data sources: Access, Oracle, Active Directory and LDAP directories, SQL Server 6.5, though for SQL Server 7 and 2000 it's more efficient to use the SQL Managed Provider.

We'll demonstrate both of these providers in the code samples in this chapter, though we'll mostly focus on the SQL provider.

ADO.NET Samples

We are now ready to see how to perform common tasks with ADO.NET. We'll present samples to read data from a database in a number of different ways, and modify the data. The database we're going to be using is the `Northwind` sample database supplied by Microsoft. This is a database of a company in the food distribution chain, which buys and sells on stocks of food. This database comes with SQL Server, MSDE and

Access. We're not going to need to understand the details of its structure here as we will be working exclusively with the Employees table of the database, which contains details of each employee: name, position, address, and other details.

MSDE is the Microsoft Database Engine, and is a version of SQL Server, but limited to five concurrent users. It's particularly useful because at the present time a version of MSDE comes packaged up with samples for the .NET platform, which means you can explore how to access SQL Server databases with ADO.NET even if you don't want to install SQL Server. The SQL samples in this chapter were actually taken using this version of MSDE, which comes with a database administrator username of sa, and no password to access the databases.

Reading a Database Using the SQL Managed Provider

Our first example will connect to the Northwind database and read the names of the employees. The employees are contained in the Employees table of this database, specifically in the FirstName and LastName columns.

For the samples in this chapter we'll use the same technique as in we have used previously; we'll create a C# Windows application, and add a list box called listBox1 to the form. We can then use the constructor of the main form to populate the list box with any data or results of our processing.

To read in the database, we create a project as just described, and first add the following line to the main code.

```
namespace ReadEmployeesSQL
{
using System;
using System.Drawing;
using System.Collections;
using System.ComponentModel;
using System.WinForms;
using System.Data;
using System.Data.SQL;
```

This ensures that we will be able to access the objects to read an SQL database.

Now we add the following to the Form1 constructor:

```
public Form1()
{
    //
    // Required for Win Form Designer support
    //
    InitializeComponent();

    //
    // TODO: Add any constructor code after InitializeComponent call
    //
    string sConn = "server=localhost;uid=sa;pwd=;database=northwind";
    string sCommand = "SELECT FirstName, LastName FROM Employees";

    SQLDataSetCommand DSCmd = new SQLDataSetCommand(sCommand, sConn);
    DataSet ds = new DataSet();
    DSCmd.FillDataSet(ds, "Employees");
```

```
        DataTable dt = ds.Tables[0];
        foreach (DataRow dr in dt.Rows)
        {
            listBox1.Items.Add(
                dr["FirstName"] + " " + dr["LastName"]);
        }
    }
```

Let's have a look at how this works.

We first set up connection and command strings. The command string gives the SQL command that we will pass to the database, while the connection string tells ADO.NET how to connect to the database.

```
        string sConn = "server=localhost;uid=sa;pwd=;database=northwind";
        string sCommand = "SELECT FirstName, LastName FROM Employees";
```

The connection string has a very similar format to connection strings in ADO. The server parameter gives the name of the machine where SQL Server is installed. uid and pwd are respectively the username and password to logon, and database gives the name of the database to connect to. On my machine, access to the database is gained with the username sa, and no password, but obviously on your machine you'll need to substitute the username and password you have set up for your SQL database.

Now we have the connection and command strings we next instantiate an object of the System.Data.SQL.SQLDataSetCommand class. This is the DataSet command object that will be responsible for talking to the database and retrieving the data from it. Notice we pass the connection and command strings as parameters to its constructor. The FillDataSet() method of this object actually executes a command and uses it to populate a DataSet. This method takes two parameters – a reference to the DataSet to be populated, and the name of the table that will be created in this DataSet to hold the data (this is important because a DataSet can hold more than one table). You'd usually select the name of the table in the actual database for this. Notice how the DataSet never directly communicates with the data source – rather the SQLDataSetCommand object acts as an intermediary and populates the DataSet with the data we need. After that we just work locally with the DataSet.

```
        SQLDataSetCommand DSCmd = new SQLDataSetCommand(sCommand, sConn);
        DataSet ds = new DataSet();
        DSCmd.FillDataSet(ds, "Employees");
```

Once the DataSet has the data in it, we access the table as the first item in the Tables collection.

```
        DataTable dt = ds.Tables[0];
```

If we'd preferred we could equally well have identified the table by name:

```
        DataTable dt = ds.Tables["Employees"];
```

Each row in the DataTable is represented by an object of class System.Data.DataRow, and is accessed through the Rows collection of the DataTable object. The DataTable contains an indexer allowing access to the values of each field in that row.

We can obtain the fields by name, as in our sample:

```
foreach (DataRow dr in dt.Rows)
{
    listBox1.Items.Add(
        dr["FirstName"] + " " + dr["LastName"]);
}
```

or, if we prefer, by index:

```
foreach (DataRow dr in dt.Rows)
{
    listBox1.Items.Add(
        dr[0]+ " " + dr[1]);
}
```

When we run our sample we get the following output:

Reading an Access Database

We'll now modify the above sample to retrieve the same information, but from the Access version of the Northwind database. This means that we'll need to use the ADODataSetCommand object to go through the OLE DB provider.

We modify the namespaces as follows:

```
namespace ReadEmployeesADO
{
using System;
using System.Drawing;
using System.Collections;
using System.ComponentModel;
using System.WinForms;
using System.Data;
using System.Data.ADO;
```

And modify the code to retrieve the data thus:

```
//
// TODO: Add any constructor code after InitializeComponent call
//
string sConn = "Provider=Microsoft.JET.OLEDB.4.0;" +
    "data source=F:\\dotNET Book\\Ch8_ADO\\northwind.mdb";
string sCommand = "SELECT FirstName, LastName FROM Employees";

ADODataSetCommand DSCmd = new ADODataSetCommand(sCommand, sConn);
DataSet ds = new DataSet();
DSCmd.FillDataSet(ds, "Employees");

DataTable dt = ds.Tables[0];
foreach (DataRow dr in dt.Rows)
{
    listBox1.Items.Add(
        dr["FirstName"] + " " + dr["LastName"]);
}
```

This code shows that the connection string for Access using the ADO managed provider is identical to what the connection string would be if we were using ADO or OLE DB directly – this applies to all providers that you might connect to with the ADO managed provider. Note that when running this code you'll obviously have to change the pathname of the access to file to match its location on your own machine.

With these changes the output is identical to the SQL version, except that we are now getting the data from the Access version of the database.

Getting Information about Columns

In the above examples we've known what data we have retrieved in what columns because we structured the SQL query specifically to return the FirstName and LastName columns of the Employees table. If we'd simply queried for everything in that table, then, unless we happened to have detailed knowledge of the Northwind database, we might not be aware of what columns had been returned. In this case we can use the Columns property of the DataTable object to retrieve details of each column.

However there is something more significant here. Our next example is going to demonstrate that the ADO.NET DataSetCommand object is also able to retrieve other information about the table. In fact, according to the documentation, when any DataSetCommand instance populates the DataSet it will first check whether there is already a table with the required name in the DataSet. If there is one, it will fill that table with the data (possibly raising an exception if the structure of that table is inconsistent with the data being returned). Since in our case there is no such table – all we've done is create the DataSet, we're relying on the SQL query to put the data in it – the SQLDataSetCommand will create an Employees table for us. In doing so it will read as much information about the structure of the table from the database as it is able to. So, for example, it will identify the primary key, which fields are required to be unique and which are allowed null values, and so on, provided that the database allows this information to be read from it – and it will make sure that the table created in the DataSet has the same properties. This is remarkable considering all this is done with just one method call, and it starts to demonstrate just what we mean when we say the DataSet is a cached copy of the database.

In this example we'll connect to the same `Northwind` database – this time to the SQL Server version – but request all the data in the `Employees` table. And instead of printing out the data in the table, we'll print out the names of the columns along with their data types, whether they are auto-increment, whether they allow null values, whether they are read-only and whether their values are required to be unique.

> *All of our following samples will use the SQL managed provider, which means we'll always also need to add a line to our code to indicate that we are implicitly using the namespace `System.Data.SQL`. You should take this to be implied in the remaining samples in this chapter.*

So we start a new C# project and amend the code as follows:

```
public Form1()
{
    //
    // Required for Win Form Designer support
    //
    InitializeComponent();

    //
    // TODO: Add any constructor code after InitializeComponent call
    //
    string sConn = "server=localhost;uid=sa;pwd=;database=northwind";
    string sCommand = "SELECT * FROM Employees";

    SQLDataSetCommand DSCmd = new SQLDataSetCommand(sCommand, sConn);
    DataSet ds = new DataSet();
    DSCmd.FillDataSet(ds, "Employees");

    DataTable dt = ds.Tables[0];

    foreach (DataColumn dc in dt.Columns)
    {
        listBox1.Items.Add(dc.ColumnName);
        listBox1.Items.Add("  DataType:  " + dc.DataType);
        listBox1.Items.Add("  Unique:    " + dc.Unique);
        listBox1.Items.Add("  AutoInc:   " + dc.AutoIncrement);
        listBox1.Items.Add("  AllowNull: " + dc.AllowNull);
        listBox1.Items.Add("  ReadOnly:  " + dc.ReadOnly);
        listBox1.Items.Add("");
    }
}
```

In this code we've populated the `DataSet` as usual, but then iterated through the `Columns` collection of the table to display information about each column.

Running the code gives this result:

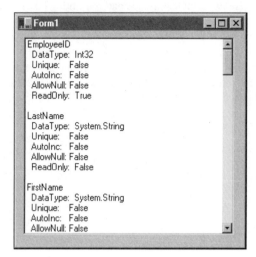

There are a couple of points to note before we go over the code. Our program hasn't quite worked perfectly. It's correctly picked up the `DataType`, `Unique`, `AllowNull` and `ReadOnly` attributes, but has failed to identify that the `EmployeeID` is auto-increment. This may be problem with the Beta 1 version of the data provider. Also this feature of picking up other data for the table only at present appears to work for SQL Server – not for using the ADO managed provider to connect to Access. It's not clear if that is a problem that will be sorted when the .NET platform is finally released.

Now we can have a look at the code that gave us this screenshot. We connect to the database as normal, and then we simply iterate through the `Columns` collection, displaying the required properties of each column:

```
foreach (DataColumn dc in dt.Columns)
{
    listBox1.Items.Add(dc.ColumnName);
    listBox1.Items.Add("   DataType:  " + dc.DataType);
    listBox1.Items.Add("   Unique:    " + dc.Unique);
    listBox1.Items.Add("   AutoInc:   " + dc.AutoIncrement);
    listBox1.Items.Add("   AllowNull: " + dc.AllowNull);
    listBox1.Items.Add("   ReadOnly:  " + dc.ReadOnly);
    listBox1.Items.Add("");
}
```

Using a DataGrid

In previous samples we manually chose which data from the `DataSet` we wanted to display and sent the results to a `ListBox`. However it is possible to automate this even more using the `DataGrid` WinForms control. Now previous incarnations of the `DataGrid` were able to link to a `Recordset` and automatically display the information from that `Recordset` – so you won't be surprised to learn that with the .NET platform comes a `DataGrid` class, actually `System.WinForms.DataGrid`, which is able to talk to `DataTables` and automatically display the information in a `DataTable`. We'll illustrate how to do this in the following sample.

Note that there is an equivalent .NET class for use in web pages,
`System.Web.UI.WebControls.DataGrid`, *which does the same thing but in the context of an ASP.NET page – so that instead of directly displaying the control, it sends HTML instructions to a web browser to display the information. We won't however be looking at the web version of the* `DataGrid` *in this book.*

Since this sample uses a `DataGrid`, we use the **Toolbox** in the developer environment to add a `DataGrid` rather than a `ListBox` to the main form:

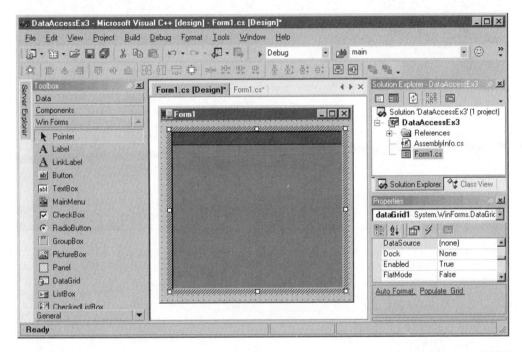

Apart from that, we create the project in the same way as the other samples in this chapter, as a C# Windows Application. Note that the `DataGrid` is by default given the name `dataGrid1`.

We add the following code to the `Form1` constructor:

```
public Form1()
{
    //
    // Required for Win Form Designer support
    //
    InitializeComponent();

    //
    // TODO: Add any constructor code after InitializeComponent call
    //
    string sConn = "server=localhost;uid=sa;pwd=;database=northwind";
    string sCommand = "SELECT * FROM Employees";

    SQLDataSetCommand DSCmd = new SQLDataSetCommand(sCommand, sConn);
```

```
      DataSet ds = new DataSet();
      DSCmd.FillDataSet(ds, "Employees");

      dataGrid1.DataSource=ds.Tables["Employees"].DefaultView;
```

Running this code gives this result:

	EmployeeID	LastName	FirstName	Title	TitleOfCourtes	BirthDate	HireDate	Ad
▶	1	Davolio	Nancy	Sales Repres	Ms.	08/12/1948	01/05/1992	507
	2	Fuller	Andrew	Vice Presiden	Dr.	19/02/1952	14/08/1992	908
	3	Leverling	Janet	Sales Repres	Ms.	30/08/1963	01/04/1992	722
	4	Peacock	Margaret	Sales Repres	Mrs.	19/09/1937	03/05/1993	411
	5	Buchanan	Steven	Sales Manage	Mr.	04/03/1955	17/10/1993	14 0
	6	Suyama	Michael	Sales Repres	Mr.	02/07/1963	17/10/1993	Cov
	7	King	Robert	Sales Repres	Mr.	29/05/1960	02/01/1994	Edg
	8	Callahan	Laura	Inside Sales	Ms.	09/01/1958	05/03/1994	472
	9	Dodsworth	Anne	Sales Repres	Ms.	27/01/1966	15/11/1994	7 H
*								

This is an impressive result considering we accomplished it in just 6 lines of code – and could have done so in 4 lines if we hadn't stored the connection and command strings in separate variables! We now have a DataGrid that allows us to view the data – and manipulate how we view it, for example changing the widths of columns, to our heart's content. It's also worth pointing out that the DataGrid can cope with hierarchies of tables, as generated by the OLE DB data shaping provider.

Modifying Data

There are three types of modification that you'll normally want to do: modify a row, add a new row or delete a row. It's very easy to perform all three types of change by calling methods on the DataTable object and on its collection of rows. Then when you want to propagate the changes from the DataSet to the underlying data source, you simply call the Update() method of the DataSetCommand object.

At the time of writing there appear to be some problems with modifying data using the pre-release version of ADO.NET that is currently available. We expect these problems to be resolved when ADO.NET is released. In the meantime the sample presented here to modify data in a data source demonstrates the way that we expect that you will be able to do so.

This sample illustrates all three forms of modification. We start up a C# Windows Application and add the following to the Form1 constructor:

```
      string sConn = "server=localhost;uid=sa;pwd=;database=northwind";
      string sCommand = "SELECT * FROM Employees";

      SQLDataSetCommand DSCmd = new SQLDataSetCommand(sCommand, sConn);
```

```
DataSet ds = new DataSet();
DSCmd.FillDataSet(ds, "Employees");

DataTable dt = ds.Tables[0];

// make sure primary key is autoincrement
dt.Columns["EmployeeID"].AutoIncrement = true;

// edit a record
dt.Rows[0]["LastName"]="Black";

// delete
dt.Rows[dt.Rows.Count-1].Delete();

// add
DataRow NewEmp = dt.NewRow();
NewEmp["FirstName"] = "Simon";
NewEmp["LastName"] = "Robinson";
dt.Rows.Add(NewEmp);

// look at state of DataSet
foreach (DataRow dr in dt.Rows)
{
    listBox1.Items.Add(dr["FirstName"] + " " + dr["LastName"] + " " +
                       dr.RowState.ToString());
}

//Update Database with DatasetCommand
DSCmd.Update(ds, "Employees");
```

Again this code shows that making changes is fairly simple.

Before making any modifications we first set the `AutoIncrement` property of the primary key:

```
dt.Columns["EmployeeID"].AutoIncrement = true;
```

This is because, as mentioned earlier, this property happened not to be set automatically when we populated the `DataSet`. If we don't set it now we'll have to manually work out a value to put in this column when we come to add a new record.

Changing a value is a simple matter of setting the relevant value in the row:

```
dt.Rows[0]["LastName"]="Black";
```

Note though that you do need to have identified the row you wish to change.

The `Delete()` method of the `Rows` collection will delete a row.

```
dt.Rows[dt.Rows.Count-1].Delete();
```

Note that this doesn't actually remove the row from the `DataSet` - it simply marks it for deletion when we want to propagate the changes back to the database. There is a separate method, `Remove()`, which will physically remove the row from the `DataSet`. However, you should avoid using that method in this context, since if you use `Remove()` then the change won't get propagated back to the data source: the row needs to be present but marked for deletion in order for the `DataSetCommand` object to be able to see that it needs to send a delete request to the data source.

Adding a new row means creating a new `DataRow` object, initializing it with the required values and adding it to the `Rows` collection:

```
// add
DataRow NewEmp = dt.NewRow();
NewEmp["FirstName"] = "Simon";
NewEmp["LastName"] = "Robinson";
dt.Rows.Add(NewEmp);
```

Once we've made all the changes, we can send them back to the database with the `Update()` method of the `DataSetCommand` object:

```
DSCmd.Update(ds, "Employees");
```

In the current version of .NET (Beta 1), this line will generate an error if we have deleted or inserted any rows. Unfortunately, to get this to work successfully, we need to define DELETE and INSERT SQL statements for the `DataSetCommand`, and set the connections we want to use for these. We also need to call `Update()` separately for the two actions:

```
// Open the connection that we'll use
// for the insert and delete commands
SQLConnection objConn = new SQLConnection(sConn);
objConn.Open();

// Add the new row
DataRow NewEmp = dt.NewRow();
NewEmp["FirstName"] = "Julian";
NewEmp["LastName"] = "Templeman";
dt.Rows.Add(NewEmp);

// Set the UPDATE command and set its ActiveConnection
DSCmd.InsertCommand.CommandText = "INSERT INTO Employees " +
                                  "(FirstName, LastName) VALUES('" +
                                  NewEmp["FirstName"] + "','" +
                                  NewEmp["LastName"] + "')";
DSCmd.InsertCommand.ActiveConnection = objConn;

// Call Update for the insert
DSCmd.Update(ds, "Employees");

// Delete a row - store its ID first to pass to the SQL statement
string strDeletedRowId =
        dt.Rows[dt.Rows.Count - 2]["EmployeeID"].ToString();
dt.Rows[dt.Rows.Count - 2].Delete();
```

```
             // Set the DELETE command and set its ActiveConnection
             DSCmd.DeleteCommand.CommandText = "DELETE FROM Employees " +
                                               "WHERE EmployeeID = '" +
                                               strDeletedRowId + "'";
             DSCmd.DeleteCommand.ActiveConnection = objConn;

             // Call Update for the delete
             DSCmd.Update(ds, "Employees");
```

RowStates

We've mentioned that the `DataSet` is able to remember changes made to it. It does this partially by use of the `RowState` property of the `DataRow` object. Each `DataRow` records its state, which can be one of five values:

1	Detached	This row is not attached to a `DataSet`.
2	Unchanged	Row has not been modified since it was placed in the `DataSet` (or since a call to `DataSet.AcceptChanges()` was made.
4	New	Row has been newly created.
8	Deleted	Row has been marked for deletion.
16	Modified	Contents of this row have been modified

We can examine the `RowState` by modifying the above code so it displays the state of each row just after we've made the changes to the `DataSet` but before we've passed them back to the data source:

```
             // edit a record
             dt.Rows[0]["LastName"]="Black";

             // delete
             dt.Rows[dt.Rows.Count-1].Delete();

             // add
             DataRow NewEmp = dt.NewRow();
             NewEmp["FirstName"] = "Simon";
             NewEmp["LastName"] = "Robinson";
             dt.Rows.Add(NewEmp);

             // look at state of DataSet
             foreach (DataRow dr in dt.Rows)
             {
                // Use C#'s ternary operator to check whether the row is marked for
                // deletion. If not, set strName to equal the name, otherwise
                // set it to the string "DELETED RECORD"
                string strName = (dr.RowState.ToInt16() != 8 ? (dr["FirstName"] +
                               " " + dr["LastName"]) : "DELETED RECORD");
                strName += ", RowState = " + dr.RowState.ToString();
                listBox1.Items.Add(strName);
             }
```

Note that in this code we've taken care to avoid displaying the contents of the row that is marked for deletion – doing so would result in a `DeletedRowInaccessibleException`, at least for the current Beta 1 version of .NET.

Running this code produces this result:

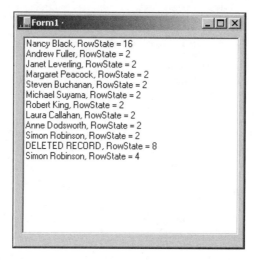

This gives the values expected from the table of possible values of the `RowState`.

Writing XML Files

Microsoft have made a big issue of the fact that ADO.NET uses XML as its standard data transmission format. In this and the next sample we're going to show how easy it is to write out and read XML data. In this example we'll read in some columns – the `EmployeeID`, `FirstName` and `LastName`, storing them in a `DataSet` as before. But instead of displaying the results in a `ListBox` we'll write out the contents to an XML file. Then in the following sample we'll read this same file back in to another `DataSet` and display its contents.

To write the results out to a file, we'll need the `FileStream` object from the `System.IO` namespace, so we need to add the appropriate using command to our source code:

```
namespace WriteXML
{
using System;
using System.Drawing;
using System.Collections;
using System.ComponentModel;
using System.WinForms;
using System.Data;
using System.Data.SQL;
using System.IO;
```

Note that you need to add a reference to the `System.Xml` namespace as well.

Now we'll add the following to the `Form1` constructor:

```
string sConn = "server=localhost;uid=sa;pwd=;database=northwind";
string sCommand = "SELECT EmployeeID,FirstName,LastName FROM Employees";

SQLDataSetCommand DSCmd = new SQLDataSetCommand(sCommand, sConn);
DataSet ds = new DataSet();
```

```
DSCmd.FillDataSet(ds, "Employees");

FileStream fstream = new FileStream(
    "Data.xml",FileMode.OpenOrCreate,
    FileAccess.Write);
ds.WriteXml(fstream);

fstream.Close();
```

To write out the file, we use the `WriteXml()` method of the `DataSet` class. This simply dumps the entire contents of the `DataSet` – data values as well as data about the structure of the table – in XML format to a stream. All we need to do to get this written to a file is make sure that the stream in question is a `FileStream`, initialized to point to the required file, with write access enabled. Simple, huh!

If we run this sample, the XML file is created in the same folder as the compiled `WriteXML` executable. The data is all there, along with the schema information for the table structure. And it's written using a fairly compact XML schema.

Reading XML Files

Now we've written the XML file, we'll have a go at reading it back. So we'll create a new C# project, `ReadXML`, and add this code to the `Form1` constructor:

```
DataSet ds = new DataSet();
FileStream fstream = new FileStream(
    "Data.xml",FileMode.Open,
    FileAccess.Read);
ds.ReadXml(fstream);
fstream.Close();

DataTable dt = ds.Tables[0];
foreach (DataRow dr in dt.Rows)
{
    listBox1.Items.Add(dr["EmployeeID"] + ": " +
        dr["FirstName"] + " " + dr["LastName"]);
}
```

Reading an XML file into a `DataSet` works in much the same way as writing it out. We simply make sure that we have created a `FileStream` instance that is attached to the required file with read access, and rely the `ReadXml` method of the `DataSet` object to pull the contents of the file out of the stream and into the `DataSet`. After that we can display the results in the normal way. If we copy the `Data.xml` file into the folder containing the new `ReadXML.exe` executable and run the program, the data from the file appears as expected. Note that once again, you need to add a reference to the `System.Xml` namespace as well:

Using the DataReader

Before we finish, we'll have a look at an alternative way that ADO.NET provides for us to read data, using the `DataReader`.

All the code used up till now is based on the `DataSet`, which is great for performing processing on local copies of the data you are interested in. Use of the `DataSet` should improve scalability for applications running on corporate networks where there is a high bandwidth giving easy access to the database server. However, the downside of disconnected datasets is the higher bandwidth requirements (as you might end up copying more data than you need from the database), and higher memory requirements (as each running copy of an ADO.NET client application keeps its own copy of a substantial part of the database). In some situations these requirements might be unacceptable. For example, if you are connecting to the database over the Internet, you might be more concerned about minimizing the bandwidth rather than minimizing the number of database connections. Similarly if you are running a web server and expect to have several hundred clients simultaneously wanting to query a table that has tens of thousands of entries, then you are not going to want each client session to have its own copy of a large `DataSet` simultaneously in memory. In such situations you can keep memory and bandwidth requirements down by being careful to use SQL statements to only retrieve the data you need from the database, but nevertheless there will be situations in which you will prefer to work in the old ADO connected Recordset way of doing things. The `DataReader` is provided for this purpose.

The `DataReader` acts rather like a recordset with a forward-only read-only "firehose" cursor. it reads one record at a time from the database, only storing the current record that you are examining in memory. If you use a `DataReader` then you don't get all the advanced facilities of the `DataSet` – the ability to handle multiple tables, examine relations and so on – but you do get a simple way to scroll through the rows in a query result.

Our next sample, the `DataReader` sample, shows how to use the `DataReader` to read records from a table – once again the `Employees` table of the `Northwind` database – and display them in a `ListBox`. We do this by adding the following to the `Form1` constructor:

```
string sConn = "server=localhost;uid=sa;pwd=;database=northwind";
string sCommand = "SELECT * FROM Employees";

SQLCommand SQLcom = new SQLCommand(sCommand, sConn);
SQLcom.ActiveConnection.Open();
SQLDataReader SQLdr = null;
SQLcom.Execute(out SQLdr);

while (SQLdr.Read())
{
    listBox1.Items.Add(SQLdr["FirstName"] + " " + SQLdr["LastName"]);
}
```

This code represents our first explicit encounter with the command object – in this case `System.Data.SQL.SQLCommand` – if we'd been using the ADO provider we'd obviously replace this with `System.Data.ADO.ADOCommand`, and similarly for the `DataReader` instance. We initialize the command object by providing it with the SQL command and connection string, and obtain the `DataReader` by calling the `Execute()` method of the command object. Once we have the `DataReader` we iterate through the data rows by calling its `Read()` method, which returns true as long as there are more rows to be read. Each time the `Read()` method is called, the `DataReader` returns to the database to retrieve the next row.

Running the above code produces this:

Exactly the same output as when using the DataSet, only the method of getting the data has changed.

Database Connections with .NET

In all the samples so far we've written all the code manually. I've done it that way because I wanted to show you how simple the code is that manipulates data using ADO.NET. However, the developer environment also provides some fairly sophisticated facilities to have code access data sources generated for you just by dragging and dropping with the mouse. In this section we'll briefly explore these facilities.

To show you the sorts of things you can do we'll create a new project, called AutoCode, which will essentially do the same thing as our previous ReadEmployeesSQL sample, which, as you might recall, displayed the names of the employees in the Employees table of the Northwind database in a list box. However, this time we won't be doing as much coding ourselves.

Automatically Setting up a Database Connection

We'll start off the project as a C# Windows application as normal, and add a listbox called listBox1 to the form. But then we'll open the Server explorer window of the developer environment. This gives us a tree view for Database Connections. We click on <Add Connection>. This leads us to a data connection wizard – the same wizard that is available from the control panel to create connections to data sources.

In the first tab we select the provider for SQL server (which is the default):

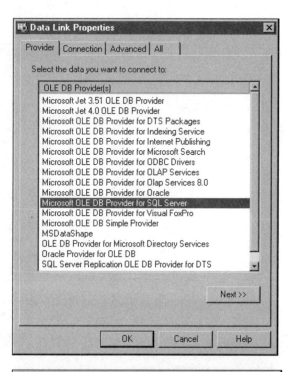

Note that the providers available are the OLE DB providers not the managed providers. A list of managed providers wouldn't be too useful at the moment because there aren't that many of them. So instead we get the full range of OLE DB providers, and the code generated will use the ADO managed provider to access the chosen data source.

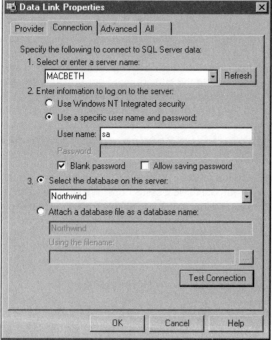

In this example I've selected the Northwind database – as a SQL Server database.

Once you click on OK and the data connection has been added you can actually view the database within the developer environment, just be clicking on the appropriate node in the Server explorer. This screenshot shows a view of the `Employees` table of the `Northwind` sample database.

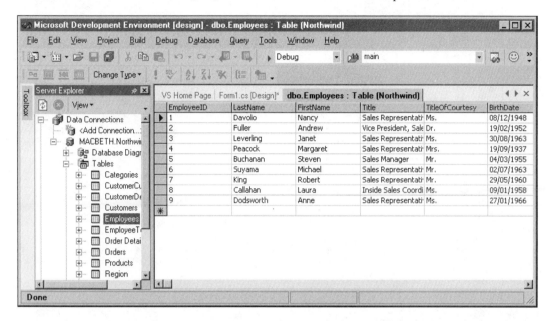

Now we have our database connection we need to get some code generated to connect to it. To do this, we make sure the Form1.cs [Design] tab is visible for the main window and click the mouse on the Employees table in the tree view in the Server explorer. Then drag this node onto the form and drop it there. This causes an `ADODataSetCommand` object and an `ADOConnection` object to be created and to appear in the main window as shown overleaf. The corresponding variables in the code are named aDODataSetCommand1 and aDOConnection1, though you can change these names from the Properties window if you want.

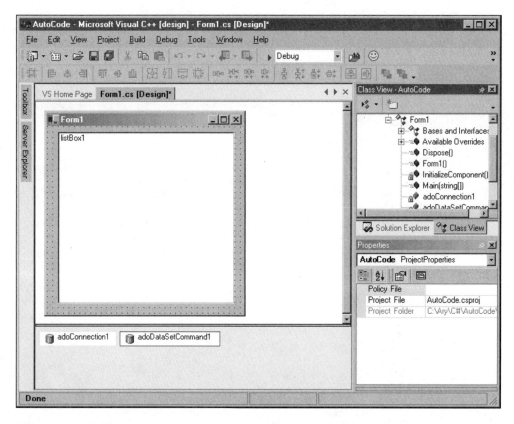

The code actually generated is quite complex, much more so than the code we have written up to now. This is because we have tended to take default values of all properties of the various ADO.NET objects, and a simple SELECT * FROM Employees statement to grab the data from the data source. The generated code explicitly specifies values of many properties of the ADO.NET objects, and uses parameters to specify the data to be retrieved from the database. This gives us a much finer degree of control, but at the expense of more complex code. Details of the properties of the ADO.NET objects and the parameters are beyond the scope of this chapter, but we'll note that they work in much the same way as ADO object parameters. The code generated for us includes the definitions of the variables representing the ADO.NET objects:

```
public class Form1 : System.WinForms.Form
{
    /// <summary>
    ///     Required designer variable
    /// </summary>
    private System.ComponentModel.Container components;
    private System.WinForms.ListBox listBox1;
    private System.Data.ADO.ADOConnection aDOConnection1;
    private System.Data.ADO.ADODataSetCommand aDODataSetCommand1;
```

As well as a complex sequence of initialization in the InitializeComponent() method of the main form class. The initialization code ensures that the DataSetCommand object will be able to read the Employees table from the data source. If you view this code in the developer environment, you will see its complexity for yourself. Indeed, the code is too complex to be reproduced in the pages of this book!

The code might be complicated, but it has saved us the bother of having to work out our own connection and command strings.

Now all that remains is for us to add the usual code of our own to instantiate and populate a `DataSet`, and use it in turn to populate the listbox.

```
//
// TODO: Add any constructor code after InitializeComponent call
//
DataSet ds = new DataSet();
adoDataSetCommand1.FillDataSet(ds);
DataTable dt = ds.Tables["Employees"];
foreach (DataRow dr in dt.Rows)
{
    listBox1.Items.Add(dr["EmployeeID"] + ": " +
        dr["FirstName"] + " " + dr["LastName"]);
}
```

Running the code now produces this result:

Summary

In this chapter we've gone over the object model for ADO.NET and seen how to use the ADO.NET classes to perform a number of common operations: reading data from a database using both a `DataSet` and a `DataReader` to get data, modifying the contents of the database, and reading and writing to XML files. We've seen that ADO.NET has a radically different object model compared to that of its predecessor ADO – ADO.NET is based more around the concept of disconnected recordsets, with the application caching a local copy of the data, which should lead to more scaleable applications. We've also seen in particular how easy it is to write out data in XML format, which will make it easy for components based on ADO.NET to talk to other software, no matter what platform it is running on.

10

Assemblies and Manifests

In this chapter we're going to look at some of the issues that arise when you start thinking about separating your code into individual components and making your code available to other applications.

We'll start with a quick look at what makes a class become a .NET component before going on to examine the basic unit used to contain .NET code, the **assembly**. We'll look at the design of assemblies and go over how this solves certain problems that used to be inherent to shared code on Windows. We'll then show you how to compile your code into an assembly, and how to turn that assembly into a **shared assembly** that's available to other applications, finishing that part of the chapter with a quick look at deployment issues.

After we've done that we'll move on to one of the great new innovations of the .NET architecture – interoperability between different languages. We'll demonstrate how this works with an example containing a VB class that inherits from a C# class and show how, when debugging, you can step seamlessly between code written in the two languages.

Components

The concept of a component has been around for many years in different forms. The idea has always been that if you can divide your code into smaller units, each of which has a well-defined behavior then your software will be a lot easier to maintain than if it is just one monolithic whole. Each component then relies only on the defined external characteristics of the other components – the 'interface' that they expose to the outside world, not on their internal implementation details. That means that you can change how you implement a component – perhaps to fix a bug or improve its performance or add some new functionality, and as long as you don't change the existing functionality as it appears to everything that calls the component, then you won't affect the rest of the application.

The other idea of components was to facilitate code reuse. Once you had some software that did something useful, you wouldn't need to write anything else to do the same thing. You just packaged your existing code up in some way that meant any other program could call it when required.

The first moves towards components can be seen in the old static libraries of a couple of decades ago – for example the well-known NAG library that was used for mathematical operations, or GINO, used for graphics. These libraries did not contain objects in the way we would understand them – they were simply collections of functions and constants. But these functions were well defined – the libraries were programming units that exposed clearly identifiable 'interfaces' – so that if you wanted to use a library you just looked up in the documentation what function did what. Later on the idea was extended to dynamic linked libraries on Windows, and the equivalent, shared libraries on Unix. These could be loaded at run-time rather than being linked in at compile-time – meaning that the size of executables was drastically reduced. In addition, only one copy of a dynamic-linked library needed to be in memory, no matter how many applications were using it at any given time.

When C++ and other object oriented languages appeared in the early 80s, they introduced the more precise idea of an **object** (which in some languages is referred to as a **class**) as an entity in a program that had both methods (functions) and state. An object became something that had a logical existence in the sense of storing data rather than just being a set of function calls – and also the concept of inheritance was introduced, by which objects could be extended to perform other tasks while still retaining the existing code base. In some ways objects became the components into which a large project was divided. However these 'components had the disadvantage that they could only be used within the same language – and even then, in practice, code reuse was limited.

The first successful moves towards defining components in a way that facilitated very easy code reuse and inter-language calls came with the introduction of **COM.** The strict binary definition for how a COM component had to interact with the outside world meant that for the first time it became easy to write component in any of several languages and to call it from other languages, and the concept of a rigidly defined and fixed **COM Interface** assisted in code reuse. However it also became apparent that this ease of use was coupled with the disadvantage of complexity. To get to grips with the workings of COM, developers needed to understand such concepts as HRESULTs, interfaces, reference counting, GUIDs and various other topics that lead to a fairly hard learning curve.

With the .NET platform these complexities have been addressed by returning to something nearer to the concept of a class in, for example, C++.

Now we've been reusing code a lot in this book – all the programs we've written in C# have been using the base classes in some way, and in some cases have inherited from them. In the .NET framework, the class is firmly established as the unit that, in programmatic terms, gives us the code reuse and exposes a fixed definition to the outside world. Added to this the system of namespaces prevents name-clashes. Also, the language independence and ease of calling components arises because the architecture of managed code, based on the Intermediate Language, ensures that classes can be called across different libraries in a consistent manner. Not only that, the .NET framework handles all this behind the scenes so that you, the developer, does not need to worry about how this happens. You just write your code, indicate which namespaces you want to be implied by default, and indicate to the compiler which libraries (stored as assemblies) you need to be able to access. If you are writing code that you intend to be used as a library, then the process is the same except that you instruct the compiler to compile to a library (DLL) rather than an executable.

So to a first approximation, a C# component could be viewed as being similar to a C# class, but with the benefit of being easy to call across DLL and language boundaries. If you want to write a component that can be reused then you just write a .NET class. In reality however, it's not quite that simple. Microsoft has laid down some guidelines concerning requirements that a class needs to meet if it is to be properly considered as a .NET component. These requirements are really to do with making sure that the component can be accessed from programs written in *any* other .NET-aware language. They can be summarized as follows.

CLS-Compliance

Recall from Chapter 1 that Microsoft has marked a portion of the facilities available in the .NET architecture and intermediate language as the common-language specification (CLS). This is the set of facilities that *any* publicly available compiler that targets the .NET platform must support. .NET components should restrict themselves to only use features in their public methods and properties etc. that are defined in the CLS – this ensures that any compiler will be able to compile code that makes full use of your component, no matter how limited the facilities available to that compiler might be.

Public Access

Perhaps rather obvious, but your class should be declared with public rather than private access. If access is private, nothing outside the assembly your class is declared in will be able to see it – which would rather restrict its usefulness as a component!

Derivation from System.ComponentModel.Component

Your class should either inherit directly or indirectly from `System.ComponentModel.Component` or implement the `IComponent` interface. This won't really affect your class – it just causes a couple of extra useful methods to be added to it which facilitate code sharing.

Names

Microsoft have issued guidelines on naming your components and the methods and properties etc. in them, so that the names are descriptive and useful. For example, individual words in the names should have their first letters capitalized, for example, `UpdateWorksheet` is fine, whereas `update_worksheet` is not. Plurals should be used correctly and verb-noun order should be consistent. For example if one of your methods is called `AppendSale`, then don't give another method the name `EmployeeAppend`. `AppendEmployee` is better because it is consistent. The guidelines also apply to namespaces in which you place your components – and you are expected to choose sensible names for your namespaces that prevent name clashes with components written by other companies – for example, if you are a company called `ComputerPictures`, and you have released a graphics library, then a sensible name for the namespace containing the classes designed to display statistical data (pie charts, graphs, etc.) would be `ComputerPictures.GraphicsLibrary.Statistics`. A namespace name such as `StatisticsCharts` would not be a good name for the namespace since another organization might conceivably create their own namespace with the same name.

Full details of these guidelines are in the MSDN documentation for the .NET platform. Whether you follow them is really up to you – if you are writing a component (class) that is only intended for use by clients written within your own organization, then you may choose not to, but following these guidelines does help to ensure your component is useful, easy to understand, and callable from any other .NET-aware program.

Assemblies

Now we've seen that the .NET component is the unit of code reuse, as far as your C# source code is concerned, we need to examine how code is actually packaged up in the file system and made available to other programs.

Previously in Windows, the unit that contained an identifiable reusable piece of code was a DLL or, later on, a COM component hosted in a DLL or executable file. Now it is the assembly. An assembly can be a single file or it can consist of a number of files. The important point about it however is that it exists as an atomic unit and is self-describing – in the sense that it doesn't only contain the Intermediate Language code but also all the other information needed to access it.

The assembly is self-describing because it contains a data structure known as a **manifest**, which contains all the information needed to describe the assembly. In particular, the manifest contains:

❑ The identity of the assembly, consisting of its name, version, and culture – the latter gives information concerning the locale.

❑ Names of all the files in the assembly (and these titles must all be in the same folder as the file containing the manifest).

❑ A short cryptographic hash of all the files in the assembly. This hash is used to detect if any of the files in the assembly have been modified or replaced since the assembly was installed. It is this hash that guarantees that even if there is more than one file in the assembly, the assembly as a whole still exists as one atomic unit. It is not possible to modify or replace some of the files independently (this would be detected by the .NET runtime when an application attempts to load the assembly because the hash would not compare correctly with the file contents. As a result, the .NET runtime would raise an exception).

❑ Details of all the types defined in the assembly, and whether they are visible to other assemblies or private to this one.

❑ Names and hashes of other assemblies that this assembly in turn will need to reference when run.

❑ Details of any security permissions that clients need to have in order to be able to run the assembly.

In many ways the manifest serves the same purpose as the type library and associated registry entries do for a COM component. The difference is that the manifest contains more information than a type library, and is directly packaged up with the code, making it impossible for manifest and code to in any way become out of sync.

It is not possible to run any managed code unless that code is packaged into an assembly, with a manifest, and the .NET runtime confirms at load time that the assembly is fine and has not been tampered with.

Recall that when you compile a C# program into an executable, what the compiler emits is not assembly language but intermediate language. In fact the compiler does more – it emits intermediate language packaged into an assembly. The same occurs if you compile to a library. Hence an assembly can be an executable (.exe) file, a DLL, or some combination of these. It may also contain resource files.

Only if you instruct the C# compiler to compile to a module will the code not be packaged into an assembly, but then it will not be possible to run the code until the module has been packaged into an assembly – which can be done with the command line tool Al (that's A-L not A-one!). A module is one of the options for types of C# project that you can create in the developer environment. You will choose this option if the code you are compiling needs to be combined with other code (other modules) in order to create a single assembly. You might also choose this option if you wish your final assembly to be broken up into several files – for example if it contains a large amount of rarely used code, it would be more efficient to have this code in a separate file so it is not loaded until it is actually needed.

Shared and Private Assemblies

There are two types of assemblies available; **private assemblies** and **shared assemblies**. By default when you compile a C# program, the assembly produced will be a private assembly – that is to say, an assembly that is only intended to be used by one application. The files that make up a private assembly must be placed either in the same folder on the Windows file system as the calling application or in a subfolder. It will not be visible to any application that is located elsewhere on the file system. If your organization produces several software packages that use the same private assembly, then it will need to be supplied separately with each package and installed separately to the folder or a subfolder where each package resides.

Defining your assembly as a private assembly makes naming it easy, since you don't need to worry about name clashes with anyone else's private assemblies. The name you give your assembly needs to be unique only within your application. And it also means there is no danger of any other software interfering with your assembly, for example by installing another assembly that claims to be a newer version of your assembly.

If you want your assembly to be available to any other software then you will need to make it a shared assembly. You would do this for example if what you have written is a generic library of useful classes, or perhaps new WinForms or WebForms controls that you want to sell for general use. If an assembly is to be shared then its naming requirements are more stringent – its name must be unique across the entire system. It's also more important to take precautions against newer versions of the component being supplied, perhaps by other companies, installed and breaking existing applications. These requirements are met by the assembly being given a **shared name** which is guaranteed to be unique. Once this has been done, the assembly is placed in the **global assembly cache**, which is an area of the file system, in the `<drive>:\WinNT\Assembly` folder reserved for shared assemblies. Microsoft has supplied a number of utilities which will take a private assembly and perform the necessary processing on it to turn it into a shared assembly – it's not something that you can do at compile time. This is deliberate since the philosophy is that making an assembly into a shared assembly is something that must be a specific decision – it should not happen by default. We'll go over precisely what shared names involve and how to create a shared assembly later in this chapter.

The Benefits of Assemblies

If you've read this far, you might be wondering what the point is of making assemblies apparently so complex. Why go to all the trouble of creating a manifest? Why all the bother of distinguishing between private and shared assemblies? What was wrong with just putting executables or DLLs in a folder, and making some registry entries to record the presence of a COM object?

Well much of the thinking behind the design of assemblies has been to eliminate certain problems that experience has shown to have occurred with the previous ways of making code available for reuse – the plain old DLL, and the COM component. To see what these problems were we'll quickly run through the history of code sharing on the Windows platform.

About 5 or 6 years ago, the standard way to share code on Windows was through DLLs, which at the time they were introduced were regarded as a good innovation over the previous static libraries. DLLs had the advantage that they could be linked in at run time and shared between simultaneously running applications, saving memory space. They contained code, usually compiled from C++, which took the form of functions or in some cases C++ classes.

When COM was introduced, we had a new way of sharing code. The DLLs were still used as one way of hosting components, but now with tight specifications governing the behavior of the code in the DLLs. The real benefit of COM was, as we've seen, the language-independence: It was extremely easy to call up a COM component from any COM-aware language, no matter what language the component had actually been written in. Not only that but components could be called across process boundaries or even machine boundaries. And the way that components were registered in the Registry gave the benefit that it was very easy to see what components were available on one machine.

Unfortunately, as tends to happen with new technologies, hindsight has shown there are disadvantages as well as advantages to using them.

Firstly, storing information in the registry may be great for seeing what software is actually on a given machine, but it also makes the process of installing software quite complex.

Having all the information about all components in one place means that information about each component has to be stored in several places. The actual code itself is in the DLL or executable in which it is hosted. Various references have to be stored in the registry, and there might even be a separate type library or marshalling DLL (though sometimes the type library is stored in the hosting DLL). Having the information about a component spread out like this means it's very easy to get out of sync. Most experienced COM developers have at some time or another found themselves using the `Regedit` registry editor tool to edit the Registry to make sure their component runs correctly.

What makes this problem more acute is that if you want a COM component to be available across the network, those registry entries need to be made on every machine on the network that it might be called from.

The other problem with COM components is that registration is always machine-wide. A registered component will be made available to every application on that machine. Quite often that's not what you want. Many organizations wrap up library code into COM components, when they only actually intend those components to be used by their own software. So the Registry gets bloated with information that's not really of any use to the system or to any other application.

Then there's the well-known issue of "DLL Hell", which equally affects both COM components and ordinary DLLs. DLL Hell is the popular name given to the situation where an application stops working because of compatibility problems between different versions of a DLL. It occurs because components are always getting improved. For example, bugs are being fixed, new functions added, classes extended, implementations made more efficient etc. The idea up to now has in theory been that when you improve a component, you always ensure it is completely compatible with previous versions of the component. Function and method signatures should remain identical and what that method does should remain the same. Then when you released a new version of something, all existing code that used the old version would still work with the new version – and perhaps even get the benefits of, for example, improved performance. The fact that this meant only one instance of the component was stored on your disk was initially an important benefit of this approach since ten or so years ago disks were small and disk space was at a premium. Nowadays, with 30GB disks commonplace, disk space is no longer an issue.

Unfortunately, experience has shown that as components get more complex, backward compatibility is impossible to rigidly maintain in practice. And this means that when you install some software which brings with it the latest version of a shared DLL, there's a risk that something else that uses that DLL will stop working. It might even be weeks before you notice the problem, and even then it's almost impossible to diagnose the cause because by then you can't remember what other software you installed when – that 's DLL Hell.

This isn't to say that DLLs and COM components were bad. They each at the time represented good innovations and brought huge benefits. When designing assemblies, Microsoft has sought to retain those benefits while addressing the accompanying problems.

We've already seen in broad terms how the problem of machine-wide registration of COM components has been addressed by the concept of private and shared assemblies. In the remainder of this section we'll examine how assemblies get round the two remaining issues: complexity of installation and DLL Hell.

Zero Impact Installs

You might notice that so far in this chapter we've not made any mention of the registry entries made in installing assemblies. The reason for that is simple –there aren't any. The point of having a manifest in each assembly is to make that assembly entirely self-describing. So there's no need to have any information about it anywhere else. The process of installing an assembly can be as simple as copying the file across – and uninstalling it might just mean deleting the file. That way not only is the installation process made easier, but there is no risk of data about an assembly becoming out of sync with the code in the assembly, causing client applications that use it to behave unpredictably or crash.

What about having a centralized record of everything installed on the computer? That was after all the aim of putting all the information about COM components in the Registry. Well the issues here are different for private and public assemblies. A private assembly is intended for use only by the application it came with. It has to reside in a subfolder of the installation folder of that application and can't be loaded by any other software. (If you do need it, it is possible to specially configure an application to load a private assembly from another location, but the intention is still that the assembly is private. You still probably wouldn't do this unless your organization wrote the assembly). In general there's simply no reason why anything else should need to know of the existence of this assembly. So for private assemblies there's no real need to know which ones are around. All that needs to be known is what software packages are installed, which will normally be done through the Windows Installer when the package as a whole is installed.

For shared assemblies there is clearly a reason for keeping a record of what assemblies are installed. However, shared assemblies must all be placed in the assembly cache, which as we mentioned earlier is contained in a particular well-known folder. So if you want to find out what shared assemblies are around, all you need to do is look in this folder. The shared assemblies will all be there, each one containing its own manifest, so you immediately have access to all the information about what classes etc. each assembly has to offer. Again, there's no need to add any information to the Registry. I should mention here that there is also a careful structure to the subfolders in the assembly cache, which we'll examine later in this chapter.

Versions

Assemblies solve the problem of DLL Hell for shared assemblies in that they are not necessarily backward compatible. Instead, the identity of each assembly is formed by the version of the assembly as well as its name – which means that it is perfectly possible to have multiple versions of the same assembly sitting side by side in the assembly cache. When a client calls up an assembly, it always indicates which version it is expecting, and will get that version, not a more recent, possibly incompatible version.

Note that versioning and side-by-side installs only apply to shared assemblies, not private assemblies. If an assembly is only intended for use by one application then there's no point having different versions of it around!

In more detail, the version of an assembly consists of four numbers, in this format:

```
Major.Minor.Build.Revision
```

The major and minor versions are regarded as incompatible, build as possibly compatible though that's not guaranteed, and revision as definitely compatible. The expectation is that if you release a new version of an assembly with new major or minor version numbers then you are declaring that it is not necessarily compatible with previous versions that had different major or minor version numbers.

The revision numbers are intended to be used for bug fixes or other patches. If you issue a new version of an assembly in which a bug fix or minor improvement is the only change you have made, and you are prepared to guarantee it is backwards compatible, then you should increase the revision number, but leave the major and minor version numbers unchanged.

When a client application requests to load an assembly of a given version, then by default the .NET runtime will locate an assembly with the requested major and minor version numbers, and the highest possible build and revision numbers. So the client gets the latest build and revision, perhaps incorporating bug fixes, but will not be given a new version of the assembly. It is however possible to override this default behavior by placing files giving instructions for versioning behavior in the folder of the client software. These files are in XML format and so are easy to edit by hand, although we won't be going into their use in this book.

Building a DLL Assembly

We've now covered a lot of theory concerning how assemblies work. It's time to put some of this theory into practice – so we're going to build a simple library along with some client code that calls it, and have a look at the assembly produced. Once we've done that we'll move on to putting more than one file into the assembly and finally converting it into a shared assembly.

The Library Project

The library we'll create contains a complex number class, `Complex`, contained in a namespace `MyMath`.

To build it we fire up the developer environment and select a Class Library Project:

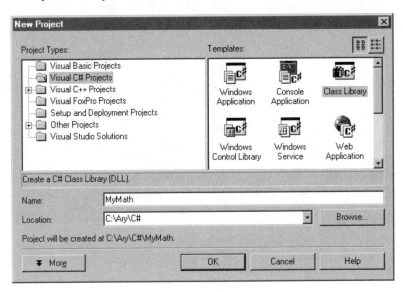

Then once the project is open we'll add the following C# code:

```
namespace Wrox.SampleCode.CSharpPreview.ChComponents.Library
{
```

```
using System;

/// <summary>
///     Summary description for Complex.
/// </summary>

public class Complex : System.ComponentModel.Component
{
    protected double x, y;

    public Complex()
    {
    }
    public Complex(double X, double Y)
    {
        x=X; y=Y;
    }

    public override string ToString()
    {
        return(x.ToString() + " + " + y.ToString() + " i");
    }

    public double Norm
    {
        get
        {
            return x*x + y*y;
        }
    }
}
}
```

From this we can see that our complex number class is very simple. It contains only constructors, a property that returns the norm of the complex number, and the `ToString()` method, overridden to display the complex number in the format `x + yi`.

> *For non-mathematical people, think of the two values x and y of a complex number as sides of a right-angled triangle. Then the norm is the square of the hypotenuse of the triangle, which if you remember your old school day math, is given by the formula in the above code, $x^2 + y^2$.*

We've derived the `Complex` class from `System.ComponentModel.Component` rather than `System.Object` in order to conform to Microsoft's guidelines for .NET components, although this doesn't have any other effect on the code we write. Note that we've also defined `Complex` as a class, though you might argue that something this simple would be better defined as a `struct`. We've done this because later on we're going to inherit another class from it – something that is not possible for a `struct`.

Once we've done this we simply compile our component in the normal way, although we will not yet be able to run it because as a library, it does not have a main program entry point.

One point that we will note is that the compiled DLL has the name `MyMath.dll`. This shouldn't come as a surprise because `MyMath` is the name we happened to give the project. However the name of the DLL will always be the name of the namespace (which was also `MyMath` at the time the project was created, though we've subsequently renamed it). If the project has a different name from the namespace then the name of the DLL would be taken from the namespace. This is important because when loading assemblies, the .NET runtime looks for files having the name of the assembly it is looking for.

The Test Harness

To run the library, we need a test harness – that is to say an executable project that calls up the library. Accordingly we'll create another C# project, this time as a Windows application project called `Client`.

Once we've created this project the first thing we need to do is ensure it references our new `MyMath` assembly. So we right-click on the **References** node in the Solution Explorer and add a reference. Since the assembly we are looking for isn't in the normal directory where all the system base class assemblies are, we need to hit the **Browse** button in the **Add Reference** dialog to navigate to the folder in which the assembly exists – if we are doing a debug build this will be the **Bin/Debug** subfolder of the folder in which we created the `MyMath` project, otherwise it will be the **Bin/Release** subfolder.

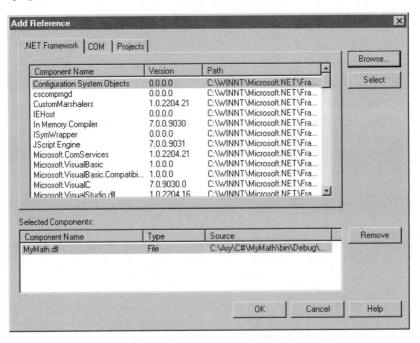

Once we have added the reference, we can refer to this class in the client code. We'll use the same technique as we introduced in chapter 7 for quickly displaying some output in a form: We'll add a list box, called `listBox1`, in the project, then add the code to perform the required processing and display the results in the list box to the constructor of the main `Form` class, which the developer environment named `Form1`, but we'll rename `FormMathHarness`. We also use the `using` command to make sure use of our new namespace is implicitly understood, and change the name of the test harness namespace so that it refers to Wrox, and so won't clash with namespaces written by any other company. Note that we've put the `Complex` class in a different namespace from the test harness (`Wrox.SampleCode.CSharpPreview.ChComponents.Library` as opposed to `Wrox.SampleCode.CSharpPreview.ChComponents` – though this doesn't actually make any difference as namespaces can be used across different assemblies).

In this code, the highlighted lines are the ones I've changed or added after the code was generated by the developer environment.

```
namespace Wrox.SampleCode.CSharpPreview.ChComponents
{
```

```
using System;
using System.Drawing;
using System.Collections;
using System.ComponentModel;
using System.WinForms;
using System.Data;
using Wrox.SampleCode.CSharpPreview.ChComponents.Library;

/// <summary>
///     Summary description for FormMathHarness.
/// </summary>
public class FormMathHarness : System.WinForms.Form
{
    /// <summary>
    ///     Required designer variable
    /// </summary>
    private System.ComponentModel.Container components;
    private System.WinForms.ListBox listBox1;

    public FormMathHarness()
    {
        //
        // Required for Win Form Designer support
        //
        InitializeComponent();

        //
        // TODO: Add any constructor code after InitializeComponent call
        //
        Complex C1 = new Complex(10.0, 10.0);
        listBox1.Items.Add("First number is " + C1.ToString());
        Complex C2 = new Complex(10.0, 20.0);
        listBox1.Items.Add("Second number is " + C2.ToString());
        double N1 = C1.Norm;
        listBox1.Items.Add("Norm of first number is " + N1.ToString());
    }
```

Now we can just compile and run the code, producing this result:

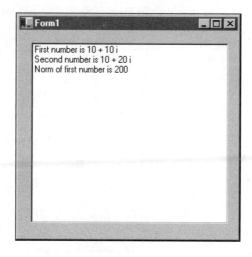

That's all we need to do to create and use a private assembly!

One point to note – we mentioned earlier that private assemblies need to be in the same folder or a sub-folder of the program that calls them. You might think we've broken that rule because we located the MyMath assembly in the folder of the MyMath project, not the folder in which we created the Client project. However when we referenced this library and built the Client project, the developer environment copied the MyMath.dll assembly across:

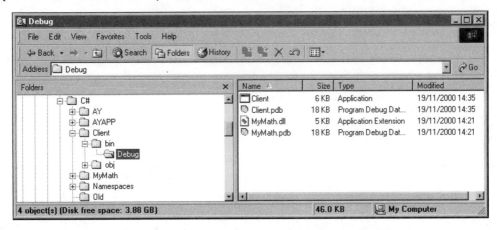

It is this copy of the assembly that now exists in the same folder as the Client.exe executable that is linked in, not the original file – as you can easily verify by removing or renaming the new copy: If you do that the client will be unable to run. Also, if we make changes to the original DLL and want it to be callable from the client, the modified version must be copied across. However it is usually best practice to recompile the client after including a new reference to the modified DLL.

Examining Assemblies with ILDasm

Now we've created our library assembly, we're going to look at a useful tool supplied with the .NET SDK that analyses the contents of assemblies. It's called ILDasm – the Intermediate Language disassembler, since it's capable of disassembling the IL in assemblies. You can run it by typing in ILDasm at the command prompt.

Once ILDasm is started, click on the File menu, select Open and browse to the assembly file you wish to examine. The following screenshot shows the results of opening up our MyMath.dll library file:

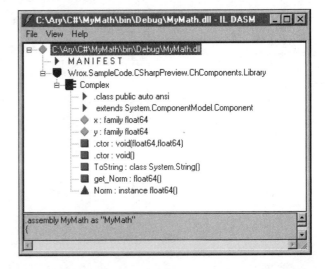

ILDasm has identified the MyMath namespace (indicated by the downward-pointing blue shield), the Complex class and its methods and propertied. It's possible from the View menu to customize precisely what information from the assembly is displayed, though by default all members of the classes are shown.

We can examine the properties of any item in more detail by double clicking on it. This is what we find for the manifest.

```
 MANIFEST                                                        _ □ ×
.assembly extern mscorlib
{
  .originator = (03 68 91 16 D3 A4 AE 33 )                // .h.....
  .hash = (52 44 F8 C9 55 1F 54 3F 97 D7 AB AD E2 DF 1D E0  // RD..U.T?.....
          F2 9D 4F BC )                                   // ..O.
  .ver 1:0:2204:21
}
.assembly MyMath as "MyMath"
{
  .custom instance void [mscorlib]System.Reflection.AssemblyTrademarkAttribut
  .custom instance void [mscorlib]System.Reflection.AssemblyCopyrightAttribut
  .custom instance void [mscorlib]System.Reflection.AssemblyProductAttribute:
  .custom instance void [mscorlib]System.Reflection.AssemblyCompanyAttribute:
  // --- The following custom attribute is added automatically, do not uncomm
  //   .custom instance void [mscorlib]System.Diagnostics.DebuggableAttribute:
  //
  .hash algorithm 0x00008004
  .ver 1:0:292:25854
}
.module MyMath.dll
// MVID: {CB057E97-03BF-4FC3-9331-4AF023D7E581}
```

The information extracted starts with an indication of which other assemblies this assembly uses – indicated by the extern keyword. In this case we only reference one other assembly, namely mscorlib.dll, the one that contains the essential system base classes. The information in the first set of curly braces refers to that assembly rather than the MyMath one. The originator field concerns a public key, which we'll explore in more detail later in the section on shared names, while the hash refers to that cryptographic hash of the contents of all the files in the assembly in question. Its presence here allows the .NET runtime to check that hashing the mscorlib assembly does generate the expected result when it loads it. It might seem strange that such a short sequence is sufficient to identify that the files are unchanged, but those 20 bytes between them can contain more than 10 to the power 48 values (that's 1 000 000 000 000 000 000 000 000 000 000 000 000 000 000 000 000 values if you write it out in full). If one of the files gets corrupted or modified, the chances of the corrupted version giving the same value of the hash are infinitesimal.

The version field indicates the version number of the mscorlib assembly that this assembly is expecting to load. As mentioned before this will normally ensure that no newer incompatible versions are loaded by mistake.

There then follows information about the contents of this assembly, including the algorithm used to generate its hash, and the current version (we didn't specify a version to the developer environment when we compiled MyMath.dll so we have been given a default version).

Although we have demonstrated ILDasm for MyMath.dll, you can use it to examine any assembly, including any of the ones in which the base classes are defined. For the present beta 1 version of the .NET platform the base class assemblies can be found in the folder `<drive>:\WINNT\Microsoft.NET\Framework\v1.0.2204`. For completeness we'll show the manifest for our client executable, Client.exe, in which you can see the dependency on MyMath.dll and some information for that library explicitly listed.

```
MANIFEST                                                               _ □ ×
.assembly extern System.WinForms
{
  .originator = (03 68 91 16 D3 A4 AE 33 )                        // .h..
  .hash = (10 EF 0B FA BE CD 77 7F 8E 21 66 D4 4E 4F CF AA  // ......w..
           4B 48 6E C7 )                                          // KHn.
  .ver 1:0:2204:21
  .config = (4D 00 69 00 63 00 72 00 6F 00 73 00 6F 00 66 00  // M.i.c.r.
             74 00 20 00 2E 00 4E 00 45 00 54 00 20 00 46 00  // t. ...N.
             72 00 61 00 6D 00 65 00 77 00 6F 00 72 00 6B 00  // r.a.m.e.
             20 00 62 00 75 00 69 00 6C 00 64 00 20 00 65 00  //  .b.u.i.
             6E 00 76 00 69 00 72 00 6F 00 6E 00 65 00 6D 00  // n.v.i.r.
             65 00 6E 00 74 00 20 00 69 00 73 00 20 00 52 00  // e.n.t. .
             65 00 74 00 61 00 69 00 6C 00 00 00 )            // e.t.a.i.
}
.assembly extern mscorlib
{
  .originator = (03 68 91 16 D3 A4 AE 33 )                        // .h..
  .hash = (52 44 F8 C9 55 1F 54 3F 97 D7 AB AD E2 DF 1D E0  // RD..U.T?..
           F2 9D 4F BC )                                         // ..O.
  .ver 1:0:2204:21
}
.assembly extern MyMath
{
  .hash = (7B F9 D2 EB 8C 56 9B C8 73 E3 4B 14 A2 96 64 93  // {....V..s.
           A8 DC AF D6 )
  .ver 1:0:292:25854
}
.assembly extern System.Drawing
{
  .originator = (03 68 91 16 D3 A4 AE 33 )                        // .h..
  .hash = (60 EE 05 E4 5F 27 3E 26 18 9C 6A 9B 19 44 99 C8  // `..._'>&..
           FF B4 05 0E )
  .ver 1:0:2204:21
  .config = (4D 00 69 00 63 00 72 00 6F 00 73 00 6F 00 66 00  // M.i.c.r.
             74 00 20 00 2E 00 4E 00 45 00 54 00 20 00 46 00  // t. ...N.
             72 00 61 00 6D 00 65 00 77 00 6F 00 72 00 6B 00  // r.a.m.e.
             20 00 62 00 75 00 69 00 6C 00 64 00 20 00 65 00  //  .b.u.i.
             6E 00 76 00 69 00 72 00 6F 00 6E 00 65 00 6D 00  // n.v.i.r.
             65 00 6E 00 74 00 20 00 69 00 73 00 20 00 52 00  // e.n.t. .
             65 00 74 00 61 00 69 00 6C 00 00 00 )            // e.t.a.i.
}
.assembly Client as "Client"
{
  .custom instance void [mscorlib]System.Reflection.AssemblyTrademarkAttri
  .custom instance void [mscorlib]System.Reflection.AssemblyCopyrightAttri
  .custom instance void [mscorlib]System.Reflection.AssemblyProductAttribu
  .custom instance void [mscorlib]System.Reflection.AssemblyCompanyAttribu
  // --- The following custom attribute is added automatically, do not unc
  //    .custom instance void [mscorlib]System.Diagnostics.DebuggableAttribu
  //
  .hash algorithm 0x00008004
  .ver 1:0:292:26264
}
.module Client.exe
// MVID: {BDA07050-C69A-4D7A-9474-9437C36CB42A}
```

Now we've generated and examined a private assembly, the next step is to convert the MyMath assembly into a shared assembly by giving it a shared name and placing it in the global assembly cache. Before we do that however, we ought to get a better understanding of these concepts. Those are the topics of the next two sections.

Shared Names

We've mentioned earlier that shared assemblies need to have so-called shared names, which are guaranteed to be unique. In this section we'll have a closer look at how this is accomplished.

Public and Private Keys

The shared names are generated using techniques from public key cryptography, so if you've not encountered this topic before we'll quickly go over what it involves. If you are familiar with public and private keys, then feel free to skip this introductory section.

The idea of public key cryptography evolved in the 1970s because of a weakness in earlier attempts to encode messages. Any encryption algorithm depended on a key – typically some set of digits that contained details of how to encode a message. For example, in a simple scheme in which each letter was mapped to a different letter (e.g. A becomes P, B becomes E, etc.), the key would consist of rules for what letter mapped to what. The problem is that if you encode a message with the key, the intended receiver needs the key to decode it. And that means that everyone you might want to send such messages to needs the keys. And that in turn implies there's a high risk that the people you're trying to hide the messages from might get their hands on the keys: There's just too many weak points in the system that might give unauthorized people that opportunity – all the people who legitimately have copies of the keys, and all the times that keys need to be communicated to these people.

Public key cryptography is based on some fairly advanced mathematical ideas, but the gist goes like this. For modern encryption methods the message is subjected to some mathematical operations, and the key takes the form of a very large number that is used in the course of those operations. And instead of one key, there are two keys, which we shall call A and B. The encryption algorithm works in such a way that if you use key A to encode a message than you need to use B, not A, to decode it again – and vice versa. So what you do is this. You publish one key – call it your **public key**. You make it available to anyone who wants it, friend or foe. Then if anyone wants to send you a secret message, they encode it with your public key. You don't tell anyone else whatsoever your other key, which becomes known as your **private key**. That means only you can decode your messages, so they stay secure. Since your private key never gets communicated to anyone else, the risk of it falling into unauthorized hands is minimized.

You can also work the other way round – encrypt a message using your private key and instruct the recipient(s) that they should use your public key to decrypt it. This means anyone can read it since everyone has access to your public key – but they can always guarantee the message genuinely came from you. No one else could send out a message claiming it came from you, because they wouldn't be able to encrypt it properly because they don't know your private key. And unless the message has been correctly encrypted using your private key then any attempt to use your public key to decrypt it will just lead to gobbledygook. It's this idea of using public keys to guarantee the authenticity of a message that is used to generate unique shared names for assemblies.

I should mention there is one other requirement for this whole concept. There should be no known practicable way to calculate what a person's private key is from their public key. Modern mathematical algorithms do currently guarantee that this is the case.

Generating Shared Names from Keys

Now that we understand how public key cryptography works we can see how this is applied to the generation of shared names.

1. First a public-private key pair is generated at random for the assembly.

2. Next, a cryptographic hash is taken of the names and contents of the files in the assembly. This hash is taken using a very simple algorithm, not using public keys. The point here is not to make it difficult to decode – just to get a small set of bits that can be used to verify the contents of the files.

3. Now the cryptographic hash is encoded using the private key for the assembly, and placed in the manifest. This is known as signing the assembly.

4. Finally, the public key is incorporated into the name of the assembly.

When an application that needs to use the shared assembly tries to call it up, the first thing the .NET runtime does is use the assembly's public key to decode that hash of the files in the assembly. Then it reads the files and independently works out the cryptographic hash for itself. If all is well the two hashes will be the same, and the .NET runtime knows it can proceed to load the assembly.

The result of all this is a very high level of security against not only name collisions, but against malicious actions by third parties. Let's see why.

The shared name is effectively unique because it contains not only the name the developer picked for the assembly, but also a randomly generated public key. The algorithm Microsoft uses to generate these keys means that the chances of the same key getting generated again are miniscule. Generating the same key again at the same time as installing another assembly with the same name on the same machine would be an absolutely unbelievable coincidence.

If any changes are made to any of the files in the assembly after the assembly is installed then this will be detected because the cryptographic hash of the new files will give a different value. The .NET runtime will see that the calculated hash is not the same as the value stored in the manifest and refuse to load the assembly.

If any malicious attempt by a third party is made to replace the manifest then the .NET runtime will again be able to detect the problem and refuse to load the assembly. This is because the third party will not know the private key for the assembly, and so will be unable to correctly encrypt the hash of the altered files.

Needless to say, this approach relies on the private key being kept private. In practice, organizations that write software will clearly implement their own policies to keep their private keys secure, only allowing access to a few trusted individuals.

It should be pointed out however that this whole process ensures only that no one else can duplicate your private key and hence replace your assembly. It is not related to the existing procedures for getting keys signed by trusted authorities, and so does not give any information on whether you as the holder of your private key are trusted to be who you claim to be. It is however still possible to do this separately, although that's beyond the scope of this chapter.

The Global Assembly Cache

Now we'll turn our attention to looking at the assembly cache in more detail. The store is located in the `<drive>:\WINNT\assembly` folder.

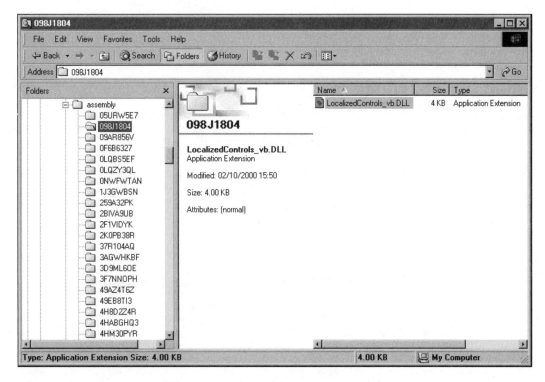

We see that in fact the store contains a large number of subfolders, each one containing one assembly. The name of each subfolder is derived from the public key of the assembly it contains – this is one mechanism by which the public key is incorporated into the identity of the assembly.

Converting a Private Assembly to a Shared Assembly

There are three stages in this process:

❑ Creating a key pair

❑ Signing the assembly with the key pair

❑ Placing the assembly in the assembly cache

We'll go through each of these steps in turn

Creating a Key Pair

The utility that you will use to create a key pair is the shared name utility, sn.exe. This is normally run from the command prompt and can perform a variety of tasks to do with generating and extracting keys, or even replacing keys in an assembly, depending on what flags are appended to the command. However, we need to run it as so:

```
sn -k key.snk
```

Where key.snk is the name of the file that the key will be stored in. It can be any name though convention seems to indicate it has the .snk extension. Running this command will cause a file with the given name to be created, which contains the public and private keys in binary format.

Signing the Assembly

Signing an assembly is normally done at compile time. You do this by indicating to the compiler, via C# attributes, that the assembly should be signed with the appropriate key file. To do this you need to open the AssemblyInfo.cs file of your project and make the changes highlighted below:

```
// Use the attributes below to control which key is used for signing.
//
// Notes:
//    (*) If no key is specified - the assembly cannot be signed.
//    (*) KeyName refers to a key that has been installed in the Crypto Service
//        Provider (CSP) on your machine.
//    (*) If the key file and a key name attributes are both specified, the
//        following processing occurs:
//        (1) If the KeyName can be found in the CSP - that key is used.
//        (2) If the KeyName does not exist and the KeyFile does exist, the key
//            in the file is installed into the CSP and used.
//    (*) Delay Signing is an advanced option - see the COM+ 2.0 documentation for
//        more information on this.
//
[assembly:AssemblyDelaySign(false)]
[assembly:AssemblyKeyFile("key.snk")]
[assembly:AssemblyKeyName("")]
```

The main change we've made is to indicate the key file we have just created using the sn utility in the assembly:AssemblyKeyFile attribute. (Note that if this key file is not in the same folder as you are compiling from then you will either need to copy it across first or specify the full path name.) By default when the project is created the key file name is left blank, which means that no signing will take place.

Once you've made this change to the project, you simply recompile it. The assembly created will now be signed with the private key contained in the specified keyfile (in this case key.snk) and so will be ready to be placed in the global assembly cache.

Placing the Assembly in the Cache

To place the assembly in the cache, you need to use another command line utility, Al (again, that's A-L not A-one!). The syntax you should type in is:

```
Al /i:MyMath.dll
```

Here, the /i flag indicates that we are placing the specified file in the assembly cache, and obviously MyMath.dll should be replaced by the name of whatever file you want to place in the assembly. If you are not running Al from the same folder that the file is in you also will need to specify the full pathname.

As a check, once we've done all three of the above steps we can see the new library in the assembly cache:

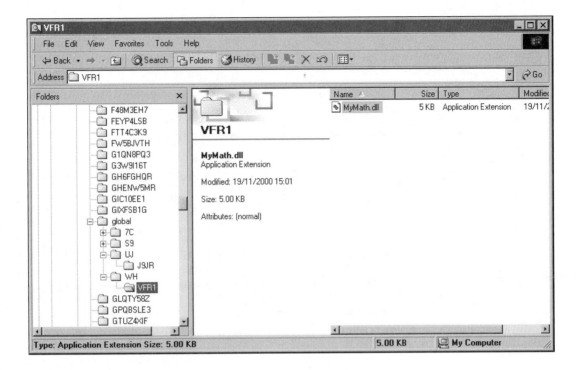

Replacing the Key File

There is one problem with the above process for moving an assembly to the assembly cache: The assembly is signed at compile time, which means that the developer responsible for compiling it needs to have access to the key file. Recall however, that we mentioned that a large organization will however almost certainly want to keep its private keys secure, allowing access to them only to a few trusted individuals – who may not be the same people as those writing the code. In this scenario, the developers writing and compiling the code simply won't be able to sign it with the organization's private key because they won't have access to the file containing it.

To get around this problem, the shared name utility can replace keys in an assembly. The idea is this: The developers work through the above procedure to place the assembly in the cache, except that the key file they create is simply a test file, which they will use while developing and testing their code. Once the code is ready to be shipped, the compiled assembly can be handed over to one of the trusted individuals, who will resign it with the 'real' key.

The syntax to resign it is:

```
sn -R <assembly-name> <key-file name>
```

So for the `MyMath.dll` case, the process would be as follows:

At some stage in the past, a trusted individual will have created the organizations key file, by running `sn` from the command line:

```
sn -k TrueKey.snk
```

When compiling, the developer creates a test key file by typing in:

```
sn -k key.snk
```

The developer compiles the assembly, using the `AssemblyKeyFile` attribute to sign it with the test key. The developer also uses the `Al` utility to place the compiled code in the assembly cache in order to test it as a shared assembly.

One the code is finished, and the assembly is ready to ship, it will be handed to the trusted individual, who will resign it:

```
sn -R MyMath.dll TrueKey.snk
```

Then the `Al` utility will be used to place the assembly in the assembly cache on whatever machines it is to be installed on (this will be done as part of the installation process when deploying the assembly):

```
Al /i:MyMath.dll
```

Before we leave this section, we'll briefly note that if you are really curious about the keys and want to look at them, running the command

```
sn -o key.snk key.csv
```

will read in the key file and store it as the named text comma-separated-values CSV file. However, your efforts won't be highly rewarded – all you'll see is a long stream of digits.

Cross-Language Features

We're going to finish this chapter with a look at how the .NET platform facilitates mixing up different languages. In particular we'll examine how you can write a class in one language that inherits from a class written in a different language, and the way you can easily debug through function calls written in the different languages.

Inheritance

We're going to demonstrate inheritance using a similar project to our test harness that demonstrated the complex number class. However this project will be written in VB. And it will feature an inherited version of the `Complex` class. The rationale is that the `Complex.ToString()` method we defined earlier displays numbers in the form $10 + 20i$ – the format normally used by mathematicians and physicists. However mechanical and electronic engineers usually write j instead of i, so they will want a different version of `ToString()`. Accordingly our VB project will feature an inherited class, `EngComplex`, which derives from `Complex` and overrides `ToString()` to display the complex number the way engineers like.

We start the project in the developer environment by selecting **Windows Application**, but as a VB project:

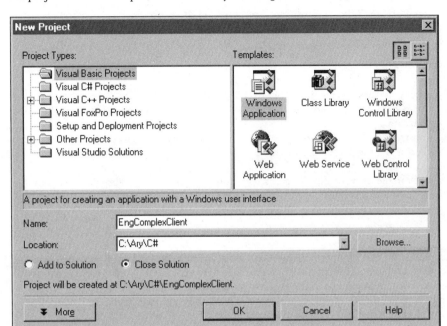

It's a measure of how well integrated the different languages are that the user interface you now get for the VB project is *exactly* the same as the user interface for a C# project. And we follow just the same procedure to add the reference to our earlier `MyMath.dll` assembly: Bring up the **Add Reference** dialog and browse to the location where the `MyMath.dll` was stored, and add it.

Now we use the toolbox to add a list box to the form – by default this list box is called `ListBox1` rather than small-L `listBox1` in C#.

Next we add the following code to our project. First we indicate that we are using the `MyMath` namespace:

```
Imports System.ComponentModel
Imports System.Drawing
Imports System.WinForms
Imports Wrox.SampleCode.CSharpPreview.ChComponents.Library
```

The VB `Imports` command does the same thing as C#'s `using` command.

Next we add the definition for the `EngComplex` class:

```
Namespace Wrox.SampleCode.CSharpPreview.ChComponents

   Public Class EngComplex
       Inherits Complex

       Public Sub New(ByVal X As Double, ByVal Y As Double)
          MyBase.New(X, Y)
       End Sub
```

```
    Overrides Public Function ToString() As String
        ToString = X.ToString & " + " & Y.ToString & " j"
    End Function

End Class
```

Without assuming a detailed knowledge of VB, hopefully you can see what's going on here. We declare a class called `EngComplex`, and indicate that it inherits from `Complex`. Next we define the constructor for this class which takes two parameters – in VB, the keyword `New` is used to indicate a constructor. The two-parameter constructor needs to simply pass through to the equivalent constructor of the `Complex` class. Again, in VB, this is indicated by the keyword `MyBase`, which indicates the immediate base class.

Finally we declare the new version of `ToString`, indicating that it overrides the version in the base class. The implementation of this function,

```
    ToString = X.ToString & " + " & Y.ToString & " j"
```

may cause you some grief if you're not familiar with VB, as the syntax here is very different to C#. The return value of a VB function is indicated not by the keyword `return`, but by setting a 'variable' with the same name as the function name to the required value. Also, note that strings are concatenated in VB using the operator `&` rather than `+` as in C#, and that the parentheses around method calls in VB are not always mandatory – hence we write = `X.ToString` rather than = `X.ToString()`.

Now we've defined the `EngComplex` class, we simply need to add some code to display a few values in the list box. We do this in exactly the same way as we did earlier in our C# client, by adding code to the `FormEngComplex` constructor:

```
Public Class Form1
    Inherits System.WinForms.Form

    Public Sub New()
        MyBase.New()
        Form1 = Me

        'This call is required by the Win Form Designer.
        InitializeComponent()

        'TODO: Add any initialization after the InitForm call
        Dim C1, C2 As EngComplex
        Dim N1 As Double
        C1 = New EngComplex(10, 10)
        ListBox1.Items.Add("First number is " & C1.ToString)
        C2 = New EngComplex(10, 20)
        ListBox1.Items.Add("Second number is " & C2.ToString)
        N1 = C1.Norm
        ListBox1.Items.Add("Norm of first number is " & N1.ToString)

    End Sub

    . . .
```

Note that again the constructor is indicated by the keyword New. If you compare this code with the C# client example you'll see that the added code is identical, apart from the different syntax due to the different languages and the fact that we are using the EngComplex rather than the Complex class.

Finally, for the code to compile, we have to set the start point by modifying the EngComplexClient project properties as follows:

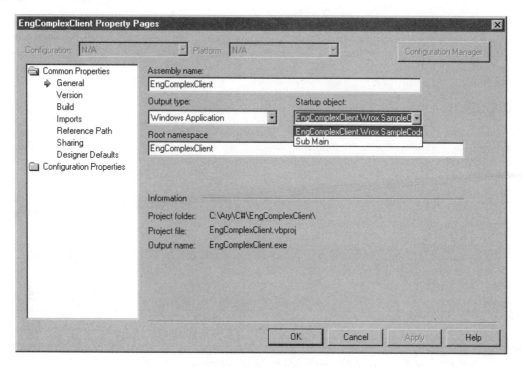

All we now need to do is run the sample. It gives this output.

showing that the overridden `ToString()` method works correctly, and also that we are able to call the `Norm` property and the constructors of the base class, written in C#, without any trouble. In fact this whole process looks so simple that it's easy to forget just what we've done. Recall again the line of code

```
Public Class EngComplex
    Inherits Complex
```

In this one statement we are declaring a class written in one language which seamlessly derives from a class that had been written in a completely different language and compiled into a library using a completely different compiler. This is something that was simply not possible to do before the .NET platform, and is a remarkable achievement.

Debugging

Now we've seen how easy it is to inherit across languages, let's see how easy it is to debug across different languages. To this end we'll set a breakpoint in the `EngComplex` constructor. Now when we start the program, it will halt execution when the variable `C1` is initialized:

```
C1 = New EngComplex(10, 10)
```

At this point the developer environment looks like this:

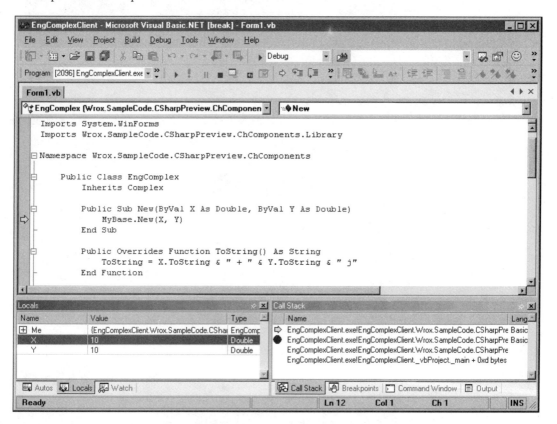

So far so good. We've halted in the right place, and the Locals window shows the values of the parameters passed in to the constructor. If we now hit *F11* (or equivalently go to the Debug menu and select Step Into) a few times, execution should step into the call to `MyBase.New()`. When we do so, this is the result:

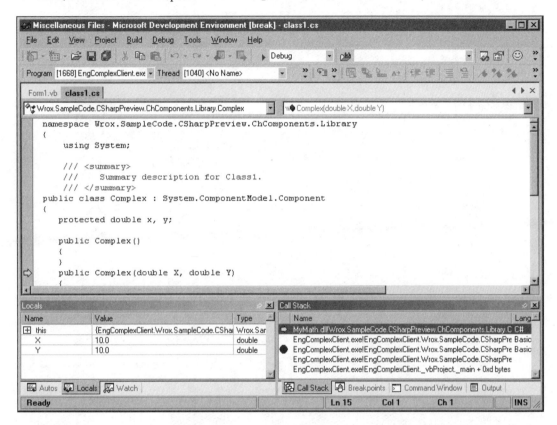

Again by comparison with Visual Studio 6, this is remarkable. We have smoothly stepped from a function written in VB to one written in C#: note the change in syntax, the changing of the VB `Me` variable to C#'s `this` in the Locals window, and the appearance of the `MyMath` DLL on the Call Stack. We don't have a new user interface to learn – that has stayed the same. The debugger hasn't raised so much as a whimper about swapping languages. And all our normal debugging facilities – including watches, the ability to look at the executable (in this case IL) code, and breakpoints have followed us through. The age of language-independent coding has truly arrived!

Summary

In this chapter we've taken a look behind the scenes at the structure of assemblies that makes code sharing and components possible on the .NET platform. We've seen how easy it is to create an assembly and make it globally available to other applications by converting it to a shared assembly. We've also looked at some of the security and other features that should keep your code safe, both from unauthorized access, and the old versioning problem – the so-called DLL Hell that existed on earlier platforms. Finally we've demonstrated how the assembly architecture really is language-independent and allows you to seamlessly integrate and inter-develop with code written in any .NET-aware programming language. The example we chose was VB and C#, but we could equally have used C++ instead. Hopefully you'll agree that the features of the .NET platform that we've demonstrated are impressive.

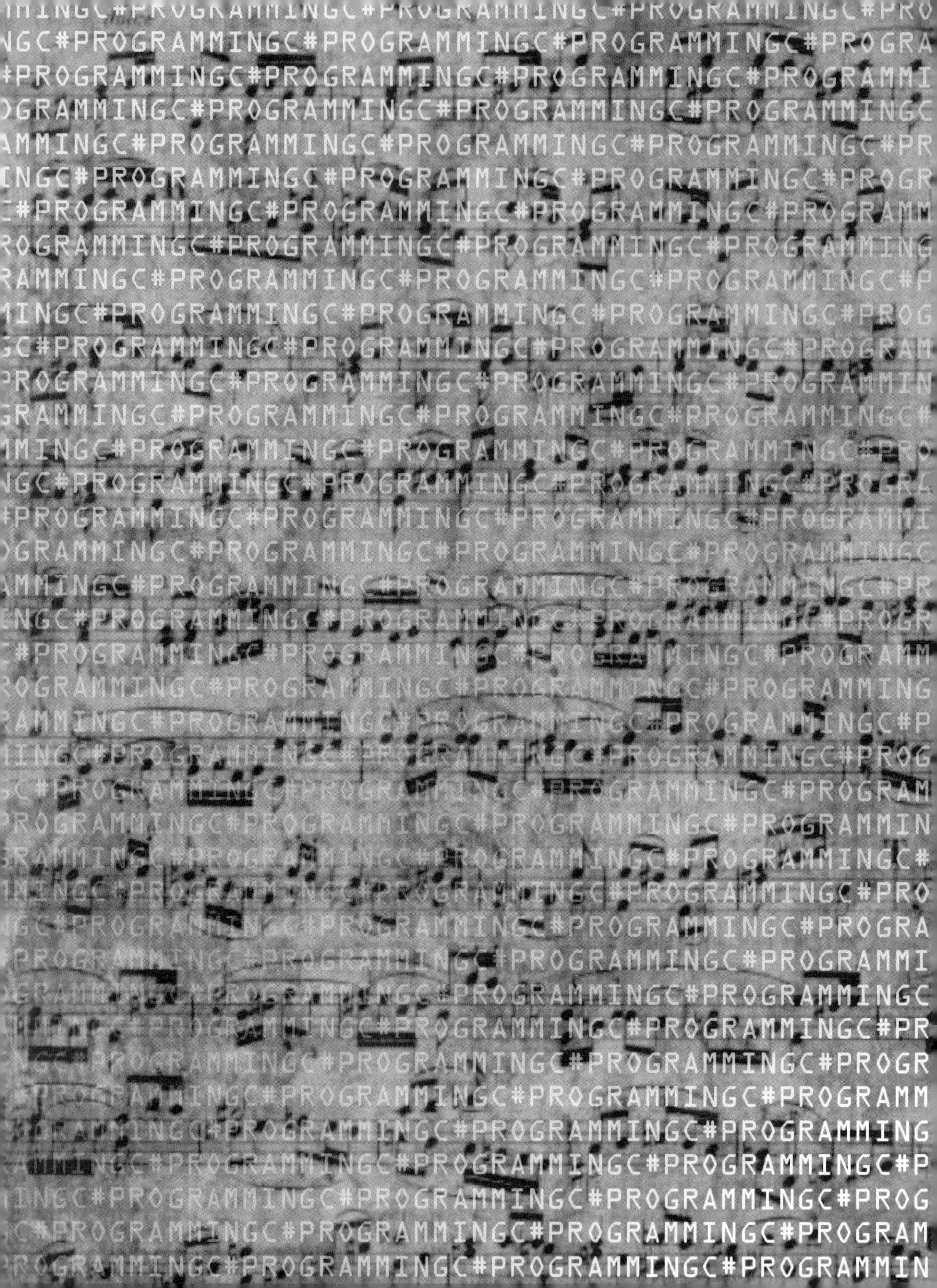
C#PROGRAMMING

11

COM Interoperability

No matter how good the .NET platform is, companies can't afford to get rid of their existing codebases just to use it and start again from scratch – not if they want to keep up with their competitors! The re-usable components and controls that they've developed represent significant investments of time and money. In order for .NET to be a practical migration path, it needs to interact well with COM.

The problem is that COM components and .NET components conform to different compiled standards: COM components to the COM binary standard, and .NET components to the Common Language Specification. The solution is a couple of programming techniques, and a set of utility programs that Microsoft has provided for generating proxy components that both standards understand:

Utility Program	Purpose
TlbImp.exe	Imports a COM type library into a proxy .NET assembly that .NET clients can reference via early binding
RegAsm.exe	Enters a .NET component into the system registry for access by COM Services, noting that it requires the CLR (Common Language Runtime) when invoked
TlbExp.exe	Exports a .NET component's type information into a type library file that COM components can reference for early binding
AxImp.exe	Creates a .NET proxy for an ActiveX control so that the control can be used in .NET WinForm applications

As you'll soon see, it's completely possible to invoke Microsoft.NET server objects from COM clients. This chapter will focus, however, on calling COM components from .NET clients because that's the situation that developers are more likely to encounter in the field.

First, we'll look at early binding and a couple of ways that .NET developers can early bind to COM objects. Next, we'll explore how late binding to COM objects can be implemented. Throughout this discussion, we'll use a sample program to make things clearer.

Our Sample Program

One of the big benefits of n-tier architectures is that the components in them can be re-used. To demonstrate the various approaches to interoperability, this chapter will re-use a COM data access object in the business object layer of a new MS.NET project.

The Legacy COM Object

The COM object, NorthwindDAL.ShippersTable, provides several methods for manipulating records in the Shippers table in SQL Server's Northwind database.

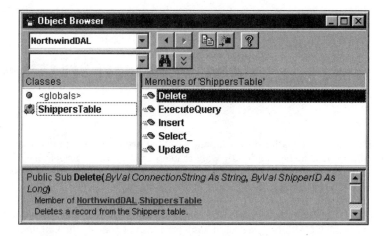

So that you can build the COM component yourself and follow along, its VB6 code is provided below and at the Wrox website (www.wrox.com). If you're typing the code in yourself, open up Visual Basic and create a new ActiveX DLL project. The code uses ADO, so you'll need to add a reference to the ADO type library (select Project | References..., and then select Microsoft ActiveX Data Objects 2.x from the Project References dialog box). After you have entered the code, you'll need to compile the project as NorthwindDAL.dll (DAL stands for "data access layer"). Keep in mind that a real, industrial-strength data access object would use stored procedures and error handling.

```
'This data access method inserts records into Shippers.
Public Sub Insert(ByVal ConnectionString As String, _
                  ByVal CompanyName As String, _
                  ByVal Phone As String)
    Dim strQuery As String
    strQuery = "INSERT INTO Shippers (CompanyName,Phone) " & _
               "VALUES ('" & CompanyName & "','" & Phone & "')"
    Call ExecuteQuery(ConnectionString, strQuery)
End Sub


'This data access method updates records in Shippers.
Public Sub Update(ByVal ConnectionString As String, _
                  ByVal ShipperID As Long, _
```

```
                        ByVal CompanyName As String, _
                        ByVal Phone As String)
    Dim strQuery As String
    strQuery = "UPDATE Shippers SET CompanyName='" & _
               CompanyName & "', Phone='" & _
               Phone & "' where ShipperID=" & ShipperID
    Call ExecuteQuery(ConnectionString, strQuery)
End Sub
```

```
'This data access method retrieves records from Shippers.
Public Function Select_(ByVal ConnectionString As String, _
                        ByVal ShipperID As Long) As ADODB.Recordset
    Dim strQuery As String
    strQuery = "SELECT * FROM Shippers WHERE ShipperID=" & _
               ShipperID
    Set Select_ = ExecuteQuery(ConnectionString, strQuery)
End Function
```

```
'This data access method deletes records from Shippers.
Public Sub Delete(ByVal ConnectionString As String, _
                        ByVal ShipperID As Long)
    Dim strQuery As String
    strQuery = "DELETE FROM Shippers WHERE ShipperID=" & _
               ShipperID
    Call ExecuteQuery(ConnectionString, strQuery)
End Sub
```

```
'This provide method executes SQL queries.
Private Function ExecuteQuery(ByVal strConnection As String, _
                        ByVal SQLQuery As String) _
                        As ADODB.Recordset
    Dim objConnection As ADODB.Connection
    Set objConnection = New ADODB.Connection
    Call objConnection.Open(strConnection)
    Set ExecuteQuery = objConnection.Execute(SQLQuery)
End Function
```

The Sample .NET Client Object

As you probably know, one of the things that business objects are responsible for is enforcing security. In our new .NET application, we'll build a .NET business object that glues some security around the legacy COM object's Insert() method. The console application below defines our .NET business object, Shipper, as well as a DriverProgram class for testing it. As we explore different ways of accessing legacy COM components, we'll implement Shipper's SecureInsert() method in different ways.

```
namespace COMInteropExample
{
using System;

//This class just serves as the driver program
//to test the business object that uses
//COM interoperability.
public class DriverProgram
```

```
{
   //Program begins here.
   public static int Main(string[] args)
   {
      Shipper objShipper=new Shipper();
      objShipper.SecureInsert(44,"WroxPress","4000280");
      return 0;
   }
}

//This business object will use several different methods to
//access the legacy COM data access object.
public class Shipper {

   public void SecureInsert(long EmployeeID,
                            string CustomerName,
                            string Phone)
   {
      //DIFFERENT IMPLEMENTATIONS WILL GO HERE.
   }
}
```

Using COM Components in C# Applications

In order to understand the differences between the various schemes for interacting with COM, we'll first need to look at the differences between early and late binding.

Early Binding and Late Binding

When a client object calls a method on a server object, it has to resolve the address of that method in memory. This process is called **binding**, and it comes in two varieties. **Early binding** occurs at compile time, when the compiler resolves the server object's interface and incorporates its metadata into the compiled client component. **Late binding** occurs at runtime, when COM Services dynamically explore the called server object to determine if it supports the requested method. As you might infer, early binding is preferable to late binding because early-bound method calls can be invoked more quickly.

Type Libraries for Early Binding

If clients are to early bind to a COM component, the component must supply a **type library** describing the methods, properties, and events in its interface. When a compiler compiles a client component, it interrogates the server's type library for the information that it needs to link into the compiled client. Like all COM components created with VB6, our `NorthwindDAL.dll` component has a type library embedded inside it. We'd like our .NET client to examine this embedded type library so that it can early bind to the COM component and thus execute faster.

Unfortunately, the COM component's type library isn't in a format that our .NET compiler can understand: it's a traditional type library and not a manifest as you'd find in a .NET assembly. How can we help our compiler understand the COM object's type library?

That's where `TlbImp.exe`, the Type Library Importer program, comes in.

Early Binding with TlbImp.exe

TlbImp can interrogate a COM component's type library, translate that type library into a .NET-compatible manifest, and produce a proxy assembly in which the manifest is encapsulated. Such a proxy assembly is called a Runtime Class Wrapper (RCW). When early binding a .NET client to the COM server, a compiler can refer to the server's RCW for the information that it needs to embed in the client. Moreover, when the .NET client executes, the RCW serves as an intermediary between the .NET client and its COM server, mapping calls between the two components.

Once you've used TlbImp.exe to generate a RCW for a COM component, it's interesting to explore that RCW with the IL Disassembler tool (ILDasm.exe) provided with the .NET SDK. In the following screenshot, I'm using this tool to explore the RCW that TlbImp created for our sample NorthwindDAL COM component:

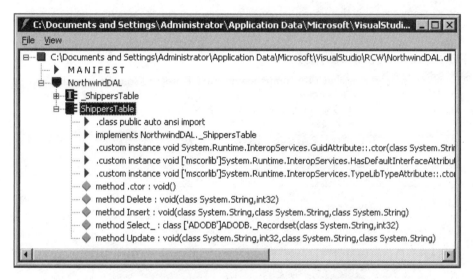

There are a couple of points that you need to be aware of when using an RCW as a bridge from a .NET client to COM server. First, because the COM server is still invoked by COM Services, the COM component must be registered with COM Services via the COM+ Administration program or regsrv32.exe. Second, like any other assembly to which the .NET client refers, the RCW must be in the .NET client's folder or in the global assembly folder.

Using TlbImp.exe from the Command Prompt

TlbImp ships with the .NET SDK, so you can download and use it for free if you don't mind running it from the command prompt.

The syntax for invoking TlbImp.exe is quite simple. You just type tlbimp, followed by the name of the COM component that you're importing. An option, /out:, controls the filename of the RCW that is produced. You need to use this option because, by default, TlbImp will name the RCW after the imported type library, and type libraries often have the same names as the COM components that contain them. To keep the RCW from overwriting the COM component, TlbImp will throw an error. Having invoked TlbImp.exe you should see the following, the /verbose switch causing the compiler to output details of what is going on:

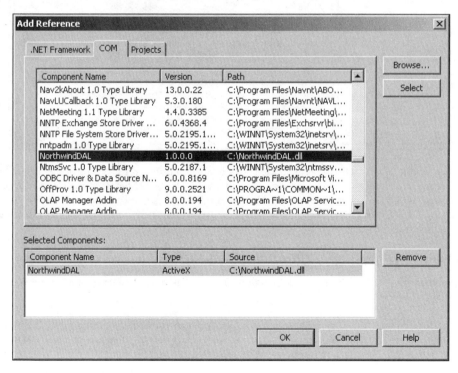

```
C:\WINNT\System32\cmd.exe                                       _|□|x|
C:\>tlbimp NorthwindDAL.dll /out:NorthwindAssembly.dll /verbose
TlbImp - TypeLib to .NET Assembly Converter Version 1.0.2204.21
Copyright (C) Microsoft Corp. 2000.  All rights reserved.
Resolving 'ADODB' as 'ADODB.dll'.
Auto importing 'ADODB' as 'ADODB.dll'.
Typelib imported successfully to NorthwindAssembly.dll

C:\>
```

> *An interesting side note is that* TlbImp *not only creates an RCW for the COM component that is applied to, but for every COM component that the COM component references as well. In the preceding screenshot, for example, you can see that an RCW was generated for the* ADODB *library, since the* NorthwindDAL *type library references it.*

As you do with any assembly that your program references, you need to mention the RCW when you invoke the C# compiler.

Using TlbImp.exe from VS.NET

VS.NET makes it simpler to use a COM component in a .NET project. You just open the Add Reference dialog (by right-clicking on References in the Solution Explorer and selecting Add Reference...), go to the COM tab, and browse to any COM component that is registered on your machine:

When you close the Add Reference window, the IDE will silently invoke the TlbImp to create an RCW for the selected component and copy the RCW to a special area in the file system (see the screenshot below). When you build a Debug or Release version of your project, the compiler will refer to the RCW for the early binding information that it needs, and will copy the RCW to the folder in which the build project is deployed.

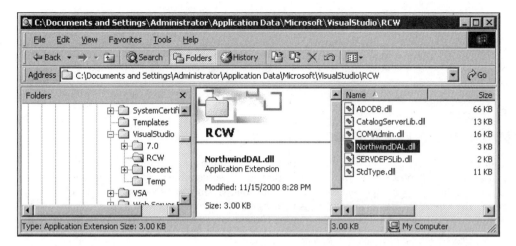

Though this approach is convenient, there's a danger to using it. When invoking `TlbImp`, the VS.NET IDE allows the program to name the RCW after the COM component that's being imported. Later, when you copy the RCW around, it would be easy to accidentally write the RCW file over the COM file, leaving COM Services unable to create the component when it needed to. So that you can give the RCW a different name, you might want to invoke `TlbImp` explicitly, from the command line, and then add a reference to the RCW by browsing to the file from the .NET Framework tab of the IDE's Add Reference dialog.

> *Since most COM components depend on other components, which will be automatically named even by* `TlbImp`, *and hence may share the same name as the original COM component, an even safer recommendation is to be very careful when moving these RCWs around not to overwrite any of the original components.*

Referencing Early-Bound COM Components from Code

In our sample problem, we want to wrap a COM data access object in a .NET business object that enforces security checks and logs usage. Once we've used `TlbImp` to create a RCW for the `NorthwindDAL.dll` and added that RCW to our project's references, writing the business object's C# code is a breeze. The COM component has become a new namespace with a `ShippersTable` class inside. In our code, we can treat `ShippersTable` as if it were a standard .NET class and remain blissfully ignorant that it's really just wrapper.

```
public class Shipper {

    private const string CONNECTION_STRING = "Provider=SQLOLEDB;" +
        "Data Source=ServerName;Initial Catalog=Northwind;User ID=sa;Password=";

    public void SecureInsert(long EmployeeID,
                             string CompanyName,
                             string Phone)
    {
        //Code here would validate the Employee ID...

        //Code here would log the employee's access...

        //This code uses the NorthwindDAL RCW that was
        //created with TlbImp. See how clean it is?
```

```
        NorthwindDAL.ShippersTable objShipperTable;
        objShipperTable=new NorthwindDAL.ShippersTable();
        objShipperTable.Insert(CONNECTION_STRING, CompanyName, Phone);
    }
}
```

Late Binding via Reflection

Although late binding slows an application's performance, there are situations in which it is unavoidable. For example, a very complex COM component might prove insusceptible to TlbImp, or the type library file (.tlb) for a third-party component might be unavailable. When you *have* to late bind to a COM component from a .NET client, the classes in the System.Reflection namespace can help.

See Chapter 6 for a discussion of reflection.

Let's take a moment to look at the major players in that namespace. Then we'll show how these players can work together to late bind to the data access object in our COM DLL.

Writing Code that Late Binds

Late binding to a COM object is a two-step process. First, you have to use the Type.GetTypeFromProgID method to get a reference to a Type object that represents the COM object's type. Next, you have to pass the Type reference to the Activator.CreateInstance method to actually create the COM object. You'll wind up with a reference to the COM object stored in an object variable.

```
Type objShipperTableType = Type.GetTypeFromProgID
                           ("NorthwindDAL.ShippersTable");
object objShipperTable = Activator.CreateInstance(objShipperTableType);
```

Once you have a reference to the COM object, you can call methods on it – but not directly. You have to use the Type object's InvokeMember method to access the COM object's features. InvokeMember takes five arguments:

- ❏ The name of the member that you are invoking.

- ❏ A value from the BindingFlag enumeration. These values indicate whether you are invoking a property, method, etc.

- ❏ A reference to a binding object. This allows you to apply language-specific binding information. You'll usually just pass it a null value.

- ❏ A reference to the COM object itself.

- ❏ The fifth argument is the most difficult to prepare. It is an array of the input arguments that you want to send to the COM method.

```
objShipperTableType.InvokeMember("Insert",
                                BindingFlags.InvokeMethod,
                                null,
                                objShipperTable,
                                aryInputArgs);
```

As you might imagine, the complexities introduced by InvokeMember and all of this indirection make your code bug-prone. For this reason, you should bullet-proof your late-binding C# code with as much exception-handling as possible.

Late Binding to our Data Access COM Component

As a demonstration, we've re-implemented our .NET business object's SecureInsert() method to access the ShippersTable COM object via late binding. The code isn't pretty, but it works.

```csharp
using System.Runtime.InteropServices;
using System.Reflection;

public class Shipper {

    private const string CONNECTION_STRING = "Provider=SQLOLEDB;" +
        "Data Source=ServerName;Initial Catalog=Northwind;User ID=sa;Password=";

    public void SecureInsert(long EmployeeID,
                             string CompanyName,
                             string Phone)
    {
        //Code here would validate the Employee ID...

        //Code here would log the employee's access...

        //This code uses reflection to late bind to
        //the data access object.
        object objShipperTable;
        Type objShipperTableType;
        object[] aryInputArgs= { CONNECTION_STRING,
                                 CompanyName,
                                 Phone };

        objShipperTableType = Type.GetTypeFromProgID
                                ("NorthwindDAL.ShippersTable");
        objShipperTable = Activator.CreateInstance(objShipperTableType);
        objShipperTableType.InvokeMember("Insert",
                                         BindingFlags.InvokeMethod,
                                         null,
                                         objShipperTable,
                                         aryInputArgs);
    }
}
```

A Final Drawback to Late Binding

In addition to being slower, late-binding applications are harder to code. Because the VS.NET IDE doesn't have access to a type library with information about the late-bound objects, it can't provide you with helpful features such as Intellisense and Auto-Data Members when you code to them. Because you don't have these editing features, it's easy to misspell method and property names. These errors slip by the compiler, causing mysterious crashes during the middle of your program's execution. You have to be careful when typing in late-binding code.

And again, be sure to provide exception handlers.

Importing ActiveX Controls

So far, we've talked about techniques for using standard COM components in .NET applications. A lot of organizations, however, have invested time, energy, and money in a particular kind of COM component, a graphical one: the ActiveX control.

There are two ways to use ActiveX controls under .NET. Visual Studio can import ActiveX controls, but the .NET SDK is also shipped with an application named AxImp.exe. This application performs the same kind of service for ActiveX controls that TlbImp.exe performs for non-graphical COM components. In other words, it generates a wrapper component containing a type library that .NET can understand, and this wrapper component is capable of marshalling calls between the .NET runtime and the underlying COM object (the control).

Using AxImp

AxImp can be run from the command line, simply passing in the path and filename of the ActiveX control library we wish to import. Note that if the library contains more than one ActiveX control, we can only import these controls in one go; we cannot import the controls one by one. As an example, let's import the MSMAPI ActiveX library. This library resides in the file MSMAPI32.ocx (in the WinNT\System32 directory), and contains two controls, MAPISession, used for logging in to a MAPI email session, and MSMAPIMessages, used for sending and receiving emails. To import these controls for use in .NET applications, we would execute the command AxImp C:\WinNT\System32\MSMAPI32.ocx:

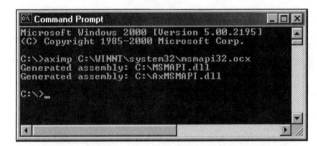

This generates three files: a .NET Windows control named AxMSMAPI.dll; a proxy .NET class library named MSMAPI.dll; and a debug file MSMAPI.pdb. The general forms of the names of these generated files are <old_ocx_name>.dll; ax<old_ocx_name>.dll, and <old_ocx_name>.pdb. However, as in the above example, numbers at the end of the name will be omitted.

> Note that in Beta 1 AxImp overwrites existing files without warning, so you need to be very careful when using this utility if the output type library will have the same name as the original COM type library.

We can use the proxy class library, MSMAPI.dll, just like any other .NET component. For example, to use this component to log on to a MAPI session and send an e-mail:

```
namespace AxImpTest
{
    using System;

    public class MSMAPITest
```

```
    {
        public static int Main()
        {
            MAPISession objSession = new MAPISession();
            MAPIMessages objMsg = new MAPIMessages();

            objSession.Password = "password";
            objSession.UserName = "me@mydomain.com";
            objSession.SignOn();
            objMsg.SessionID = objSession.SessionID;
            objMsg.Compose();
            objMsg.MsgSubject = "MAPI Control Test";
            objMsg.MsgNoteText = "The message body";
            objMsg.RecipAddress = "you@yourdomain.com";
            objMsg.ResolveName();
            objMsg.Send(null);
            objSession.SignOff();

            return 0;
        }
    }
}
```

We can compile this console application using the command-line compiler; we simply need to add a reference to the `MSMAPI.dll` library:

```
csc aximptest.cs /r:system.dll /r:msmapi.dll
```

Adding Controls to the Toolbox

The other DLL generated by `AxImp` – the proxy Windows control (`AxMSMAPI.dll`) – can be added to a form and used just like a normal .NET Windows control. We can add controls to the toolbox simply by right-clicking on one of the tabs in the toolbox, and selecting **Customize Toolbox...** from the context menu. From the dialog box, select the **.NET Framework Components** tab, and browse to the `AxMSMAPI.dll` file:

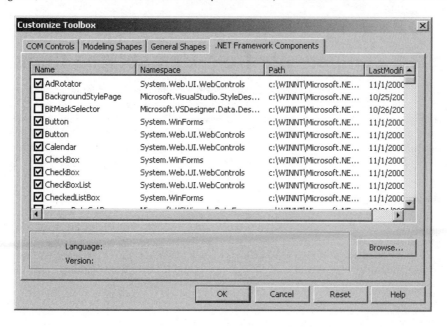

The **Customize Toolbox** dialog also allows us to add ActiveX controls directly, without the need to run `AxImp` ourselves. Visual Studio will automatically generate the necessary proxies when the controls are added to the form. To do this, we just select the **COM Controls** tab and select or browse to the ActiveX controls we want to add. This approach allows us to add controls individually, rather than adding all the controls in a particular library.

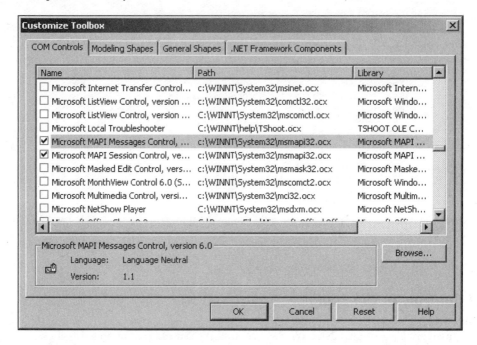

Once the controls have been added to the toolbox, we can simply drop them onto a form, and Visual Studio will take care of all the code needed to initialize the controls, so we can use them like normal WinForms controls.

Calling C# Components from Unmanaged Code

The previous section covers the most likely scenario developers face as they migrate applications to the .NET Framework – calling existing COM components from managed code – but what if you need to integrate your shiny new .NET components into an existing, COM-based application? As you might have guessed, the .NET Framework comes with tools that allow us to do this, too. However, before we look at these, a quick word of warning: migrating .NET components to unmanaged code means that they will lose the fancy new features of the .NET Framework, such as cross-language support.

RegAsm.exe

When you use the Visual Basic `CreateObject` or Visual C++ `CoCreateInstance` function to request a COM object, COM Services looks in the Registry for the metadata necessary to instantiate it. Therefore, if we want to use a .NET component from a COM client, we need to export the component's metadata from its manifest to the system Registry, where COM Services can find it. The `RegAsm` utility lets us do just that.

When we execute RegAsm passing in the name of a .NET component, the program makes an entry for our component in the system Registry. This allows COM Services to provide instances of objects in our component to requesting clients.

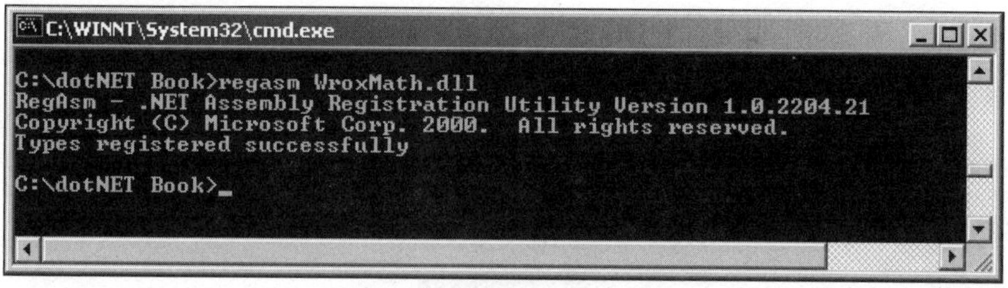

A RegAsm Sample

To demonstrate this process, I have constructed a simple MS.NET component, WroxMath, which contains a class called Calculator that can Add(), Subtract(), Multiply(), and Divide() two integers.

The code for Calculator follows, and it can also be downloaded from the Wrox website (http://www.wrox.com). After you have typed the code in, compile it to a .NET component (csc /t:library WroxMath.cs), and register the component with COM using RegAsm (as in the screenshot above). Although it's a good idea to give an assembly file the same name as the component it contains, it doesn't really matter what you name the file; when RegAsm imports the component into the Registry, it generates the class's Prog ID by combining the MS.NET namespace and class name.

```
namespace WroxMath
{
using System;

public class Calculator
{
   public Calculator()
   {
   }

   public int Add(int FirstNumber, int SecondNumber){
      return FirstNumber + SecondNumber;
   }

   public int Subtract(int FirstNumber, int SecondNumber){
      return FirstNumber - SecondNumber;
   }

   public int Multiply(int FirstNumber, int SecondNumber){
      return FirstNumber * SecondNumber;
   }

   public int Divide(int FirstNumber, int SecondNumber){
      return FirstNumber / SecondNumber;
   }
}
}
```

To test this, we'll use a very simple Windows Script Host file in VBScript to late bind to our .NET component. Type in the script below in your favorite text editor and save it to the desktop with a `.vbs` extension:

```
Dim objCalculator
Set objCalculator = CreateObject("WroxMath.Calculator")
Call MsgBox(objCalculator.Add(57,4))
```

When we execute the script, it will use COM Services to obtain a reference to the .NET `Calculator` component and invoke the `Add()` method on it, displaying the results returned from that method in a message box:

RegAsm Snags

There are a couple of snags to avoid when using `RegAsm` to expose a .NET component through COM Services.

First, if you're going to access your .NET components from older languages such as VBScript, don't use C#'s new `long` datatype. VBScript can't marshal the 64 bits. Use the `int` type instead (32 bits).

Second, remember that the registry entries just redirect COM Services to your .NET code; your .NET code will be executed, and COM Services needs to know where to find it. With that in mind, make sure that there's a copy of the assembly either in the global assembly folder (typically, somewhere under `C:/WINNT/assembly`) or in the same folder as the application. You'll know that COM Services is not able to find your assembly file if you get an error message similar to this one:

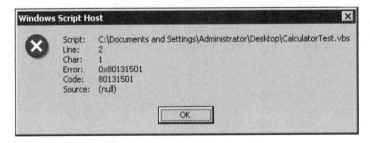

For more information on adding assemblies to the Global Assembly Cache, please see Chapter 10.

Registry Entries Created by RegAsm

It's an interesting exercise to use Regedit to find the entries for your .NET component that RegAsm makes in the system Registry. Look closely at the `(Default)` value in the screenshot below; you'll see that it points to `MSCorEE.dll`. This DLL file denotes the .NET execution engine (hence the EE), and its entry in the Registry lets COM Services know that the component should be created in that engine's process:

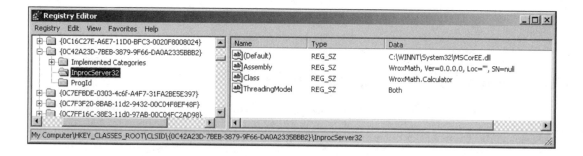

Exporting Type Libraries

As you probably know, VBScript uses late binding – that's why it was able to create our .NET object in the example above. If a COM client wants to early bind to an MS.NET component, we have two options. Firstly, we can tell `RegAsm` that we want to generate a type library using the `/tlb` switch:

```
RegAsm WroxMath.dll /tlb:WroxMath.tlb
```

Alternatively, we can use the Type Library Exporter program, `TlbExp.exe`. This can interrogate an assembly's manifest and use it to produce a type library file that COM clients can use for early binding during compilation. It works much the same as `TlbImp`; we pass in the name of the assembly from which the type library will be generated, and the filename of the type library we want to generate:

```
TlbExp WroxMath.dll /out:WroxMath.tlb
```

The generated type library looks like this when viewed in OLE View:

Projects which reference this type library can now make use of early binding, for example to take advantage of Intellisense when using Visual Basic.

Unsafe and Unmanaged Code

We've seen how to use COM components in managed code, and how to call .NET assemblies as though they were COM components, but there's one more way we can interact with unmanaged code. Before we look at this, though, it's worth quickly reiterating what managed code is, and how it differs from unsafe code.

"Unsafe" Doesn't Mean "Unmanaged"

Contrary to popular belief, there's a difference between code that is *unmanaged* and code that is *unsafe*.

Unmanaged code is not managed by the Common Language Runtime. Such code includes executables created with VB6, or stand-alone VC++ programs without managed extensions.

Unsafe code *is* managed by the CLR: it just includes constructions and idioms that the C# compiler typically frowns on. By placing code in blocks delimited with the unsafe keyword, the C# developer is free to use all the dangerous pointer trickery that he or she desires. Source code in unsafe blocks just slips by some of the compiler's more stringent restrictions. However, when compiled, it is unable to escape the watchful eye of the CLR.

Unmanaged Code: PInvoke

In this chapter, we've focused on using COM classes in .NET applications, but C# permits another kind of interoperability as well: the ability of managed C# code to invoke unmanaged functions stored in DLLs. Originally intended to provide access just to the Windows API, .NET's Platform Invocation Services (PInvoke) can now also expose functions in DLLs other than the operating system ones.

Unlike code in unsafe blocks, code called by PInvoke truly is "unmanaged" and outside the authority of the CLR.

How PInvoke Is Used

To use Platform Invocation Services to call an unmanaged, external function, we must declare the target function at the top of a C# file. Providing no implementation, this declaration gives the target function's name, lists its input arguments, and associates the function with the name of the DLL in which the function is stored. This simple console application example uses the Windows API to create a message box:

```
namespace UnmanagedExample
{
using System;

class PInvokeExample
{
    //Declare the external, unmanaged function.
    [sysimport(dll="user32.dll")]
    public static extern int MessageBoxA (int Modal,
```

```
                                        string Message,
                                        string Caption,
                                        int Options);

        //Program starts here.
        public static void Main (string[] args)
        {
            //Invoke the unmanaged function using PInvoke.
            MessageBoxA(0,"PInvoke worked!","PInvoke Example",0);
        }
    }
}
```

When the code calls the unmanaged function, `PInvoke` loads the function's DLL into memory, locates the address of the function, and marshals the C# input arguments to types that the DLL function will understand. Then `PInvoke` activates the function, moving the application's thread-of-execution into the unmanaged DLL. As example above shows, a call to an unmanaged function looks just like the call to an ordinary, managed one.

An important thing to note about the above code is the use of the `extern` keyword in the unmanaged function's declaration. This indicates that the function is defined externally, so we don't have to supply a definition within our code itself; this is used in conjunction with the `sysimport` attribute to indicate that the definition is provided in `user32.dll`.

Marshaling Structs

Underneath the hood, `PInvoke` and COM Interoperability use the same marshaling service to move simple numbers, floats, and references between managed and unmanaged code. If we want to marshal more complex data structures (such as `structs`), we have to provide the runtime with explicit instructions on how to do so.

To provide this information, we use the `StructLayout` attribute. We simply declare a `struct`, modify it with `StructLayout`, and then reference that `struct` when we declare the external function. For example, if we export the following `struct` (which resides in the `Calculator` class):

```
using System.Runtime.InteropServices;

// Set the StructLayout attribute.
// As well as Sequential layout, we can specify LayoutKind.Explicit.
// We would then need to specify a FieldOffset attribute for each field.
[StructLayout(LayoutKind.Sequential)]
public struct Rectangle {
    int length;
    int breadth;
}
```

It will be passed to COM as:

```
struct tagCalculator$Rectangle
{
long length;
long breadth;
} Calculator$Rectangle;
```

Note that only fields are exported; methods and properties of the struct are ignored.

Aliasing Methods

Handily, PInvoke allows us to refer to external functions by names other than those embedded in their DLLs. To rename an external function, we just add a name value to the sysimport command that declares it:

```
//Declare the external, unmanaged function.
[sysimport(dll="user32.dll",name="MessageBoxA")]
public static extern int ErrorMessage(int Modal,
               string Message,
               string Caption,
               int Options);
```

The name value in the preceding code snippet, for instance, would allow the client to invoke the MessageBoxA function with the more meaningful ErrorMessage.

```
//Program starts here.
public static void Main(string[] args)
{
    //Invoke the unmanaged function using PInvoke.
    ErrorMessage(0,"PInvoke worked!","PInvokeExample",0);
}
```

Code Access Security with PInvoke

The Common Language Runtime is able to keep close tabs on managed code to make sure that it doesn't do anything malicious. When a program's thread-of-execution moves from managed code into unmanaged code, however, the CLR isn't able to enforce security any more. For this reason, classes that use PInvoke to execute unmanaged code need to be fully trusted in the execution environment. Furthermore, classes that access *those* classes will also require full trust.

Consider carefully whether the functionality of PInvoke is worth the security hole that it can open up.

Platform Independence with PInvoke?

While it's true that PInvoke buys us the rich functionality of the entire Windows API, the .NET base classes give us most of it, and in a nice object-oriented fashion to boot. When we use the base classes, we make it easier for other developers to understand our code, because the .NET base classes are the element common to all the .NET development languages.

Furthermore, using the base classes instead of invoking the Windows API increases the chances that our code will one day be portable to other platforms. Theoretically, .NET code that executes in one environment should execute in any other environment that is equipped with a base class library and a CLR. When we dip into the underlying operating system, we violate the insulation that .NET provides and destroy any chance of platform independence.

Although platform independence is *somewhat* speculative right now, why not prepare for a possible future?

Summary

Our organizations don't have to throw away their existing COM components and ActiveX controls in order to use the .NET Framework. Instead, a suite of utility programs and programmatic techniques allow our new .NET applications to interact with legacy COM code. In this chapter we've seen both how to call COM components from our C# programs, and how our .NET assemblies can be called from existing applications.

In addition to COM Interoperability, C# offers Windows API interoperability in the form of Platform Invocation Services (`PInvoke`). Although easy to use and potentially quite powerful, `PInvoke` may introduce issues regarding security and platform independence, and as such should be used with caution.

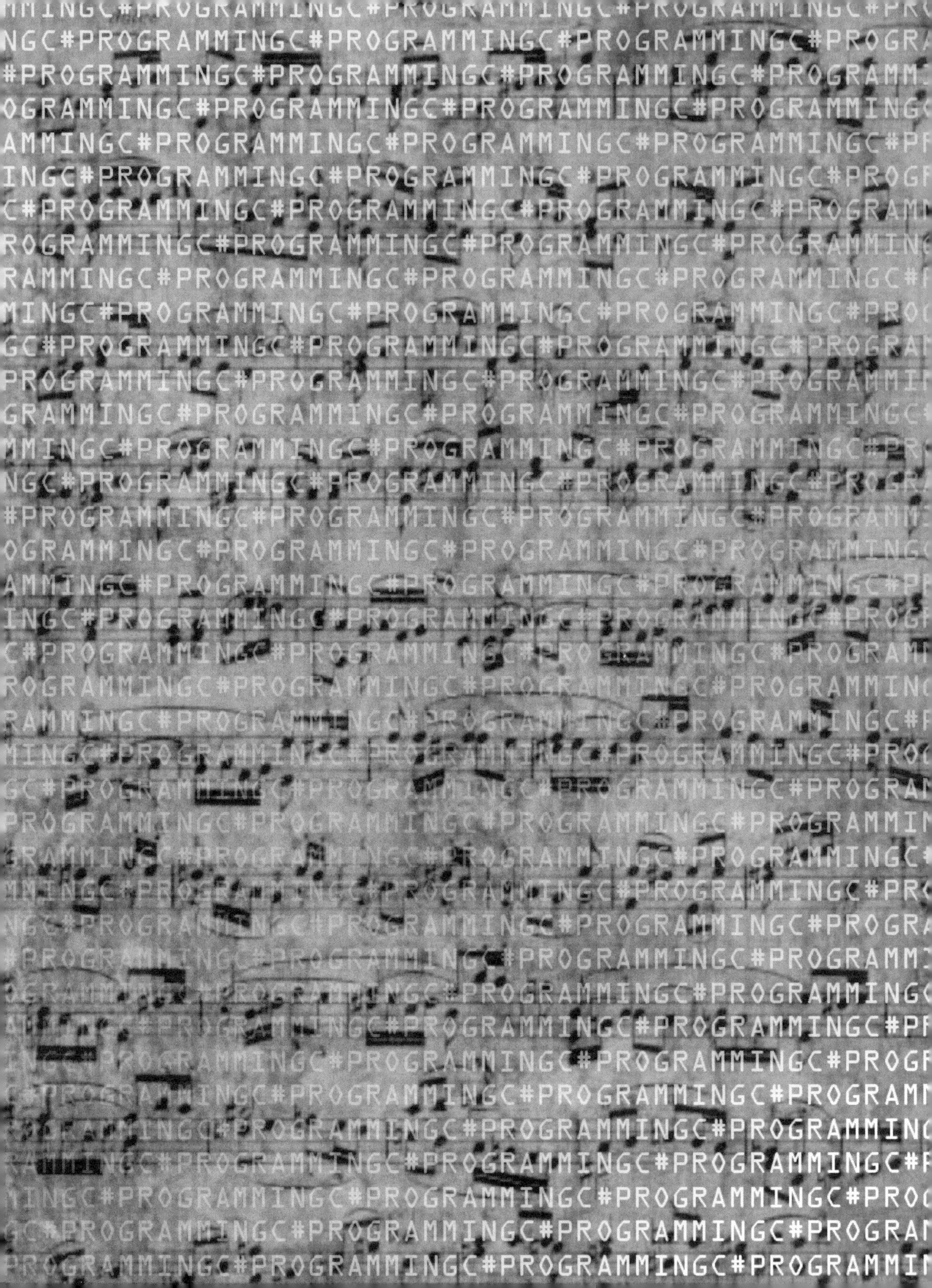

12

COM+ Services

Overview of Component Services

This chapter targets people who have some experience with Microsoft Transaction Server (MTS) and wish to get up to speed quickly with COM+ Services, MTS's latest incarnation.

This first section gives a brief refresher of some component services concepts, while the rest of the chapter deals with what's new in COM+.

Re-usable, Robust Enterprise Functionality

In the development of enterprise-scale applications, many kinds of functionality need to be used over and over again. One example is transaction support, the ability to group related operations together so that they succeed or fail as a single unit.

MTS bundled up transactional support into a neat package that developers could use and re-use. MTS has been superseded by COM+ Services, so let's start talking in those terms.

Component Administration

An application is an administrable group of components. The COM+ Services administration program, available from Start | Programs | Administration | Component Services, is an MMC snap-in which allows you to create applications and fill them with COM components that are on your machine. You can import both registered and unregistered components.

Once components are imported into COM+ Services applications, the administration program allows you to set those applications' properties. The most important property is called the `Activation` property. When a client tries to create a component, the `Activation` property of that component's application determines the process in which the component is created. Components in library applications are created in the same process as the client creating them.

Surrogate processes provide a place for components to live when they are requested by clients on remote machines. They provide a degree of fault tolerance; if the surrogate process fails, the remote client is untouched. For efficiency's sake, COM+ provides a setting with which you can make a surrogate process live through inactive periods in which it receives no requests from clients.

Some applications contain components that need to be tied down so that not just anyone can create them. Those components might provide access to sensitive information, or even expose a method for purging the whole database. For safety reasons, COM+ allows you to restrict applications to clients in certain security roles.

The creation, population, and configuration of an application can be a time-consuming task. COM+ allows you to export applications to re-distributable files that you can run on other machines.

Services Provided

We'll begin our exploration of COM+ Services' transaction support now.

Supporting Transactions

All transactions must show atomicity, consistency, isolation, and durability. The Distributed Transaction Coordinator (DTC) acts as the overseer, ensuring that these conditions are met, directing the different participants in transactions, and negotiating between them.

When a client creates a component that is configured in COM+, COM+ Services creates a wrapper object called an `ObjectContext`. The `ObjectContext` exposes the object's COM+ settings and transactional information.

Using methods and objects exposed in `mtxas.dll`, a COM+ component can obtain a reference to its `ObjectContext` and use that reference to commit transactions or roll them back.

Configuring Transaction Levels

Transactional components need to have their transactional levels set. An object's transaction level determines if and how an object participates in transactions. For components to make use of COM+'s transaction support effectively, they need both code and configuration. With .NET, you no longer need the administration program to do this. Transaction level can be set programmatically or with the COM+ Services classes.

Transaction Level	Notes
Not Supported	The object cannot participate in transactions.
Supported	The object can participate in a transaction initiated by its client, but does not need a transaction in order to execute, and will not initiate one when invoked outside of a transaction.

Transaction Level	Notes
Required	The object can only execute within a transaction. If called by a client participating in a transaction, the object will join that transaction. If called by a client not in a transaction, the object will create its own, new transaction.
Requires New	The object generates its own, new transaction with every call. If this new method is committed, its work will persist even if the client is calling from a transaction that fails.

In the real world, Supported and Required are the only transaction level values that most people ever use.

The Danger of Transactions

Transactions must be used prudently. While executing, a transaction can create locks on the resources participating in it, blocking other clients from access to those resources. For this reason, transactions can represent bottlenecks in application performance. They should be used sparingly.

> *For a more comprehensive guide to how VB, COM, and MTS work together, see* Professional Visual Basic 6 MTS Programming, *Wrox Press, ISBN 1861002440.*

Conserving Server Resources

In today's networked world of internet applications, it's feasible for several thousand remote clients to simultaneously make requests on a single server. If the fulfillment of each request involves the instantiation of an object, the sudden demand on the server's resources could cause the server to degrade or even crash. Clearly, internet applications demand that object lifetime be controlled efficiently and intelligently.

Applications like IIS don't allow unlimited simultaneous requests. Only a specified number of requests per CPU are typically allowed, 25 being the default in IIS.

Another approach would be to require clients to create objects only at the time that they need them and to destroy them as soon as they are through with them. Thus, by using objects sparingly, clients could help reduce the total number of objects on the server at any one time. Unfortunately, there are at least two flaws with this approach. First, its puts an awful lot of responsibility on the developer writing the client code, and, second, the server still has to do the work of creating and destroying objects.

JIT Activation

One solution that COM+ Services provides is JIT (Just-In-Time) activation. When an object is configured for JIT activation, it lives only while a method on it is being called. After a method call is complete, the server deactivates the object, reclaiming the object's resources so that they can be used for other tasks. When another call to the object is made, COM+ Services activates the object again, quickly reassembling it for the short time that it will do its work. Of course, COM+ uses load balancing to make sure that it isn't constantly creating and destroying objects willy-nilly. See the *Component Load Balancing* section later on in this chapter.

With JIT activation, clients create objects whenever they want to and keep them for as long as they need them. They remain blissfully ignorant that they are actually holding a stub which waits until it has an actual reference before calling the object. Clients only know that, when they ask that stub to do some work, the work gets done.

Object Pooling

Object pooling is another way to minimize the performance hit that objects exact on servers. This is very similar to the IIS pooling model. When a class is configured for object pooling, the system maintains a pool of instances of that class. When a client requests an object, it receives a reference to one of the instances from the pool, if one is available. If no instance is available, the client must wait for one to be created or for an existing one to become available if the pool has reached its maximum number of objects.

The administration program allows administrators to configure the minimum and maximum number of objects maintained in an object pool. It also allows for the specification of a time-out value. If a client doesn't receive a requested object from the pool within the period indicated by the time-out value, an error event will be generated.

Objects must be Stateless

In order for objects to employ JIT activation and object pooling, they must be stateless (this also helps to ensure isolation in transactions). When a method is called, all the information that the object needs to perform that method must be passed in as arguments to the method; you can't rely on information being maintained in the object's properties.

Remember that under JIT activation an object's resources are continually being reclaimed for other purposes. Under object pooling, the same object instance is being passed around from client to client. Under these conditions, there's no guarantee that the value of an object's properties will be consistent or meaningful from one method call to another.

Because the developer cannot maintain state in objects, he/she must do so elsewhere – on the client (probably in browser cookies), or in a database. Microsoft's .NET has introduced a new Session State Store which makes it easier than ever to store session state in SQL Server.

What's New in COM+?

Installation

COM+ is an integral part of the Windows 2000 operating system and not just add-on program. It's there as soon as you install the OS.

The COM+ Catalog

MTS stored information about its components in the system registry; COM+ uses both the registry and the new Registration Database for storing component metadata. When abstracted, the combined information store is known as the COM+ Catalog.

You manipulate values and components in the COM+ Catalog from the administration program. Behind the scenes, this program automates the COM+ object model to manipulate values in the Catalog. You too can reference the COM+ object model for building automatic setup packages, profiling components, and soon.

New Services

Component Load Balancing

For some heavily hit Internet applications, the resource conservation provided by JIT activation and object pooling just isn't enough. In such situations, developers need to distribute the workload from a single server to several, making a "web farm" of cooperating machines. The Component Load Balancing (CLB) provided by COM+ Services allows developers to accomplish this.

When a client requests a component, a single server on the network – the CLB server – selects an eligible server machine from a list that it maintains to provide the component. Afterwards, subsequent communication between the client and the component server is done directly, without the help of the CLB server. As you might imagine, this is a very efficient arrangement.

The algorithm that the CLB server uses to pick server machines is a hybrid of other popular algorithms used today. Many schemes use a "round robin" algorithm and simply go down a list of available machines, doling out object requests to the servers in an even, alternating fashion. Other schemes are more sophisticated and subject participating servers to a response time analysis in order to determine their relative capacities. Like a round-robin algorithm, Microsoft's scheme does iterate through a list of servers, but one in which the servers are ordered by response time. Because stronger servers appear first in the list, more object requests are directed to them. The efficiency of this algorithm ensures that server resources are used to their maximum efficiency, and that application users enjoy an optimal usage experience.

Because CLB introduces redundancy to a server network, it's a godsend when a server goes down. But what happens when the CLB server itself crashes? To prevent disaster, developers can use Microsoft Clustering to provide a backup CLB server which will come online and assume the responsibilities of the failed one.

There are several issues to consider when deciding whether to use CLB in an enterprise application. First, at the time of writing this, only machines running Windows 2000 Advanced Server or Windows 2000 DataCenter Server can be used as Component Load Balancers. Second, because instances of load-balanced objects may hop from machine to machine between method calls, load-balanced objects must be stateless. Third, objects cannot use CLB and object pooling together for an obvious reason: CLB distributes a virtual pool of objects across the entire cluster of server machines.

Events

What Events are for

Events are a form of bi-directional, asynchronous communication between server objects and their clients. When an error occurs, or when an unusual situation is encountered, a server object can raise an event that alerts its client or clients, who can then take appropriate action. The nice thing about events is that a server object doesn't have to know who its clients are. It just raises the event and goes about its merry business, oblivious to how many or how few clients are listening.

A server might raise an event to tell a client that a background processing job – such as the saving of a file to a disk – has completed. Or a server object might raise an event many times in succession, periodically informing a client about the progress of an operation so that the client can update a progress bar. There are many other circumstances where events play an invaluable role. In fact, the whole Windows operating system is an event-driven one in which window objects respond to events such as key-presses and mouse clicks.

317

Limitations of COM's Event Model

Classic COM's event model was an internal one; it required that both client objects and server objects be equipped with special code for implementing events.

Specifically, clients and servers had to know the `IConnectionPoint` interface. Client objects used this interface to add references to themselves to a linked list of pointers maintained by server objects. When a server object wanted to raise an event, it iterated through its list, notifying each client by activating its associated pointer.

This boilerplate code bulked up client and server classes, and was another layer of complexity that developers had to deal with.

Strengths of COM+'s Event Model

COM+ introduces a new, external event model that is much simpler than its predecessor. It requires a minimum amount of boilerplate code in client and server objects. Instead, the intelligence for handling communication between clients and servers is centralized in COM+ Services, wherein the relationship between the clients and servers is configured.

Here's the workflow for creating an event relationship with COM+:

1. Create a COM DLL that defines an event class. An event class is just a list of unimplemented methods that serves as a model for servers who raise events and clients who handle them.

2. Use the COM+ administration program to register the event class DLL with COM+ Services.

3. Create a client component that references the event class DLL and implements the interface defined in it.

4. Register the client component as a subscriber with COM+ Services.

5. Create a server component that references the event class DLL and uses it when it wants to raise an event.

6. Register the server component as a publisher with COM+ Services.

Now, when the server object raises an event, COM+ Services will serve as an interceptor for this event, relaying notification of it to all the client components that have registered as subscribers to its event class.

When you configure an event relationship, you must remember to activate it using the Properties window. Another option on this window allows you to turn on queuing for the event, which we will discuss shortly.

A Limitation of COM+'s Event Model

In this current iteration of COM+ Services, server objects can only raise events to client objects located on the same physical server; it's impossible to use the new event model and load balancing at the same time.

Queuing

Normally, messages from client objects to server objects are delivered synchronously; the client makes a request of the server object and waits until this request is fulfilled and control is returned from the server. There are situations, however, in which communication must occur asynchronously. Here are a couple of examples.

Consider a sales application used by a remote user from his laptop. Throughout the day, the salesman takes orders and enters them into his machine. At night, in his hotel perhaps, he connects with his organization's server and uploads the day's sales information to it. Queuing would allow the salesman's laptop to maintain a "sending" queue of requests to an object on the main server. When he connected with the server, COM+ Services could play back the requests from the sending queue to the server object, asking it to enter the sales information in the database. The strength of this approach is that the same server object could be used for connected and disconnected machines.

A second example involves an e-commerce application. Imagine that, during the course of a busy day of transactions, the server on which the business objects reside goes down. Without queuing, the e-commerce application would generate errors as it hopelessly attempts to instantiate necessary objects on the unavailable server. With queuing, COM+ Services could store requests to the unavailable objects in a "receiving" queue and send each customer on his merry way. Later, when the unavailable server came back up, a qualified user could replay the stored messages from the receiving queue, allowing them to instantiate the now-available objects and use them to perform order processing.

Queuing requires that Microsoft Message Queuing (MSMQ) be installed on the target machine.

Using COM+ under .NET

Using COM+ Services with .NET Components

As this chapter has demonstrated, COM+ Services have a wealth of enterprise functionality that would be very difficult and time-consuming to duplicate. Although COM+ Services were originally designed for use with COM components, it would nice if .NET components could also use them. The problem is that compiled .NET components (that is, assemblies) and compiled COM components adhere to different structural standards; COM components conform to COM's binary model and .NET components conform to the strictures outlined in the Common Language Specification. In order to make .NET components make use of services originally designed for components that fit a different model, there are two basic challenges that need to be met.

First, .NET components need to be able to access the objects in the COM+ Services object model so that they can refer to them in code.

Second, .NET components need to be compiled, packaged, and registered in such a way as to be recognizable by COM+ Services.

To meet the first goal, Microsoft provides the attributes and classes in the `Microsoft.ComServices` namespace. To meet the second goal, they provide the `RegSvcs.exe` registration program. Developers can use these tools together to COM+ enable .NET components.

Let's take a closer look at this process.

The Microsoft.ComServices Namespace

For an example, let's consider the order entry system for a hypothetical book distributor. In this system, a certain function does two things: 1) it debits a customer's credit card account for the cost of a book, and 2) it records the sale of the book in a shipment table in the database.

This system has a function in a class library requiring transactional support. This function debits a credit card account and then inserts a record into the shipment table, and we don't want one operation happening without the other. We want atomicity.

```
//This function's work needs to succeed or fail as a unit.
public void PlaceOrder(object objCardInfo, object objOrderInfo)
{
//Operation 1: Debit the credit card.
//Imagine code here...

//Operation 2: Record a shipment to be fulfilled.
//Imagine code here...
}
```

If you've ever done any MTS or COM+ programming, you'll know that we need the `ObjectContext` object in order to join operations 1 and 2 atomically. Fortunately, this COM+ Services object, along with many others, is exposed to .NET components via the `Microsoft.ComServices` namespace. `ContextUtil` is the name of the .NET object that wrappers COM's `ObjectContext`. The screenshot here shows the classes in `Microsoft.ComServices`:

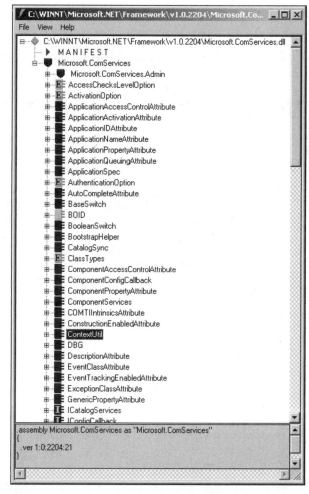

`ContextUtil` exposes .NET versions of all the functions that you remember from the `ObjectContext` object in COM. Here are the methods of the `ContextUtil` object:

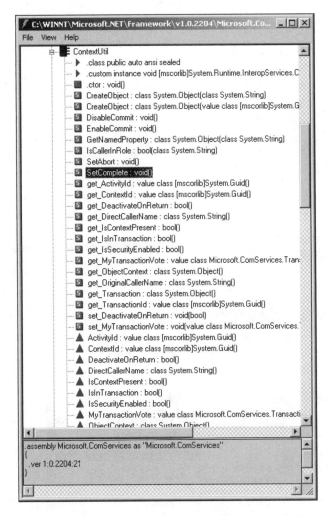

To endow our example function with transactional support, we'll need two of these functions.

If everything goes well and the transaction should be committed, our function will call `ContextUtil`'s `SetComplete method`. If an error occurs during processing and both operations should be rolled back, our function will call `SetAbort`. If you recall, these method calls are indirect messages to the DTC.

```
//This function's work needs to succeed or fail as a unit.
public void PlaceOrder(object objCardInfo, object objOrderInfo)
{
    try
    {
    //Operation 1: Debit the credit card.
    //Imagine code here…
```

```
    //Operation 2: Record a shipment to be fulfilled.
    //Imagine code here...

    //Commit the transaction.
    ContextUtil.SetComplete();
    return;
    }

    //This block will be activated if an error occurs.
    catch (Exception e)
    {
    ContextUtil.SetAbort();
    return;
    }
}
```

We have used the `ContextUtil` object from the `Microsoft.ComServices` namespace to make our function into a transaction. But how do we tell Visual Studio what transaction setting we require? That's what we will look at next.

Recommending Configuration Options

Remember the MTSTransactionMode option in VB6's property window? By setting it, you could tell MTS what transaction levels your COM components required.

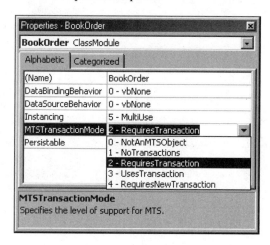

.NET provides the same type of service, in the form of an `attribute`: `[Transaction]`. By prefacing a class with the `Transaction` attribute, you can tell COM+ Services what sort of transaction levels your .NET components require:

```
namespace CSharpPreview
{
    using System;
    using System.Runtime.CompilerServices;
    using Microsoft.ComServices;

    [Transaction(TransactionOption.Required)]
    public class BookOrder : ServicedComponent
```

```
    {
        public void PlaceOrder(object objCardInfo, object objOrderInfo)
        {
            //Imagine code for placing the order here...
        }
    }
}
```

The `Transaction` attribute lets COM+ Services know the proper transaction level for our component so that we don't have to set it ourselves. As an added bonus, it implicitly invokes `SetComplete` if the function exits normally (without raising an exception).

`TransactionOption` is, of course, an enumeration, with values of `Required`, `None`, `Ignored`, `Supported`, and `RequiresNew`. These values represent possible settings in the COM+ administration program.

> *Note that we also derive our class from the `System.ServicedComponent` abstract class; we will look at this class in more detail shortly.*

Now that we know how to set up a transactional component, we can proceed with building one.

Building a Transactional Component

In this section, we will build a transactional component that will delete a row from the `Employees` table in the `Northwind` database. The code will delete a row from the `Northwind` database before attempting another connection. This means that the delete operation will always take place, but as the code takes place in a transaction, all of the actions are rolled back if any of them fail. To demonstrate that the component is transactional, we will attempt to connect to a non-existing database after deleting the row; this allows us to confirm that the roll-back of the deletion operation really does take place.

Building the Class

Start by selecting File | New Project and then select Class Library, as we want to build our transaction into a class so that it's recognized by Component Services. Name the project transaction then rename the class file changename.cs in the Properties window. In the Solution Explorer window right click on References and then add references to `Microsoft.ComServices` and `System.Data.dll`, and enter the following code into the `changename.cs` file:

```
namespace transaction
{
    using System;
    using System.Data;
    using System.Data.SQL;
    using System.IO;
    using Microsoft.ComServices;
    using System.Runtime.InteropServices;

    /// <summary>
    ///     Summary description for Class1.
    /// </summary>
    [Transaction(TransactionOption.Required)]
    public class changename : ServicedComponent
    {
```

```
    public changename()
    {
        //
        // TODO: Add Constructor Logic here
        //
    }

    public void changemethod()
    {
        string sConn = "server=Ephemeral;uid=sa;pwd=;database=northwind";
        string sCommand = "SELECT EmployeeID, FirstName, LastName " +
                          "FROM Employees";
        string sConn2 = "Provider=nonsense";
        string sCommand2 = "SELECT title FROM titles";

        SQLDataSetCommand DSCmd = new SQLDataSetCommand (sCommand, sConn);
        SQLDataSetCommand DSCmd2;

        DataSet ds = new DataSet();

        DSCmd.FillDataSet(ds, "Employees");

        DataTable dt = ds.Tables[0];

        try
        {
            // Delete the last row in the dataset
            string strEmpID =
                dt.Rows[dt.Rows.Count - 1]["EmployeeID"].ToString();
            dt.Rows[dt.Rows.Count - 1].Delete();

            // Update the database
            DSCmd.DeleteCommand.CommandText =
                "DELETE FROM Employees WHERE EmployeeID='" + strEmpID + "'";
            SQLConnection objConn =
                    new SQLConnection("Ephemeral","sa","","Northwind");
            objConn.Open();
            DSCmd.DeleteCommand.ActiveConnection = objConn;
            DSCmd.Update(ds,"Employees");

            // Attempt to connect using an incorrect connection string
            DSCmd2 = new SQLDataSetCommand(sCommand2, sConn2);

            // Complete the transaction if all went well
            ContextUtil.SetComplete();
        }
        catch (Exception e)
        {
            Console.WriteLine(e.Message);

            // Abort the transaction since an exception was raised
            ContextUtil.SetAbort();
            return;
        }
    }
}
}
```

Let's go through this code and see how the transaction is going to work:

```
public void changemethod()
{
    string sConn = "server=Ephemeral;uid=sa;pwd=;database=northwind";
    string sCommand = "SELECT EmployeeID, FirstName, LastName " +
                        "FROM Employees";
    string sConn2 = "Provider=nonsense";
    string sCommand2 = "SELECT title FROM titles";
```

changemethod() is the method we are going to call to perform our transaction. We declare string variables to connect to the database. sConn and sCommand hold a connection to the Northwind database. sConn2 holds an invalid connection, which we will use to check that the deletion is rolled back.

```
SQLDataSetCommand DSCmd = new SQLDataSetCommand (sCommand, sConn);
SQLDataSetCommand DSCmd2;

DataSet ds = new DataSet();

DSCmd.FillDataSet(ds, "Employees");

DataTable dt = ds.Tables[0];
```

Here we set DSCmd to connect to the Northwind database. We don't set the invalid DSCmd2 here – we want that to fail, so we will do it within our try block to catch any exceptions that are thrown. We then set up our datasets, and fill ds with information from the Employees table:

```
try
{
    // Delete the last row in the dataset
    string strEmpID =
        dt.Rows[dt.Rows.Count - 1]["EmployeeID"].ToString();
    dt.Rows[dt.Rows.Count - 1].Delete();

    // Update the database
    DSCmd.DeleteCommand.CommandText =
        "DELETE FROM Employees WHERE EmployeeID='" + strEmpID + "'";
    SQLConnection objConn =
            new SQLConnection("Ephemeral","sa","","Northwind");
    objConn.Open();
    DSCmd.DeleteCommand.ActiveConnection = objConn;
    DSCmd.Update(ds,"Employees");

    // Attempt to connect using an incorrect connection string
    DSCmd2 = new SQLDataSetCommand(sCommand2, sConn2);

    // Complete the transaction if all went well
    ContextUtil.SetComplete();
}
catch (Exception e)
{
    Console.WriteLine(e.Message);

    // Abort the transaction since an exception was raised
    ContextUtil.SetAbort();
```

```
            return;
        }
    }
    }
}
```

In the `try` block, we delete a row from the `Employees` table, and then attempt the invalid connection. For simplicity's sake, we'll just delete the last row in the dataset. When the second attempted connection is unsuccessful, an exception will be thrown and program control will jump to the `catch` block. The row deletion will then be rolled back, and the error code written to the console.

We could now compile and register this class to be used by another program, but this will be left until later as we want to see how the class operates. We will therefore build a client now for use with this class.

Building the Client

Keep the `transaction` project open, and from the **File** menu select **Add Project**, select **Console Application** as the project type and name the project `Console`. We need to add a reference to the `changename` class, so right-click on References in the **Solution Explorer**, click on the **Projects** tab and select the **transaction** project. Now add the following code to the `Main()` function:

```
public static int Main(string[] args)
{
    //
    // TODO: Add code to start application here
    //
    transaction.changename Text = new transaction.changename();
    Text.changemethod();
    Console.WriteLine("Done");
    return 0;
}
```

This just creates an object called `Text`. This object is an instance of the `changename` class, found in the `transaction` namespace. We then call the `Text.changemethod()` method which performs our transaction, and then display a line to the console so we can see when our program has finished running.

Now we want to see what happens when we run our component. We need to set the client program as the startup project, since our transactional component doesn't have an entry point, so click on the **Console** project in the **Solution Explorer**, and then from the **Project** menu select **Set as StartUp Project**. We can now run our project by clicking on the run button or pressing *Ctrl-F5*.

When we do this, the following should show up in the console window (this shows that an exception has been thrown and has been caught):

```
Unknown connection option in connection string: Provider
Done
Press any key to continue
```

Now open up the database and have a look at the `Employees` table; you should see that the last row hasn't been deleted, since the change was rolled back after we attempted the second connection and the transaction failed. You can check that the row is actually deleted if the transaction is committed by commenting out the line:

```
DSCmd2 = new SQLDataSetCommand(sCommand2, sConn2);
```

We have looked at how transactions worked, and built a component that uses transactions. We will now look at how you would register a class so that it could be called from other projects.

Registering .NET Components with COM+ Services

Once we've coded our .NET component and compiled it to an assembly DLL, we still have to get it into COM+ Services. You can try adding the assembly DLL to a COM+ application in the same way that you would add a COM DLL – by browsing to it – but this approach won't do you much good. The assembly doesn't have a type library recognizable by COM embedded inside it. Among other things, we're going to have to generate one of these for our .NET component.

Fortunately, Microsoft provides the RegSvcs.exe as part of the .NET SDK. This command line program expedites the process of adding .NET assemblies to COM+ applications. In fact, it does several things, in the following order:

1. It loads and registers the assembly.

2. It creates a type library for the assembly.

3. It imports the type library into a COM+ Services application.

4. It uses metadata inside the DLL (remember our transaction level attribute?) to properly configure the .NET component inside its COM+ Services application.

RegSvcs.exe Syntax

The syntax for invoking RegSvcs.exe isn't complicated, but you'll probably want to invoke the program from a command prompt rather than from the system's Run prompt, so that you'll have time to read any error messages that it might spit out (It's pretty particular about the attributes that you use in your .NET class).

```
RegSvcs BookDistributor.dll [COM+AppName] [TypeLibrary.tbl]
```

The brackets around [COM+AppName] and [TypeLibrary.tbl] indicate that those arguments are optional. If you don't provide the name of a COM+ application, RegSvcs.exe will create one with the same name as your component. If you skip naming the type library, it will create one of those too.

If all's well, `RegSvcs.exe` will effectively import your .NET component into COM+ Services:

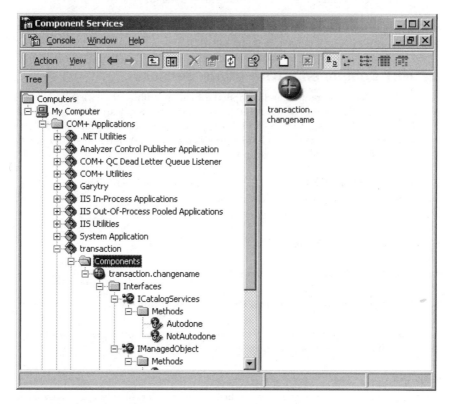

Using other COM+ Services

In our sample code, the `ContextUtil` object and the `Transaction` attribute endowed our .NET component with COM+'s transaction support. Now we'll explore how .NET components can exploit some of COM+ Services' more advanced features such as object pooling and JIT activation.

The System.ServicedComponent Class

.NET components that use COM+ Services are still executed by the .NET runtime; COM+ simply maintains the information about the components' contexts, so that rollbacks and so on can be performed. The `System.ServicedComponent` class gives the .NET developer some control over how COM+ Services treats components' contexts. By inheriting from the `System.ServicedComponent` abstract class, .NET developers can turn COM+ Services on and off for components and intercept events in shared objects' lifetimes.

```
public class BookOrder : ServicedComponent
{
    public override void Activate()
    {
    //The Activate message from COM+ Services
    }

    public override void Deactivate()
```

```
    {
    //The Deactivate message from COM+ Services
    }

    public override bool CanBePooled()
    {
    return false;
    }
}
```

You can see this in action by adding the following methods to your changename class in your transaction project. You will then be able to see when the activation and deactivation of the Text object in the console project takes place:

```
public override void Activate()
{
    Console.WriteLine("Activate");
}

public override void Deactivate()
{
    Console.WriteLine("Deactivate");
}
```

JIT Activation

You will have noticed the Activate and Deactivate methods in the System.ServicedComponent interface. These methods are invoked when JIT activated components are activated and deactivated by COM+ Services. They present an opportunity for your component to do whatever cleanup and state storage work it needs.

Object Pooling

Using COM+'s Object Pooling Service in a .NET component requires that the component's class be modified with the [CanBePooled] attribute. As the following snippet of code reveals, various arguments allow you to set the minimum pool size, maximum pool size, and creation timeout period.

```
[ObjectPooling(MinPoolSize=1, MaxPoolSize=100, CreationTimeOut=30)]
public class BookOrder:ServicedComponent
```

Additionally, the CanBePooled() method from the ServicedComponent interface must return True.

The AutoComplete Attribute

Remember the code for our transaction function? In form, it's a lot like MTS code that you may have written in VB6; you call SetComplete() at the function's normal exit point, or SetAbort() at the error handler if the function terminates abnormally. Most implementations differ very little from this format. To save you calling SetComplete(), .NET provides the [AutoComplete] attribute.

```
[AutoComplete]
public void PlaceOrder(object objCardInfo, object objOrderInfo)
{
//Operation 1: Debit the credit card.
```

```
//Imagine code here…

//Operation 2: Record a shipment to be fulfilled.
//Imagine code here…

return;
}
```

Prefacing a function with [AutoComplete] is a short-hand way of saying to the compiler, "The function is automatically committed unless it is explicitly rolled back using SetAbort()".

The Strength of the Attributed Approach

Do all these classes, attributes, and interfaces seem like a lot of trouble just to use COM+ Services? In relative terms, they're not.

With attributes, you can use COM+ Services with objects created in any .NET language. VB6, for example, wouldn't let you create pooled COM components. Under .NET, such restrictions are lifted, and you can use any .NET language to create COM+-enabled components that are as simple or complex as you like.

Even better, the attributed approach is a non-invasive one. By pasting attributes onto the front of classes and methods, you can COM+-enable them without altering their implementations.

Summary

MTS provided component services that developers could easily use in their enterprise applications: transaction support, security, object pooling, and JIT activation. COM+ Services made these services an integral part of the Windows 2000 operating system and provided new services such as message queuing and events.

Attributes and classes in the Microsoft.COMServices namespace give the .NET developer access to the power of COM+ Services. This namespace provides a ContextUtil class, which gives us access to a component's object context.   We saw how to use this class to implement COM+ transaction under .NET. We also looked at the SystemServicedComponent class, which allows us to implment object pooling, and the AutoComplete attribute which enables auto-completing transactions.

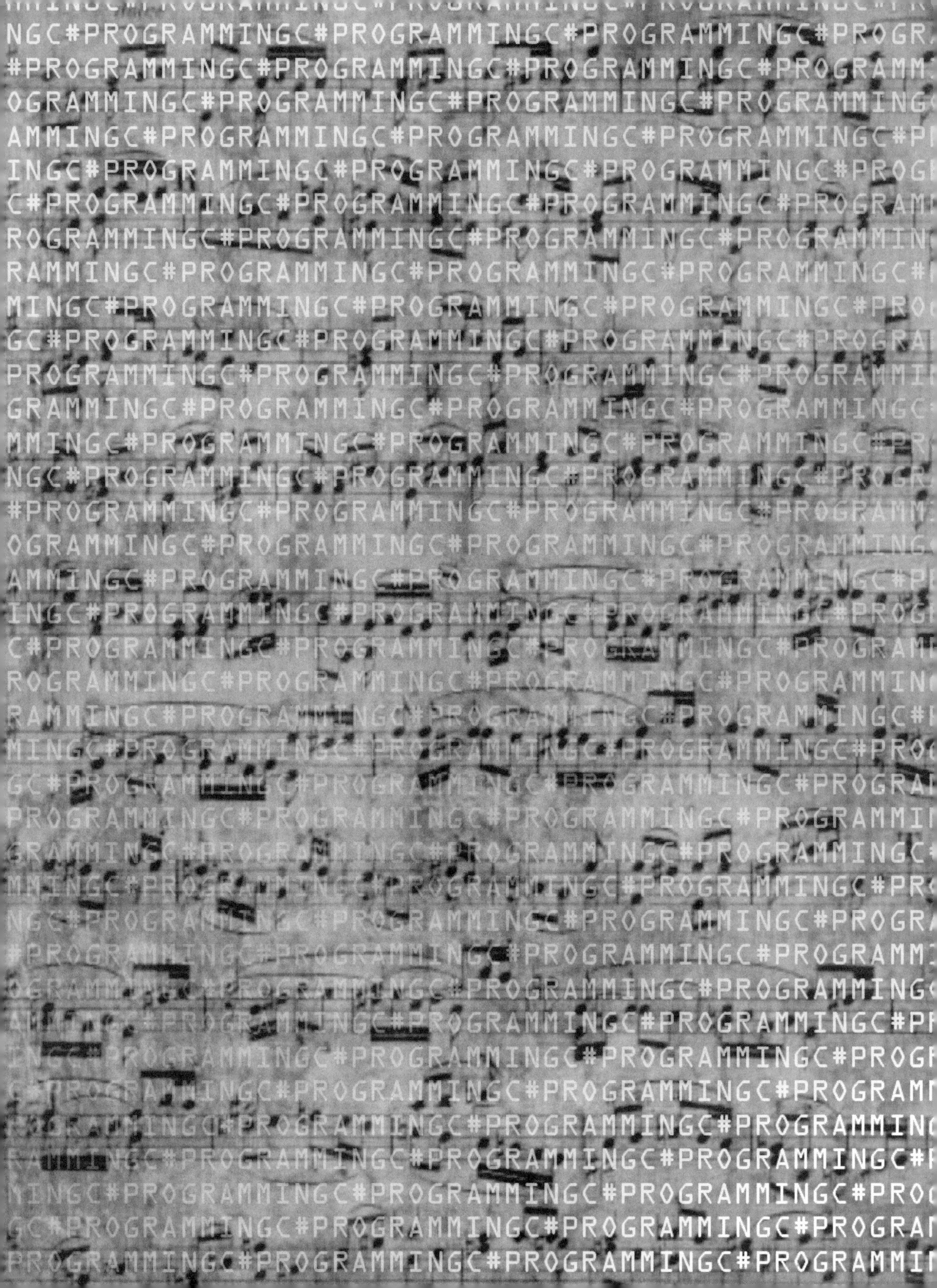

13

ASP.NET

ASP.NET (Active Server Pages.NET) is being introduced as a major component of the .NET platform with the intention of becoming a replacement for ASP. And it's no exaggeration to say that it is likely to completely revolutionize the writing of dynamic web pages.

In this chapter, we'll explain how to write ASP.NET pages and something of what goes on behind the scenes when an ASP.NET page is processed. Since ASP.NET is an evolution of ASP – albeit a rather dramatic evolution – we'll start by explaining how ASP.NET differs from ASP. Note that this chapter presumes that you understand HTML and have some familiarity with the principles (though not necessarily the programming details) of ASP.

ASP is based on the principle that, in a web page, HTML code is interspersed with scripting code that will be run each time the page is requested, dynamically generating the appropriate HTML output. Strictly speaking, the output is not necessarily HTML – for instance, it may include DHTML, XML, or, for mobile phones, WML and WMLScript – but the principles remain identical and we'll concentrate on HTML in this chapter. For example, an ASP page to display the current date and time might look like this:

```
<%option explicit%>
<!DOCTYPE HTML PUBLIC "-//W3C//DTD HTML 3.2 Final//EN">
<HTML>
<HEAD>
</HEAD>
<BODY>
Current Date and Time is
<%=Now%>
</BODY>
</HTML>
```

ASP.NET follows the same general principles, but makes vast improvements in a number of key areas and makes your life as an ASP.NET page writer much easier. In fact, ASP.NET makes a lot of coding so much easier that you'll not actually see that much C# code in this chapter, because so many of the tasks that would previously have been accomplished using server-side scripts can now be performed with simple ASP.NET tags.

New Features of ASP.NET

The main changes with ASP.NET are as follows:

Compiled Code

Whereas the scripting code in traditional ASP pages was interpreted each time the page was run, ASP.NET pages are each compiled into a .NET class the first time the page is requested. The compiled class is cached for subsequent page requests, leading to a huge improvement in performance. The ASP.NET runtime will automatically detect if any changes are made to the source code for ASP.NET page and, if necessary, recompile the .NET class. It's not even necessary to stop the World Wide Web Service for this to happen. If a new version of the source code is written to the file, existing running requests will be serviced using the old version of the class, while all new requests that come in will be serviced with the new version. The old version will be removed from the cache as soon as all existing requests are complete.

Support for Languages

In ASP, the code had to be written in a scripting language – normally VBScript or JScript. With the .NET platform this has changed – at present the compiled code can be written in C#, VB or JScript, and other languages will probably be added to this list in future. Indeed VBScript no longer exists as a separate language, having been absorbed into VB.

Developer Environment

Whereas ASP pages were normally written with Visual Interdev, which provided only limited developer and debugging support through the script debugger, ASP.NET pages can be written using the same Developer Environment as we've been using throughout this book for .NET components and standalone C# applications (as well as C++ and VB applications). This also means that ASP.NET developers get access to the same debugging facilities as developers of standalone applications get.

Server Controls

In ASP, if you wanted to display, say, a drop-down list box, you'd have to actually put the HTML code in your ASP pages. The ASP script engine had no concept of what a drop-down list box was – so you had to explicitly place in the file all of the HTML code that would be passed to the browser. That has changed with ASP.NET because Microsoft has written a large number of server controls, such as list boxes, buttons, and even a full-scale calendar control. These are essentially .NET components that can generate the appropriate HTML code for you, and which you can call up with simple ASP.NET tags. For example, to generate a list box in your HTML page, you might write:

```
<asp:ListBox  id=MyListBox runat=server>
   <asp:ListItem runat=server ID=Item1>Item1</asp:ListItem>
   <asp:ListItem runat=server ID=Item2>Item2</asp:ListItem>
</asp:ListBox>
```

The `runat="Server"` attribute indicates that this tag needs to be processed by the ASP.NET runtime on the web server before the page is returned to the browser, and ensures that the HTML needed to create (or if no such control exists in HTML, simulate) your requested control gets generated automatically. This frees you up to concentrate on the business logic of your page. Unless you're trying to do something pretty advanced or exotic, you don't need to worry about the precise HTML syntax to get the control you want. For something like a textbox, you might not save that much effort, but if it's a calendar control – for which there is no single corresponding tag defined in the HTML protocols and which therefore has to be constructed using a lot of HTML code – the saving to you in terms of development time is huge.

There are also server-side validation controls that arrange to have data validation performed on the data supplied by the user in HTML forms – again saving you from having to write boilerplate HTML or client-side script code to carry out this kind of routine work.

Browser Independence

With ASP.NET you don't need to spend as much time worrying about the capabilities of the particular browser making the request. This is a direct result of the server-side controls. When the ASP.NET runtime processes a control, it automatically checks from the HTTP request headers what type of browser is making the request, and can therefore generate a page tailored to that browser. For example, it might send out JavaScript to perform client-side data validation for a modern browser, whereas an old browser making the same request, but being incapable of running client-side scripts, would get back plain HTML which sends the user's input back to the server for data validation. Again, all this happens without you as the ASP.NET page developer having to worry about it.

Separation of User Interface from Business Logic

With ASP, the `.ASP` file tended to contain all the programming logic that decided what data to send to the browser. Intermingled with this was the HTML that actually created the user interface. This made it more difficult to maintain the code. Admittedly, it was possible, with careful use of included files and function calls, to separate these out to some extent but the process was always somewhat clumsy. It was also possible in principle, to use COM components to separate out code logic from the user interface, but most ISPs wouldn't allow their users to do this because such code could present a security risk to the servers.

ASP.NET makes it much easier to separate out these aspects of your code. This is partly because of the server-side controls – which allow you to just indicate the type of control you want, rather than having to explicitly type in the HTML user-interface tags – and partly because of a new concept, `Codebehind`, in which an alternative file is explicitly indicated as the location where much of the compiled code is contained. We'll examine `Codebehind` later in the chapter.

Now, we are going to see how some of the changes listed above are of benefit in practice, and we'll do this by generating a series of simple ASP.NET pages. Then we'll step back a little, to examine the object model that is working behind the scenes to make it all possible.

Our First ASP.NET Page

To illustrate the general principles of writing and compiling an ASP.NET page, we'll start off with a simple page that displays the current date and also calculates the squares of the numbers from 1 to 10. To keep things simple at the start, this page doesn't use any server controls or other advanced features of ASP.NET. We'll come to those later.

Naturally, the language we use for our code will be C#.

To create the page, we fire up the developer environment and create a new project, selecting a Web Application under Visual C# projects as the application type:

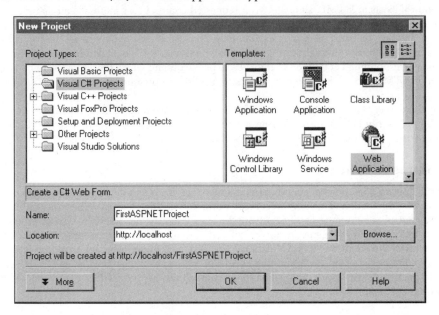

I've imaginatively picked FirstASPNETProject as the project name. This is not going to be the name of any of our ASP.NET pages, but is the collective name of the whole project – the set of pages we will ultimately create in a given virtual directory.

Notice also that the default location that the developer environment has suggested for the project is given as an HTTP URL rather than a file system path. Accepting this location will cause almost all of the files in the project to be created under the home directory for the default web site on your server. The project solution file, <ProjectName>.sln (and its associated .suo file) however, are created in a different location, at <drive>:\Documents and Settings\<UserName>\My Documents\Visual Studio Projects. You'll need to remember this location, since this is the file you double-click in Windows Explorer to start up the development environment to work on the project. You'll also need this file if you intend to use source control tools.

> *Before creating this project, you need to make sure that the FrontPage Server extensions are not only installed, but also configured for the web site you intend to use in IIS. If the FrontPage Server extensions are not configured, the developer environment will refuse to create the project. To configure the FrontPage Server extensions, you should open the Internet Services Manager and then right-click on the chosen web site. From the context menu that pops up, select* All Tasks, *then* Configure Server Extensions. *You'll then be taken through a short wizard that asks you for some information and configures the extensions for you. Note also that, at present, you must have installed IIS and the server extensions (though not necessarily have them configured) before you even install the .NET SDK and the developer environment – otherwise IIS will not be able to process ASP.NET pages correctly.*

When the project has been created, you'll see that a number of files have been created under the <ProjectName> subfolder of the IIS home directory for the web site (normally inetpub/wwwroot):

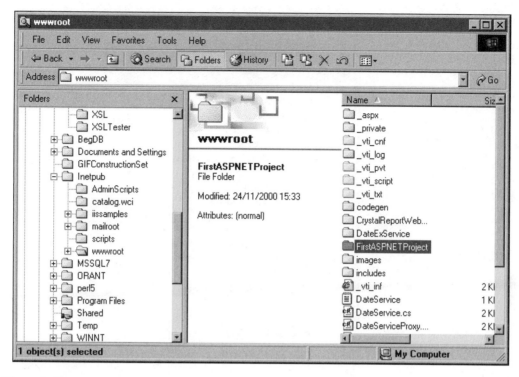

The main files are:

`WebForm1.aspx`	The actual ASP.NET page that is requested by the browser. ASP.NET pages have the `.aspx` extension, which will be recognized by IIS as indicating that the ASP.NET runtime must be used to process requests for the page. You can rename this file after creating the project.
`WebForm1.cs`	Contains any background C# code for the business logic which you don't want mixed up with the UI code in the `WebForm1.aspx` file. `WebForm1.cs` doesn't show up in the Solution Explorer, but you can see it by selecting **View Code** from the page's context menu (if you want to see the HTML code, you need to select **View Designer** and then **HTML** at the bottom).
`Config.web`	Contains various settings governing the web site, in XML format so you can easily modify them. This is an added benefit of ASP.NET – configuration settings are stored in plain text files making administration easier. However, use of these files is beyond the scope of this chapter.

The remaining files are, for the most part, simply the standard project files created with any C# project to give compilation information, etc., and, as such, you'll rarely want to modify them directly.

In the **Solution Explorer** in the developer environment, the screen looks like this:

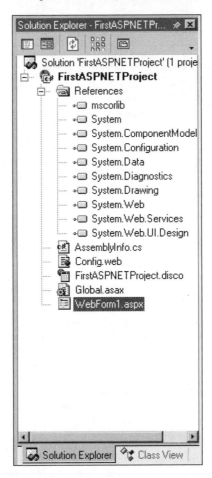

Here, we can see that a couple of web-related base class namespaces, `System.Web` and `System.Web.UI.Design`, have been automatically referenced in the project.

`WebForm1.aspx` isn't a particularly informative name for a web page so we'll change it to `DateSquares.aspx`. We do this in the developer environment by right clicking on that file in the **Solution Explorer** and picking **Rename** from the **context** menu (you might be asked to first close the editor window on the file, if it is open). When you do this, the `WebForm1.cs` file will be automatically renamed too. By the way, don't try simply renaming the files in Windows Explorer – that would be a great way to break your project!

Now we can examine the code that the wizard has generated for us. Open the newly renamed `DataSquares.aspx` file in the developer environment's editor and make sure the HTML view tab is selected. We can then see the following ASP.NET code:

```
<%@ Page language="c#" Codebehind="DataSquares.cs" AutoEventWireup="false"
Inherits="FirstASPXProject.WebForm1" %>
```

```
<html>
  <head>
    <meta name="GENERATOR" Content="Microsoft Visual Studio 7.0">
    <meta name="CODE_LANGUAGE" Content="C#">
  </head>
  <body>

    <form method="post" runat="server">

    </form>

  </body>
</html>
```

Most of this is boilerplate HTML code that sets up the framework for the page, laying out the `<head>` and `<body>` elements. There is also a `<form>` element in the page body. This is based on the assumption that almost any useful dynamically generated web page is going to have a form somewhere to accept user input. That's why the default name for the page was `WebForm1.aspx`. In fact, in ASP.NET parlance, the page that has been generated for us is technically known as a **Web Form**.

There are two new things in this page that won't be familiar to an ASP programmer. One is that the `<form>` element has the `runat="server"` attribute. As we mentioned earlier, this indicates that it is a server control and will be processed by the ASP.NET runtime to generate the corresponding HTML code – though it happens that, in the case of a simple form element like this, the generated HTML code will be almost identical to what we see in the ASP.NET page.

The other new element is the first line of the file:

```
<%@ Page language="c#" Codebehind="DataSquares.cs" AutoEventWireup="false"
Inherits="FirstASPXProject.WebForm1" %>
```

The `<%@ ... %>` block contains information about the ASP.NET file, much as the `<%@ ... %>` block in ASP pages did. However, for ASP.NET, the information contained is somewhat different. In ASP, the information was just there for the benefit of the script engine; here it is to enable the compiler to generate the correct .NET class that will have the responsibility of responding to requests for this page. We start off with the language used – in this case "C#". (The alternative values, at the moment, are "VB" and "JScript".) `Codebehind` indicates the name of the file in which this class is defined and `Inherits` indicates the name of the class. To keep things simple for the time being, we won't worry about the `Codebehind` file just yet. Suffice to say it contains a namespace called `FirstASPXProject` (the name of our project), in which a class called `WebForm1` is defined.

Adding Code to the Page

We're now ready to add our own code to the new ASP.NET page. In the editor we'll modify the wizard-generated code as follows:

```
<%@ Page language="c#" Codebehind="DataSquares.cs"
Inherits="FirstASPXProject.WebForm1" %>

<html>
  <head>
    <meta name="GENERATOR" Content="Microsoft Visual Studio 7.0">
```

```
        <meta name="CODE_LANGUAGE" Content="C#">
    </head>
    <body>

        <h1> First ASP.NET Page</h1>

        Today's date is
        <% = DateTime.Now.ToString() %>

        <p>
        First 10 squares are
        <%
            int i;
            for (i=1 ; i<=10 ; i++)
            {
                Response.Write("<br> " + i.ToString() + " squared = " +
                                (i*i).ToString());
            };
        %>

        <form method="post" action="DataSquares.aspx" runat="server">
        </form>

    </body>
</html>
```

What we've added starts off with the title, using raw HTML. Then we use a <% =...%> block to delimit a block of code in which we use the System.DateTime base class to generate the current date and time. Recall that we introduced this class in Chapter 7, in which we showed how to use its static property, Now, to obtain the current date-time. We don't need to explicitly specify that we are using the System namespace because the command:

```
using System;
```

is present in the Codebehind file.

Finally, we have added a standard C# for loop to iterate over the numbers from 1 to 10, this time in a <%...%> block. Just as in ASP, the <%...%> encloses code that will be executed, while <% = ...%> encloses code that evaluates to an expression which will be added to the response stream. The Response.Write() method is also available, just as it was in ASP, as an alternative way of adding output. The only overt difference between our code and the code you would find in an ASP page is that we are able to use C# as our language – though, obviously, behind the scenes our ASP.NET code is being compiled whereas an ASP page would not be.

We can run the code in just the same way as running a standalone application from the developer environment – by going to the Debug menu and selecting Start. Doing so produces this output:

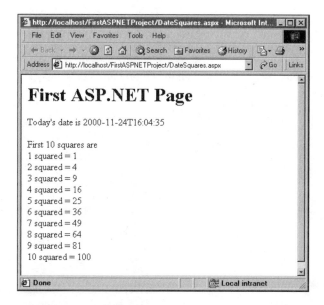

Just as for a standalone application, we can also set breakpoints and examine the values of variables using the Watch window.

Alternatively, you can test the same ASP.NET page by firing up a web browser and typing in the URL of the page (the .aspx file) – though in this case you don't get the benefit of all the debugging facilities of the developer environment.

Writing a Server Control

The DateSquares page we've just developed doesn't make use of the server-side web controls available with ASP.NET. To see how to use those, we'll create another page – a very simple list server registration form which contains three items in the HTML form: a text box, a set of radio controls, and a button to submit the information. The page we will create will look like this:

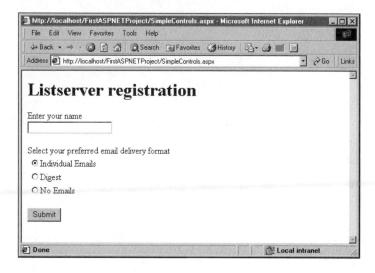

The page isn't really complete – a real list server registration form would ask for a lot more information – such as your email address! But it'll do to illustrate the principles involved with server controls.

To create the new page, go to the **Project** menu in the developer environment and select **Add New Item**. In the resultant dialog box, select **Web Form** and hit the **Open** button to actually create the page. We'll give our new page the name `SimpleControls.aspx`.

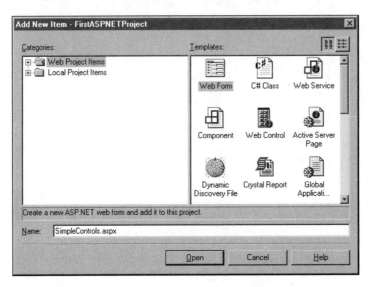

Now open the page and add the following to the wizard-generated ASP.NET code:

```
<%@ Page language="c#" Codebehind="SimpleControls.cs"
         Inherits="FirstASPXProject.SimpleControls" %>

<html>
   <head>
      <meta name="GENERATOR" Content="Microsoft Visual Studio 7.0">
      <meta name="CODE_LANGUAGE" Content="C#">
   </head>
   <body>

      <form method="post" action="SimpleControls.aspx" runat="server">

         <h1> Listserver registration </h1>
         Enter your name<BR>
         <asp:TextBox Runat=server />

         <p>Select your preferred email delivery format
         <asp:RadioButtonList Runat=server>
            <asp:ListItem Runat=server
                    ID=Individual Selected>Individual Emails</asp:ListItem>
           <asp:ListItem Runat=server ID=Digest>Digest</asp:ListItem>
           <asp:ListItem Runat=server ID=NoEmails>No Emails</asp:ListItem>
         </asp:RadioButtonList>

         <p>
```

```
              <asp:Button Text=Submit Runat=server />
          </form>

      </body>
  </html>
```

Again, we start off with pure HTML that gives the title. Then we create the textbox with the tag `asp:TextBox`. The syntax is similar to XML, hence the XML-style close to the tag, `/>`. The `runat=server` attribute is once again present to indicate this element must be processed by the ASP.NET runtime before the output is sent to the browser. Note that server-side tags seem generally to be case-insensitive. Quote marks are optional provided there are only alphanumeric characters and no spaces in the attribute values.

The `RadioButtonList` control is more complex since it must contain a number of list items. Hence there are separate opening and closing tags around the element, with the closing tag appearing in more traditional HTML style, `</asp:RadioButtonList>`. The elements `asp:RadioButtonList` and `asp:ListItem` are used to indicate a list of radio buttons and an individual button within the list, respectively.

Finally we add the Submit button, using a similar syntax and with the tag `asp:Button`. This actually generates an HTML Submit button, and we also need to indicate the text to appear on the button, via the attribute `Text`.

Before we can run this page, we need to make one change to our project. ASP.NET projects have the concept of a **Start Page** – this is the page at which execution of the project will always start if we run it from the developer environment, and it is still set to the first page we created, `DataSquares.aspx`. We need to change the start page so that, when we run the project, our new `SimpleControls.aspx` will be run first. To do this, we right-click on the `SimpleControls.aspx` node in the solution explorer and select **Set As Start Page** from the resultant context menu.

Once the page is running, it is instructive to view the HTML that is actually sent to the browser by using the **View Source** option in the browser. The results will, to some extent, depend on the browser because of ASP.NET's ability to customize code to the capabilities of each browser. However, viewed on Internet Explorer 5.5, the HTML returned by the server is as follows, with the content that was generated by the server controls highlighted:

```
<HTML>
<!-- Header stuff removed for clarity -->
<BODY>
  <FORM id=ctrl1 name=ctrl1 action=SimpleControls.aspx method=post>
    <INPUT type=hidden
          value=YTB6LTEwNTA1MDcwODZfX194028c9312 name=__VIEWSTATE>
    <H1>Listserver registration </H1>Enter your name<BR>
    <INPUT id=TextBox1 name=TextBox1>
    <P>Select your preferred email delivery format

    <TABLE border=0>
      <TBODY>
        <TR><TD><SPAN value="Individual Emails">
          <INPUT id=RadioButtonList1_0 type=radio CHECKED
                value="Individual Emails" name=RadioButtonList1>
          <LABEL for=RadioButtonList1_0>Individual Emails</LABEL>
        </SPAN></TD></TR>
```

```
            <TR><TD><SPAN value="Digest">
              <INPUT id=RadioButtonList1_1 type=radio
                    value=Digest name=RadioButtonList1>
              <LABEL for=RadioButtonList1_1>Digest</LABEL>
            </SPAN> </TD></TR>
            <TR><TD><SPAN value="No Emails">
              <INPUT id=RadioButtonList1_2 type=radio
                    value="No Emails" name=RadioButtonList1>
              <LABEL for=RadioButtonList1_2>No Emails</LABEL>
            </SPAN></TD></TR>
          </TBODY>
        </TABLE>
        <P><INPUT id=Button1 type=submit value=Submit name=Button1>
    </FORM>
  </BODY>
</HTML>
```

A couple of points emerge from this code.

Firstly, ASP.NET has added a hidden control to the page:

```
<INPUT type=hidden value=YTB6LTEwNTA1MDcwODZfX194028c9312 name=__VIEWSTATE>
```

This control is there for the ASP.NET runtime's own use – it gives information to ASP.NET about the state of the page and all the controls in it. In general, behind the scenes, ASP.NET uses hidden controls to preserve information between pages concerning values entered in the user controls on the page, and to indicate how a page has been requested. Remember that HTTP is a stateless protocol and that ASP.NET preserves this. Apart from the usual session cookies, once a page has been dispatched back to the browser, ASP.NET does not store any information about the page. Any information that the user has entered or that needs to be preserved between page requests must be stored via hidden controls in exactly the same way that it would have been with ASP pages. The difference with ASP.NET is that the ASP.NET runtime is, to some extent, able to automatically add hidden controls to the pages to do this, without any explicit coding.

A second point of interest from the code concerns the set of radio buttons. The RadioButtonList server control is a good example of an ASP.NET control that has no counterpart in HTML. The closest HTML comes is the <input> element with the attribute type=radio, which defines a single radio button. Radio buttons that have the same value for the name attribute are treated as a group in browsers, to the extent that selecting any one such radio button automatically deselects all the others in that group. Our server-side RadioButtonList control has generated all of the HTML necessarily to construct a number of radio buttons in the same group, and even to lay them out in a table to ensure they are arranged neatly.

Finally, note that ASP.NET has automatically generated IDs for the <input> elements that appear in the HTML output. This is another example of how ASP.NET is able to automatically take care of work that would previously have been done by the page developer. Incidentally, the id attributes in the asp:ListItem server controls are not related to the HTML IDs in the page generated. The id attribute in server controls serves the different (although related) purpose of allowing the control to be identified in the server-side compiled code. We'll see an example of this later on.

Server Controls Available

Microsoft has written a large number of server web controls that offer different user interface elements similar to the radio button list. These controls are all represented by classes belonging to the `System.Web.UI.WebControls` namespace, and the full list is, at present:

Tag	Purpose
`asp:AdRotator`	AdRotator component.
`asp:Button`	Submit, Cancel, or other general-purpose button.
`asp:Calendar`	Calendar control, allowing user to select dates or ranges of dates.
`asp:CheckBox`	Single checkbox.
`asp:CheckBoxList`	A list of checkboxes.
`asp:DropDownList`	Drop-down list box.
`asp:Hyperlink`	HTML anchor tag.
`asp:Image`	GIF, JPEG, or other image.
`asp:ImageButton`	Similar to `asp:Button` but displays a specified image file instead of a conventional button.
`asp:Label`	Plain text – roughly equivalent to an HTML span tag. Using this control gives programmatic access to areas of text output.
`asp:LinkButton`	Hyperlink that is displayed as a button.
`asp:ListBox`	Single or multiple selection listbox.
`asp:Panel`	Highlighted area of text.
`asp:RadioButton`	Single radio button.
`asp:RadioButtonList`	Group of radio buttons.
`asp:Repeater`	Allows some HTML construct on the page to be repeated. You separately write a server-side template that indicates the nature of the item to be repeated.
`asp:Table`	An HTML table.
`asp:TableCell`	Cell in a table.
`asp:TableRow`	Row of a table.
`asp:Textbox`	Textbox.

Full details of the syntax used for each of these elements is given in the documentation with the .NET SDK.

In addition to these controls are a couple that can be connected to an ADO.NET data source, so they automatically display the results of a query against that data source.

Control	Purpose
`asp:DataGrid`	Displays data in a grid.
`asp:DataList`	Displays data as a list.

We won't be going into these controls in this chapter.

We should also mention that a number of available controls are known as HTML controls. These are server-side controls but work somewhat differently, allowing you to specify the precise HTML that should be sent to the browser, rather than simply indicating the type of control that you wish. To this extent they can be seen as not such high level abstractions as the web controls. You're unlikely to want to use them unless you have some special requirements to manually fine-tune the HTML sent out (and, of course, if you do need to do that, you can just avoid the server controls altogether and code up the raw HTML in your page just as you would have done in ASP). The HTML controls available are:

`HtmlAnchor`	`HtmlButton`	`HtmlForm`	`HtmlGenericControl`
`HtmlImage`	`HtmlInputButton (Button)`	`HtmlInputButton (Reset)`	`HtmlInputButton (Submit)`
`HtmlInputCheckBox`	`HtmlInputFile`	`HtmlInputHidden`	`HtmlInputImage`
`HtmlInputRadioButton`	`HtmlInputText (Password)`	`HtmlInputText (Text)`	`HtmlSelect`
`HtmlTable`	`HtmlTableCell`	`HtmlTableRow`	`HtmlTextArea.`

Again, we won't be covering these controls in this chapter.

Writing a Validation Control

We're now going to extend our small `listserver` registration page by adding two examples of a new type of server control which validates the input that the user enters. The server control we'll use is called the `RequiredFieldValidator`, and its purpose is to check that some data has been entered.

Validating a TextBox

To validate that the user types in something in the textbox, we amend that part of the code as follows:

```
<h1> Listserver registration </h1>
Enter your name<BR>

<asp:TextBox id=TextName Runat=server />
<asp:RequiredFieldValidator ControlToValidate=TextName runat="server">
    You must supply your Name
</asp:RequiredFieldValidator>
```

The first change is that we've given the `TextBox` control an ID, for which we've chosen the name `TextName`. The reason for doing this is so that we can refer to it in the validation control.

Next, we add the code for the `RequiredFieldValidator`. It follows the same format as the server controls we've already introduced. The `ControlToValidate` attribute indicates the ID of the control that we are validating, while text inside the element is the error message that will be displayed if validation fails.

How the `RequiredFieldValidator` works depends very heavily on the browser. For a modern (uplevel) browser such as IE5, it will add some client-side JavaScript to the returned page which checks that there is data in the relevant HTML `<input>` element when the user attempts to hit the Submit button, and displays an error message instead of submitting the form if there is none. For older (downlevel) browsers, the `RequiredFieldValidator` won't add any HTML to the page the first time round, but will validate the data on the server when the user hits the Submit button and return an error message if appropriate. In other words, when the user hits the Submit button, ASP.NET will see (from the `__VIEWSTATE` hidden control) that data has been submitted. The field validator control will process the data, and if the result is an error, ASP.NET will return the original page to the browser with the errors in the user input flagged.

Validating a Selection

The `RequiredFieldValidator` control isn't limited to text boxes. It can also validate the selection made in a `RadioList`, `ListBox`, or `DropDownList` server control. In these cases the validation works somewhat differently: You indicate to the validator which field is selected initially, and the validation will be considered to have failed if the user has not selected a different option from this one in the list.

We'll demonstrate this in our listserver registration page by validating the chosen delivery format. We'll do this by adding another option to the list, called `<--Select a Format-->`, which will be the initially selected option, and by requiring the user to select another option from the list. Since, in web pages, this technique is more commonly applied to list boxes and dropdown lists rather than sets of radio buttons, we'll also use a listbox rather than a set of radio buttons. This has the extra benefit of demonstrating how easy it is to swap to a listbox – we just change the `asp:RadioButtonList` element to an `asp:ListBox` element, and don't need to modify anything else – despite the fact that the HTML which will be generated for a listbox is completely different from that which will be generated for a set of radio buttons.

With these changes, the ASP.NET code looks like this:

```
<p>Select your preferred email delivery format
<br>
<asp:ListBox  id=ListDeliveryTypes runat=server>
   <asp:ListItem Runat=server
       ID=NotSelected Selected><--Select a Format--></asp:ListItem>
   <asp:ListItem Runat=server ID=Individual>
      Individual Emails
   </asp:ListItem>
   <asp:ListItem Runat=server ID=Digest>Digest</asp:ListItem>
   <asp:ListItem Runat=server ID=NoEmails>No Emails</asp:ListItem>
</asp:ListBox>
<asp:RequiredFieldValidator ControlToValidate=ListDeliveryTypes
          InitialValue="<--Select a Format-->" runat="server">
   You must select a delivery format
</asp:RequiredFieldValidator>
<p>
<asp:Button Text=Submit Runat=server />
```

Note that we've also had to supply an ID to the `ListBox` control, so that we can identify it in the `ControlToValidate` attribute of the `RequiredFieldValidator` control.

Now if we run the page we see this:

And, if we hit the Submit button without inputting any data, this happens:

Other Validation Controls

The `RequiredFieldValidator` is the simplest of the validation controls. Microsoft has supplied a number of others. At the time of writing, the complete list is as follows:

Control	Purpose
CompareValidator	Compares the values of two controls for equality or inequality.
CustomValidator	Calls a user-defined function to carry out the validation.
RangeValidator	Checks if an entry falls within a given range.
RegularExpressionValidator	Checks that an entry matches a pattern specified by a regular expression.
RequiredFieldValidator	Checks that the user has modified an entry (that its value is different from a specified initial value, which defaults to an empty string).
ValidationSummary	Polls the other validators on the page to make sure that all entries are valid.

Modifying the Appearance of Controls

If the appearance of controls were fixed, their usefulness would be quite limited. In real life, organizations want their web pages to have a unique corporate style – a particular font, background-image, or color scheme – possibly implemented using style sheets.

Accordingly, the server controls have a large number of possible attributes that indicate how they are to be displayed. We're going to demonstrate some of these by having a bit of fun with our list server registration page – by modifying some of the colors, fonts, etc. around the text box.

To do this, we modify the code for the text box as follows:

```
<h1> Listserver registration </h1>
<asp:Label ForeColor="#0033cc" Font-Bold Font-Italic Runat=server>
Enter your name</asp:Label>
<br>
<asp:TextBox id=TextName Text="<--Your Name-->"
             Height=25 Width=200 Runat=server />
<asp:RequiredFieldValidator ControlToValidate=TextName
       InitialValue="<--Your Name-->" Font-Size=20 BackColor="#33ffcc"
       runat="server">
    You must supply your Name
</asp:RequiredFieldValidator>
```

Most of these changes should be self-explanatory from the code. We've specified the width and height of the textbox, and the font-size and background color of the error message if it appears. While we're at it, we've also added an initial text value to the textbox, so it initially displays `<--Your Name-->` instead of being empty. This means that, in order for the `RequiredFieldValidator` control to work correctly, we need to add an `InitialValue` attribute specifying the text that will cause an error – this attribute would normally default to an empty string.

One other change we've made is to put a server `Label` control around the text above the textbox. A `Label` simply displays plain HTML, so you might wonder what the point of it is. However, by putting it into a control we can specify its attributes – in this case, foreground color and that the text is italic and bold – using the same format as all the other controls. More importantly, it means we will have programmatic access to modify this text when we come to learn how to modify server controls using C# code – which we'll do later in this chapter.

Now, if we run the page and hit the Submit button without putting a valid name in the text box, we get the following:

There are quite a large number of attributes that can modify the appearance of controls. It's not really possible to give an exhaustive list here but main ones are:

BackColor	Enabled	Font-Size	Text
BorderColor	Font-Bold	Font-Strikeout	ToolTip
BorderStyle	Font-Italic	Font-Underline	Visible
BorderWidth	Font-Name	ForeColor	Width
CssClass	Font-Overline	Height	

The names of these attributes should be self-explanatory. We'll just remark here that `CssClass` allows you to associate an element with the class of a style sheet. You should also bear in mind that, in the above list, not all attributes make sense for all controls. Also, the ASP.NET runtime might not attempt to render some attributes in all browsers simply because some attributes may be beyond the capabilities of some browsers to render.

How it all Works: the ASP.NET Object Model

We've come a long way in terms of the functionality of our list server registration page, without having to write much ASP.NET code. And in fact, we've got this far without writing *any* compiled C# code – apart from briefly in our `DateSquares` page. If you look back over the chapter, you'll see that all the server controls and the data validation checks have been carried out solely using ASP.NET tags.

However, there is a limit as to what we can do without writing our own actual programming code. In particular, our page doesn't really respond when you click the Submit button. It just comes back again, remembering the values that we typed into the controls. To improve on this we need to start writing some C# code – and that means now is a good time to try to understand what's going on behind the scenes. How the .NET components fit into the picture, what is going on in the Codebehind page, and how the ASP.NET object model works.

The Codebehind Page

So far we've hinted at the fact that ASP.NET pages are each compiled into a class – a .NET component – and it is this class that is executed when the page is requested. We've also indicated that the name of this class is specified as an attribute in the initial `<%@Page` command in the `.aspx` file and is defined in the file specified in the Codebehind attribute. For example, in the DataSquares.aspx page we have:

```
<%@ Page language="c#" Codebehind="DataSquares.cs" AutoEventsWireup="false"
Inherits="FirstASPXProject.WebForm1" %>
```

While, for SimpleControls.aspx, the listserver registration page, we have:

```
<%@ Page language="c#" Codebehind="SimpleControls.cs" AutoEventsWireup="false"
Inherits="FirstASPXProject.SimpleControls" %>
```

If we take a look at the `SimpleControls.cs` Codebehind page (right click on the ASP.NET page and select View Code) we see the following code, which we'll step through piece by piece now.

The page starts off by declaring a namespace and indicating a number of namespaces whose use should be understood implicitly:

```
namespace FirstASPNETProject
{
    using System;
    using System.Collections;
    using System.ComponentModel;
    using System.Data;
    using System.Drawing;
    using System.Web;
    using System.Web.SessionState;
    using System.Web.UI;
    using System.Web.UI.WebControls;
    using System.Web.UI.HtmlControls;
```

Then the `SimpleControls` class – the class that represents our page – is actually declared, along with default implementations of three methods: `Page_Load()`, `Init()`, and `InitializeComponent()`:

```
/// <summary>
///     Summary description for WebForm1.
/// </summary>
public class SimpleControls : System.Web.UI.Page
{
    protected System.Web.UI.WebControls.Button Button1;
    protected System.Web.UI.WebControls.RequiredFieldValidator
                                              RequiredFieldValidator2;
    protected System.Web.UI.WebControls.ListBox ListDeliveryTypes;
    protected System.Web.UI.WebControls.RequiredFieldValidator
                                              RequiredFieldValidator1;
    protected System.Web.UI.WebControls.TextBox TextName;
    protected System.Web.UI.WebControls.Label Label1;

    public SimpleControls()
    {
        Page.Init += new System.EventHandler(Page_Init);
    }

    protected void Page_Load(object sender, EventArgs e)
    {
        if (!IsPostBack)
        {
            //
            // Evals true first time browser hits the page
            //
        }
    }

    protected void Page_Init(object sender, EventArgs e)
    {
        //
        // CODEGEN: This call is required by the ASP+ Windows Form Designer.
        //
        InitializeComponent();
    }

    /// <summary>
    ///     Required method for Designer support - do not modify
    ///     the contents of this method with the code editor.
    /// </summary>
    private void InitializeComponent()
    {
        this.Load += new System.EventHandler (this.Page_Load);
    }
}
}
```

Page_Load is called when the page is loaded, while Init(), which in turn calls
InitializeComponent(), is called earlier on when the component is initialized. Of these, you are most
likely to want to modify the Page_Load() method, and to perform tasks such as reading data from data
sources and setting up the values in various controls.

Apart from the fact that it contains the definition of the class, the main significance of the Codebehind page is that you can use it as a place to store other methods, etc., that you may come to write. Whereas, in ASP you would write functions in the scripting language you are using to perform routine tasks, in ASP.NET it makes more sense instead to have methods in the page class – and you can then call these methods in the C# code in the .aspx file. That way you can minimize the amount of C# code in the .aspx file and so achieve greater separation of the compiled C# code from the user-interface and HTML code. If this sounds a bit confusing, it'll probably become clearer when we write some more C# code in a few pages time.

The ASP.NET Object Model

In this section we'll take a closer look at some of the classes used in ASP.NET.

The main page class is derived from the Page class, in the System.Web.UI namespace. Tracing back the hierarchy, System.Web.UI.Page is derived from System.Web.UI.TemplateControl, which in turn is derived from System.Web.UI.Control and also features in the hierarchy of the classes that represent the various server controls.

The easiest way to investigate what methods and properties are available to us in our main page class is to use the WinCV .NET class viewer that we introduced in Chapter 7 to examine the System.Web.UI.Page class.

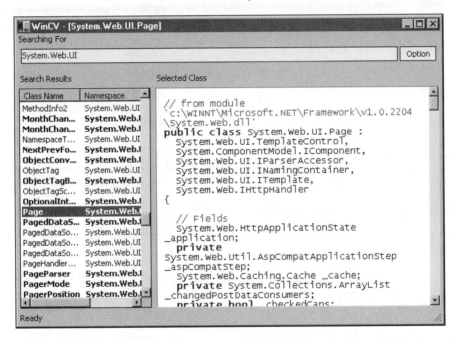

Once again, the member methods, fields, and properties are really too numerous to list here, but the most useful properties you will find include the following:

Name	Class	Purpose
IsPostBack	bool	True if the page has been called by the client hitting the Submit button to send data from an HTML form.

Table continued on following page

Name	Class	Purpose
IsValid	bool	True if all the validation controls on the page indicate that the data they are responsible for is valid.
Request	System.Web.HttpRequest	Equivalent to the Request object in ASP.
Response	System.Web.HttpResponse	Equivalent to the Response object in ASP.
Application	System.Web.HttpApplication State	Equivalent to the Application object in ASP.
Session	System.Web.SessionState. HttpSessionState	Equivalent to the Session object in ASP.

The properties `Request`, `Response`, `Application`, and `Session` tell us how Microsoft have managed to totally change what goes on behind the scenes in ASP.NET when compared to ASP, but while keeping a huge amount of backwards compatibility in ASP.NET pages. By making these .NET classes available as properties in the `Page` class, we can get to exactly the same functionality using the same syntax as with the equivalent former ASP intrinsic objects. For example, the `HttpRequest` class defines the properties `Form` and `QueryString`, which respectively retrieve the `POST` and `GET` data submitted with the HTTP header information in the page request from the browser – just as the equivalent properties of the ASP Request object did. Similarly, in our earlier `DateSquares` page, we had the code:

```
for (i=1 ; i<=10 ; i++)
{
    Response.Write("<br> " + i.ToString() + " squared = " +
                    (i*i).ToString());
};
```

We are now in a position to understand what is going on – this code is actually calling the `Write` method of the `HttpResponse` instance referred to by the `Response` property of the class that instantiates the page.

The ASP.NET Object Model and Server Controls

We are actually dealing with .NET components when we create server controls as well. For example, consider this tag from our list server registration page:

```
<asp:TextBox id=TextName Text="<--Your Name-->"
Height=25 Width=200 Runat=server />
```

What this tag actually causes to happen is that an object of class `System.Web.UI.WebControls.TextBox` is instantiated – and it is this object that is responsible for figuring out the appropriate HTML code to send to the browser. Not only that, but a field is created in the `SimpleControls` page class, called `TextName`, which refers to this object (the name of the field comes from the ID attribute of the ASP.NET element). It's rather as if you'd added a line in the `Codebehind` file like this:

```
TextBox TextName;
```

However, the ASP.NET tag does more than that. It sets the `Text`, `Height`, and `Width` properties of this `TextBox` object to the indicated values, and then calls a method on it which causes the appropriate HTML text to be output to the browser. If we so chose, we could do all of that programmatically in C# code but, provided you know all the values of the attributes at compile time, it's a lot easier to just use the ASP.NET tags.

Now that we understand how the ASP.NET object model works in relation to server controls, we are in a position to be able to manipulate them programmatically. We're going to do this in the next section, in which we put some more dynamic output in our list server registration page.

Manipulating Server Controls

We're going to finish off this chapter by extending the `SimpleControls` page to illustrate how to manipulate the web controls from C# code. We will end up with a page that looks roughly the same, but which is able to detect when the user has hit the Submit button and respond with a slightly different output. We're also going to populate the list box programmatically rather than using ASP.NET tags.

To preserve the current `SimpleControls` page in the code that's available for download from the Wrox Press website, www.wrox.com, we'll actually create a new page, `SimpleControls2`, so copy and paste the code from `SimpleControls` to the new file. (To keep things simple we'll omit the extra attributes that changed the colors and fonts.) The other changes we will make are to add IDs to the `Label` and `Textbox` so that we can access them programmatically, and to remove the `asp:ListItem` tags from the `ListBox` element. This leaves the following ASP.NET code:

```
    ...
        <form method="post" runat="server">
            <h1> Listserver registration </h1>
            <asp:Label ID=LabelName Runat=server>Enter your name</asp:Label>
            <BR>
            <asp:TextBox id=TextName runat="server" />

            <asp:RequiredFieldValidator ControlToValidate=TextName runat="server"
                                        ID=RequiredFieldValidator1>
                You must supply your Name
            </asp:RequiredFieldValidator>
            <p>Select your preferred email delivery format
            <br>

            <asp:ListBox id=ListDeliveryTypes runat="server">
            </asp:ListBox>

            <asp:RequiredFieldValidator ControlToValidate=ListDeliveryTypes
                    InitialValue="<--Select a Format-->" runat="server"
                    ID=RequiredFieldValidator2>
                You must select a delivery format
            </asp:RequiredFieldValidator>
            <p>
            <asp:Button Text=Submit Runat=server />
        </form>
    ...
```

By itself, this would produce a page with an empty list box, but we'll now add the entries back inside the `Page_Load` method in the Codebehind page:

```
protected void Page_Load(object sender, EventArgs e)
{
    if (ListDeliveryTypes.Items.Count == 0)
    {
        ListDeliveryTypes.Items.Add("<--Select a Format-->");
        ListDeliveryTypes.Items[0].Selected = true;
        ListDeliveryTypes.Items.Add("Individual Emails");
        ListDeliveryTypes.Items.Add("Digest");
        ListDeliveryTypes.Items.Add("No Emails");
    }
    if (!IsPostBack)
...
```

Inside the `Page_Load()` method, we add the code that inserts the required items into the list box and ensures that the first item is initially selected. The reason for the initial test of whether there are any items already in the list box is that I found on some occasions `Page_Load` was getting called twice before the page loaded – it's not clear what the reason for this is, or if this is a due to a bug in the current version of the .NET SDK. Note that we've also had to explicitly declare the list box in order to access it programmatically.

At this point it doesn't look like we've gained anything – the code we've added does exactly what our earlier ASP.NET tags did. But the point is that we now have much more dynamic control over what goes in the list box. With the ASP.NET tags we had to know what the items to go in the list box were at compile time, since they were hard-coded into the `.aspx` page. Now, although we happen to have hard-coded the strings, we could equally well have, for example, read them in from a database at run time. We've also, to some extent, separated the business logic from the layout code.

That has sorted out the list box. We now wish to make some changes to the code so that it displays a different message when you click on the **Submit** button. The change we will make is that, when the user clicks **Submit**, the intro to the initial text box will read "you selected the name..." and both the textbox and the list box will become disabled.

Our first task is to check whether the page has been called because the **Submit** button has been pressed. In ASP we would have had to do this by explicitly examining the POST data to see if it contains any data from the forms in the page. In ASP.NET, we have an easier way of doing this – by examining the `IsPostBack` property of the `SimpleControls2` class.

The easiest and neatest way to code up these changes would be to insert them in the `Page_Load()` function, but to illustrate a different way of doing it, we'll add the code to the ASP.NET page itself:

```
<form method="post" action="SimpleControls2.aspx" runat="server">

<%
    if (IsPostBack)
    {
        if (TextName.Text != "<--Your Name-->")
        {
            LabelName.Text = "Your name is";
            TextName.Enabled = false;
        }
        ListDeliveryTypes.Enabled = false;
    }
%>

<h1> Listserver registration </h1>
<asp:Label ID=LabelName Runat=server>Enter your name</asp:Label>
```

Now all we have to do is test the page. On first running it we see the following:

To check that the validator controls still work, we'll hit Submit without inputting any data. This results in the following:

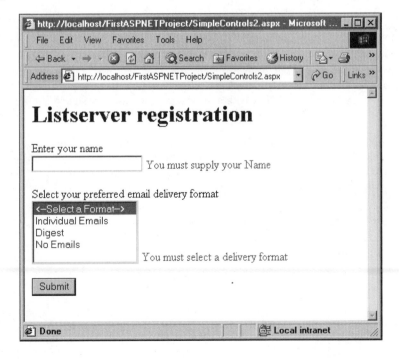

If we now type in some data and hit Submit again, we get this:

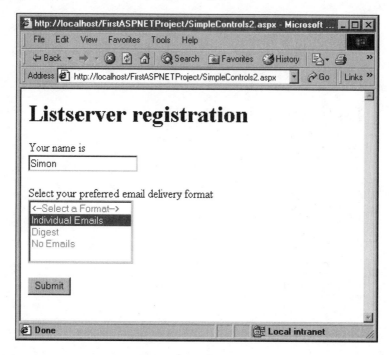

This confirms that our code has worked fine. Note that although it's hard to see in the screenshot, the textbox and list box are actually grayed out and won't accept any input.

Uploading Files

We'll just add one more feature to our sample: the ability to upload files from the client to the server. It's slightly contrived in this instance, but well worth demonstrating. This was of course possible in ASP, but only with a third-party component (unless you fancied scanning through the binary form data manually). However, it's now easy to do in ASP.NET with no extra components, so we'll add a new page to our sample to let users upload their resumes to demonstrate this new feature.

Firstly, we'll need to add a form to our page. This will contain an HTML input box with `type=file` to our form to allow the user to specify the file to upload. Note that there's no server-side equivalent to this element, and that the form must run on the client. We'll also add a hidden input element to store the username passed in from the previous page:

```
<%@ Page language="c#" %>
<html>
   <head>
      <title>Upload Resume</title>
   </head>
   <body>
      <h1>Upload your Resume</h1>
      <p>Please use this page to upload your resume onto our server.</p>
      <form method="post" action="Upload.aspx" name=frmUpload ID=frmUpload
            enctype="multipart/form-data">
```

```
<input type="file" id="myFile" name="myFile"><br><br>
<input type="hidden" id="TextName" name="TextName"
       value="<%= Request['TextName'] %>">
<input type="submit" id="btnSubmit" value="Post file!">
<hr><br>
```

Next, we have to handle the uploaded file. We'll do this in two ways. Firstly, we'll save the uploaded file onto the server. We'll save all the files with the name `resume.txt` in a subfolder named according to the user's name, in the folder `C:\resumes` (which we're assuming already exists). To avoid overwriting files if one user with that name has already submitted a resume, we'll add extra folders distinguished by an incrementing number. For example, the first resume submitted by a user named John Smith will be saved in the folder `resumes\John Smith`, the second in `resumes\John Smith1`, etc.

Secondly, we will display the text on the browser in a textarea. Admittedly, it is slightly perverse to send the data back to the client after we've just uploaded it, but this does illustrate nicely how to read the file.

Handling Uploaded Files

Our next step is therefore to add code to our ASP.NET page to check whether a file has been uploaded, and if it has, to handle it appropriately. The `Request` object now has a `Files` collection, which contains an object of class `System.Web.HttpPostedFile` for each file that was uploaded from the client. So, to determine whether the user has uploaded a resume, we just need to check the `Count` property of this collection. If it's greater than zero, a file has been uploaded, and we can get a reference to it. We're only allowing one file to be uploaded, so we can just get the first item in the collection:

```
<%
  if (Request.Files.Count > 0)
  {
      string strName = Request["TextName"];
      System.Web.HttpPostedFile objFile = Request.Files[0];
```

Next, we'll save the file to the specially created directory, using the `System.IO` classes we saw in Chapter 7. In a real application, of course, we wouldn't want to allow just anyone to upload files to the server, and we would also want to perform some checks on any files which were uploaded, such as checking their `ContentType` and `ContentLength`. However, we will forsake these checks in the interests of simplicity for this sample.

We set our `Directory` object, `objDir`, to point to the folder `C:\resumes\`*username*, where *username* is the name the user submitted in the form. We then run through a `for` loop, incrementing a counter on each iteration, appending this to the username and checking whether the folder with this name exists. When we've found a folder that doesn't already exist, we create it by calling the `CreateSubdirectory()` method of its parent folder, and save the uploaded file as `resume.txt` in this folder:

```
System.IO.Directory objDir = new System.IO.Directory
                                ("c:\\resumes\\" + strName);
int i;
for (i=1; objDir.Exists; i++)
    objDir = new System.IO.Directory
                    ("c:\\resumes\\" + strName + i);
objDir.Parent.CreateSubdirectory(objDir.Name);
objFile.SaveAs(objDir.FullName + "\\resume.txt");
```

Now we've saved the file, we'll display its contents in a textarea on the client. We read the contents of the file into an array of bytes using the `Read()` method of the file's `InputStream`. We then create an `Enumerator` object to iterate through this array one byte at a time and store it in a string. Finally, we write this string to the client inside the `<textarea>` tags:

```
                int iFileLength = objFile.ContentLength;
                byte[] arrBytes = new byte[iFileLength];
                objFile.InputStream.Read(arrBytes, 0, iFileLength);
                System.Collections.IEnumerator enumBytes =
                                         arrBytes.GetEnumerator();
                string strContent = "";
                while (enumBytes.MoveNext())
                    strContent += Convert.ToChar(enumBytes.Current);
                Response.Write("File uploaded: <b>" + objFile.FileName +
                            "</b><br>");
                Response.Write("<p>The text of the file you submitted is:");
                Response.Write("</p><textarea name='txtDisplayFile' " +
                            "id='txtDisplayFile' cols=80 rows=15>" +
                            strContent + "</textarea>");
        }
```

Otherwise, if no file has been uploaded, we just ask the user to select a file:

```
                else
                {
                    Response.Write("Please select a file.");
                }
            %>
        </form>
    </body>
</html>
```

Our new page will look like this after we've uploaded a file:

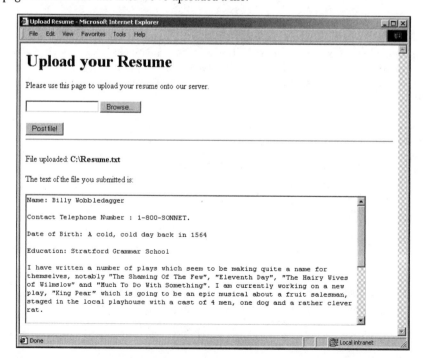

Summary

In this chapter we've gone over the ASP.NET object model and written some simple ASP.NET pages. In the process we've shown how the ASP.NET and .NET architecture give us a conceptually very simple object model that not only makes writing dynamic pages extremely simple, but also results in a very high level of backwards compatibility with ASP – in the sense that all the intrinsic objects available from ASP pages are replaced by objects that can be accessed with the same syntax in ASP.NET. We've also seen that the ASP.NET tags give you a large amount of functionality that you can access without needing to write any compiled C# code.

For organizations that wish to host dynamic web sites, ASP.NET is going to be a huge bonus, leading to web pages that are easy to write and maintain yet at the same time give high performance and powerful functionality.

For further information regarding ASP.NET, visit `http://www.asp.net`.

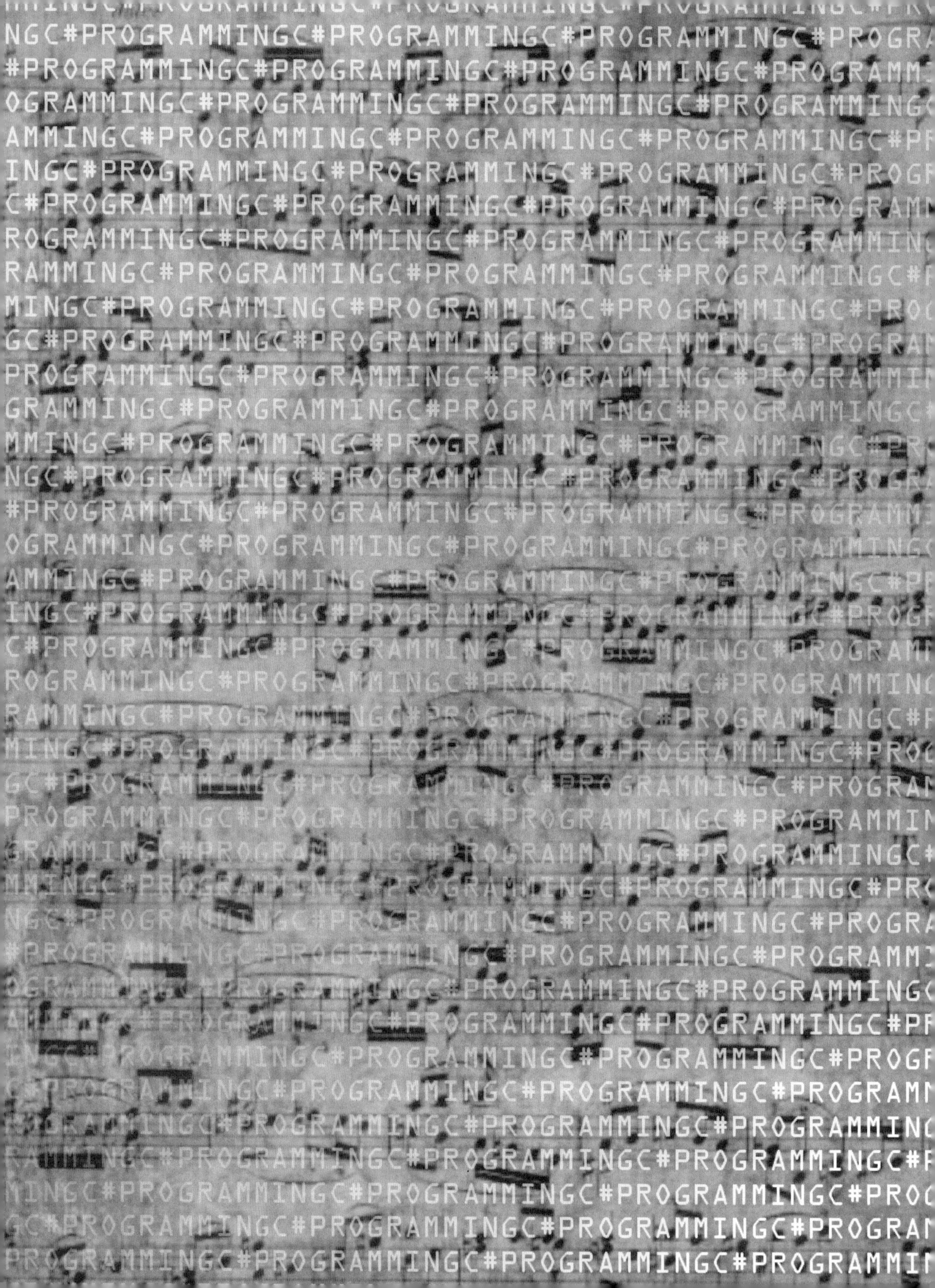
C#PROGRAMMING

Web Services

In this chapter we're going to look at how the .NET platform makes it easy for you to write web services in C#. We'll start off by looking at precisely what a web service is, as the concept may not be familiar to everyone. We'll have a quick look at the protocols that are working behind the scenes to make your web services work, and then we'll move straight on to how to create a web service. We'll do this in two ways – by creating a simple text file and using a full-blown developer environment project – and we'll test the service from Internet Explorer. Next we'll show you how to create a client if you actually want to access the web service from a program running on the client machine rather than from a standard web browser. Finally we'll take a look at the mechanism provided to allow clients to discover what web services are available at a given web site.

What is a Web Service?

In the early days of the Internet, web pages were generally static HTML – which meant a given web page would always display exactly the same information independent of when and by whom it was viewed. Then ASP and other scripting techniques became popular, which meant that pages could dynamically respond to requests for particular information (such as searches) or could look up information in a database and return whatever was in the database at that time. The usefulness of web pages increased hugely. It also meant that users on client machines could use their web browsers to check their email, for example, or perform systems management, on servers over the Internet. However, the big restriction that still existed is that users were confined to doing what that particular page had been structured to do, and viewing the data with whatever user interface was written on the server for that page. If, say, the web page was designed to show a list of products ordered by price, but you from your browser wanted to see them ordered by shipment time then you were stuck – unless of course you had access to the web server to rewrite the pages served up. Similarly, if, instead of wanting to view the site with a standard web browser, you actually wanted to run some software that would extract information from a web page, then that software had to work with the user-interface HTML code returned from the page – it couldn't just directly query the site for the information it needed.

Web Services are a way of overcoming that limitation and allowing software to be written and run on the client machine, which can use the data provided by the server in whatever way it wishes – provided of course that appropriate permissions have been set up. The idea is this: instead of supplying information via HTML, the page makes available a series of function calls. These function calls might look up information in a database or they might be used to supply information to the server. The point is that these functions work exactly the same as method calls in any .NET component – they take parameters and may return a value, except that they are callable over the Internet. The data concerning which function is to be called, the values of any parameters, and any return value of the function are transmitted across the net via standard HTTP-based protocols. The whole concept looks something like this:

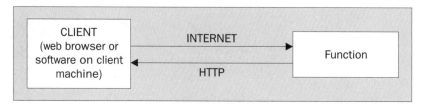

The concept can be viewed in one of two different ways:

❑ **The Ultimate Distributed Application**. The main trend in application architecture over the last few years has been to componentize an application. To split it into smaller units, each of which can be maintained independently of the others. And the more you can design the architecture so you can just replace one unit (component) independently of the others, the lower will be the cost of maintaining the application, and the longer its life is likely to be. A web service takes this idea to the limit – if functions are called using standard HTTP-based protocols over the Internet then the component that calls them can be located anywhere that is connected to the Internet, and there are no restrictions on what platform it might be running on or what language it should be written in.

❑ **A Fully Customizable Web Page**. This is the idea that we mentioned at the beginning of the chapter. If a web page exposes a series of function calls rather than a fairly fixed, albeit dynamically generated, user interface, then clients have much more freedom to use the page in whatever way they wish. For example, suppose you are a news agency, gathering the latest news stories and selling them on to other organizations to publish. You can make the stories available via a web service, and then your clients can use this service to update their own web pages using their own software whenever they wish.

Protocols Needed

While a web service is a powerful concept, it's only going to work if there is a standard protocol available for calling up the functions exposed, something that is universally agreed on. Such a protocol has now been available since at least 1999 – **SOAP (Simple Object Access Protocol)**. SOAP is an XML application and can essentially be thought of as defining the appropriate elements to specify function names and the names, values, and data types of parameters. Microsoft has also added a protocol of its own – **SDL (Service Description Language)**. The SDL is another XML schema, but in this case its purpose is to define the function calls available at a particular URL. If you see a page written in SDL, you'll find it simply lists what functions are available and what parameters they take.

Microsoft has also introduced the idea of a **Discovery File**. Discovery files are files with the .disco extension, and provide information to help browsers determine URLs at a given web site at which web services are available. The discovery file itself contains information for the server, in XML format, which instructs the server about how to respond when the disco file is requested. When the web server receives a request from a browser for a discovery file, it processes the file to generate a list of some or all of the URLs on the site at which web services are available. This list is also returned to the browser in XML format. We'll look at discovery files later on in this chapter.

This all means that, if you are looking to see if any web services are available at a site, you might first send a request with the URL of a discovery file, which will result in a response indicating the appropriate URLs at which the services are located. Suppose you have now identified a service at a certain URL. You would then put in a request for that URL. Depending on what information you append to the URL, the server might respond with an HTML web page that contains a form allowing you to call various functions, a description in SDL of these functions, or might actually invoke one of the functions. Later in the chapter we'll see how to use the URL and the HTTP GET header information to achieve each of these results.

Of course all of this is only going to work with some fairly complex code running on the server. The software (perhaps script or a component) that processes the request for the web service is going to have to figure out from the GET header information what the client wants done, understand SOAP format, extract the parameters, call the appropriate function, then package the results back up in SOAP format. If you were going to develop all this by yourself, that would be a formidable task. The first step Microsoft took towards making this process easier was the introduction of the SOAP toolkit. Designed to work with ASP, this toolkit automated some of the process of coding up pages that could interpret and respond to SOAP requests.

With the introduction of ASP.NET however, the coding up of web services has taken another a huge leap forward, so that writing web services is now as easy as writing ordinary ASP.NET pages. Now all you need to do is write the actual function implementations in your preferred language – C# or VB – and the ASP.NET runtime will automatically take care of receiving calls in any of the above protocols, calling out the appropriate functions with the correct parameters, and converting the results into SOAP format for returning to the browser. A separate tool will set up equivalent functions that can be distributed to the clients. These client functions look externally exactly like the same C# or VB functions that you've placed on the server, but are implemented to convert their parameters into SOAP format and package them off to the server.

What this means is that you don't need to know anything about the underlying protocols in order to write either the web services themselves or the software on the client machine that calls them. ASP.NET takes care of converting data to and from SOAP and SDL for you on both the client and server side. Because of this, we won't go into the details of the SOAP or SDL protocols in this chapter, although you will see examples of them in some of the screenshots. If you do need more details, you can find the SOAP specifications at http://www.w3.org/TR/SOAP/ and details about SDL in the Microsoft .NET documentation.

Our First Web Service

We're going to start off by showing you how simple it is to create a web service without even using the developer environment. The service we create is a simple date service. It exposes two functions, one that returns the current date as a human-friendly string, and one that adds a given number of days to the current date and again returns the result as a human-friendly string. Perhaps not the most exciting of methods, but they'll do to illustrate the principles involved.

To create this web service, simply create a new text file in the home directory of the default web site – for the default IIS settings, that is add the following code: the `inetpub/wwwroot` folder. Call this file `DateService.asmx`:

```
<%@ WebService Language="C#" class="DateService"%>
using System;
using System.Web.Services;

public class DateService : System.Web.Services.WebService
{

    [WebMethod]
    public string CurrentDate()
    {
        return DateTime.Now.ToLongDateString();
    }

    [WebMethod]
    public string AddToToday(int nDays)
    {
        DateTime NewDate = DateTime.Now.AddDays(nDays);
        return NewDate.ToLongDateString();
    }
}
```

As you can see, what we've done is type in some C# code for a class that implements the two methods we want to make available over the Web. The only remarkable points to note about the code are that we've derived `DateService` from the `System.Web.Services.WebService` class and we've assigned the `[WebMethod]` attribute to our two functions. And, of course, this is not scripting code but C# compiled code.

The `WebService` base class gives us some useful properties that let us access the `Session`, `Server`, and `Application` ASP.NET objects, for example, as well as a couple of other web-related objects. The `[WebMethod]` attribute must be included as this informs the compiler that this method is intended to be callable over the web, not just internally within the program.

There's also a `<%@WebService... %>` tag at the top of the file. This tag is needed to inform the ASP.NET runtime that this page is to be processed as a web service. Although, on looking at the contents of the file, you might be forgiven for thinking otherwise, remember that this is an ASP.NET page after all, not a C# source code file!

The amazing thing is that this is all we need to do! Our web service is now up and running. The first time a browser requests this page, the ASP.NET runtime will see from the `.asmx` extension that this page is a web service. It will therefore compile the file into a .NET class that can respond as a web service, and then call up this class. As with ASP.NET pages, it will cache the compiled executable so it doesn't need to be recompiled for future requests.

Let's see what happens if we use Internet Explorer to request our new page:

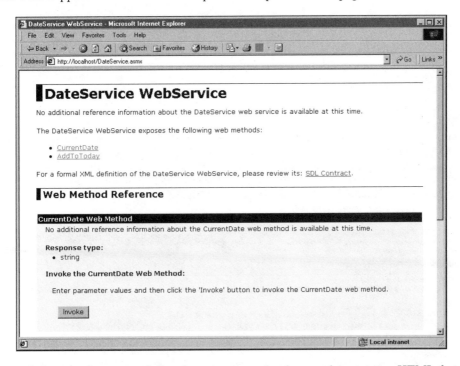

The compiled service has responded to the raw request for the page by returning HTML that describes the services available and invites the user to actually call any of the functions. The part of the page that is invisible contains a button that will call the AddToToday() method, as we can see if we scroll down:

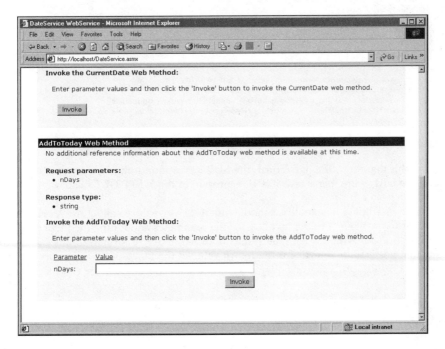

We have three options from this page. We can:

❑ View the SDL contract. This means look at the raw SDL data that describes what functions are available and what parameters they require. The SDL is described as a "contract" since it can be seen as playing that role – indicating what functions the server guarantees to supply; just the same way as a COM interface is sometimes described as a contract.

❑ Invoke the `AddToToday` method.

❑ Invoke the `CurrentDate` method.

You'll only be interested in the SDL contract if you want to work directly with the SDL protocol for any reason. As you don't need that to write and use web services we won't go into it in this chapter but, so you can get an idea of what SDL looks like, we'll present the screenshot you get if you click the **SDL Contract** link. As you can see, the SDL indicates the two available functions, `AddToToday` and `CurrentDate`. The collapsed nodes near the bottom of the screenshot give information about the parameters required and their data types.

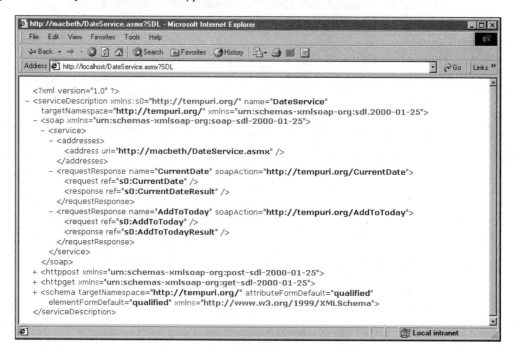

We note from this that the ASP.NET returns the SDL description if the web service is called with `?SDL` appended to the URL – in other words if SDL is present in the HTTP GET header information.

We're more interested here in actually using the function, so we'll try calling the `AddToCurrentDate` function, typing in the value 4 in the text box for the parameter and hitting the **Invoke** button. This results in a new browser window, with the results returned in SOAP format. In this case the only information that needs to be returned is the return value of the function, though more generally there may also be final values of `[out]` and `[in,out]` parameters that need to be returned as well:

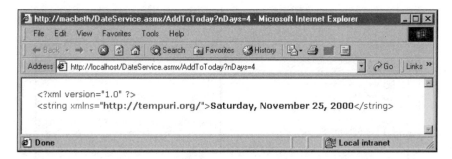

We can also see from this that the ASP.NET runtime actually calls the method if the method name is appended to the URL after a forward slash (/) and the parameters are indicated in the HTTP GET header information when the page is requested.

I should emphasize that all the action here is happening on the server, with the ASP.NET runtime responding to the requests for the `DateService.asmx` page by looking at the information following it. There is nothing remarkable happening on the client. The form asking the client to invoke the functions is just that – a simple form that uses the user input to append the appropriate text to the URL before submitting the request. One point I will draw attention to in the HTML code that is returned from the page is a reference to the `.disco` file in the header information.

```
<!DOCTYPE HTML PUBLIC "-//W3C//DTD HTML 4.0 Transitional//EN">
<!-- saved from url=(0031)http://macbeth/DateService.asmx -->
<HTML>
<HEAD>
<TITLE>DateService WebService</TITLE>
<META http-equiv=Content-Type content="text/html; charset=iso-8859-1">
<LINK href="DateService.asmx?disco" type=text/xml rel=alternate>
<STYLE type=text/css>
... etc.
```

The `<LINK>` tag informs the browser of alternative URLs that give versions of this document. Here the server has returned a line informing browsers that know how to use `.disco` files where the nearest one can be found. We will examine `.disco` files later in the chapter. A default discovery file is placed in the root directory for the web site when the .NET platform is installed.

So far we've seen how to create the simplest possible web service. We've seen how that service can be conveniently called from HTML. We're now going to look at how the developer environment can be used to create basically the same web service, but with more supporting infrastructure in place.

Creating a Web Service with the Developer Environment

To create a web service we start a new project in the developer environment, selecting C# Web Service as the type of project. We'll call this service `DateExService`. `DateExService` will implement exactly the same functions as `DateService` so we keep the name similar.

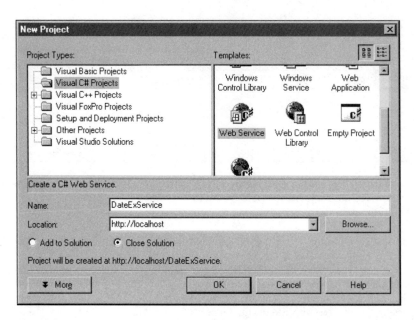

This will cause a folder called `DateExService` to be created inside the default web directory. A number of files will be created in this folder, including the usual C# project files, and also:

- ❑ `WebService1.asmx` – the page that is requested by the browser. The equivalent of the `.aspx` file for ordinary ASP.NET pages.

- ❑ `WebService1.cs` – the `Codebehind` page that contains the actual C# code.

- ❑ `DiscoFile1.disco` – a discovery file that will return details of web services available in this folder and subfolders.

As usual, we can if we wish, rename any of these files to names more relevant to our project, though we won't bother doing so here.

If we look at the contents of `WebService1.asmx`, we'll find the following:

```
<%@ WebService Language="c#" Codebehind="WebService1.cs"
Class="DateExService.WebService1" %>
```

In other words, in the wizard-generated project, there is no direct code in this page – it has all been relegated to the `Codebehind` file.

Looking at the `Codebehind` file, we find a framework definition for the class that will represent the web service. As before, it is derived from `System.Web.Services.WebService`. However, now we find automatically generated code for a number of methods has been prepared for us, to perform such tasks as any extra processing needed to initialize the component. There's also a sample `HelloWorld` method commented out there to show us how to write methods for web services.

```
namespace DateExService
{
using System;
```

```
using System.Collections;
using System.Configuration;
using System.ComponentModel;
using System.Data;
using System.Diagnostics;
using System.Web;
using System.Web.Services;

/// <summary>
///     Summary description for WebService1
/// </summary>
public class WebService1 : System.Web.Services.WebService
{
    public WebService1()
    {
        //CODEGEN: This call is required by the ASP.NET Web Services Designer
        InitializeComponent();
    }

    /// <summary>
    ///     Required method for Designer support - do not modify
    ///     the contents of this method with the code editor
    /// </summary>
    private void InitializeComponent()
    {
    }

    /// <summary>
    ///     Clean up any resources being used
    /// </summary>
    public override void Dispose()
    {
    }

    //WEB SERVICE EXAMPLE
    //The HelloWorld() example service returns the string Hello World
    //To build, uncomment the following lines then save and build the project
    //To test, right-click the Web Service's .asmx file and select View in
    //Browser
    //
    //[WebMethod]
    //public string HelloWorld()
    //{
    //    return "Hello World";
    //}
}
}
```

Although there's a lot of code here, it doesn't really differ in principle from the short web service `DateService.asmx` that we created earlier using the text editor. There's just framework code there to get us started if we want to do anything complex, such as requiring initialization of the class. We're not going to need anything like that for this example – instead we'll just add the methods to give us the same functionality as the original `DateService` service. So we'll add this code:

```
public override void Dispose()
{
}

[WebMethod]
public string CurrentDate()
```

```
    {
        return DateTime.Now.ToLongDateString();
    }


    [WebMethod]
    public string AddToToday(int nDays)
    {
        DateTime NewDate = DateTime.Now.AddDays(nDays);
        return NewDate.ToLongDateString();
    }
```

Our project can now be compiled and called up in exactly the same way as we called up the `DateService` service from web browsers.

At this point you might be thinking that it looks like creating a project in the developer environment hasn't really gained us anything. For this particular project, that's basically correct. We have extra files and code that we wouldn't really need unless we were doing something more complex. But, if you are writing a more complex service, you'll probably appreciate having the extra facilities of the developer environment available. Also, if your web service uses ADO.NET to extract data from a backend database, you can drag and drop ADO.NET classes from the Toolbox and Server explorer straight into your project, and hence get the C# code that instantiates these objects and connects to the database automatically written for you by the developer environment, in just the same way as if you were creating a Windows or WebForms project.

We've now covered the basics of creating a web service. Next we'll look at how we can get the .NET platform to generate the code that we'd need to access it programmatically from a client machine.

Creating a Client

To create a class that implements a web client is actually fairly simple – though it can be broken down into two aspects. Firstly, we need to create a library assembly to be installed on the web client machine, and which contains a class that will handle calling up the service methods. Secondly, we will write the actual client that uses this class. The class that handles calling up the web service methods is known as a **web proxy** since it looks on the outside just like the web service – it exposes the same function calls. However, internally the implementations of these functions simply package the parameters up using the SOAP protocol to send to the real web service.

Creating the Proxy

To do this we first need to run the command line utility `WebServiceUtil`. To create a proxy for our `DateExService` service, the syntax is:

> WebServiceUtil /c:proxy /pa:http://localhost/DateExService/WebService1.asmx?sdl
> /out:c:\inetpub\wwwroot\DateExService\DateExServiceProxy.cs

From this we see that we supply three command line flags to the `WebServiceUtil` program. `/c:proxy` indicates that we wish to create a client proxy, `/pa:<url>` indicates the URL of the page that we wish to create the proxy for, and `/out:<name>` specifies the name of the output file.

Running `WebServiceUtil` with these parameters causes a C# source file, `DateExServiceProxy.cs`, to be created. This code defines a class, `WebService1`, which is derived from `System.Web.Services.Protocol.SoapClientProtocol`. Amongst other things, the `SoapClientProtocol` base class supplies methods to modify aspects of how the client operates – for example, whether cookies are stored and whether the username and password are to be sent to the server. The base class also implements the functions that perform the work of converting parameters into the required XML-SOAP format.

We don't really need to understand the workings of the `WebService1` proxy class. We simply need to know that it exposes two public methods – `AddToDay()` and `CurrentDate()` – which have identical signatures to the equivalent functions in the real web service and which generate the HTTP requests to call those functions over the Web. However, for completeness here is the definition of the class as generated by `WebServiceUtil`:

```
//----------------------------------------------------------------------
/// <autogenerated>
///      This class was generated by a tool.
///      Runtime Version: 1.0.2204.21
///
///      Changes to this file may cause incorrect behavior and will be lost if
///      the code is regenerated.
/// </autogenerated>
//----------------------------------------------------------------------

using System.Xml.Serialization;
using System.Web.Services.Protocols;
using System.Web.Services;

public class WebService1 : SoapClientProtocol {
   public WebService1() {
      this.URL = "http://localhost/DateExService/WebService1.asmx";
   }
[System.Web.Services.Protocols.SoapMethodAttribute("http://tempuri.org/AddToToday"
)]
   public string AddToToday(int nDays) {
      object[] results = this.Invoke("AddToToday", new object[] {nDays});
      return (string)(results[0]);
   }
   public System.IAsyncResult BeginAddToToday(int nDays,
                           System.AsyncCallback callback, object asyncState)
   {
      return this.BeginInvoke("AddToToday", new object[] {nDays},
                                          callback, asyncState);
   }
   public string EndAddToToday(System.IAsyncResult asyncResult)
   {
      object[] results = this.EndInvoke(asyncResult);
      return (string)(results[0]);
   }
[System.Web.Services.Protocols.SoapMethodAttribute("http://tempuri.org/CurrentDate
")]
   public string CurrentDate()
   {
      object[] results = this.Invoke("CurrentDate", new object[0]);
      return (string)(results[0]);
```

```
      }
    public System.IAsyncResult BeginCurrentDate(System.AsyncCallback callback,
                                                           object asyncState)
    {
       return this.BeginInvoke("CurrentDate", new object[0], callback,
                                                           asyncState);
    }
    public string EndCurrentDate(System.IAsyncResult asyncResult)
    {
       object[] results = this.EndInvoke(asyncResult);
       return (string)(results[0]);
    }
  }
}
```

WebServiceUtil only gives us the source code – we still need to compile it into an assembly before it can be incorporated into other projects.

> *Note that you don't have to use WebServiceUtil if you don't want to – but the alternative is to code up the source file for the proxy class by hand, which you'll probably find a lot less convenient!*

You can compile the C# source code using the csc command at the command line, providing you specify it is a DLL you want to compile (/t:library), supply the name of the DLL and you include referenced to all the relevant libraries. However, personally I find it easiest to create a new project in developer environment to do this. So we create a new project, called DateExProxy, specifying C# library as the project type. Then we use the **Add Existing Item** menu option to add the proxy file – in our case this is DateExServiceProxy.cs – to the project.

Before we can compile to the library we need to make a couple of changes to the project. Firstly, the WebService1 class needs to be in a namespace. (In your projects you might also wish to rename WebService1 to a more user-friendly class name though we won't do so here.)

So we modify the source code thus:

```
  ...

  using System.Xml.Serialization;
  using System.Web.Services.Protocols;
  using System.Web.Services;

  namespace DateExProxy
  {

  public class WebService1 : SoapClientProtocol {
     public WebService1() {
        this.Path = "http://localhost/DateExService/WebService1.asmx";
     }

  // code removed for clarity

     }
  }

     }
```

We also need to add the `System.Web.Services` namespace to the list of project references.

Having done that we can compile the project and now have an assembly that can be used to call the `DateExService` remotely.

Creating the Web Service Client

The last step in this it to create an actual client. In our case, it'll basically be a small test harness to check that the web proxy class works correctly, though obviously in real life the web clients will be a lot more substantial. So we create a new C# Windows application project called `DateExClient`, and add our newly created assembly to the list of references for this project. We also need to make sure `System.Web.Services` is added to the references.

As with Windows projects we've created in previous chapters, we'll add a list box called `listBox1` to the form. Then we'll add this code to the `Form1` constructor:

```
public Form1()
{
    //
    // Required for Win Form Designer support
    //
    InitializeComponent();

    WebService1 SoapClient = new WebService1();
    listBox1.Items.Add(SoapClient.CurrentDate());
```

In other words, we just instantiate an instance of the `DateExProxy.WebService1` proxy class and call its `CurrentDate()` method exactly as if we were doing so directly on the web service itself. The difference is that here we are calling a proxy which will implement the `CurrentDate()` method by packaging up the call using the SOAP grammar and sending it off over the Internet to the web service. (Note the URL of the web service was hard coded into the `WebService1` class by the `WebServiceUtil` program.)

One more change to the code – weneed to ensure that the `DateExProxy` namespace is understood by default:

```
namespace DateExClient
{
using System;
using System.Drawing;
using System.Collections;
using System.ComponentModel;
using System.WinForms;
using System.Data;
using DateExProxy;
```

Running the client now gives this result.

And we now have a client application which is able to call up our web service over the Internet – and all for very little actual coding work.

Discovering Services

We've mentioned earlier that `.disco` files are used to reveal to clients where services are. We'll finish this chapter by taking a quick look at what's in the `.disco` files.

If we examine the contents of the `default.disco` file in the `inetpub/wwwroot` folder, this is what we see.

```
<?xml version="1.0" ?>
<dynamicDiscovery xmlns="urn:schemas-dynamicdiscovery:disco.2000-03-17">
<exclude path="_vti_cnf" />
<exclude path="_vti_pvt" />
<exclude path="_vti_log" />
<exclude path="_vti_script" />
<exclude path="_vti_txt" />
</dynamicDiscovery>
```

I should emphasize that this isn't what gets returned to the client when the file is requested – just like `.aspx` and `.asmx` pages, `.disco` pages are processed on the server first.

The contents of this file essentially tell the server to dynamically check what web services are available when the discovery file is requested, but to exclude certain folders from its search. The folders listed in the file above are the ones that are used internally in the implementation of the FrontPage server extensions – so they're not going to contain any files of direct interest to browsers, hence their exclusion.

If we request this file from a web browser, this is what gets returned:

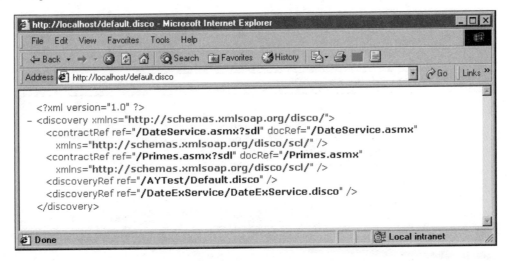

This contains a list of web services available. In this list we see the `DateService` and `DateServiceEx` services that we created, as well as a couple of other services (`FirstService` and `MathService`) that I've written, and some `CrystalReportWebFormViewer` URLs – these are from a service that is automatically installed with the PDC version of the .NET platform.

Notice that the discovery file doesn't return all URLs for web services on a site, but only those in the same folder as itself. However, as you can see in the above screenshot, it also gives the locations of all other discovery files in subfolders, so the user can then look up each of these discovery files to find what services are available in those folders. The `DateExService\DateExService.disco` discovery file is the one that the developer environment created for us when we created the `DateExService` project. Its contents are identical to the `default.disco` file displayed above, but when it is requested it is processed to give the web service in the `DateExService` directory and its subfolders, as shown in the following screenshot.

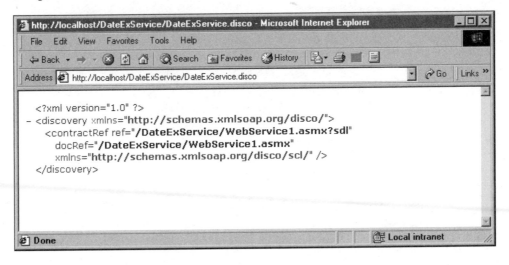

Alternatively you can get the discovery information by appending ?disco to the web service URL:

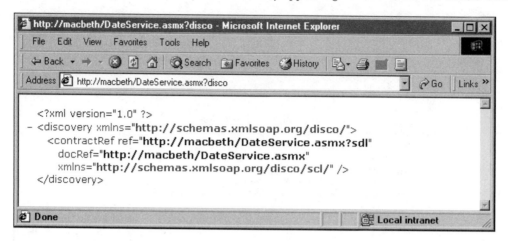

Summary

In this chapter we've seen how easy the .NET platform makes it for you to both create and use web services. Creating a web service can be as easy as writing a short text file containing C# code, while the WebServiceUtil command line utility, along with the .NET base class SoapClientProtocol, provide between them all the functionality you need to code up an assembly that calls a given web service. Using these tools frees you from needing to have any knowledge of the underlying XML grammars, SOAP and SDL, that are used to call the web services.

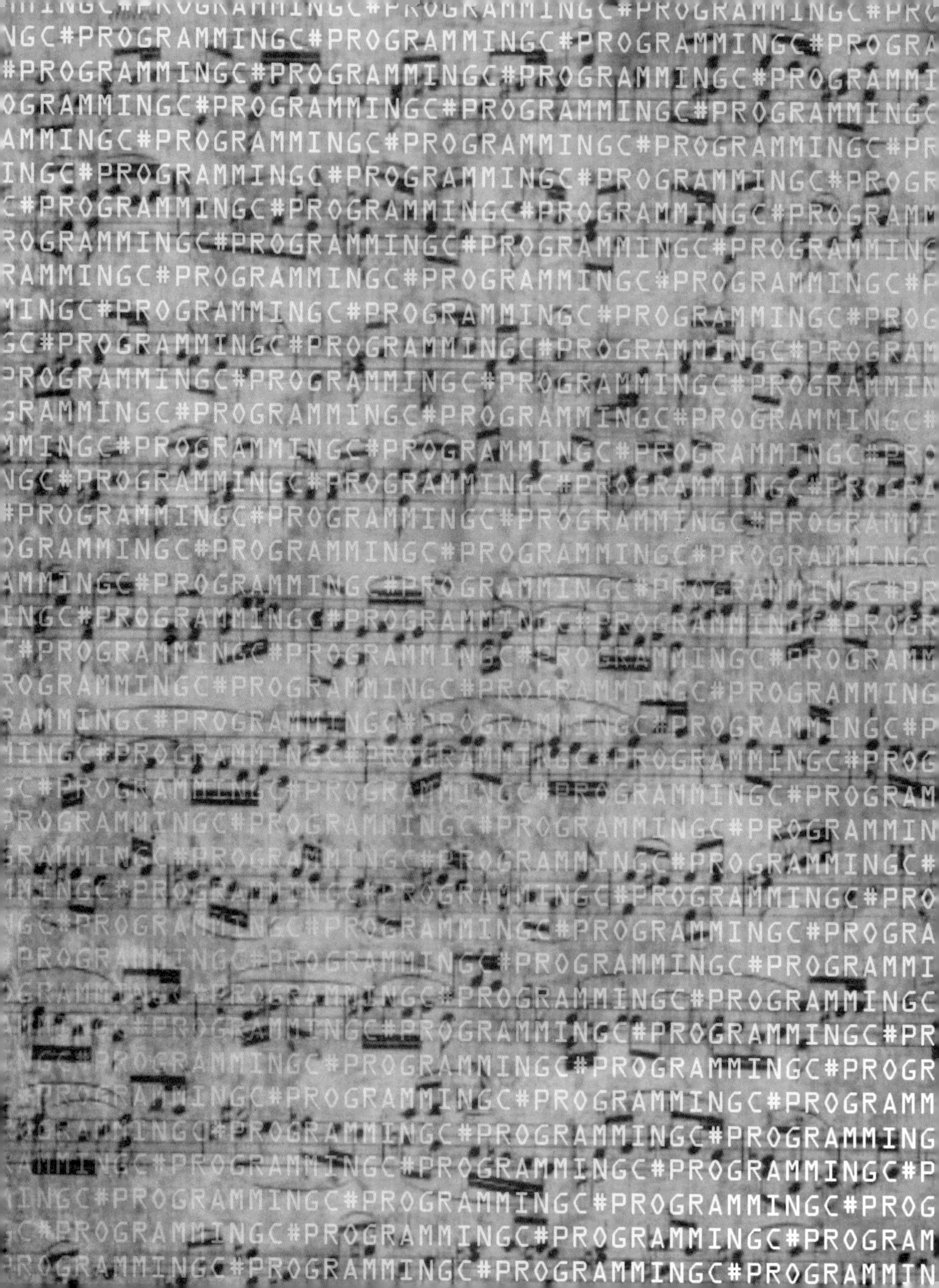
C#PROGRAMMING

Index

A Guide to the Index

The index is arranged hierarchically, in alphabetical order, with symbols preceding the letter A. Most second-level entries and many third-level entries also occur as first-level entries. This is to ensure that users will find the information they require however they choose to search for it

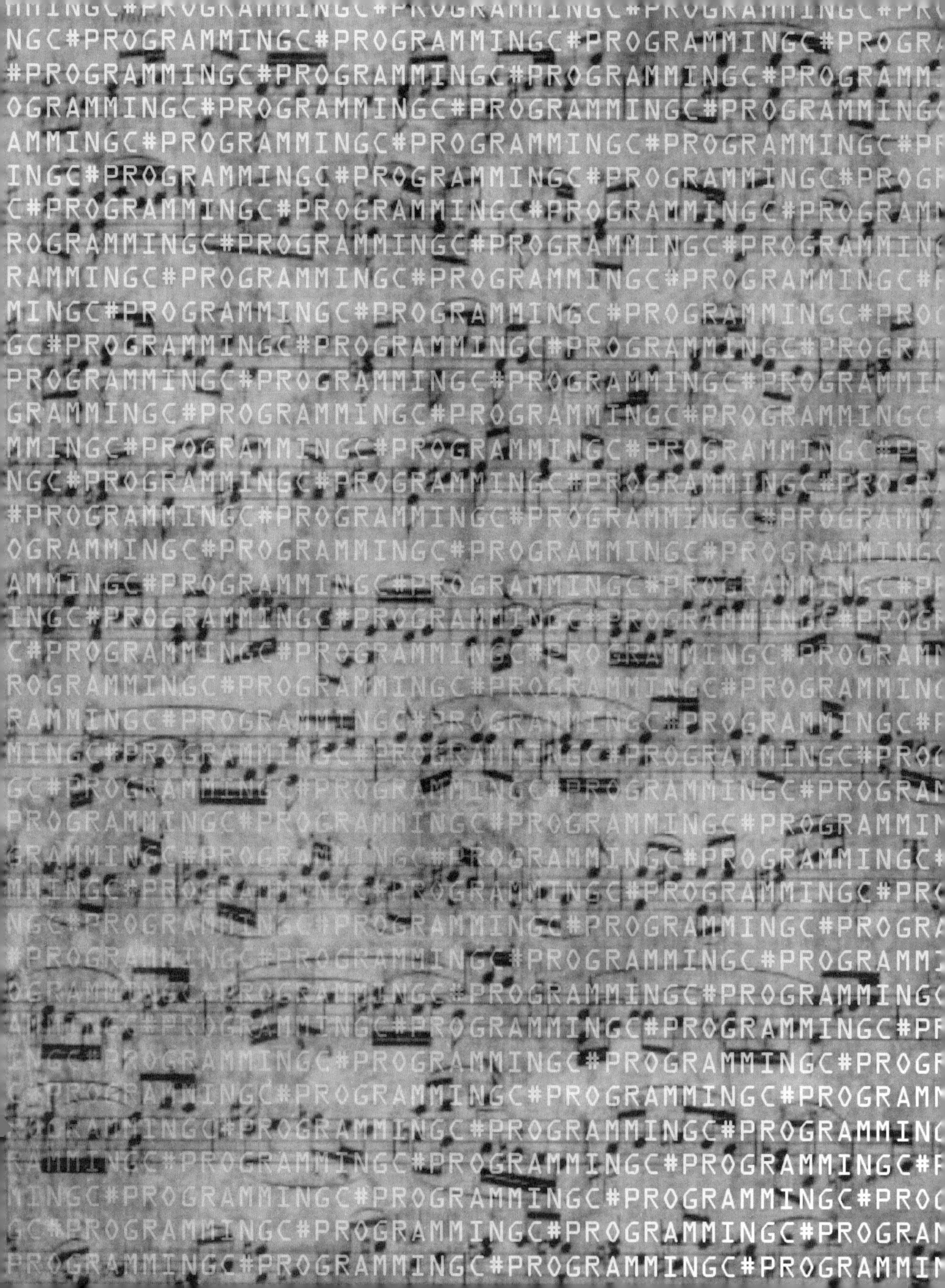
C#PROGRAMMING

wrox
PROGRAMMER TO PROGRAMMER™

Wrox writes books for you. Any suggestions, or ideas about how you want information given in your ideal book will be studied by our team. Your comments are always valued at Wrox.

Free phone in USA 800-USE-WROX
Fax (312) 893 8001

UK Tel. (0121) 687 4100   Fax (0121) 687 4101

C# Programming with the Public Beta - Registration Card

Name _____
Address _____
_____
_____
_____
City_____ State/Region _____
Country_____ Postcode/Zip _____
E-mail _____
Occupation _____
How did you hear about this book? _____
☐ Book review (name) _____
☐ Advertisement (name) _____
☐ Recommendation _____
☐ Catalog _____
☐ Other _____
Where did you buy this book? _____
☐ Bookstore (name)_____ City _____
☐ Computer Store (name)_____
☐ Mail Order _____
☐ Other _____

What influenced you in the purchase of this book?
☐ Cover Design
☐ Contents
☐ Other (please specify) _____

How did you rate the overall contents of this book?
☐ Excellent   ☐ Good
☐ Average   ☐ Poor

What did you find most useful about this book? _____

What did you find least useful about this book? _____

Please add any additional comments. _____

What other subjects will you buy a computer book on soon? _____

What is the best computer book you have used this year? _____

Note: This information will only be used to keep you updated about new Wrox Press titles and will not be used for any other purpose or passed to any other third party.

wrox

PROGRAMMER TO PROGRAMMER™

NB. If you post the bounce back card below in the UK, please send it to:

Wrox Press Ltd., Arden House, 1102 Warwick Road,
Acocks Green, Birmingham B27 6BH. UK.

——— *Computer Book Publishers* ———